SEEKING

EMPLOYMENT IN

CRIMINAL

JUSTICE

AND

RELATED

FIELDS

THIRD EDITION

D1542314

J. SCOTT HARR, JD • KÄREN M. HESS, PhD

Attorney at Law
Instructor, Normandale
Community College

President, Institute for
Professional Development
Instructor, Normandale
Community College

Wadsworth
Thomson Learning™

Australia • Canada • Denmark • Japan • Mexico • New Zealand • Philippines
Puerto Rico • Singapore • South Africa • Spain • United Kingdom • United States

DEDICATED TO THE PURSUIT OF DREAMS

We look forward to hearing from our readers who call with the exciting message, "I got the job!" This book is for you. Good luck!

We also wish to provide a special dedication to Henry Wrobleski, former coordinator of the law enforcement department, and Pam Reierson, former media specialist, Normandale Community College, both of whom have contributed a great deal to the advancement of criminal justice and private security as true professions.

Illustrations by Officer Joe Guy, Roseville Police Department
A note on the artwork: Officer Joe Guy relieves the stress of police work by drawing. We thank him for his contributions which add a light touch to a serious subject.

Design, graphics and index by Christine M. H. Orthmann.

COPYRIGHT © 2000 Wadsworth, a division of Thomson Learning. Thomson Learning is a trademark used herein under license.

All Rights Reserved. No part of this work may be reproduced, transcribed, or used in any form or by any means-graphic, electronic, or mechanical, including photocopying, recording, taping, Web distribution, or information storage and retrieval systems-without the prior written permission of the publisher.

Printed in the United States of America
  2 3 4 5 6 7 03 02 01 00 99

For permission to use material
from this text, contact us:
Web: www.thomsonrights.com
Fax: 1-800-730-2215
Phone: 1-800-730-2214

Text and Cover Printer: Mazer Corporation

ISBN: 0-534-52156-8

For more information, contact
Wadsworth/Thomson Learning
10 Davis Drive
Belmont, CA 94002-3098
USA
www.wadsworth.com

International Headquarters
Thomson Learning
290 Harbor Drive, 2nd Floor
Stamford, CT 06902-7477
USA

UK/Europe/Middle East
Thomson Learning
Berkshire House
168-173 High Holborn
London WC1V 7AA
United Kingdom

Asia
Thomson Learning
60 Albert Street #15-01
Albert Complex
Singapore 189969

Canada
Nelson/Thomson Learning
1120 Birchmount Road
Scarborough, Ontario M1K 5G4
Canada

CONTENTS

SECTION FOUR: YOUR FUTURE IN YOUR CHOSEN PROFESSION   283

FIGURES

TABLES

FOREWORD

Abraham Lincoln once said, "Prepare yourself for the day opportunity presents itself, and you will be rewarded." The process of entering a career in criminal justice or private security usually consists of several steps to "prepare yourself."

Philosophical questions regarding your goals must be resolved by practical approaches. As an applicant, you will be seeking to reach one of your most important goals in life. Whatever the situation, you are more likely to realize success if you are prepared to present yourself in the best possible manner to a prospective employer. Different expectations are held by employers and future employees in a situation where there is the beginning of a career.

This book is a genuine contribution to the future of young Americans seeking employment in such careers as law enforcement, juvenile justice, corrections or any of the numerous areas within the private security profession. J. Scott Harr and Kären M. Hess have been heralded by many as being the best in providing information, guidance and direction to those seeking a career in the public or private sectors of the criminal justice system. The authors give applicants a realistic, factual approach in conveying to the reader "this is what it's all about."

The past and present dynamics of seeking employment projected into the future suggest great optimism for applicants who pursue careers and job hunting with a positive attitude. This book goes as far as our knowledge takes it today. It is the best resource for the 21st century and gives the aspirant an enlightened, positive approach to job seeking in these highly competitive fields.

Henry M. Wrobleski
Former Coordinator of Law Enforcement
Normandale Community College

ACKNOWLEDGMENTS

We wish to personally express appreciation to the criminal justice, security and other professionals who have contributed to this book, which is richer because of their personal sharing:

Russell M. Anderson, Field Supervisor and Investigator, Wisconsin Alliance for Fair Contracting;

Richard D. Beckman, Sergeant, Cloverdale (California) Police Department;

Brian Beniek, Officer, Plymouth (Minnesota) Police Department;

Jack R. Cahall, Past Chair, Crime Abatement Committee, New Orleans, Louisiana;

Jim Chaffee, Director of Security, Walt Disney Pictures and Television;

Jim Clark, Chief, Eden Prairie (Minnesota) Police Department;

Dennis L. Conroy, PhD, Sergeant and Director of the Employee Assistance Program, St. Paul (Minnesota) Police Department;

Driggs, John H., Licensed Clinical Social Worker, St. Paul, Minnesota;

Timothy E. Erickson, Assistant Professor, Metropolitan State University;

Lawrence J. Fennelly, Sergeant and Crime Prevention Specialist, Harvard University Police Department;

Bill B. Green, Manager, Security Services, Rosemount, Inc.;

Joe Guy, Officer, Roseville (Minnesota) Police Department;

Marsh J. Halberg, Attorney, Thomsen & Nybeck, P.A.;

Sheldon T. Hess, MD, General Internist, Health Partners;

Robert B. Iannone, CPP, President, Iannone Security Management, Inc.;

Gil Kerlikowske, Police Commissioner, Buffalo (New York) Police Department;

Molly Koivamaki, Emergency Management Coordination, Eden Prairie (Minnesota) Police Department;

John Lombardi, Professor of Criminal Justice and Criminology, Albany State College;

John J. Maas, Deputy Chief, U.S. Probation/Pretrial Services Officer, South Dakota;

Brenda P. Maples, Lieutenant, Memphis (Tennessee) Police Department;

Robert Meyerson, Trooper I, Minnesota State Patrol;

Linda S. Miller, Sergeant, Bloomington Police Department; Executive Director, Minnesota Community Policing Institute;

Obershaw, Richard J., Grief Center, Burnsville, Minnesota;

Marie Ohman, Executive Director, Minnesota Board of Private Investigators and Protective Agents;

Penny A. Parrish, Public Information Officer, Minneapolis (Minnesota) Police Department; Parrish Institute of Law Enforcement and Media;

Richard W. Stanek, Sergeant, Minneapolis (Minnesota) Police Department;

Michael P. Stein, Chief, Escondido (California) Police Department;

Albert J. Sweeney, Captain Commanding, Training and Education Division, Boston (Massachusetts) Police Department;

Timothy J. Thompson, Director of Safety and Security, University of St. Thomas;

Kenneth S. Trump, Assistant Director, Tri-City Task Force Comprehensive Gang Initiative; Director of Safety and Security, Parma (Ohio) City School District; National School Safety Consultant;

Luis Velez, Captain, Colorado Springs (Colorado) Police Department;

Henry Wrobleski, Former Coordinator, Law Enforcement Department, Normandale Community College; and

Monte D. Zillinger, Special Agent in Charge, Burlington Northern Railroad.

We wish to thank the reviewers of the first and second editions: Frank P. Alberico, Joliet Junior College; Tim Apolito, University of Dayton; Robert H. Burrington, Georgia Police Academy; Dean J. Champion, Minot State College; Paul V. Clark, Community College of Philadelphia; William J. Halliday, Brookdale Community College; Robert Ives, Rock Valley College; Joseph Macy, Palm Beach Community College; Charles E. Myers; Aims Community College; James E. Newman, Rio Honda College; Daniel W. Nolan, Gateway Technical College, Kenosha; and Carroll S. Price, Penn Valley Community College.

Further thanks go to the reviewers of the third edition for their comments and suggestions in preparing this latest revision:

Jerald C. Burns, Alabama State University

Gregory B. Talley, Broome Community College

Joy Thompson, University of Wyoming

We also wish to acknowledge Christine Hess Orthmann for her careful, accurate manuscript preparation, Carol Dunsmore for her friendship and assistance with developing the second edition, Diane Harr for her assistance reviewing the initial manuscript and West/Wadsworth Publishing Company editors Sabra Horne and Shannon Ryan for their encouragement and assistance.

Scott would also like to personally thank Henry Wrobleski for being the kind of mentor that everyone should have, but few have the privilege of associating with. For reasons I'll never fully understand, Hank saw something in me worth cultivating and encouraging, which has opened doors and personal and professional development in ways I couldn't have done alone. The only way I can adequately repay him is to serve in this role to others. Thank you, Henry. Kären would also like to thank Henry (Hank) Wrobleski for launching her writing career in criminal justice over 20 years ago and for being a good friend all those years. Thanks, Hank.

Finally, a profound thanks to our families for their patience and encouragement.

INTRODUCTION

"The longest journey begins with but a single step."

—Anonymous

In the first two editions of this book, we began this introduction by stating that the purpose of this book is simple: to help you develop a job-search STRATEGY to help you land your "dream" job. We remain correct about the need to develop a strategy. But we've learned, as a result of personal experience and from those who have used this book, that there isn't much about the world of job seeking that is simple. It's difficult to come to grips with just what career one is best suited for, and it's tough to get a job. It can be equally challenging to keep a job, and dealing with job changes or job loss can be particularly difficult. Why? Because work is such an important part of our lives . . . and this is why it is even more important to have a strategy to find meaningful work.

Webster's Dictionary defines *strategy* as "a careful plan or method . . . the art of devising or employing plans. . . toward a goal." Your goal is TO GET A NEW JOB! Whether it is to enter into a profession or to advance within your current profession, it all sounds so simple. Most of us have had no trouble getting work--flipping burgers, washing dishes, baby-sitting. Do not let this lull you into a false sense of security as so many others have. Assuming that getting a job—any job—is easy is a disastrous mistake.

You have chosen to pursue employment in a field that has become exceptionally popular. Increasing numbers of individuals are acquiring the prerequisites necessary to enter the criminal justice and security professions, and many individuals are exceeding these requirements. Municipal police departments have received over 1,000 applicants for single job openings! Additionally, once in the profession, relatively few people leave, so jobs do not open up rapidly. Lateral transfers often fill new jobs with experienced individuals.

The days of walking into an agency or department with little or no preparation and expecting to be offered a job are gone. In Minnesota, where we practice, the average length of time it now takes for someone to find work after completing the educational requirements for a career in law enforcement is two years. A carefully planned job-search strategy has become more important than ever. Anyone seeking a job must prepare themselves to succeed in this endeavor.

In addition to the vast number of applicants who possess the minimum qualifications, many applicants have excellent experience. Applicants may have worked out of state as law enforcement officers, corrections officers or as private security officers. Military experience has also proven to be very beneficial in the job search, as has advanced college education. Others have worked at several different jobs in the field and come to a job interview with experience in other areas of criminal justice or security.

In fact, some agencies and departments require applicants to have a Bachelor's degree. And some applicants have Master's degrees, law degrees, PhDs and a myriad of specialty certifications. In addition, many people have taken advantage of volunteer opportunities related to the field, such as police reserves, volunteer rescue/firefighting and civilian police support jobs. Such work not only provides valuable experience, but also demonstrates that the individuals can be trusted in a field demanding unqualified ethics. Other vocational and volunteer positions show the applicant is truly well-rounded. In short, many applicants begin their job search with exceptional qualifications, making them most attractive candidates.

Do not get discouraged. While all of this may be overwhelming, it should not cause you to give up. You *will* eventually get a job. When and what that job will be depends on your job-hunting strategy. While job hunting sometimes takes longer than anticipated and has occasional discouragements, it is also challenging, exciting and eventually fruitful.

Reflecting on what little was required not too many years ago of those seeking employment in law enforcement, corrections or security work, it is amazing what is expected of job candidates and professionals in criminal justice and security today. Communication skills, computer knowledge, business sense, all are necessities now.

This book addresses both the public and the private sector. It discusses career opportunities throughout the criminal justice system, including law enforcement, the practice of law, courts, corrections and related local, state and federal agencies. It also discusses career opportunities within private security because private security and law enforcement are complementary professions. A private security job can be a stepping stone into a police job. Many students majoring in law enforcement have jobs in private security. Even entry-level security jobs are becoming harder to obtain. Additionally, private security is recognized as an attractive field. Pay, hours and assignments at the management level often are better than in the public sector. Conversely, a police job can lead to a position as a security director or any of numerous other jobs in the field of criminal justice. Because the fields of criminal justice and private security have so many specific jobs, you can pursue whatever type of position appeals to you. Whether it be on the line or in administration, you *can* find your niche in these rewarding career areas. Further, lateral transfers between both professions are occurring more often. You have an opportunity to position yourself for any number of truly rewarding jobs.

This book also addresses promotions and the career ladder. Traditionally, these professions have promoted from within. The ability to advance through the ranks requires many of the same attributes that apply to the entry-level job seeker. But, it also requires an effective strategy. The skills discussed here apply equally to getting a new job in a new field and to getting promoted. You've got to have a plan—a strategy.

We have added a chapter entitled "Job Loss and Change: The Road Less Traveled." With job change seemingly inevitable, sometimes not by your choice, job loss has its own special needs. We not only want to help you get that dream job, but we also want to provide some assistance in dealing with job loss as well.

Keep in mind that this book was written for individuals throughout the country and is, therefore, general. Each state has different laws which you must be aware of, for example, laws regarding licensure requirements, use of polygraph testing and the like. In addition, every employing agency will have its own individualized requirements, for example, what areas in a background investigation will be of particular concern or what types of physical agility testing will be given. Find out what your state and the agency you are interested in require and expect of applicants.

Recognize that searching for a job actually becomes a job in itself. The first step is to develop a personal job-hunting strategy. Always remember, however, your job-hunt strategy should not control you—you should control it. A planned strategy will make the entire process more tolerable, successful and even enjoyable.

To help you develop such a strategy and get the job you seek is the purpose of this book. The first section gives a general overview of the world of work (Chapter 1). This is followed by a discussion of career opportunities in law enforcement, the most visible component of the criminal justice system (Chapter 2), opportunities in courts and corrections (Chapter 3) and opportunities in private security (Chapter 4). The section concludes with an exploration of factors to consider when selecting a career (Chapter 5).

The second section focuses on preparing for the job search, including physical fitness and testing (Chapter 6), other tests that might be encountered (Chapter 7), desirable attributes to develop and present (Chapter 8) and the resume (Chapter 9). The section concludes with a critical component of being prepared—facing the risks of failure and building upon them should they occur (Chapter 10).

Section Three presents very specific job-seeking strategies to help you land your "dream job." These strategies are important during the application process (Chapter 11), when presenting yourself (Chapter 12) and during an interview (Chapter 13).

The fourth and final section discusses how you can succeed on the job once you get it, including making it through probation (Chapter 14) and enhancing your chances for promotion (Chapter 15). The final chapter address job loss and change and how you move through such set-backs (Chapter 16).

Throughout the book you will be asked to become actively engaged with the topic being discussed, to write down your ideas and plans. Such instances will be indicated like this:

 by an arrow.

You may want to keep a journal handy for this purpose. The more you interact with the content in this book, the more you will get out of it and the more effective your job-search strategy is likely to be.

Each chapter includes *Insiders' Views* of the topic, written by individuals in the field. These brief, personal essays are based on experience and give a variety of perspectives on what is or might be important in seeking a career in law enforcement, corrections, private security or related fields in criminal justice, as well as learning how others have succeeded. The idea for these personal contributions resulted from the enthusiastic reception of speakers sharing similar ideas at our job-seeking seminars. Most job seekers never get a chance to find out what really goes on in the minds of those doing the hiring. The *Insider's Views* fills this void. Repetition occurs within these personal essays. Although the individuals were asked to write about their experience with the topic of the chapter, many felt compelled to add information and advice about other areas as well. As areas are repeated, you will come to realize how critical certain aspects of the job-seeking process are. Every contributor talks about them.

You may also find some contradictions with what is said in the text. Use your own judgment as to whose advice you feel suits *you* best. Often no "right" answer exists.

Each chapter concludes with a series of *Mind Stretches* to get you thinking about the topic as it relates to your particular interests and talents. Again, to get the most out of this book, *do* take time to work through these Mind Stretches, either mentally or in your journal. We have been impressed by our students who have organized job-hunting support groups which discuss issues pertaining to their efforts, including reviewing these Mind Stretch questions together.

Let your first reading be only the beginning. As you get into your job search, use the book as a reference. In addition, libraries and bookstores have a tremendous amount of information on the many important aspects of job searching. Keep practicing your skills such as working up great responses to those "most commonly asked" interview questions. Look at interviews that do not result in a job as opportunities to practice your interviewing skills. Continue to role-play interviews whenever you get the chance.

Experts say that most people will have between *five* and *twenty* careers—not just jobs, *careers*—during a lifetime. The job-hunting process is, indeed, continuing, so become skilled at it. No one should feel trapped in a job they dislike. Pursue a new one. Or grow in your present job.

I am genuinely interested in your job search. I have experienced the excitement of being "the one" selected, the bitter disappointment and pain of not being "the one" and the frustration of being cut at an early stage of a hiring process as well as after making it into the finals. Believe me, I know what it is like. That is precisely why I have written this book. I want you to get the job you want in the field you choose.

We wish you the best of luck in your job search. Here's to developing the skills and strategy that will get you the job you really want!

> *Having once decided to achieve a certain task, achieve it at all costs of tedium and distastes. The gain in self-confidence of having accomplished a tiresome labor is immense.*
>
> —*Arnold Bennett*

J. Scott Harr, 1999

ABOUT THE AUTHORS

The authors of this book are committed to the advancement of the professionalism of criminal justice. Both Scott and Kären have been teaching college-level law enforcement classes for many years and have a number of other criminal justice related texts on the national market. Their joint publications with West/Wadsworth include *Criminal Procedure* and *Constitutional Law for the Criminal Justice Professional*.

Scott is an attorney and legal investigator in the Twin Cities. For over 11 years he served as the public safety director for a rapidly growing suburb of Minneapolis, Minnesota. He also has served as a police officer for two other cities. In addition, Scott has served as a firefighter and emergency medical technician. He is licensed as a lawyer, a police officer and a private investigator. He teaches courses in criminal procedure, constitutional law, juvenile justice, private security and criminal justice job-seeking skills.

Scott's family, wife Diane and his two children, Kelsey and Ricky, have provided more support than they could know. Their interest in the project and contributions throughout helped make it a reality. Their smiles, laughter and demands that he put the work down and listen to their piano practice helped him maintain his priorities. His hobbies include cars (he holds an NHRA gas dragster license and owns a 1967 GTO), bicycling and snowmobiling.

Kären is the executive director of Innovative Programming Systems, Inc. and president of the Institute for Professional Development. She holds a PhD in English and a second PhD in criminal justice. Kären conducts in-house workshops on writing effective reports. She has also published extensively. West/Wadsworth publications include *The Police in the Community: Strategies for the 21st Century* (2nd edition), *Criminal Investigation* (5th edition), *Criminal Procedure, Introduction to Law Enforcement and Criminal Justice* (6th edition), *Juvenile Justice* (3rd edition), *Management and Supervision in Law Enforcement* (2nd edition), *Police Operations* (2nd edition) and *Private Security* (4th edition).

Kären has been married for 37 years to husband, Sheldon, and has two grown children. Christine Hess Orthmann, her highly valued assistant, does research, writing, proofing and indexing on the texts. Tim Hess is a captain in the Air Force.

SECTION ONE

THE CHALLENGE

There are two things to aim at in life;
first, to get what you want; and,
after that, to enjoy it.
Only the wisest . . . achieve the second.

—*Langdon Smith*

Nothing great was ever achieved without enthusiasm.

—*Ralph Waldo Emerson*

Before beginning your job search, you should fully understand what it is you are getting into. Work is so vitally important that choosing a line of work deserves far more effort than many people consider giving. It is by taking an educated look at the real world of work that you begin a *realistic* job search. You've probably read startling statistics about the rate of change facing employees and the job market. These dramatic changes are directly affecting, and will continue to affect, the service sector, including employment in criminal justice and private security services. Chapter 1 addresses how these changes have affected the job market and what the career you're seeking might look like in the twenty-first century.

Chapter 2 discusses careers in law enforcement, the most visible and familiar component of the criminal justice system. It examines where employment opportunities exist—on the federal, state, county and local levels. Chapter 3 examines careers in the courts and corrections. Corrections is a rapidly expanding field due to the country's increasing intolerance of repeat offenders, the "three strikes and you're out" approach and the mandatory serving of sentences. Included in this chapter is information on careers in probation and parole.

Chapter 4 explores careers in the private sector. Privatization is a current trend, with private security growing much faster than any segment of the criminal justice system. Numerous career opportunities are found in the private security profession, including not only the familiar security officer but alarm services, armed courier services, executive protection services, private corrections and the like. Chapter 5 examines the steps for choosing a career and what factors to consider. It helps you look at the entrance requirements in light of your background, experience and personal likes and dislikes.

If after reading this section you are convinced that a career in criminal justice or private security is for you, read on. The rest of the book provides strategies and techniques to help you get the job you seek. These fields are demanding, and so is the road to employment.

You have made an important decision by taking this step to develop your job-search strategies. Let's get started!

CHAPTER 1

EMPLOYMENT TRENDS: THE WORLD OF WORK

Most of our adult lives are spent working. Taking into account commuting time, overtime, thinking about our jobs, and worrying over work, we spend more of our waking hours in the office, at the factory, on the road, behind the desk, than we do at home.

—*The Joy of Working, p. ix.*

Do You Know:

➢ What the "hierarchy of needs" is?
➢ What role work has in meeting our needs?
➢ What most people rank as the two most important factors in a job?
➢ How many job and career changes the average person will make in a lifetime?
➢ How our labor force is changing in terms of age, gender, race and skill level?
➢ Why it is crucial to keep current with technology?
➢ What job areas will expand?
➢ What the projections look like for jobs in criminal justice and security?
➢ What factor education will play in future work?

INTRODUCTION

Work. For most of us, work is a large part of who we are, occupying a vast amount of our time and, to a great degree, shaping how we think about ourselves. The fact that you have invested your time, energy and money into working with this book says it is important to you too.

This chapter examines why work is so important to most people, what needs it fulfills and how these needs may change. It then presents a brief history of how work has evolved to its present state and some of the massive changes that have occurred, including the impact of technology. This is followed by a look at the changing job market and jobs of the future, including growth trends in the service sector and the need for more education. The chapter concludes with some myths and realities about jobs of the future.

THE IMPORTANCE OF WORK

Working *is* important. It provides you with income, to be sure. But work is so much more. Work helps form your identity, and it makes a statement about who you are. According to well-known psychologist Abraham H. Maslow, work meets *all* five levels of human needs. Maslow developed a hierarchy of needs ranging from the most basic physical needs to the most complex self-actualization needs, with security, social and esteem needs in between. According to Maslow, once a person's needs are satisfied at the lowest level, he or she is able to move up the hierarchy to the next level. Maslow acknowledged, however, that few people ever reach the highest level—self-actualization.

According to Maslow's "hierarchy of needs," physical needs are the most basic of human needs and self-actualization needs are the most complex. Security, social and esteem needs fall in between.

This hierarchy is illustrated in Figure 1-1.

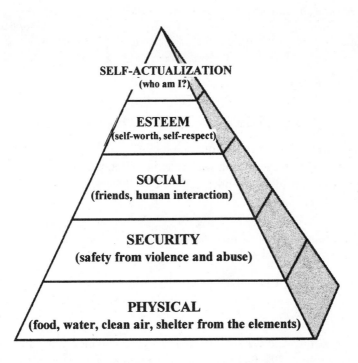

FIGURE 1-1   Maslow's Hierarchy of Human Needs

These needs and their job-related counterparts in a *satisfying* job are often as follows:

➢   Physical: Good working conditions, rest periods, labor-saving equipment, sufficient income, heating/air conditioning

➢   Safety: Safe working conditions, good supervision, job security, training in survival

➢   Social: Feeling of belonging to a "job family," agency/department/organization spirit, after-hours get-togethers, picnics and softball games

➢   Esteem: Challenging job, promotions, titles, community recognition, awards

➢   Self-Actualization: Opportunity for growth and development, discretion/decision-making authority, contributing to society/organization

Work has the potential to meet all five levels of human needs; however, only truly *satisfying* jobs will actually fulfill every level.

According to Mendofik (1995, p. 41):

> The most efficient, productive individuals have reached the plateau of "Maslow's Hierarchy of Needs" by progressing through the lower levels. Maslow's ascending progression evolves in the following manner. The individual's physiological needs (food and shelter) are satisfied. He feels security in his environment, and there is an absence of threat to his stability.
>
> The next level nurtures his need for affiliation with others, or organizations. Having accomplished these, the psychological needs of achievement and self-esteem become targets of fulfillment.
>
> At the plateau, Maslow claims we reach self-actualization. This is a level of personal development where basic needs are fulfilled and we enrich ourselves and our environment by contributing in a significant, positive manner. We are confident in our ability and proficient in our craft.

 Think for a few minutes about what's important to **you** in the career you select. Which level(s) of need will influence you the most? Jot down your responses in your journal.

WHAT'S IMPORTANT ON THE JOB

What's important to you as you consider your career? A study conducted by *Psychology Today* had participants rank what was important to them on the job. The factors they used are listed below. Rank them yourself, using 1 for the most important and 17 for the least important.

_____ Amount of freedom you have on your job.
_____ Amount of fringe benefits.
_____ Amount of information you get about your job performance.
_____ Amount of job security.
_____ Amount of pay.
_____ Amount of praise you get for a job well done.
_____ Chances for getting a promotion.
_____ Chances for taking part in making decisions.
_____ Chances to accomplish something worthwhile.
_____ Chances to do something that makes you feel good about yourself.
_____ Chances to do things you do best.
_____ Chances to learn new things.
_____ Friendliness of people you work with.
_____ Opportunities to develop your skills and abilities.
_____ Resources you have to do your job.
_____ Respect you receive from people you work with.
_____ How you are treated by the people you work with.

You may be interested to know that in the *Psychology Today* survey, "Chances to do something that makes you feel good about yourself" was ranked first, and "Chances to accomplish something worthwhile" was ranked second. However, how other people rank the factors is not important. What *is* important is how *you* ranked them.

In a survey, most people ranked "Chances to do something that makes you feel good about yourself" as the most important factor in a job; "Chances to accomplish something worthwhile" ranked second.

 Think carefully about your top rankings and how well they would be met in your chosen field. Again, record your thoughts in your journal.

Work satisfies so many human needs that those who find themselves without meaningful employment usually experience a sense of loss. If your work is unfulfilling, your needs must be met elsewhere or anxiety, frustration or even depression may result. If you are suddenly unemployed, such as in the case of an unexpected layoff, your lifestyle may become seriously disrupted. Losing a job and being unable to find other work has driven some to such self-destructive behaviors as alcoholism and other substance abuse and even suicide. Truly, work is important as something positive to do to meet your needs—not only your financial needs, but your identity and self-esteem needs.

For these reasons it is important to give careful thought to what work you pursue. This book will help you decide what you want to do with your working life. You will have a chance to look at what is important to you and what you have to offer employers. Many people spend more time planning their next vacation than they do planning what they're going to do for the rest of their lives. To do so is risky, as Cornish (1983, p. 5) suggested 15 years ago:

> Choosing a career has never been as difficult as it is today. There are far more occupations than ever before with new ones springing up every day, and the older occupations are changing radically. Add to that the fact that people are living longer and adopting new lifestyles, and it's no wonder that the notion of a lifelong commitment to a single career now seems a trifle quaint . . . .
>
> Choosing a career—and sticking to it—used to be a lot easier. In bygone times, a boy would naturally follow the occupation of his father, easily picking up needed skills while still a toddler. By the time he reached adulthood, he would be fully trained and ready to earn his living. A girl would learn the homemaking skills from her mother and by the time she reached her teens was ready to run a home on her own.

It is even harder 15 years later. Mackay (1993, p. 37) states: "Statistics show that during your lifetime you are likely to make 10.2 job changes. That's shocking enough, but in addition, you are likely to make five career changes."

Statistics indicate the average person is likely to make more than 10 job changes and 5 career changes in a lifetime.

In addition, according to Hammonds (1994, p. 78), behind the buzzwords associated with work is a radical redefinition of labor:

> Mobility. Empowerment. Teams. Cross-training. Virtual offices. Telecommuting. Reengineering. Restructuring. Delayering. Outsourcing. Contingency. If the buzzwords don't sound familiar, they should: They are changing your life. The last decade, perhaps more than any other time since the advent of mass production, has witnessed a profound redefinition of the way we work.

WHAT HAPPENED? A brief look at the evolution of work in the United States is revealing.

A BRIEF HISTORY

You may be familiar with futurist Toffler's "three waves" theory, which uses the comparison of ocean waves and sweeping major changes in society:

➤   The Agricultural Revolution
➤   The Industrial Revolution
➤   The Technological Revolution

Toffler suggests that the first wave, the Agricultural Revolution, occurred about 8,000 B.C., sweeping aside 45,000 years of cave dwelling. The second wave, the Industrial Revolution, came around 1760, turning our landscape from that of "amber waves of grain" and "fruited plains" to that of smokestacks. This second wave was not without its resistors. A group of workers, called Luddites, systematically destroyed machinery they saw as a threat to manual laborers. But the wave engulfed America, forcing many farmers into factories to labor as blue-collar workers in the new era of industrialization.

Pulley (1997, pp. 15–16) notes that the Industrial Revolution had an impact on more than just how and where people worked—it changed the way people identified with each other and how they viewed themselves. Whereas the Agricultural Age saw family members working in the fields together, the Industrial Age fractionated families, sending its members, young and old, into the factories to labor as nameless "cogs" in the massive machine:

> As people spent more time in the factory than with the family, the importance of work grew. Increasingly it became the principle source of people's identity. For instance, in preindustrial society it was more common to identify yourself in terms of your birthplace or family membership, such as "I'm John of Winchester," or "I'm William's son." In industrialized society people began to tie identity to work . . . . The workplace became the main organizing feature of our life and the source of our identity, status, income, and affiliations. And by the 20th century, identity became specifically tied to *organizations*.

Pulley (p. 16) further notes that, over time, these organizations became increasingly "paternalistic," taking care of their employees by providing such benefits as health care insurance, retirement pensions, social functions and activities, as well as rewards for company loyalty, such as bonuses, watches, plaques and dinners. Pulley contends: "Out of this grew the implicit and pervasive understanding between workers and organizations that is now coming apart at the seams—the belief that hard work and loyalty will be exchanged for promotions and job security."

Gradually, the dominance of factories and industrialized business ebbed and a new era—"the information age"—was born. This third wave, the Technological Revolution, began in the mid-fifties and again changed the face of the American workplace. Brains rather than brawn became important, and white-collar workers began displacing blue-collar workers. Again, resistance has occurred. Many people, similar to the Luddites, have rebelled against computers, fax machines and voice mail systems. But the third wave *is* here.

OUR CHANGING WORLD

Pulley asserts the third wave is putting an end to the assumptions previously mentioned—that hard work and loyalty will be rewarded with job security. The job turnover rate is at an all-time high, leaving many with feelings of collapse and insecurity (Pulley, pp. 16–17):

> When our building-block assumptions are pulled out from under us, we often experience a psychological crash that feels as personally damaging as the Kobe earthquake that struck Japan in 1995. . . . What was learned from this disaster, however, is that wood-frame-and-stucco buildings do not survive an earthquake because they do not yield. . . . Likewise both we as individuals and our organizations will need built-in flexibility to weather the future. . . . Our world no longer has the stability and predictability of earlier times. Workers in the information age need to use their minds and hearts, not just their hands.

Others, however, believe this "instability" will have a positive impact on contemporary workers as they strive to continuously move up into better and more challenging positions. Tevlin (1999, p. D5) notes: "As the Great Depression produced a generation of 'organization men,' whose fear of unemployment generated loyalty to their employers, the current period of nearly full employment will create generations of confident and increasingly assertive workers, some experts say."

The Tofflers (1990, pp. 2–5) suggest: "We are witnessing the massive breakdown of America as we knew it and the emergence of a strange, new 21st-century America whose basic institutional structures have yet to be formed." They note that in the past, immigrants who spoke little or no English and poor, uneducated Americans were able to fit into the mainstream because jobs required muscle power rather than mind power. This is no longer true. Those on the "bottom rung" are more likely to stay there.

According to Bradsher (1995, p. 4A): "New studies on the growing concentration of American wealth and income challenge a cherished part of the country's self-image: They show that rather than being an egalitarian society, the United States has become the most economically stratified of industrial nations." Sawyer (1997, p. A13) reports: "The gap between rich and poor has widened in 44 states over the last two decades." He continues:

> The Census Bureau reported that [in 1996], the top 20 percent of families earned 49 percent of the money, up from 43.8 percent in 1967. Those in the bottom 20 percent earned 3.7 percent of the nation's income . . ., down from 4 percent in 1967. The middle 60 percent—households earning roughly $15,000 to $68,000 a year—have also lost out during this period. They used to earn 52.3 percent of the money but now take just 47.4 percent.

The Tofflers caution that:

> It is simple-minded to blame crime on poverty. There are plenty of societies in which poverty does *not* produce crime. But it is equally witless to assume that millions of poor, jobless young people—not part of the work-world culture and bursting with energy and anger—are going to stay off the streets and join knitting clubs.

More importantly, say the Tofflers, as social disapproval has less and less power, "law enforcement must take over." In other words, the role of law enforcement, the courts, corrections and security will be even more critical in the years ahead.

The Growing Importance of Criminal Justice and Security

Americans have paid tremendous attention to crime and expect it to be contained. Eskridge (1999, p. 9) states:

> Concern for criminal activity in our society runs from the suites to the streets. While overall crime rates seem to have stabilized for now, the visible increase in violent crime is a cause of great concern. As a result, crime continues to be one of the most significant social-political issues of the day.

Other Changes

In the next century:

➢ White dominance of the United States will end.
➢ America will grow "grayer."
➢ Legal and illegal immigrants will flood into the country.
➢ Minorities and women will make significant gains.

These changes are producing amazing opportunities for everyone interested in criminal justice and security careers, particularly those who understand and prepare to address these changes.

Important changes have also taken place in several values:

<u>Then</u>	<u>Now</u>
A warm, secure family life	Soaring divorce rates
Participation in a great ennobling nation-state	Vietnam, Watergate, Desert Storm, MonicaGate, the Kosovo Crisis
Hope of heaven and the afterlife	Weakening of the church
Childhood as a carefree time	Children committing violent crimes and being victimized

Naisbitt (1982), in his classic *Megatrends*, identified 10 fundamental shifts which will have a great impact on the future of all Americans:

Old—Moving From	New—Moving Toward
Industrial society	Information society
Forced technology	High Tech/High Touch
National economy	World economy
Short-term view	Long-term view
Centralization	Decentralization
Institutional help	Self-help
Representative democracy	Participatory democracy
Hierarchies	Networking
The North (physically)	The South
Either/or stance	Multiple options

Such changes greatly affect the workplace and work force. In addition to these changes, according to *Future Work* (1991, p. 2): "The North American work force faces wrenching changes in its structure and composition." Among the changes are the following (pp. 2–8):

➢ The continuing aging of the work force will create problems and opportunities. . . . By 2010, one-quarter of the U.S. population will be at least 55.
➢ Older Americans will increase in number and grow in influence.
➢ Hispanics will be the largest fast-growing minority population in the United States.
➢ Women will move gradually into the executive suite.
➢ New critical skills are emerging.

> The labor force in America is undergoing many changes, including an increasing percentage of older people, an increasing percentage of women, a decreasing percentage of "white" people and a greater reliance on critical technical skills.

Many of the emerging "critical skills" are the direct result of technological advances. This is definitely the case in all areas of criminal justice and security employment.

THE IMPACT OF TECHNOLOGY

What remains fascinating is how the working world continues to evolve. The changes in work have been greatly affected by technological advances. Technology is changing so fast it is almost impossible to keep up, much less predict what is ahead. More than ever, successful job seekers will position themselves to showcase their computer knowledge and skills. It is strongly recommended that you bring your computer skill level up as high as possible. While many computer classes are more exotic than typing, you simply must be comfortable at a keyboard.

To illustrate, a woman had finally worked her way up to a good position with a Fortune 500 corporation after many years with the company. All employees were warned years in advance of the eventual transition the company would make towards becoming more computerized. Classes were offered; encouragement was provided. Still, the woman resisted training and getting "up to speed." Eventually, changes affecting the industry necessitated major downsizing. Those lacking computer skills were first to go, regardless of years of service or other contributions to the company. Acquiring computer skills and keeping current with technology is *that* important.

> Technology is a powerful, rapidly changing force in today's working world. To stay competitive and ensure your value in the work force, keep current with technology.

Technology is not the only driving force behind the changing job market, however. Economic and political forces also have influenced the job market.

CHANGES IN THE JOB MARKET

According to the 1998–1999 edition of the *Occupational Outlook Handbook*, the labor force of the future is projected to change in some important ways:

➤   The labor force will become increasingly diverse (p. 1):

> The labor force growth of Hispanics, Asians and other races will be faster than for blacks and white non-Hispanics. Despite relatively slow growth, white non-Hispanics will have the largest numerical growth between 1996 and 2006. Between 1996 and 2006, women's share of the labor force is projected to slowly increase from 46 to 47 percent.

➤   The labor force will become older (p. 2):

> Workers over age 45 will account for a larger share of the labor force as the baby-boom generation ages.

A LOOK AT JOBS OF THE FUTURE—WHERE WILL YOU FIT IN?

As we enter the twenty-first century, interest has heightened in looking ahead at what our world of work might be like. Certain trends are pointed out repeatedly:

➤   The labor force will continue to grow.
➤   The total number of jobs will increase rapidly.
➤   The most rapid growth will be in jobs in the *service sector* (which includes criminal justice and security).
➤   Blue-collar jobs will decline slightly.
➤   More education will be needed for more jobs.
➤   An alarming number of young people will not be qualified for the new jobs.
➤   More workers will be between the ages of 25 and 54.
➤   Women and minorities will account for a greater share of the work force.

Growth in the Service Industries

According to the *Occupational Outlook Handbook* (1998, p. 2): "Industry employment growth is projected to be highly concentrated in service-producing industries. . . . Employment in service-producing industries will increase faster than average, with growth near 30 percent." Meyers (1999, p. D5) adds: "The assembly line has been in decline in the United States for more than a generation. Work more closely tied to worker skills—the vaunted 'service economy'—now represents more than three in four jobs in the nation." Careers within the criminal justice field and private security fall within the services category. Figure 1-2 illustrates the projected changes in employment in service-producing industries.

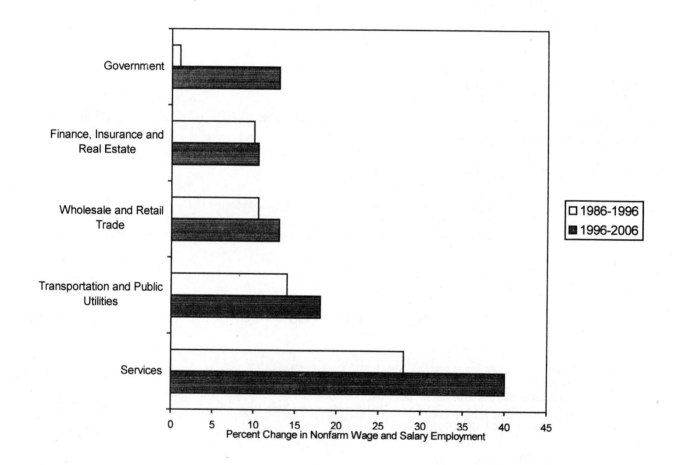

FIGURE 1-2   Percent Change in Employment in Service-Producing Industries, 1986–1996 and Projected 1996–2006

SOURCE: *Occupational Outlook Handbook, 1998–1999 Edition.* Washington, DC: Bureau of Labor Statistics, January 1998, p. 2.

Moreau (1996, p. 53) includes social-services workers in the top 10 jobs with the fastest growth for the period of 1992–2005—ranked second at 136 percent. *The Top 100: The Fastest Growing Careers for the 21ˢᵗ Century* (1998) includes police officers, detectives, corrections officers and security consultants and technicians. According to this document:

> The employment outlook for police detectives is expected to be much faster than the average through the year 2005. High estimates call for an increase of nearly 77 percent over the next decade, to more than 104,000 detectives. Even the lowest estimate calls for an increase of 60 percent over the next decade, to 94,000 detectives.

Regarding corrections officers (p. 91):

> Employment in this field is expected to increase much faster than the average for all jobs. It is estimated that another 142,000 jobs will be created within the next fifteen years, an increase in employment of 61 percent. The ongoing war on drugs, new tough-on-crime legislation, and increasing mandatory sentencing policies will add more prison beds and more corrections officers.

The employment outlook is equally positive for security consultants and technicians (p. 345):

> Security services is one of the largest employment fields in the United States. About 883,000 persons are employed . . . . The demand for guards and other security personnel is expected to increase much faster than the average through the year 2005, as crime rates rise with the overall population growth. The highest estimates call for more than 1.25 million guards to be employed by the year 2005.

Trends in the changing work force show service-producing industries, including criminal justice and security, will account for most of all job growth. Furthermore, these services will remain the fastest growing major industry during the next decade.

A Need for More Education

New service industry jobs will require enhanced skills and proficiencies, and many will demand successful applicants possess college degrees and other certifications. Data from both the U.S. Labor Department and the U.S. Census Bureau forecast service jobs becoming higher skilled during the next century (Meyers, p. D5). Ironically, such requirements will lead to both higher and lower unemployment: more joblessness for those who can't read or who don't possess marketable skills, and less joblessness among those with higher education.

According to the *Occupational Outlook Handbook* (p. 4): "Of the 25 occupations with fast growth, high pay, and low unemployment that have the largest numerical growth, 18 require at least a bachelor's degree." Furthermore (p. 5): "Occupations that require a bachelor's degree are projected to grow the fastest, nearly twice as fast as the average for all occupations. All of the 20 occupations with the highest earnings require at least a bachelor's degree."

According to Hammonds (p. 86): "Certainly, education forms a foundation for the new workplace: The continuing growth in professional and technical occupations will demand ever-higher capabilities of Americans." The reality is that a high school diploma, while perhaps meeting the bare requirements for some jobs, will seldom be sufficient to assure career advancement opportunities. As Hammonds (p. 77) stresses: "Constantly in training, you must acquire new skills to keep up with new technologies." Imel (1994) also suggests: "Because the future will belong to the knowledge worker, instill in learners the concept of lifelong learning."

> It is projected that more than half of the new jobs created by the year 2000 will require a level of education beyond high school. Criminal justice and security agencies nationwide are also raising the educational requirements of applicants. To stay competitive, you must seek higher education.

The importance of education is discussed more fully in Chapter 8.

Myths vs. Reality in Jobs of the Future

Imel discusses several "myths and realities" about jobs in the future, including the following:

➢   Myth: "Forty Years and Out." Reality: Individuals can no longer plan on spending their entire working lives with one organization.
➢   Myth: A college education will guarantee a good job. Reality: Between now and 2005, an estimated 30 percent of new graduates will either be unemployed or underemployed.
➢   Myth: Technology will simplify work. Reality: What technology has done is eliminate many low-level jobs and increased the skill levels required for those that remain.
➢   Myth: Job growth will level off. Reality: The United States is still creating about 2 million new jobs every year. . . . According to BLS [Bureau of Labor Statistics] projections, service industries will provide more than half of new job growth in this period.

KEEPING UP-TO-DATE

One excellent source for finding help in planning careers that require college or technical degrees is the *Professional Careers Sourcebook*, published by Gale Research Publishing, Detroit. It contains job descriptions and the names and addresses of associations able to provide further information on career possibilities.

Another excellent source for keeping current on jobs and employment trends is the *Occupational Outlook Handbook*, produced by the U.S. Department of Labor. Updated every two years, this resource describes about 200 occupations, offering information on the nature of the work involved, salaries, work environments, necessary education and training, and job outlook. It also includes a listing of sources of state and local job information. It can be purchased at any U.S. government bookstore or by calling the office of the Superintendent of Documents in Washington (202-783-3238). You might also want to check with your local library, state agencies and employment offices, as well as your state department of education, state job services agencies and state labor departments.

CONCLUSION

The days of picking one career and sticking with it for 40 years are over. Statistics show the average person is likely to make more than ten job changes and five career changes in a lifetime. Trends in the changing work force show service-producing industries, including criminal justice and security, will account for most of all job growth. Furthermore, these services will remain the fastest growing major industry during the next decade. It is also projected that more than half of the new jobs created by the year 2000 will require a level of education beyond high school. Criminal justice and security agencies nationwide are raising the educational requirements of applicants. Therefore, to stay competitive, you must seek higher education and keep current with technology.

INTRODUCING THE INSIDERS' VIEWS

Because the first chapter of this book is titled **Employment Trends: The World of Work**, the contribution from Dr. Cahall was selected to introduce you to the valuable information provided by our guest writers. They were asked to provide their own thoughts about jobs in criminal justice or related fields and how to obtain them. Their perspectives are unique, as is the case with Dr. Cahall's view of how business and criminal justice must work together to make the system work. Some contributors hand you information on a silver platter. Others encourage you to think about the profession you wish to pursue and how best to get there. Whichever angle a particular writer pursues, think about the important insights you are being given from those "on the inside." The world of work is, indeed, changing. It's no longer "us versus them." Rather, as Dr. Cahall explains, communities must work together to meet their common goals. The successful job applicant, and then successful criminal justice or security professional, will realize that a well-rounded, educated person is what employers want and need.

AN INSIDER'S VIEW

NEW ORLEANS—"THE GOOD, THE BAD AND THE UGLY!"

Jack R. Cahall, Ph.D.
Past Chair, Crime Abatement Committee
Chamber—New Orleans, Louisiana

The Good. New Orleans, located in Orleans Parish (County), Louisiana, is a corporate city/parish of about a half million people. The total metro area, including New Orleans, has a population of about 1,250,000. And, of course, millions of visitors and daily inbound commuters raise that number even higher. Approximately 2,000 police personnel, including civilian employees, are charged with keeping the peace and protecting the parish's citizens.

Major events in the New Orleans area which involve the police include:

➢   Mardi Gras — Annual Madness!
➢   JazzFest — Worldwide musical attraction.
➢   Casino and River Boat Gambling.
➢   French Quarter — A street party every, and all, night!
➢   World-class aquarium and zoo.
➢   Saints football — If they win, a blast!
➢   Crescent City Classic — A world-class 10K street race.
➢   Great food, friendly people — Laissez-faire attitude.
➢   Southern European/Caribbean cultural blend.
➢   Ethnic diversity.
➢   Semi-tropical climate — HOT!

A great place to live! A great place to work . . . but maybe not in law enforcement?

The Bad. The area is hurricane-prone, and since the city lies below sea level, the whole region is prone to flooding. The large, festive street crowds that sometimes become unruly, coupled with the high crime rate, create intense requirements for police services. Low police pay forces many to work paid overtime details just to make ends meet. Furthermore, a federal lawsuit settlement includes affirmative action hiring and promotion quotas. It's a struggle.

The Ugly. The stressful working conditions require psychologically and physically fit, educated police, yet it is difficult to attract and keep such officers when the pay is so inadequate. The taxpayers, particularly the business community, feel overtaxed and underprotected. This climate can fuel the ever-present danger of overreacting—brutality and financial temptations, bribes, kickbacks and drugs.

To counter the "ugly," middle management, the 5–10 year veteran and future police leaders *must* stay informed and maintain sharp job skills through continuing education and community involvement. Citizens *must* be encouraged to support and approve salary restructuring to allow adequate compensation for law enforcement officers.

Twenty-first century law enforcement personnel *must* make every effort to encourage civilian and business participation in the planning and operation of law enforcement agencies. The citizens will not support law enforcement that lapses into a siege-like mode—an "us versus them" or "give us the funds and we'll decide how to spend it" attitude. Only those police agencies operating under sound business practices will be successful and have total community support.

———————

Dr. Jack R. Cahall is the president and principal stockholder of several businesses, including electrical engineering and sales firms and real estate ventures. He is a graduate of the Harvard School of Business Administration, was one of three participants to complete the three-year curriculum in one year and finished in the top 10 percent of his class. He also attended the U.S. Army Warfare School, Fort Bragg, North Carolina; was a Green Beret and studied military engineering. Dr. Cahall served in both the Korean and Vietnam wars.

Dr. Cahall has been a member of the Chamber for New Orleans and the River Region, Louisiana, has chaired the Crime Abatement Committee and served as the program director for the "Adopt-A-Cop" program. He is also a member of the International Association of Chiefs of Police, holding a certificate of training from the International Symposium on Terrorism. His honors include a certificate of merit from the City of New Orleans, a Special Officer's Commission from the New Orleans Police Department, being named Honorary Captain of the New Orleans Police Department, receiving the U.S. Defense Industry Award (Republic of Korea) in 1987 and receiving the Delta Airlines Presidential Recognition Award in 1986.

AN INSIDER'S VIEW

WHAT YOU'LL NEED TO SUCCEED IN THE 21ST CENTURY

Timothy E. Erickson
Assistant Professor
Metropolitan State University

In the early 1900s August Vollmer, Chief of Police in Berkeley, California, had a vision that included a place for college-educated peace officers within the field of law enforcement.

Since the days of Vollmer, this vision has been revisited periodically in the form of such events as the *Wickersham Report* of the 1930s and the *President's Commission on Law Enforcement and Administration of Justice* in the 1960s. In fact, the cry for college-educated peace officers has come from several quarters within this century, but until rather recently, few real efforts have occurred to make this vision a reality.

During the 1970s substantial amounts of money were spent by the federal government in the form of LEAA grants to help working peace officers attain postsecondary education. In 1977 Minnesota became the first state to require as a state standard, a minimum level of postsecondary education as an entry requirement for the peace officer position. In 1989 two separate proposals were introduced at the congressional level which would provide resources directed toward programs designed to provide college-level education for peace officers.

While these efforts are laudatory, the law enforcement profession has only been slowly nudged to the precipice. It is time for individual practitioners to take proactive steps to ensure this vision for themselves. In other words, peace officers need to "fish or cut bait."

The increasing complexity of the issues in our society—issues individual peace officers must address—has become an incredible burden. Rapid advances in theory, knowledge and technology, rapidly changing demographics, and newly developing and evolving social problems ranging from ecology to global political realities—all point toward the need for continual growth in peace officer education.

In addition, peace officers interact daily with other professionals in the criminal justice system, all of whom have at least one undergraduate degree. Most have graduate-level educational experiences. Add to this the fact that the educational level of all citizens is increasing dramatically (approximately 40 to 60 percent of current high school graduates will go on to some form of postsecondary education experience), and it becomes clear that if peace officer education does not at least keep pace with these changes, individual officers will be "left in the dust."

All of the preceding information aside, individuals entering law enforcement professions owe it to themselves to aspire to higher educational levels and to make a commitment to lifelong learning. This is important for several reasons.

First, broadly based, postsecondary liberal arts education prepares individuals for a wide range of professional opportunities both within and outside the law enforcement profession. Recent research indicates that most adults will have the opportunity to make major career changes anywhere from three to six times during their life spans. It would be tragic if those choosing law enforcement as one of their careers were not in a position to have similar opportunities.

Second, although no scientific or empirical evidence indicates that increased education results in increased performance levels of peace officers, numerous recent perceptual studies report that citizens have more confidence in and esteem for more highly educated officers.

Third, law enforcement executives are constantly expressing the need for more officers who have:

➢ Well-developed verbal and written communication skills.
➢ Excellent critical thinking and decision-making skills.
➢ Highly developed ethical and moral standards.
➢ The ability to analyze complex public policy issues and social trends.

Such attributes are developed in the broad-based, interdisciplinary liberal arts curriculum available through postsecondary educational experiences.

Finally, and perhaps most important, postsecondary education will prepare peace officers to grow personally. If allowed to, the law enforcement environment can become a narrow, isolated, cynical place, not unlike a prison. Postsecondary education, continuing education, commitment to lifelong learning and an appreciation for diversity can help peace officers keep the walls from closing in on them.

We in law enforcement do not have the luxury to wait for our agencies or our governments to provide education fo us. We must recognize that education is as important to our "officer survival skills" as our firearms and other weapons training. Education does not need to be a state mandate or a department policy. It can be our individual choice, a gift to ourselves. No group of professionals is more deserving.

Timothy E. Erickson is an assistant professor at Metropolitan State University in Minnesota. He has been employed in the field of criminal justice for 26 years, serving as a police officer, police sergeant and sergeant investigator for the St. Paul (Minnesota) Police Department. He also served as the education coordinator for the Minnesota POST Board. Mr. Erickson is also a licensed secondary education teacher, holds an MAT (broad area social science) and an MSE (educational counseling) degree.

MIND STRETCHES

1. Imagine you have a crystal ball—what changes do you see in the world of work five years from now? Ten years from now? Fifty years from now?

2. What role do you think education will play in the future?

3. Do you think work will become more specialized or more generalized in the future? Why? How will your job goals be affected?

4. What do you think will happen to current age limitations on jobs? Why?

5. What jobs do you think will become more necessary in the future? Less necessary?

6. Is your community changing? How? What about neighboring communities?

7. Why do you think more people don't pursue advanced education or specialized training? Are these reasons legitimate?

8. Recognizing that our entire society is always changing, what importance will you place on continuing to grow and change yourself?

9. Is always striving to improve yourself important to you? Is there a danger in not continuing to grow and change?

10. Can you think of jobs that do not now exist but will within the next 10 or 20 years?

REFERENCES

Bradsher, Keith. "America, Land of Inequality." (Minneapolis/St. Paul) *Star Tribune,* April 18, 1995, p. 4A.

Cornish, Edward, ed. *Careers Tomorrow: The Outlook for Work in a Changing World* (selections from *The Futurist*). Bethesda, MD: World Future Society, 1983.

Eskridge, Chris W. *Criminal Justice: Concepts and Issues*, 3rd ed. Los Angeles: Roxbury Publishing Company, 1999.

Future Work. Bethesda, MD: World Future Society, 1991.

Hammonds, Keith H. "The New World of Work." *Business Week,* October 17, 1994, pp. 76–87.

Imel, Susan. *Jobs in the Future: Myths and Realities*. ERIC, Clearinghouse on Adult, Career and Vocational Education, 1994.

Mackay, Harvey. "Perfectly Positioned." *Successful Meetings,* February 1993, p. 37.

Mendofik, Paul J. "Career Development." *Law and Order,* May 1995, pp. 41–45.

Meyers, Mike. "More Brain, Less Brawn." (Minneapolis/St. Paul) *Star Tribune*, April 11, 1999, p. D5.

Moreau, Dan. "Great for Grads Job Mart." *Kiplinger's Personal Finance Magazine*, January 1996, pp. 51–53.

Naisbitt, John. *Megatrends: Ten New Directions Transforming Our Lives*. New York: Warner Books, 1982.

Occupational Outlook Handbook, 1998–1999 Edition. Bulletin 2500. Washington, DC: Bureau of Labor Statistics, January 1998.

Pulley, Mary Lynn. *Losing Your Job—Reclaiming Your Soul*. San Francisco: Jossey-Bass Publishers, 1997.

Sawyer, Joel. "Gap between Poor, Rich Continues to Grow, Reports Says." (Minneapolis/St. Paul) *Star Tribune*, December 17, 1997, p. A13.

Tevlin, Jon. "Change Will Come Slowly." (Minneapolis/St. Paul) *Star Tribune*, April 11, 1999, p. D5.

Toffler, Alvin and Heidi. "The Future of Law Enforcement: Dangerous and Different." *FBI Law Enforcement Bulletin,* January 1990, pp. 2–5.

The Top 100: The Fastest Growing Careers for the 21st Century. Chicago: Ferguson Publishing Company, 1998.

CHAPTER 2

CAREERS IN LAW ENFORCEMENT

The very first step towards success in any occupation is to become interested in it.

—*John Dewey*

Do You Know:

➢ What two courses futurist Alvin Toffler says law enforcement can take?
➢ What societal changes have had an impact on the law enforcement profession?
➢ Why specialization within the law enforcement profession is important?
➢ How job prospects look for those interested in the field of juvenile justice?
➢ What percentage of time is spent on patrol or doing routine paperwork and how much time is actually taken up with chases and shoot-outs?
➢ What twelve federal agencies you might consider in seeking employment in law enforcement or a related field? Six state agencies? Three county agencies? Two local agencies?
➢ Where the greatest employment potential is usually found?
➢ At what jurisdictional levels civilian positions in law enforcement are available?
➢ How common promotions in law enforcement are?
➢ What career options exist in community crime prevention and the "helping" professions?
➢ How specialized training or expertise may benefit a law enforcement professional?
➢ What the availability of international jobs in law enforcement is?

INTRODUCTION

This chapter discusses the largest and most visible component of the criminal justice system—law enforcement. It begins with a brief overview of the evolution of law enforcement and important changes occurring within the profession. This is followed by a discussion of what the law enforcement profession entails in reality as opposed to what is often seen in movies and on television. Next, a close-up look at the variety of employment available in law enforcement is presented, followed by an explanation of where specific opportunities exist at the federal, state, county and local levels. This includes a brief look at the salaries that might be expected and the compensation packages often provided. The chapter concludes with a discussion of career opportunities in areas closely related to and supportive of law enforcement.

THE EVOLUTION OF LAW ENFORCEMENT

It has been said that the best way to know where you are going is to look at where you have been. Law enforcement has deep roots in the past. Be it the Code of Hammurabi (2200 B.C.), the Justinian Code (A.D. 527), Leges Henrici (A.D. 1100s), the Magna Carta, the United States Constitution or the world A.C. (after computers), law enforcement has played an extraordinary role in the development of civilization. Whether the system was that of a Hue and Cry (A.D. 800s), a Watch and Ward (1200s) or one of the more modern approaches to enforcing the law, such as constables, Bow Street Runners (London's first detectives), Bobbies, deputies, marshals, or police officers, its members have always been valuable societal resources.

For those involved in law enforcement, "job security" is not an issue. No matter what social policies are in place, no matter what resources are available, the law will need to be enforced, and people will continue to call for help.

While our technology becomes increasingly sophisticated and our society itself more complex, a certain segment of our population will continue to prey upon the weak. Similarly, there will continue to be individuals who, for whatever reason, are unable to care for themselves. The equipment may change, but the challenge will remain—*to protect and to serve.* How this challenge is approached has changed over the centuries.

Recall from Chapter 1 Toffler's "three waves" theory of sweeping major changes in society:

➢   The Agricultural Revolution
➢   The Industrial Revolution
➢   The Technological Revolution

Tafoya (1990, p. 15) uses Toffler's wave analogy to describe changes in law enforcement. The first wave was the Metropolitan Police Act of 1829, the first major reform in law enforcement, which brought order and a military model to law enforcement. The second wave occurred nearly 100 years later:

> A century later in the 1930s, August Vollmer and O.W. Wilson, two American police pioneers, advanced the goal of "professionalizing" law enforcement. Their efforts ushered in the "second wave" of major law enforcement reform. Standardization, specialization, synchronization, concentration, maximization, and centralization dominated law enforcement during this era.

The third wave began with the civil unrest of the 1960s and 70s. Law enforcement professionals began questioning the military model and the bureaucracy associated with policing. In the past, the majority of law enforcement officers had a military background and were used to accepting orders without question. This is no longer true of today's more highly educated young workers who are used to thinking for themselves. Tafoya (p. 15) suggests: "Today, there is ample evidence to indicate that insofar as dealing with people is concerned, the good ole days may best serve as memories, not models for future personnel practices." According to Tafoya (p. 13), almost a decade ago Toffler spoke to a group of law enforcement executives at the FBI Academy and suggested:

> . . . because change was taking place so rapidly, tremendous social pressures were occurring and will continue to ferment and explode unless opportunities were created to relieve those pressures.

> According to Toffler, law enforcement, like society, has two possible courses of action. The first is to cling to the status quo; the second to facilitate social change.

Futurist Alvin Toffler believes law enforcement may take one of two courses: cling to the status quo or evolve to facilitate social change.

Our criminal justice system has a rich history. The fact that the field is so historically based and tends to be so conservative may help to explain why more reliance may have been placed on past tradition than on future advancement. Some believe that the profession of law enforcement has actually changed little over the centuries except, of course, for some advances in technology. But change is certainly occurring now.

Change *always* creates tension. Here the tension is between a profession very much rooted in history and tradition and a society always on the move. As recently as the past decade, law enforcement has become recognized as a profession. New responses to new challenges are sure to emerge.

THE CHANGING LAW ENFORCEMENT PROFESSION

Fulton (1998, p. 98) asserts: "Change is inevitable in any police organization." Leonard (1997, p. 63) contends: "Change can be simple or complicated, fast and furious or slow and unnoticeable. It can come in many shapes and forms. One thing is for sure, though, it will come." He adds that, just as change is inevitable, so is an inherent fear of change: "The fear of change exists because change goes against an individual's comfort zone." Nonetheless: "Change is an inevitable part of police work, even if police organizations have historically resisted it."

One of *the* most important changes is the flood of immigrants, legal and illegal, who cluster together in poor neighborhoods with high crime rates, thereby presenting a tremendous challenge to law enforcement. Officers must guard against stereotyping immigrants. In addition, many immigrants come from cultures where uniformed officers are feared, not respected. Further, many will become victims because they do not know our laws or our customs and are easy targets for predators.

No one can argue that our world is changing, perhaps faster than we can keep up with. Technologically speaking, it seems that the "good guys" are always racing just to keep up with the firepower of the "bad guys." For example, while the criminal element has been using semiautomatic weapons for years, many police agencies in the United States are still using revolvers. Further, prisons and jails, for the most part, are full or overflowing, and the courts are requiring more correctional authorities to either build more facilities or release more prisoners. The release of nonrehabilitated prisoners will certainly affect most police agencies and their personnel in the near future.

An even greater problem may be the increasing significance of the subculture of the illegal drug world and the spin-offs that are adversely affecting more and more people and their organizations (including families). This problem permeates our society and presents a tremendous challenge.

Even as the makeup of our community is changing, the majority of police agencies still provide the same style of law enforcement service they always have. How these services are provided will need to be reexamined if law enforcement and the entire criminal justice system are to keep up with the developing needs of society. One of the biggest changes that immediately comes to mind is the increasing educational requirements for police officers. As the profession of law enforcement has become recognized as a true profession, the need for education has increased. Police must keep up with the times and the expectations of the community they serve. Another important change is in the makeup and expectations of those entering law enforcement. There was a time when law enforcement was a job that *men* did upon returning from military service, perhaps because they had no other skills or abilities. In some jurisdictions an individual can still get hired as an officer without any necessary prior training, be handed a badge and a gun, and be expected to enforce the law—or business regulations. Such agencies are facing extinction, however. As noted by Sharp (1995, p. 68):

> The vast majority of law enforcement administrators believe the role of officers will change dramatically in the early years of the 21st century. That change was summed up by Virginia's Assistant Attorney General James Gilmore. He told an assembly of administrators . . . that police used to get by with a badge, baton, and gun. Today, he said, they must be part-time lawyers, scientists, social workers, psychologists, and full-time heroes to replace the drug dealers.

Without question, the civilianization of criminal justice is not just something being considered; it's happening. Why? It's cheaper. Civilian positions don't require the ongoing training required of sworn police personnel, and in some cases they don't have the higher pay or added benefits either. And sometimes nonsworn personnel provide a different perspective than a police officer.

For example, some departments assign juvenile cases to juvenile justice specialists rather than police officers. These specialists might have a degree in social work but not be police-licensed. Or a crime lab employee might specialize in a certain area of investigation, but again, not be a sworn police officer.

The trend towards *community-oriented policing* is a relatively new field that will provide many opportunities for civilian and sworn personnel. According to Miller and Hess (1998, p. 21): "Community policing is a philosophy that emphasizes working proactively with citizens to reduce fear, solve crime-related problems and prevent crime."

Community policing is proactive rather than reactive, seeking to identify and solve problems rather than simply reacting to incidents as they occur. Problem solving is a vital component of community-oriented policing. It requires officers to identify problems through personal experience, through talking with residents or through calls for service. They must then analyze the problems, develop a response or solution and then assess the effectiveness of the response.

Often it is a police officer who is detailed to such community-oriented work, but it doesn't need to be. There are civilian crime prevention officers and community liaisons. Some civilian employees work as crime victim advocates or other resource personnel to help the community. Even evidence-room technicians need not necessarily be sworn personnel. The field of criminal justice will continue to use their personnel in different ways, not only to provide a better level of service but to save money as well.

Societal changes affecting the law enforcement profession include the increasing number of immigrants, the increased availability of powerful weapons and firearms to criminals, overcrowded correctional facilities, the expanding drug problem, a greater need for educated law enforcement personnel, a shift in the characteristics of those entering the law enforcement profession and an emphasis on community-oriented policing and problem solving.

Another major change impacting the criminal justice field is advancing technology. As noted by Domash (1998, p. 24): "Computer technology has . . . revolutionized the law enforcement industry." For example, the application of digital technology to law enforcement offers significant enhancements to crime scene processing and communication among officers (p. 25). Digital cameras allow immediate "processing" and permit images to be downloaded to department computers for rapid, efficient circulation among personnel. Digital two-way radios are being developed to enable officers at the local, state and federal levels to communicate readily with each other regardless of distance.

Law enforcement gear is also going high tech, with major improvements being made to body armor and higher caliber weapons (p. 25). Finally, police vehicles and traffic devices are helping to improve the safety of the officers, as well as the citizens, on the streets.

OFFICERS OF THE FUTURE

As the needs of our society change, so will the profession of law enforcement and the expectations of those entering or remaining in this field. Education will continue to be viewed as important, including specialized education. Applicants who are skilled in foreign languages or have experience with groups, such as juveniles or people with disabilities, will be particularly attractive to employers. Technical skills such as computer literacy will, no doubt, look attractive to employers as well.

Society is changing and, as a result, professions are changing as well. To meet the increasing demands of our world, people need to become specialists. Attorneys specialize in certain areas of law, physicians specialize within the medical field and, more and more, those in criminal justice and related fields are specializing.

While most officers do, and possibly should, begin their careers as generalists, most upwardly mobile, successful professional police officers will specialize: juvenile specialists, crime prevention specialists, polygraph specialists, and the list goes on. As technology continues to develop, specialists in these areas will be sought. As our society changes, becoming older and more diverse in demographic and cultural makeup, other needed specialties will emerge as well.

A need exists for specialization within the law enforcement field. While a majority of officers begin as generalists, those who wish to progress up the ladder of responsibility and salary will usually need to specialize.

This does not mean that the day of the "generalist" police officer on patrol is nearing an end. It is highly likely that patrol officers will continue as the backbone of any law enforcement agency. The fact is, every aspect of our world is becoming more complex and specialized. Those who are successful today recognized a decade or two ago what the future would need. The people putting themselves in a good position for future advancement will be able to successfully work toward the future.

Planning for the future may be as general as obtaining a generalized advanced education to effectively interact with those of similar educational levels in other professions. It may be acknowledging the increasing cultural diversity of the United States and learning a foreign language or two. It may be acquiring a degree in management, law, computer science, public relations or psychology. Our world is complex and no doubt will require significantly more of law enforcement professionals than in the past. It's your call. *Anything* you can do to set yourself positively apart from others is important. If you have the chance to acquire specialized skills, take that chance. Don't merely keep up with the others. Take advantage of the myriad of opportunities available to meet the challenge and forge ahead.

A Special Challenge—The Juvenile Officer

Although theoretically the juvenile justice system is separate from the criminal justice system, it is inextricably linked with that system. And because of the growing amount of juvenile delinquency and serious, violent offenses committed by youth, the juvenile justice system is expanding at a phenomenal rate and should be a major employer of personnel in the years ahead. Careers in juvenile justice include such areas as group home child care workers/counselors, intake officers and child care workers in juvenile detention facilities or correctional facilities, boot camps, juvenile probation, etc.

Work in the juvenile justice system is very challenging, and the need for juvenile officers is growing.

The juvenile officer faces a particular challenge in that the system "lumps" youths who are violent criminals together with youths who commit relatively minor offenses (such as smoking) and youths who are victims of neglect or abuse. According to Drowns and Hess (2000, p. 2):

> Our juvenile justice system is a complex, changing network that is apart from, yet a part of, the broader criminal justice system. It is apart *from* that system in that it is charged with protecting youths from harm, neglect and abuse, both emotional and physical. This protection frequently involves the criminal justice system as well as numerous public agencies and organizations. The juvenile justice system is a part *of* the criminal justice system in that it is charged with dealing with youths who break the law, and some juveniles may end up in the adult system.

If you enjoy working with youths, a career in the juvenile justice system may be right for you. If you think you might be interested in this area of law enforcement, start volunteering with some youth groups to gain experience in working with youths and to confirm that this is, indeed, an area of special interest to you.

IS LAW ENFORCEMENT FOR YOU?

To make informed decisions about your career, you must gather factual data. Some of this information comes from within. Do you possess the personal attributes needed to be a police officer? Can you give orders? Can you take orders? Can you remain calm under stress? Can you treat people professionally and apply the law equally? Can you work the hours under the conditions required by the job? Can you control innate and acquired drives and impulses under various environmental situations, some of which may be ambiguous?

You also need to consider objective, external data. Much of what happens within the law enforcement profession is not common knowledge. Consequently, many people considering employment in law enforcement may find themselves relying on inaccurate data. Unless you have a personal friend or relative in law enforcement, you are likely to obtain what you know about the field from where most people do: television or the movies.

It Isn't So

Because of the popularity of police investigators and detectives, movies and television shows about them abound. But the primary goal of such shows is to entertain, not to educate. Sensationalism is much more likely than realism. Television may lead you to believe police work falls into one of two categories: driving through downtown at night with siren blaring and red lights flashing or investigating macabre crimes in obscure locations.

A major public misconception about police work is that it is primarily oriented toward catching criminals. *Nash Bridges, NYPD Blue, Homicide* and other television dramas about law enforcement depict police continuously involved in high-speed chases, exciting and dangerous shoot-outs and other dramatic criminal-catching activities. In fact, according to official estimates, 80 percent of police work consists of routine paperwork and patrol.

The law enforcement profession is grossly misrepresented in television shows and movies. In reality, about 80 percent of duty time is spent on patrol and doing routine paperwork. "Action" such as investigations, high-speed chases, shoot-outs and other dramatic criminal-catching activities consumes only about 20 percent of the time on duty.

"Actually, I was hoping the job would be a little more like Miami Vice."

To select a career based on fiction is to set yourself up for disappointment. No one knows better than those in the profession that television shows and movies don't exactly "tell it like it is." The uniforms, the cars, the equipment, the apparent prestige and the legal authority combine to make for a romantic ideal. This is why the media loves to portray detectives as such colorful characters. Don't be fooled. Take a hard look at the law enforcement profession as you make realistic, informed decisions about your future career.

According to the *Occupational Outlook Handbook* (1998, p. 346), 40-hour workweeks are typical for law enforcement officers, although paid overtime is common. Because most communities require round-the-clock police protection, officers (typically junior officers) are needed to work the night, weekend and holiday shifts. Also, keep in mind that you will not begin your career as a detective—it may be a goal that requires many years to achieve. Other significant points to consider about pursuing a career as a police officer, detective or special agent include (p. 345):

➢   Police work can be dangerous and stressful.
➢   The number of qualified candidates exceeds the number of job openings in federal law enforcement agencies and in most state, local, and special police departments.
➢   Opportunities will be best in those urban communities whose departments offer relatively low salaries and where the crime rate is relatively high.

Large, urban departments may offer the widest variety of positions, as well. According to *The Top 100: The Fastest Growing Careers for the 21st Century* (1998, pp. 269–270):

> In very large city police departments, officers may fill positions as police chiefs, precinct sergeants and captains, desk officers, booking officers, police inspectors, identification officers, complaint evaluation supervisors and officers, crime prevention police officers, and internal affairs investigators, whose job it is to police the police. Some officers work as plainclothes detectives in criminal investigation divisions. Other specialized police officers include police reserves commanders; police officer commanding officers III, who act as supervisors in missing persons and fugitive investigations; and police officers III, who investigate and pursue nonpayment and fraud fugitives. Many police departments employ police clerks, who perform administrative and community-oriented tasks.

The possibility of officer assaults and fatalities is one aspect of the job many prefer not to think about. Nevertheless, grim statistics attest to the potential violence that law enforcement officers may encounter on the job. In an article titled "Police Deaths Slightly Lower in 1998" (1999, p. 11), data from the National Law Enforcement Officers Memorial Fund and the Concerns of Police Survivors indicate there were 155 federal, state and local law enforcement fatalities during 1998, compared to 160 during 1997. Hall (1998, p. 6) adds: "For far too many years to count, on average, every week, at least one law officer somewhere in this country is murdered."

Another hazard of the job involves the reality of communicable diseases. Officers called to the scene of an accident may come in contact with blood or other bodily fluids. Officers attempting to arrest or contain drunken, high, violent, excited or otherwise "altered" individuals may be bitten, scratched, spit on or worse, increasing their chances of contracting diseases, some of which may be fatal. Many agencies now make hepatitis vaccinations available and have regular HIV testing for officers involved in needle pricks and other high-risk incidents— incidents that may be as deadly as an assault.

These statistics are presented not to discourage or frighten you from considering a career in law enforcement; they are meant to raise your awareness about some of the potential hazards of a very worthwhile profession. Caution, alertness and good judgment are critical, possibly lifesaving, qualities every good officer should possess. You must also consider the level of education, training and other qualifications needed to be considered for a law enforcement position. As noted in the *Occupational Outlook Handbook* (p. 346): "Candidates must be U.S. citizens, usually at least 20 years of age, and must meet rigorous physical and personal qualifications. . . . [P]ersonal characteristics such as honesty, good judgment, integrity, and a sense of responsibility are especially important in law enforcement work." Additionally: "In larger police departments, where the majority of law enforcement jobs are found, applicants usually must have at least a high school education. Federal agencies generally require a college degree. A few police departments accept applicants as recruits who have less than a high school education, but the number is declining." It is further noted: "Police departments are encouraging applicants to take postsecondary school training in law enforcement."

EMPLOYMENT OUTLOOK

The outlook for jobs in law enforcement is positive, yet over the next decade, the field is expected to grow more slowly than the average for all occupations due to the "continuing budgetary constraints faced by law enforcement agencies" (*Occupational Outlook,* p. 347). Nonetheless:

> The opportunity for public service through law enforcement work is attractive to many. The job is challenging and involves much responsibility. Furthermore, in many agencies, law enforcement officers may retire with a pension after 20 or 25 years of service, allowing them to pursue a second career while still in their 40s. Because of relatively attractive salaries and benefits, the number of qualified candidates exceeds the number of job openings in Federal law enforcement agencies and in most State, local, and special police departments—resulting in increased hiring standards and selectivity by employers. Competition is expected to remain keen for the higher paying jobs with State and Federal agencies and police departments in more affluent areas.

The Top 100 (p. 272) reports: "Employment of police officers is expected to increase through the year 2005. People today are becoming increasingly security conscious and concerned about drug-related crimes." It also states (p. 106): "The employment outlook for police detectives is expected to be much faster than the average through the year 2005. High estimates call for an increase of nearly 77 percent over the next decade, to more than 104,000 detectives."

Some aspects of law enforcement require careful, realistic consideration. But these fields continue to draw people to them. Ask a hundred officers why they're in it, and you'll hear a hundred different responses. And, yes, police officers complain a lot—about the hours, the pay and the administration. But there is something about law enforcement that gets in your blood.

LAW ENFORCEMENT—UP CLOSE

The allure of being a police officer makes this profession extraordinarily popular. The public generally believes that being a police officer means wearing a uniform and pushing a squad car around town. Few people outside the field have any idea of the variety of employment available. Consider the vocational spectrum shown by the following partial listing of positions, many obtained by reviewing the 1999 *International Association of Chiefs of Police Membership Directory*:

Arson Investigator	Document Specialist	Police Surgeon
Attaché	Emergency Management Coordinator	Polygraph Operator
Ballistics Expert	Evidence Technician	Professor
Booking Officer	FBI Special Agent	Psychiatric Advisor
Border Patrol Officer	Fingerprint Expert	Public Relations Officer
Chaplain	Firearms Instructor	Public Safety Director
Chief of Police	Forensic Scientist	Radio Communications
Chief of Staff	Gaming Enforcement Agent	Records Management Director
Commander of Field Operations	Gang Investigator	Scientist
Commissioner	Inspector	Security Specialist
Communications Officer	Instructor	Secret Service Agent
Community Safety Coordinator	Intelligence Officer	Serology Specialist
Community Service Officer	Investigator	Sheriff
Conservation Officer	Jailer	Street Crimes Specialist
Crime Lab Technician	Juvenile Specialist	Superintendent of Police
Crime Prevention Specialist	K-9 Handler	S.W.A.T.
Customs Officer	Narcotics Agent	Traffic Officer
Data Processing Specialist	Operations Specialist	Training Director
Deputy	Patrol Officer	Treasury Agent
Deputy Chief	Personnel Specialist	Trooper
Detective	Photographer	Undercover Operative
Detention Officer	Pilot	Undersheriff
Director of Research and Development	Police Attorney/Legal Advisor	U.S. Marshal
Director of Scientific Services	Police Psychologist	Water Patrol
Director of Standards and Training	Police/School Liaison Officer	Witness Protection Agent

WHERE OPPORTUNITIES EXIST

To begin your look at law enforcement, consider the basic jurisdictions in which you might work. Jurisdiction in this sense basically addresses both *where* particular agencies work and *what* their enforcement emphasis is. The primary jurisdictional levels are federal, state, county and local.

While law enforcement officers may enforce the law wherever they happen to be, different levels of law enforcement agencies have different areas of responsibility. For example, while Secret Service agents are law enforcement officers, they do not do traffic enforcement. Similarly, local law enforcement officers are seldom called on for diplomatic protective service. The following descriptions of federal, state, county and local agencies are adapted from *Introduction to Law Enforcement and Criminal Justice,* 6th edition (Wrobleski and Hess, 2000, pp. 16–19. Reprinted by permission).

Federal Agencies

Data from "Fed Law Enforcement Is a Growth Industry" (1996, p. 5) indicates: "While Federal agencies from the Department of Energy to the Department of Labor are being downsized as the 'era of big government' wanes, law enforcement appears to be moving briskly in the opposite direction, with more than 41,000 criminal investigators now working for 32 Federal agencies and a proposed increase of nearly 14 percent in the Justice Department's fiscal 1997 budget."

The Federal Bureau of Investigation (FBI). The FBI is the primary investigative agency of the federal government. Its special agents have jurisdiction over more than 200 federal crimes. Responsibilities include investigating espionage; interstate transportation of stolen property and kidnapping; unlawful flight to avoid prosecution, confinement or giving testimony; sabotage; piracy of aircraft and other crimes aboard aircraft; bank robbery and embezzlement; and enforcement of the Civil Rights Act.

In addition to these numerous responsibilities, the FBI provides valuable services to law enforcement agencies throughout the country. The *Identification Division* is a central repository for fingerprint information, including its automated fingerprint identification system (AFIS), which greatly streamlines the matching of fingerprints with suspects. The *National Crime Information Center* (NCIC) is a computerized, electronic data exchange network developed to complement computerized systems already in existence and those planned by local and state law enforcement agencies. The *FBI Laboratory*, the largest criminal laboratory in the world, is available without cost to any city, county, state or federal law enforcement agency in the country. *Uniform Crime Reports* (UCR), another service provided by the FBI, is a national clearinghouse for United States crime statistics.

The Federal Drug Enforcement Administration (FDEA). FDEA agents seek to stop the flow of drugs at their source, both domestic and foreign, and to assist state and local police in preventing illegal drugs from reaching local communities. They become involved in surveillance, raids, interviewing witnesses and suspects, searching for evidence and seizing contraband.

The U.S. Marshals. In 1789 Congress created the office of U.S. Marshal. Marshals are appointed by the president and are responsible for (1) seizing property in both criminal and civil matters to satisfy judgments issued by a federal court, (2) providing physical security for U.S. courtrooms, (3) transporting federal prisoners and (4) protecting government witnesses whose testimony might jeopardize their safety.

The Immigration and Naturalization Service (INS). The Immigration and Naturalization Service has border patrol agents who serve throughout the United States, Canada, Mexico, Bermuda, Nassau, Puerto Rico, the Philippines and Europe. They investigate violations of immigrant and nationality laws and determine whether aliens may enter or remain in the United States.

The Bureau of Prisons (BOP). The Bureau of Prisons is responsible for the care and custody of persons convicted of federal crimes and sentenced to federal penal institutions. The Bureau operates a nationwide system of maximum-, medium- and minimum-security prisons, halfway houses and community program offices.

The Bureau of Customs. The Bureau of Customs has agents stationed primarily at ports of entry to the United States, where people and/or goods enter and leave. Customs agents investigate frauds on customs revenue and the smuggling of merchandise and contraband into or out of the United States.

The Internal Revenue Service (IRS). The Internal Revenue Service, established in 1862, is the largest bureau of the Department of the Treasury. Its mission is to encourage the highest degree of voluntary compliance with the tax laws and regulations. Internal Revenue Service agents investigate willful tax evasion, tax fraud and the activities of gamblers and drug peddlers.

The U.S. Secret Service. The Secret Service was established in 1865 to fight currency counterfeiters. In 1901 it was given the responsibility for protecting the president of the United States, the president's family members, the president-elect and the vice president.

The Bureau of Alcohol, Tobacco and Firearms Tax (BATF). The Bureau of Alcohol, Tobacco and Firearms Tax is primarily a licensing and investigative agency involved in federal tax violations. The Firearms Division enforces the Gun Control Act of 1968.

Postal Inspectors. Postal inspectors enforce federal laws pertaining to mailing prohibited items such as explosives, obscene matter and articles likely to injure or cause damage. Any mail that may prove to be libelous, defamatory or threatening can be excluded from being transported by the postal service. Postal inspectors protect the mails and recipients of mail. They also investigate any frauds perpetrated through the mails such as chain letters, gift enterprises and similar schemes.

The Coast Guard. The Coast Guard assists local and state agencies that border the oceans, lakes and national waterways. They have been actively involved in preventing the smuggling of narcotics into this country.

The Military Services. The armed forces also have law enforcement responsibilities. The uniformed divisions are known as the Military Police in the Army, the Shore Patrol in the Navy and the Security Police in the Marine Corps and Air Force. The military police are primarily concerned with the physical security of the various bases under their control. Within each operation, the security forces control criminal activity, court-martials, discipline, desertions and the confinement of prisoners.

Even if you are not interested in the military as a career, it is a great background when job seeking. The military is particularly well suited for those who are younger and less certain as to what career direction to take. Any military experience is better than just throwing those years away aimlessly wandering from job to job. Military experience is usually directly applicable to successful employment in law enforcement.

Military law enforcement assignments such as the military police provide exceptional experience. Other non-law enforcement assignments, however, also provide proof that the individual can take orders, assume responsibility and successfully accept challenges.

Federal agencies to consider when looking for a job in law enforcement or a related field include (1) Federal Bureau of Investigation; (2) Federal Drug Enforcement Administration; (3) U.S. Marshals; (4) Immigration and Naturalization Service; (5) Bureau of Prisons; (6) Bureau of Customs; (7) Internal Revenue Service; (8) U.S. Secret Service; (9) Bureau of Alcohol, Tobacco and Firearms Tax; (10) Postal Inspectors; (11) Coast Guard and (12) military services.

New recruits with most federal law enforcement agencies throughout the country receive their initial training at the Federal Law Enforcement Training Center (FLETC) in Glynco, Georgia.

Sources of further information regarding federal law enforcement careers are provided at the end of this chapter.

State Agencies

Many federal agencies have state counterparts. State agencies with law enforcement responsibilities may include state bureaus of investigation and apprehension and state fire marshal divisions as well as departments of natural resources, driver and vehicle services divisions, departments of human rights and state police and highway patrol. For state troopers seeking additional specialization, most states have specialized units such as canine units, aircraft units, special response and tactical teams, investigation units and executive protection teams.

State Bureau of Investigation and Apprehension. The Bureau of Investigation and Apprehension places investigators throughout the state to help investigate major crimes, organized criminal activity, and the illegal sale or possession of narcotics and prohibited drugs; conduct police science training courses for peace officers; provide scientific examination of crime scenes and laboratory analysis of evidence; and maintain a criminal justice information and telecommunications system.

State Fire Marshal Division. Designated state fire marshals investigate suspicious and incendiary fire origins, fire fatalities and large-loss fires; tabulate fire statistics; and provide education, inspection and training programs for fire prevention.

State Department of Natural Resources (Fish, Game and Watercraft). Conservation officers investigate complaints about nuisance wildlife, misuse of public lands and waters, violations of state park rules and unlawful appropriation of state-owned timber. They also dispose of big game animals struck by motor vehicles, assist state game managers on wildlife census projects and assist in identifying needed sites for public access to lakes and streams. The department also issues resident and nonresident boat licenses and licenses for hunting, fishing and trapping.

Driver and Vehicle Services Division. The *Motor Vehicle Section* registers motor vehicles, issues ownership certificates, answers inquiries, returns defective applications received through the mail, licenses motor vehicle dealers, supplies record information to the public and in some states, registers bicycles. The *Driver's License Section* tests, evaluates and licenses all drivers throughout the state; maintains accurate records of each individual driver including all violations and accidents occurring anywhere in the United States and Canada; interviews drivers whose record warrants possible revocation, suspension or cancellation; records the location of every reported accident; assists in driver education efforts and administers written and road tests to applicants.

Department of Human Rights. The Department of Human Rights enforces the Human Rights Act, which prohibits discrimination on the basis of race, color, creed, religion, national origin, sex, marital status, status with regard to public assistance or disability in employment, housing, public accommodations, public service and education.

State Troopers—State Police and State Highway Patrol. Some state police enforce all state laws; others enforce only traffic laws on highways and freeways and are usually designated as state highway patrols. A major difference between these two types of troopers is that the state police generally have more investigative duties than do the state highway patrol. Usually, *state police* do not work within municipalities that have their own forces, except on request.

Most *highway patrol* agencies enforce state traffic laws and all laws governing operation of vehicles on public highways in the state. They usually operate in uniform, drive distinctively marked patrol cars and motorcycles and engage in such activities as (1) enforcing laws regulating the use of vehicles, (2) maintaining preventive patrol on the highways, (3) regulating traffic movements and relieving congestion, (4) investigating traffic accidents and (5) making surveys and studies of accidents and enforcement practices to improve traffic safety. In contrast, the state police typically have specialized units of special agents or criminal investigators, plainclothes detectives who investigate various violations of state law such as drug trafficking.

State agencies with law enforcement responsibilities include (1) state bureaus of investigation and apprehension, (2) state fire marshal divisions, (3) departments of natural resources, (4) driver and vehicle services divisions, (5) departments of human rights and (6) state police and highway patrol agencies.

Again, sources of further information regarding state law enforcement careers are provided at the end of this chapter.

County Agencies

The two main types of county law enforcement agencies are the county sheriff and the county police. Another officer of the county is the coroner or medical examiner.

The County Sheriff. Many state constitutions have designated the sheriff as the chief county law enforcement officer. The sheriff is usually elected locally for a two- or four-year term, an obvious mixing of police and politics.

State law establishes the sheriff's powers and duties. Each sheriff is authorized to appoint deputies and, working with them, to assume responsibility for providing police protection, as well as a variety of other functions including (1) keeping the public peace, (2) executing civil and criminal process throughout the county (such as serving civil legal papers and criminal warrants), (3) maintaining and staffing the county jail, (4) preserving the court's dignity and (5) enforcing court orders.

The hundreds of sheriff's departments vary greatly in organization and function. In some states, the sheriff is primarily a court officer; criminal investigation and traffic enforcement are delegated to state or local agencies. In other states, notably in the South and West, the sheriff and deputies perform both traffic and criminal duties. The sheriff's staff ranges from one (the sheriff only) to several hundred, including sworn deputies as well as civilian personnel. One major difference between sheriffs' officers and municipal police departments is that sheriffs often place greater emphasis on civil functions and operating corrections facilities.

The County Police. The county police are often found in areas where city and county governments have merged, such as in Florida. County police departments are headed by a chief of police, usually appointed from within the department.

The Coroner or Medical Examiner. The office of coroner has a history similar to that of the sheriff and comes to modern law enforcement from ancient times. The coroner's principal task is to determine the cause of death and to take care of the remains and personal effects of deceased persons.

The coroner need not be a medical doctor or have any legal background to be elected. In some jurisdictions, however, the coroner has been replaced by the medical examiner, a physician, usually a pathologist who has studied forensic science.

County agencies with law enforcement responsibilities include (1) the county sheriff, (2) the county police and (3) the county coroner or medical examiner.

Local Agencies

Local agencies include township and special district police, the constable, the marshal and municipal police.

Township and Special District Police. The United States has approximately 19,000 townships, which vary widely in scope of governmental powers and operations. Most townships provide a limited range of services for predominantly rural areas. Some townships, often those in well-developed fringe areas surrounding a metropolitan complex, perform functions similar to municipal police.

The Constable. Several states have established the office of constable, especially in New England, the South and the West. The constable is usually an elected official who serves a township, preserving the peace and serving processes for the local justice court. The constable may also be the tax collector or be in charge of the pound, execute arrest warrants and transport prisoners.

The Marshal. In some parts of the United States, a marshal serves as a court officer, serving writs, subpoenas and other papers issued by the court and escorting prisoners from jail or holding cells in the courthouse to and from trials and hearings. The marshal also serves as the bailiff and protects the municipal judge and people in the court. In some jurisdictions, the marshal is elected; in other jurisdictions, the marshal is appointed.

Municipal Police.   The United States has more than 40,000 police jurisdictions and approximately 450,000 police officers, all with similar responsibilities but with limited geographical jurisdictions. The least uniformity and greatest organizational complexity are found at the municipal level due to local autonomy. The majority of these police forces consist of fewer than 10 officers, yet this is what most people think of when they think of law enforcement.

Local agencies and offices with law enforcement responsibilities include (1) township and special district police, (2) the constable, (3) the marshal and (4) municipal police.

JURISDICTIONS COMPARED

Each agency level has its own particular benefits. Federal work may be prestigious and dynamic, and also usually has the best pay and benefits. However, it also usually has higher standards and often requires relocating. Because of the large number of people employed by the federal system, the bureaucracy can be frustrating, with a possibility of feeling engulfed in the numbers. Federal benefits are excellent, however, and transfers within the system are available. On the other hand, likely transfers can substantially interfere with today's common two-profession families. Age may also be a drawback. You cannot be older than 35 at the time you are hired because of laws governing retirement in the federal law enforcement system.

Employment with local law enforcement has its own benefits, frequently associated with being part of a more concentrated law enforcement effort. One community benefit of having a local police department is local identity and control. Many officers enjoy being a recognized part of a smaller community. Smaller agencies may have fewer transfer or promotional opportunities, but may also permit officers to assume more responsibilities on the job.

Usually, the larger the geographic jurisdiction, the greater the number of employment opportunities. In considering where you might find your best employment potential, consider which governmental agencies have the greatest number of employees because with numbers go advancement potential. Remember, however, that it is also easy to feel lost in the sheer numbers.

Some departments are also more aggressive in their hiring of women and minorities, although generally the employment outlook has improved tremendously for both of these groups over the last quarter century. For example, according to a survey by the National Center for Women in Policing (NCWP) of the nation's 100 largest law enforcement agencies, the number of women police officers grew from 2 percent to 12 percent between 1972 and 1997 ("The Future of Women in Policing: Mandates for Action," 1999, p. 53).

Local police departments offer more than half the jobs available, and of these, nearly three-fourths of full-timers are "sworn" personnel as compared to civilian. However, a significant number of civilian opportunities also exist, as shown in Table 2-1.

To find the greatest employment potential, consider agencies that have the greatest number of employees. Remember, more than half of all law enforcement positions are found in local police departments, and civilian opportunities exist at all three levels—federal, state and local.

TABLE 2-1 Employees in State and Local Law Enforcement Agencies (by Type of Agency, United States, 1996)

Type of Agency	Number of Employees					
	-----------------Full-time----------------			*-----------------Part-time----------------*		
	Total	Sworn	Nonsworn	Total	Sworn	Nonsworn
Number	921,978	663,535	258,443	97,770	47,712	50,058
Local police	521,985	410,956	111,029	61,453	30,976	30,477
Sheriff	257,712	152,922	104,790	22,412	10,845	11,567
State police	83,742	54,587	29,155	1,303	132	1,171
Special police	56,229	43,082	13,147	12,003	5,202	6,801
Texas constable	2,310	1,988	322	599	557	42
Percent	100%	72.0%	28.0%	100%	48.8%	51.2%
Local police	100	78.7	21.3	100	50.4	49.6
Sheriff	100	59.3	40.7	100	48.4	51.6
State police	100	65.2	34.8	100	10.1	89.9
Special police	100	76.6	23.4	100	43.3	56.7
Texas constable	100	86.1	13.9	100	93.0	7.0

SOURCE: *Census of State and Local Law Enforcement Agencies, 1996.* Washington, DC: U.S. Department of Justice, Bureau of Justice Statistics Bulletin, June 1998, p. 2. (NCJ-164618)

SALARIES

Simply put, no police officer is ever going to get rich from a government payroll. This is not to say that law enforcement personnel are destined to be destitute. On the contrary, law enforcement pay at the federal, state, county and local levels is certainly comfortable. When you consider the benefits associated with government work—for example, retirement plans, medical coverage, sick time and vacation time, together with job security that is usually better than in the private sector—work in law enforcement is well compensated.

In many jurisdictions, additional opportunities can be taken advantage of to make law enforcement employment even more attractive. Most jurisdictions, for example, have opportunities for some part-time work. Not only could this be overtime work (usually paying more than the 40-hour-per-week pay scale), but local businesses often hire police at good pay for security work, traffic control for special events, etc. While it is usually something other than money that motivates the professional law enforcement officer, salary is an important consideration. Different jurisdictions pay differently, and advancement offers pay incentives.

Federal Salaries

Jobs in law enforcement at the federal level fall under the *General Schedule,* or *GS,* system. This salary scale has 15 grades (GS-1 to GS-15), defined according to level of responsibility, type of work and required qualifications. Salary increases as the grade increases. Each grade has 10 steps. Currently, depending on experience, the starting grade level for jobs in criminal justice at the federal level is usually between GS-5 and GS-7. Various localities may have separate pay scales, but for "the rest of us" (RUS), there is the RUS general pay scale. The 1999 RUS General Schedule Pay Chart is shown in Table 2-2.

TABLE 2-2   1999 RUS General Schedule

GRADE	STEP									
	1	2	3	4	5	6	7	8	9	10
1	$14,146	$14,617	$15,089	$15,557	$16,029	$16,305	$16,768	$17,237	$17,256	$17,699
2	15,905	16,283	16,810	17,256	17,449	17,963	18,476	18,990	19,503	20,017
3	17,354	17,932	18,510	19,088	19,666	20,244	20,823	21,401	21,979	22,557
4	19,481	20,130	20,779	21,428	22,077	22,726	23,375	24,024	24,673	25,322
5	21,797	22,523	23,249	23,975	24,702	25,428	26,154	26,880	27,607	28,333
6	24,295	25,105	25,915	26,725	27,535	28,345	29,154	29,964	30,774	31,584
7	26,998	27,898	28,798	29,698	30,597	31,497	32,397	33,297	34,197	35,097
8	29,900	30,896	31,892	32,889	33,885	34,881	35,877	36,873	37,870	38,866
9	33,026	34,127	35,228	36,329	37,430	38,531	39,632	40,733	41,835	42,936
10	36,370	37,582	38,794	40,006	41,218	42,431	43,643	44,855	46,067	47,279
11	39,960	41,291	42,623	43,955	45,287	46,619	47,951	49,282	50,614	51,946
12	47,891	49,488	51,084	52,681	54,277	55,874	57,470	59,067	60,664	62,260
13	56,951	58,849	60,747	62,645	64,544	66,442	68,340	70,238	72,137	74,035
14	67,298	69,542	71,785	74,029	76,272	78,515	80,759	83,002	85,245	87,489
15	79,162	81,800	84,439	87,077	89,715	92,354	94,992	97,630	100,268	102,907

SOURCE: *Pay Structure of the Federal Civil Service, 1999.* Washington, DC: U.S. Office of Personnel Management, 1999.

State, County and Local Salaries

According to *The Top 100*, salaries for detectives and police officers vary greatly, according to location and the size of the population served. The average starting salary for all police officers is $18,900 but may range from $15,000 in smaller towns and cities to $26,500 in larger cities (p. 272). Salaries of police detectives range from $18,900 to $40,300 (p. 106). A summary of police salary scales, based on a survey of the 100 largest cities in the country, is presented in Figure 2-3. Note that salaries for all ranks are highest in the West and lowest in the Southeast.

Table 2-3   Police Salary Scales

Rank	USA Average (100 largest cities)	West[a]	Central[b]	Midwest[c]	Northeast[d]	Southeast[e]
Officer	$30,760	$36,906	$29,609	$31,110	$29,606	$23,675
Sergeant	45,868	53,143	42,760	43,919	50,300	35,633
Lieutenant	54,813	64,339	50,188	54,640	56,347	40,874
Captain	60,528	73,493	57,152	57,975	64,453	44,825

NOTE: Footnotes denote which states are in each of the five regions. The number in [brackets] indicates how many of the 100 largest cities are found within that state.
[a] Alaska [1], Arizona [3], California [16], Hawaii [1], Idaho [0], Nevada [1], Oregon [1], Utah [0], Washington [3] – 9 states; 26 cities
[b] Colorado [3], Kansas [1], Montana [0], Nebraska [2], New Mexico [1], North Dakota [0], Oklahoma [2], South Dakota [0], Texas [10], Wyoming [0] – 10 states; 19 cities
[c] Illinois [1], Indiana [2], Iowa [1], Kentucky [2], Michigan [2], Minnesota [2], Missouri [2], Ohio [6], West Virginia [0], Wisconsin [2] – 10 states; 20 cities
[d] Connecticut [1], Delaware [0], Maine [0], Maryland [2], Massachusetts [1], New Hampshire [0], New Jersey [2], New York [3], Pennsylvania [2], Rhode Island [0], Vermont [0], Virginia [5] – 12 states; 16 cities
[e] Alabama [3], Arkansas [0], Florida [5], Georgia [2], Louisiana [3], Mississippi [1], North Carolina [3], South Carolina [0], Tennessee [2] – 9 states; 19 cities

SOURCE: Adapted from "Police Salary Scales." *Police*, August 1997, pp. 20–21. Compiled by the Bobit Research Department, June 1997. Reprinted by permission.

Fringe Benefits

According to *The Top 100* (p. 272):

> Because most police officers are civil service employees, they receive generous benefits, including health insurance and paid vacation and sick leave, and enjoy increased job security. In addition, most police departments offer retirement plans and retirement after twenty or twenty-five years of service, usually at half pay.

Promotions and Transfers

The Top 100 (p. 271) notes:

> Advancement in these [law enforcement] occupations is determined by several factors. An officer's eligibility for promotion may depend on a specified length of service, job performance, formal education and training courses, and results of written examinations. Those who become eligible for promotion are listed on the promotional list along with other qualified candidates. Promotions generally become available from six months to three years after starting, depending on the department.

Law enforcement has definite upward salary limitations, but the main frustration for most is that promotions are limited, corresponding to the number of officers in the particular department. Larger city departments usually offer greater numbers of advancement opportunities, whereas police forces in smaller communities are typically more limited by the rank and number of law enforcement personnel needed (*The Top 100*, pp. 271–272). The fact is, most police officers will retire at the employment level at which they were hired. While intermediate supervisory positions between patrol officer and chief exist, there are far fewer of these than there are officers. A major contributing factor to police "burnout" is that many officers consider lack of promotion as a lack of recognition.

> Promotions in law enforcement are limited, and most police officers retire at the employment level at which they were hired.

As noted earlier, many other employment opportunities exist in specialty positions within a department. Becoming a specialist in such areas as traffic enforcement, accident investigation, juveniles, narcotics enforcement, K-9 handling or internal affairs may prevent officers from falling into a rut.

Promotions and transfers generally come from within a department. Not only would the administration know the individual, but the promotion would serve as recognition for that officer's work. There are, however, benefits to bringing in an outsider, particularly if no one from within the department is qualified or if internal problems require someone without prior ties to the department. Promotional opportunities outside one's department are occurring more often. The career ladder is the focus of Chapter 15.

Like other professions, getting ahead in law enforcement requires both time and commitment—sometimes combined with luck. People do make sergeant, lieutenant, captain and chief. But you can't rise to the top without landing that first entry-level position. From there, your job-seeking skills become job-advancing skills.

You may also find a career in a field related to law enforcement.

CAREER OPTIONS RELATED TO LAW ENFORCEMENT

The more regular hours, the varied and interesting assignments and the relative lack of danger are just a few factors that might motivate you to consider some exciting careers that *support* law enforcement. You can work out of a police station or sheriff's office without being subjected to some of the negatives of police work.

Community Crime Prevention

The last decade has seen an increasing interest in and reliance on community crime prevention. While some law enforcement agencies have sworn officers conduct such work, others assign civilians. Crime prevention specialists have the luxury of working with the community in a positive effort *before* crisis occurs, with the hope of *preventing* crime. Or, they may be the contact that lends valuable assistance after a crisis. Crime prevention specialists educate the community about such issues as locks, lighting, alarms and personal safety. It is an excellent opportunity to be creative because much of crime prevention involves developing programs, designing brochures, presenting speeches and even directing videos and slide presentations. Salaries vary, but the more regular schedule and the opportunity to step into the private sector make this an area worth considering.

Animal Control

Animal control is one area within the realm of community service that can effectively serve as both an entry-level stepping stone to a job in law enforcement or as a specialty area that many find rewarding in itself. If you have a special interest in animal welfare, this is an area where you can get paid for doing what you love.

Other Areas

Other positions traditionally filled by sworn personnel are now often being filled by nonsworn personnel. Examples include juvenile specialists, communications directors and dispatchers. The simple reason for this trend is economic. Nonsworn personnel may be every bit as qualified and yet not need to be paid at the salary level of sworn, often unionized, personnel.

> Civilians are becoming more common in various careers that support traditional law enforcement, including crime prevention specialists, animal control officers, juvenile specialists, communications directors and dispatchers.

THE HELPING PROFESSIONS

The "helping" professions provide a host of jobs for assisting others. This area includes the entire range of rehabilitation workers from treatment center technicians to counselors and social workers to psychologists and psychiatrists. Employment in these areas is extremely satisfying and requires a special commitment to helping others. These professions are often well suited to those who may have had similar problems, giving them special insights that can help guide others. If you have a past record that could interfere with becoming a law enforcement officer, these alternative areas may still be open.

> A career in one of the "helping" professions also supports law enforcement and includes positions such as treatment center technicians, counselors, social workers, psychologists and psychiatrists.

ADVANCED JOBS

Criminal justice provides many opportunities in areas requiring special expertise. While these require advanced training, they also offer higher salaries. Attorneys, for example, can be intimately involved in the criminal justice process from either perspective: prosecution or defense. A law degree is an excellent education for any area of law enforcement, whether the person wants to use it in a courtroom or "in the trenches." This topic is discussed further in Chapter 3.

The criminal justice system needs every type of specialist, including psychologists, physicians, scientists, accountants and engineers. The FBI, for example, specifically seeks people with very specialized training.

Working in law enforcement with specialized degrees can provide attractive pay and benefits. The downside, however, is that your work may not vary and travel may be a requirement. In particular, federal agencies may require a number of relocations throughout a career. Such relocations can be viewed as exciting opportunities or as extreme inconveniences.

Almost *any* specific area of interest you have can be successfully woven into a satisfying career. Police officers with law degrees, psychology degrees or medical degrees are of great worth to their departments. In addition, the many skills that can be taken into the private sector can not only fill important department needs, but also create attractive and lucrative specialty positions. Expertise in such areas as drawing, photography, computers, firearms, flying or even public relations can help any professional on the move.

> Specialized training or expertise, whether in the form of a law degree, a talent for drawing or the ability to pilot an aircraft, can benefit any law enforcement professional seeking advancement.

INTERNATIONAL JOBS

The vast majority of career areas have a new emphasis on international employment. Law enforcement is no exception. Many people are eager to travel, and if it can be part of their job, all the better.

International jobs are available in law enforcement, but obtaining them is not easy. Most overseas positions are classified jobs with special requirements such as security clearances and confidentiality. Because of such factors as jurisdiction, these jobs tend to be covert, with danger being a real element. Federal agencies such as the FBI, Drug Enforcement Administration and Secret Service have agents around the world. Although it is not part of the criminal justice or law enforcement field, the Central Intelligence Agency (CIA) also offers opportunities for excitement and travel. Again, travel can be a perk as well as a potential difficulty.

> As the field of law enforcement expands, so does the geographic availability of jobs. International job opportunities in law enforcement are slowly increasing, but obtaining them is still difficult.

CONCLUSION

A multitude of agencies exist for those considering a career in law enforcement or related fields, including federal agencies, state agencies, county agencies and local agencies. To find the greatest employment potential, consider agencies that have the greatest number of employees. Remember, more than half of all law enforcement positions are found in local police departments, and civilian opportunities exist at all three levels—federal, state and local.

Civilians are becoming more common in the various careers that support traditional law enforcement, including crime prevention specialists, animal control officers, juvenile specialists, communications directors and dispatchers. A career in one of the "helping" professions also supports law enforcement and includes positions such as treatment center technicians, counselors, social workers, psychologists and psychiatrists.

Keep in mind a need exists for specialization within the law enforcement field. While a majority of officers begin as generalists, those who wish to progress up the ladder of responsibility and salary will usually need to specialize. Specialized training or expertise, whether in the form of a law degree, a talent for drawing or the ability to pilot an aircraft, can benefit any law enforcement professional seeking advancement. Also consider that as the field of law enforcement expands, so does the geographic availability of jobs. International job opportunities in law enforcement are slowly increasing, but obtaining them remains difficult.

ADDITIONAL CONTACTS AND SOURCES OF INFORMATION

AFOSI, Public Affairs Office
1535 Command Drive, Suite B-304
Andrews AFB, MD 20762-7000
(301) 981-6860

American Federation of Police
3801 Biscayne Boulevard
Miami, FL 33137
(305) 573-9819

American Police Academy
1000 Connecticut Avenue NW, Suite 9
Washington, DC 20036
(202) 293-9088

Applying for Federal Jobs—A Guide to Writing Successful Applications and Resumes for the Job You Want in Government
by Patricia B. Wood. May be ordered from:
Workbooks, Inc.
9039 Sligo Creek Parkway, #316
Silver Springs, MD 20901
Phone/FAX (301) 565-9467
Also available:
    The 171 Reference Book; The 171 Writing Portfolio; Promote Yourself! How to Use Your Knowledge, Skills and Abilities . . . and Advance in the Federal Government

Border Patrol hiring
(912) 757-3001, extension 9916

Bureau of Indian Affairs
(202) 208-3711

Drug Enforcement Administration (DEA)
Washington, DC 20537
(202) 401-7834

FCF Jobs
P.O. Box 2176
Brunswick, GA 31521-2176
Web site: http://www.gate.net/~fcfjobs
    Federal Law Enforcement Careers ($9.95)
    State Trooper Careers ($9.95)
    Federal Law Enforcement Testing Guide ($6.95)
    State Handgun Laws ($4.95)

International Association of Chiefs of Police (IACP)
515 North Washington Street, 4th Floor
Alexandria, VA 22314
(703) 836-6767

International Security and Detective Alliance (ISDA)
P.O. Box 6303
Corpus Christi, TX 78466-6303
(512) 888-6164

International Union of Police Associations
1421 Prince Street, Suite 330
Alexandria, VA 22314
(703) 549-7473

National Association of Investigative Specialists (NAIS)
P.O. Box 33244
Austin, TX 78764
(512) 719-3595

National Park Service
1849 C Street NW
Washington, DC 20240
(202) 208-6843

National Police Officers Association of America
P.O. Box 22129
Louisville, KY 40252-0129
(800) 467-6762

National United Law Enforcement Association
256 East McLemore Avenue
Memphis, TN 38106
(901) 774-1118

The Top 100: The Fastest Growing Careers for the 21st Century. Published and distributed by:
            Ferguson Publishing Company
            200 West Madison Street, Suite 300
            Chicago, IL 60606
            (312) 580-5480

U.S. Customs
Job hotline number: 1-800-944-7725

AN INSIDER'S VIEW

IT'S NOT LIKE ON TV

Dennis L. Conroy, Ph.D.
Director of the Employee Assistance Program
St. Paul (Minnesota) Police Department

It is crucial for anyone anticipating a career in law enforcement or private security to realize they will get a view of the world no one else has. They will do and see things that are boring, exciting and amusing. They will also do and see things that are painful, tragic and sometimes terrifying. Careers in law enforcement and private security can be rewarding, but the applicant must also remember there may very well be a "price to pay."

Very few, if any, people entering law enforcement know what they are getting into. *It's not like on television*. The endings aren't always successful, and officers don't always get respect. Those entering law enforcement look forward to becoming a police officer and intend to wear the uniform with pride. The lessons these new officers learn are often very difficult to accept and frequently result in alcoholism, physical problems, divorce and even suicide.

The first lesson new officers learn is that not everyone respects police officers simply because *they are police officers*. Officers soon learn that a large number of people they deal with do not even want them around most of the time. Some will call officers names like "Pig," lie to them, fight with them and even spit on them—just because they are officers. Officers subjected to such treatment discover they are not even permitted to respond except to defend themselves from the most grievous physical harm. Even in that response, they will frequently be challenged on the level of force used and will have to justify such actions later.

The next step in the discovery process occurs when officers learn they are *expected* not to respond when spit on. Being spit on is considered "part of the job." Officers learn that everyone else in the criminal justice system demands respect and inflicts sanctions on those refusing to comply. Can you imagine a defendant spitting on a prosecutor or a judge in a courtroom with impunity? But officers are prohibited from imposing their own sanctions.

New officers are usually shocked at the amount of pain and suffering in the world. Most police officers have grown up without exposure to situations requiring police intervention. They have not seen young children, or even babies, who have been beaten or killed simply for crying. They have not had to talk with and console an elderly couple whose house has been burglarized by teenage vandals, their world invaded and destroyed for no apparent reason. They have probably never had to console a rape victim and tell her that her "hell" may only be starting because if she wants to prosecute the offender she will have to relive the experience time and again and defend her own morality each time.

As new officers learn these lessons, they respond, they change. Officers learn that to work with these problems day after day, they must build a suit of armor to protect themselves. They build this armor by (1) becoming less personally involved and (2) not believing in anyone or anything. While such armor protects officers from work-related issues, it also changes them as individuals.

Many officers find they become cynical and isolated. They lose the capacity to believe in anything or anybody because they have seen or experienced so much disappointment in performing their duties. They see humanity at its worst and the system in almost constant failure. It becomes increasingly difficult to believe in successful outcomes. This cynicism is not only an "at work" attitude, but soon pervades every aspect of the officers' lives.

As officers become more and more cynical, they believe less and less in successful outcomes and begin to invest less and less in personal relationships. This can lead to isolation and loneliness. Officers in the end may have no one but themselves, and they are not sure that they can even believe in themselves.

If applicants know they are likely to experience change, this change can be monitored and, along with the law enforcement career, have a positive outcome. Officers will find rewards in the little things they can do to help individuals they come in contact with. They can brighten a small child's life by just a smile or brief "Hello." They can make an elderly couple feel a bit more secure by driving by and taking the time to wave, showing them that someone cares. As a result, the officers feel better knowing that they made even the smallest difference in the lives of those they have sworn to "protect and serve."

Dennis L. Conroy *is a sergeant with the St. Paul (Minnesota) Police Department. He has been a police officer for over 20 years. He has worked as a patrol officer, patrol supervisor, vice-narcotics investigator, juvenile investigator, trainer and Employee Assistance Program director.*

Dr. Conroy has a Ph.D. in Clinical Psychology and conducts a psychology practice and consulting business. He is the lead author of Officers at Risk: How to Identify and Cope With Stress.

AN INSIDER'S VIEW

A WEALTH OF OPPORTUNITIES

Molly Koivamaki
Emergency Management Coordinator
Eden Prairie (Minnesota) Police Department

The job of civilian crime prevention specialist is the best, in my opinion, because it provides the excitement of working in law enforcement without "getting your hands dirty." This unique position has enjoyed increasing popularity over the past few years.

As a crime prevention specialist, I provide service to units within the police department as well as to citizens and businesses in the community. I analyze calls for service and police reports to provide the patrol division information on where certain types of crimes are likely to occur. This helps the division plan more efficient, directed patrol activity.

In return, patrol officers, particularly those on night shifts, inform me about such things as businesses with open doors or crime victims who may need special attention. I then follow up on the information and inform the officers of the outcome. This system of communication is successful because it is informal and gives officers a way to monitor activities or situations that may otherwise go unchecked.

I help the investigation division by "running interference" with crime victims. This allows the detectives to spend time investigating crimes and not getting too involved with the victims' personal problems. Crime victims' needs range from simply wanting someone to talk to about the crime, to requiring assistance in getting emergency housing or transportation.

Most police agencies provide standard crime prevention programs. Crime prevention specialists coordinate a variety of programs, such as neighborhood watch and apartment watch groups, McGruff programs and school-based safety programs. The police administration relies on the crime prevention specialist to enforce the alarm ordinance, compile monthly and annual reports and do special projects.

I also:

- Plan the review for all new construction permits submitted to the city.
- Do public speaking, addressing civic groups and organizations on a *wide* variety of topics such as personal safety, home security and the like.
- Arrange meetings for police officers to address groups.
- Conduct business crime prevention sessions on such topics as shoplifting awareness and prevention, bank robbery awareness, employee theft and physical security.

Being a part of the criminal justice system is *not* limited to being a cop on the street. Of the many benefits I enjoy in my nonsworn position in our police department, I think I have better hours and less danger, while interacting with the public on a primarily positive basis.

I think many appealing jobs are not considered because they are not the jobs TV portrays as "cop jobs." In fact, these other jobs open up a whole new world of potentially satisfying and exciting employment. Give them a look.

Molly Koivamaki has taken advantage of opportunities not always associated with traditional law enforcement work. By developing her position of crime prevention specialist with a rapidly growing metro area police department, she quickly made a name for herself as an expert in this expanding area of law enforcement. Developing her expertise in the areas of both commercial and residential crime prevention, as well as personal safety, she combined this interest with the current interest communities have in emergency management. As the newly appointed emergency management coordinator for her city, Ms. Koivamaki continues to recognize the opportunities in very important areas within the field that others fail to and continues to grow as a professional dedicated to the overall field of public safety.

MIND STRETCHES

1. What do most people think of when they think of a "police job"? Where did you acquire the information on which you base your answer?

2. Do you see law enforcement changing to respond to new challenges?

3. Why might you *not* want to consider a job as a police officer "on the street"?

4. Do "nonsworn" law enforcement positions, such as civilian crime prevention specialists, have career benefits not available to police officers? What negatives would you want to be aware of in considering a career such as a community service officer?

5. What other vocational or avocational skills could blend well with a police career? Can you think of unique skills that could make a candidate for a job more attractive to a hiring agency?

6. Why might someone interested in a career in policing fail to consider other jobs in the security or criminal justice fields?

7. Can law enforcement continue as it has been in serving communities, or is some change inevitable? What change do you foresee, if any? What can you begin doing right now to meet the challenge?

8. Why do you think the entertainment field is so obsessed with law enforcement? Do you think this obsession helps or hurts the profession? Why?

9. What is your favorite television police show? Why? Do you think television and the movies have influenced your career choice?

10. Are police salaries more or less than you had anticipated? Does salary affect your decision as to what field of employment you will eventually pursue? Why or why not?

REFERENCES

Domash, Shelly Feuer. "Technological Change Spurs Growth in Policing Industry." *Police*, August 1998, pp. 24–31.

Drowns, Robert W. and Hess, Kären M. *Juvenile Justice*, 3rd ed. Belmont, CA: West/Wadsworth Publishing Company, 2000.

"Fed Law Enforcement Is a Growth Industry." *Law Enforcement News*, April 30, 1996, p. 5.

Fulton, Roger. "Managing Change." *Law Enforcement Technology*, June 1998, p. 98.

"The Future of Women in Policing: Mandates for Action." *The Police Chief*, March 1999, pp. 53–56.

Hall, Dennis. "Officer Death Toll in 1997 a Tragic Reminder to Us All." *Police*, September 1998, p. 6.

Leonard, Karl S. "Making Change a Positive Experience." *Law and Order*, May 1997, pp. 63–64.

Miller, Linda S. and Hess, Kären M. *The Police in the Community: Strategies for the 21st Century*, 2nd ed. Belmont, CA: West/Wadsworth Publishing Company, 1998.

Occupational Outlook Handbook. 1998–1999 Edition. U.S. Department of Labor. Bureau of Labor Statistics. Washington, DC: U.S. Government Printing Office, January 1998.

"Police Deaths Slightly Lower in 1998." *Law Enforcement Technology*, February 1999, p. 11.

Sharp, Arthur G. "The 21st Century Cop." *Law and Order*, February 1995, pp.68, 73.

Tafoya, William L. "The Future of Policing." *FBI Law Enforcement Bulletin*, January 1990, pp. 13–17.

The Top 100: The Fastest Growing Careers for the 21st Century. Chicago: Ferguson Publishing Company, 1998.

Wrobleski, Henry M. and Hess, Kären M. *Introduction to Law Enforcement and Criminal Justice*, 6th ed. Belmont, CA: West/Wadsworth Publishing Company, 2000.

CHAPTER 3

CAREERS IN THE COURTS AND CORRECTIONS

The pessimist complains about the wind; the optimist expects it to change; the realist adjusts the sails.

—Anonymous

Do You Know:

➤ How a law degree may be useful to someone not seeking to become a lawyer?
➤ Besides lawyers, what other professionals work in our nation's courts?
➤ What the purpose of corrections is in our criminal justice system?
➤ What the primary difference between adult corrections and juvenile corrections has traditionally been and whether this is still the case?
➤ Who the majority of corrections employees are?
➤ What corrections officers do and how the future looks for those seeking this job?
➤ What the primary difference is between probation and parole and whether one officer can manage both probationers and parolees?
➤ How the job outlook is for probation and parole officers?
➤ What impact home detention and electronic monitoring have on jobs in corrections?

INTRODUCTION

As you learned in Chapter 2, an incredible variety of jobs are available within the law enforcement profession—everything from patrol officer to police surgeon—assuring a niche for almost every interest. Beyond that, the criminal justice field offers even more than you may have ever considered. You may be destined for a job you have never thought of or even knew existed—until now.

Directing your career toward one of these other areas could open a whole new world of employment satisfaction. The criminal justice system is so complex it needs a tremendous number of participants. While many of these jobs may not appear as glamorous as those frequently depicted on television, they are extremely important and provide exceptional opportunities.

This chapter presents the numerous job opportunities within the other two components of the criminal justice system—the courts and corrections. It begins with a focused look at the judicial system in the United States and the critical role played by lawyers. It also discusses numerous other careers within this system that might interest those wishing to become part of criminal justice. The chapter then presents a focused look at corrections in the United States, including the adult and juvenile systems as well as careers at the federal, state and local levels.

OPPORTUNITIES IN OUR JUDICIAL SYSTEM—THE COURTS

Before exploring the various jobs within the judicial system, let's briefly review the nature of our legal system. It is highly complex and by its very nature, adversarial. This means that the accused is pitted against the government prosecutor and that the entire affair is presumed to involve a challenge of the individuals as well as a challenge to the system. While this process has been accused of being too involved and full of loopholes and technicalities, one thing is for sure: the system requires a lot of employees.

Lawyers

When you think of job opportunities within the legal system, you usually begin by thinking of attorneys. If you are like a lot of other people, you may not think too highly of lawyers. This negative view has existed for centuries. In fact, toward the end of Shakespeare's *Henry VI*, one of the rebels against the king expresses the desire of many people throughout history when he states: "The first thing we do, let's kill all the lawyers."

Lawyers are essential in our courts, however. The judicial process generally requires at least two lawyers—one representing the state, or "the people," (the prosecutor) and one representing the defendant (the defense attorney). Each lawyer must represent his or her client aggressively within the boundaries of the law.

Many people who don't understand the system look down on defense lawyers because of what their clients have been accused of doing, when in actuality, defense lawyers are simply doing their job by aggressively representing the client. In addition, some people may feel the system is unfair because it seems to favor the wrongdoer with such rules as prohibiting certain evidence from being admitted. Although some attorneys find this side of the system unappealing and may prefer to be a prosecutor, many attorneys find working for the defense a great challenge. Whichever side a trial lawyer chooses, some of the best known attorneys began their careers as prosecutors or defense lawyers because this is where a great deal of trial experience can be obtained in a relatively short time. For those who enjoy trial work, this is the place to be.

The practice of law requires a law degree, otherwise known as a doctor of law or a juris doctorate. To obtain this degree you must complete three to four years of intense study beyond the bachelor degree level. The competition for getting into law school is intense, requiring a strong academic background and experience. The demands of obtaining a law degree are both difficult and expensive. Law school is very competitive and the level of student ability is extremely high.

Attorneys can practice in many areas besides criminal law. There are corporate, insurance and personal injury lawyers. Some lawyers specialize in bankruptcy or divorce law, while others are committed to working with the poor and disadvantaged. Others are able to use their degrees in their current jobs as their employers discover it helpful to have people knowledgeable about the law on staff. Others simply enjoy the academic challenge of attaining this level of degree and continue in their present line of work.

A trend developing in criminal justice is for employees to obtain law degrees to help them achieve professional goals, which may or may not include the traditional practice of law. This trend has generated so many lawyers that the salaries are not what they once were.

A career option for those seeking active employment in our nation's courts is that of law. In fact, many already employed in the field of criminal justice are pursuing law degrees to help them achieve their professional goals, even if they do not include the traditional practice of law.

According to Kaplan (1995, p. 76): "For some young lawyers, associate positions at large, prestigious firms are just way stations before locking into the perfect job." Kaplan continues:

> These lawyers are using big firms as launching pads to find jobs in the law that are compatible with their values, personalities and lifestyles. The jobs they find may not be the most lucrative ones in the legal field, but, for the lawyers who have them, they are the most fulfilling.

While attorneys are generally the group that others in the criminal justice fields love to hate, many non-lawyer job opportunities exist within our judicial system that people find fascinating, lucrative and very satisfying. In fact, most people are not aware of the multitude of other careers within the courts.

Legal Assistants and Paralegals

Whether they are called legal assistants or paralegals, these professions have generated a great deal of interest recently. They require considerably less schooling than a law degree and often pay very well. Many people in these fields believe they get the opportunity to do almost as much as the lawyers. Because they often do much of the interacting with the clients and witnesses and working up the cases, there can be a great deal of job satisfaction. Because all states require a license to actually practice law, legal assistants and paralegals must work under a supervising lawyer.

These jobs are rapidly increasing because such persons are able to complete a great deal of the work needed by lawyers or firms at a fraction of the cost. With all professions investigating ways to reduce costs, having such necessary work performed by those other than lawyers is simply a smart business decision. This is certainly an opportune time to consider this area of work if it interests you.

Court Reporters

You've all seen them on television or in the movies. Court reporters type a coded script into what appears to be a scaled-down typewriter. Everything is entered verbatim, so that later the entire transcript of a hearing or trial can be typed out completely. This important skill is currently in high demand.

What may appear to be a rather mundane job is, in fact, a very rewarding one. Not only are these professionals right in the middle of very interesting events, but the pay is excellent. Many court reporters have their own lucrative businesses, while others work for judges. In addition to opportunities in the courtroom, reporters are needed to document depositions in other types of legal proceedings, such as in law offices or elsewhere (perhaps a hospital room, if a witness is seriously injured or otherwise unable to attend a more formal proceeding). The fact that every word must be accurately recorded keeps this job from being as dull as one might think.

Bailiffs

Bailiffs are officers, usually deputy sheriffs, who are assigned to facilitate the court process. While some are sworn, armed law enforcement officers, others are not. Duties of the bailiff include maintaining order in the court and helping to move those involved with the court process, including defendants and the jury. If a particular assignment requires a sworn officer, all the regular requirements for any police officer apply. Nonsworn bailiffs may require less education or experience.

Clerks

Court clerks play many roles that assist the administration of justice. The role of the clerk includes maintaining accurate records and ensuring that court schedules are made and kept. The system, whether criminal or civil, revolves around records and paperwork, and it is the duty of the clerks to see that all records are properly maintained. While many of these positions are clerical, those who work their way up to be *the* Clerk of Court attain a position that is both prestigious and well paying.

Others Who Are Necessary to the System of Justice

One of the wonders of the criminal justice field is the number and types of jobs that are available. If you are interested in criminal justice as a career path, so many particular niches exist that regardless of your interests, you should find a place that suits you.

Psychologists, social workers and case managers are involved with both the adult and juvenile systems. Chemical dependency and domestic abuse counselors work hand in hand with financial, marriage and vocational counselors. Because our legal system seeks to help people who become involved with the system, including those who are being punished, almost every job that people have in the helping professions outside the legal system can be found within the system. It is the opportunity to positively affect the lives of those who find themselves in the legal system that appeals to those who enjoy being a part of it.

In addition to becoming a lawyer, a multitude of other career alternatives exists for those wishing to work in a courtroom setting. Possibilities to consider include jobs as a legal assistant or paralegal, court reporter, bailiff, clerk, psychologist, social worker, case manager or a variety of counseling positions.

So, whether you like to work with the young or the old, those accused of committing a crime or those victimized by it, or even if you enjoy administrative work, the legal system has a place for you.

Because the judicial system has so many job opportunities, there is work for all levels of education, experience and background. Employment in the courts and, indeed, in the entire field of criminal justice is not limited to those wishing to maintain traditional police-type jobs. Criminal justice opens up areas of work for those who may not be interested in patrol work, as well as for those who could not find work in this particular area. For example, many people who found themselves "on the other side" of the law at some point in their lives are now playing valuable roles in the criminal justice field. Some believe that those who have been in trouble themselves, and possibly even served jail or prison time, can address the issues and concerns of those presently involved better than those who have merely read about it. Similarly, many exceptional chemical dependency and domestic abuse counselors have police records dating back to before they received treatment. Such experiences give them an insight that proves very valuable to those now needing help. And while these individuals may not be able to ever get a job as a police officer because of their records, their records may turn out to actually help them in finding their own very important role in the system.

You should never be discouraged about not meeting the requirements of one particular area of criminal justice employment because so many others exist, each with its own unique set of requirements and opportunities. If a specific area of employment interests you, learn about the various opportunities that may best suit you, find out what the job requirements are and develop a strategy to get that job and carve out your own important niche within the system.

OPPORTUNITIES IN OUR JUDICIAL SYSTEM—CORRECTIONS

Kelly (1996, p. 134) states:

> Working in the field of corrections can provide three things that many people are looking for in a job: opportunity, mobility, and a challenging, rewarding career. The number of incarcerated individuals in the United States has grown beyond 1.5 million and is increasing every year. . . . A career in corrections demands a strong sense of responsibility, respect for authority, and sensitivity towards others.
>
> By far, the most available jobs in this field are those of correctional officers and juvenile caseworkers.

The corrections portion of our criminal justice system serves several purposes:

➢   To punish offenders.
➢   To rehabilitate wrongdoers.
➢   To make society safer for the public.

The purpose of corrections is to punish and rehabilitate offenders while protecting the public and making our society safer.

Some of these goals can be accomplished at the same time, by the same workers. For instance, corrections officers accomplish all three goals by keeping offenders incarcerated. Specific rehabilitative services, however, require specific training. Also, different systems such as the juvenile and the adult systems emphasize different areas.

Adult and Juvenile Corrections

Like law enforcement and the courts, corrections is divided into an adult and a juvenile system. The overall goal of the adult system is often punishment; the goal of the juvenile system is more likely to be treatment and rehabilitation.

Typical of state statutes regarding *adult offenders* is Chapter 609 of the Minnesota Statutes, which states that the purpose of the adult criminal code is:

> To protect the public safety and welfare by preventing the commission of crime through the deterring effect of the sentences authorized, the rehabilitation of those convicted, and their confinement when the public safety and interest requires.

In contrast, typical of state statutes regarding *juveniles* is Chapter 260 of the Minnesota Statutes:

> The purpose of the laws relating to juvenile courts is to secure for each child alleged or adjudicated to be delinquent is to promote the public safety and reduce juvenile delinquency by maintaining the integrity of the substantive law prohibiting certain behavior and by developing individual responsibility for lawful behavior. This purpose should be pursued through means that are fair and just, that recognize the unique characteristics and needs of children, and that give children access to opportunities for personal and social growth.

The trend of punishing adults and "treating" juveniles seems to be reversing itself to some extent. More emphasis is being placed on the *treatment* of adult offenders. At the same time, more traditional penalties, such as incarceration and even manual labor, are being used more frequently as "treatment" for juvenile offenders. Nonetheless, some people prefer working with juveniles because the system still is more treatment oriented, and our society holds the belief that youths are generally as capable as, if not more than, adults in redirecting their lives. It is particularly satisfying to see young people getting their lives straightened out.

The primary difference between adult corrections and juvenile corrections has traditionally been the *punishment* of adults and the *treatment* of juveniles, although this difference seems to be reversing itself to some extent.

Is the field of corrections as exciting as being in on the action-packed arrest? (Remember, that's only 20 percent of police work.) Maybe not. But then, police work doesn't offer the long-range benefits of really helping people to change. Many police officers express frustration over seeing only the misery caused by crime and not having a positive influence on people, as those who work in corrections often do, particularly those who work in probation and parole, as will be discussed shortly. But first, let's look at the most prevalent professional in the corrections field—the corrections officer, or C.O.

Corrections Officers

Corrections begins after the arrest and involves everything from the initial "booking" (fingerprinting, photographing, etc.) to long-term "guarding." Some positions involve counseling inmates, while others are limited to an armed position in a watchtower.

For some, work in corrections is a step towards getting somewhere else. It is a legitimate "stepping stone" to other jobs in law enforcement. It is also, however, an opportunity to be part of a whole other world of the criminal justice system, which many find appealing. In 1997 nearly 400,000 individuals were employed in adult corrections at the state and federal levels (Camp and Camp, 1997, pp. 108, 112). The majority of correctional employees (51.7 percent) worked as correctional officers, as shown in Table 3-1. The remainder held administrative and service positions or were employed as probation and/or parole officers. Keep in mind these figures do not account for the thousands of individuals employed in the juvenile corrections system.

TABLE 3-1   Total Number of Employees and Number Employed as Correctional Officers in Adult Correctional Systems (by Sex, Race and Jurisdiction, as of January 1, 1997)

Jurisdiction		Total	Sex		Race	
			Male	Female	White	Non-White
State DOCs*	All Employees	369,918	253,170	116,748	262,421	107,497
	Correctional Officers	195,241	154,030	41,211	132,897	62,344
Federal DOCs	All Employees	29,636	21,723	7,913	20,064	9,572
	Correctional Officers	11,136	9,833	1,303	7,027	4,109
TOTAL	All Employees	399,554	274,893	124,661	282,485	117,069
	Correctional Officers	206,377	163,863	42,514	139,924	66,453

* Includes Washington, DC

SOURCE: Adapted from George M. Camp and Camille Graham Camp. *The Corrections Yearbook, 1997*. South Salem, NY: The Criminal Justice Institute, 1997, pp. 108, 112.

As noted by the *Occupational Outlook Handbook* (1999, p. 339):

> Correction officers are responsible for overseeing individuals who have been arrested, are awaiting trial or other hearing, or who have been convicted of a crime and sentenced to serve time in a jail, reformatory, or penitentiary. They maintain security and observe inmate conduct and behavior to prevent disturbances and escapes.

It is worth making the distinction here between corrections officers and detention officers. Though they both perform their functions behind bars, and their jobs are similar in some ways, their jobs are also different in several critical ways. One major distinction is the different constitutional justifications for doing what they do. Individuals held in detention have not yet appeared before the court and, therefore, retain the presumption of innocence. Consequently, any punitive aspect of the correctional environment is not justified with such "inmates." The officer's duty regarding such individuals is to keep them safe and secure until they can be brought before a judge.

Hill (1997, p. 2) has compiled a competency profile of correctional officer traits and skills, presented in Figure 3-1. This profile offers a glimpse at some of the duties, roles and responsibilities of correctional officers.

A CORRECTIONAL OFFICER ensures the public safety by providing for the care, custody, control and maintenance of inmates; and to carry out this mission, must:

I. Manage and communicate with inmates—
    A. Orient new arrivals on rules, procedures, and general information of facility/unit.
    B. Enforce rules and regulations.
    C. Conduct cell inspections (for contraband, obstructions, sanitation, jammed locks, etc.).
    D. Establish rapport (introduce self, use good body language, listen, etc.).
    E. Provide verbal and written counseling (i.e., disciplinary behavior, informational, confidential).
    F. Write disciplinary and incident reports.

II. Intervene in crises and manage conflicts—
    A. Employ the use of force continuum (minimum, less-than-lethal, lethal).
    B. Direct inmate movement.
    C. Observe, monitor and supervise movement of inmates/inmate property.
    D. Properly identify and escort inmates individually or in groups.
    E. Implement schedules for controlled movement of inmates at specified times.
    F. Restrict movement during scheduled physical counts of inmates.
    G. Receive/issue inmate passes/appointment slips.
    H. Implement emergency operating plans.
    I. Enforce custody/privilege/disciplinary restrictions.
    J. Receive/recommend inmate requests for bed, cell, or unit move.
    K. Maintain key, tool, and equipment control.
    L. Inspect keys, equipment, tools, and beepers.
    M. Report broken/missing keys, equipment, and tools.
    N. Inventory keys, equipment, and tools at the beginning and end of shift.
    O. Maintain physical control of keys, equipment, and tools.
    P. Log keys, equipment, and tools in the work area.

III. Maintain health, safety, and sanitation—
    A. Report changes in behavior.
    B. Search persons, personal property, and units.
    C. Report security violations.
    D. Submit health, safety, and sanitation recommendations to appropriate departments.
    E. Implement proper health procedures for inmates with infectious diseases.
    F. Implement health/safety memos and posters.
    G. Develop cleaning schedule.
    H. Supervise cleaning schedule.
    I. Ensure proper handling/labeling of hazardous materials.
    J. Supervise hygiene habits of inmates.

IV. Communicate with staff—
    A. Establish positive rapport with other staff.
    B. Maintain constant communication with other staff and vigilance as to their work.
    C. Operate communication equipment per established guidelines.
    D. Document incidents, write reports, write recommendations going through chain-of-command.
    E. Brief oncoming staff for next shifts.
    F. Explain unusual procedures to staff.
    G. Participate in staff meetings.

FIGURE 3-1   **Competency Profile of Correctional Officer (continued on next pages)**

V. Participate in training—
   A. Participate in mandatory/elective training.
   B. Read daily log book and other information.
   C. Review new/updated post orders, administrative regulations, and memos.
   D. Participate in cross-training.
   E. Review and simulate emergency procedures (fire drills).
   F. Pursue continuing education opportunities.
   G. Seek additional training opportunities.

VI. Distribute authorized items to inmates—
   A. Order/request authorized items.
   B. Take inventory of and distribute authorized items.
   C. Document the distribution of authorized items.

CORRECTIONAL OFFICER TRAITS & ATTITUDES

Professional	Empathetic	Positive role model	Flexible	Leader
Dependable	Perceptive	Emotionally stable	Punctual	Assertive
Consistent	Neat	Self-motivated	Sincere	Adaptable/change-oriented
Compassionate	Fair	Sense of humor	Optimistic	
Analytical	Ethical	Cooperative	Credible	

KNOWLEDGE & SKILLS

Knowledge of:
Laws of jurisdiction
Policies & procedures
Force/necessary use of
Agency mission/purpose
Ethnic diversity
Equipment/tools
Available training
Stress management

Skills:
Written communication
Non-verbal communication
Stress management
All prison equipment/tools
Searching
CPR/First Aid
Leadership
Public relations
Management
Interpersonal communication

FIGURE 3-1   (Continued)

```
TOOLS & EQUIPMENT

    Radios                        Helmets (riot/protective)      Weapons:
    Mechanical restraints (cuffs,  Polycaptor/riot shields          Rifle/Shotgun
        waist chains, leg irons,   Stun shields                     Handgun (37/38 mm)
        flex-cuffs, soft restraints) Body armor (vests, etc.)       Gas Gun
    Badge                         Protective CPR/First Aid masks    Dispersal of grenades
    Whistle                       Generators                       Rubber bullets
    Leather duty belts with       Light stands                     Chemical agents
        accessories               Computers                           (CN/CS/mace)
    Personal alarm devices/TAC    Telephone/paging systems         Gas masks
        alarms                    Airpacks/SCBA
    Keys                          Binoculars
    Flashlight                    Audio/visual aids
    Electronic control devices    Equipment for opening/
        (Taser/stun gun)              closing cell doors
    Batons (straight/PR-24/riot)  Sallyports, entry gates,
    Gloves (protective/leather/       corridor grills
        duty)                     ID cards
    Uniforms/footwear
```

FIGURE 3-1   (Continued)

SOURCE: Gary Hill. "Correctional Officer Traits and Skills." *Corrections Compendium*, Vol. XXII, No. 8, August 1997, p. 2. Reprinted by permission of CEGA Publishing.

The working conditions in correctional institutions may be stressful or occasionally dangerous, as inmate riots have been known to claim the lives of corrections officers. As with law enforcement and life on the outside, security in correctional institutions must be provided 24 hours a day. Most corrections officers work 8 hours a day, 5 days a week, but the hours may occur during the night shift, and the days may fall on weekends or holidays. Overtime work is also common (*Occupational Outlook Handbook*, p. 340).

For those seeking employment as a correctional officer, consideration must be given to educational requirements and other qualifications. Kelly (p. 134) notes: "As with any profession, education is a major factor for a successful career in corrections. . . . Increasingly, employers are looking for individuals with postsecondary education in psychology, sociology, criminal justice, and related fields." According to a survey of corrections agencies, 14 states and the Federal Bureau of Prisons require correctional officer recruits to have completed some college coursework, if not a two-year degree (Hill, pp. 3–6). Many agencies also expect newly hired correctional officers to complete a training program prior to actual work in the facility. Nationwide, such programs range from zero preservice hours in Wyoming to 640 hours in Michigan, with an average of 229 hours (Camp and Camp, p. 122).

The *Occupational Outlook Handbook* adds (p. 340): "Most institutions require that correctional officers be at least 18 or 21 years of age, have a high school education or its equivalent, have no felony convictions, and be a United States citizen." Further requirements may include physical and mental fitness, previous work experience and a valid driver's license. The *Occupational Outlook Handbook* (p. 340) states: "Strength, good judgment, and the ability to think and act quickly are indispensable."

Regarding salaries, the *Occupational Outlook Handbook* (p. 340) reports:

> According to a 1996 survey . . ., Federal and State correctional officers' annual salaries averaged about $26,100 and ranged from a low of $17,300 in South Carolina to a high of $41,700 in Rhode Island.
>
> At the Federal level, the starting salary was about $20,200 to $22,600 a year in 1996; supervisory correctional officers started at about $28,300 a year. Starting salaries were slightly higher in selected areas where prevailing local pay levels were higher. The annual average salary for correctional officers employed by the Federal Government was $33,540 in early 1997.

Benefits commonly available to corrections officers include uniforms or a clothing allowance to buy their own work clothes, medical and dental insurance, disability and life insurance, vacation, sick leave and retirement pensions (*Occupational Outlook Handbook,* p. 340).

Corrections is considered a growth industry. The outlook for jobs for corrections officers at all levels—local, state and federal—is favorable over the next decade, given the projected increases in the number of individuals incarcerated across the country. According to *The Top 100: The Fastest Growing Careers for the 21st Century* (1998, p. 91): "Employment in this field is expected to increase much faster than the average for all jobs. It is estimated that another 142,000 jobs will be created within the next fifteen years, an increase in employment of 61 percent. The ongoing war on drugs, new tough-on-crime legislation, and increasing mandatory sentencing policies will add more prison beds and more corrections officers."

A career in corrections, while demanding and challenging, can be extremely rewarding. Consequently, as noted by Stephens (1999, p. 29): "The field has become much more competitive in recent years. . . . This means that people today choosing correctional careers are, increasingly, those who are preparing for it. Vanishing from the landscape are those people simply experimenting with corrections as one among several career options."

While a majority of this discussion on corrections officers has focused on those individuals working in prisons, jail officers are another group whose employment outlook appears bright. According to Schmalleger (1999): "Significantly, one of the fastest-growing sectors of today's jail population consists of sentenced offenders serving time in local jails because overcrowded prisons cannot accept them."

Figure 3-2 shows how the population of jail and prison inmates has steadily risen since 1990. Various projections estimate the U.S. prison population will exceed 2 million by the year 2002 (Schmalleger, p. 488). Considering the new crime bill, the passage of "Three Strikes and You're Out" laws, the increased use of mandatory life sentences without parole and the efforts to achieve an 85 percent mandatory service of one's sentence, the need for corrections officers will be even greater in the years to come.

A career option for those seeking work in corrections is that of a corrections officer. Corrections officers make up over half of all employees in corrections today. Duties include maintaining the security and safety of persons being held within the correctional facility, enforcing rules and regulations and possibly providing a degree of counseling to inmates. Present and predicted increases in inmate populations mean more corrections officers will be needed in the future.

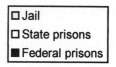

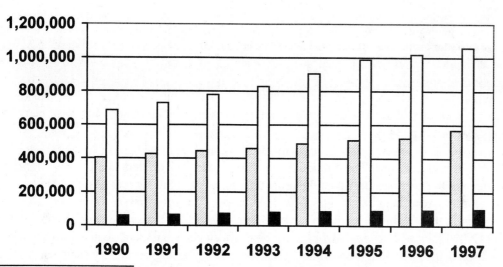

FIGURE 3-2   Number of Persons Held in State or Federal Prisons or in Local Jails, 1990–1997

SOURCE: Darrell K. Gilliard and Allen J. Beck. Prison and Jail Inmates at Midyear 1997. Bureau of Justice Statistics Bulletin, January 1998, p. 2. (NCJ-167247)

For prospective criminal justice applicants interested in long-term personal interaction, the fields of probation and parole are worth considering.

Probation and Parole Officers

Careers in probation and parole are other options for those seeking work in the field of corrections. Like corrections officers, probation and parole officers counsel offenders, but they also evaluate their progress in becoming productive members of society (*Occupational Outlook Handbook,* p. 340).

> The primary difference between probation and parole is that probation is an alternative to incarceration, while parole is supervised release from incarceration before the expiration of the sentence. Each involves considerable interaction with offenders, and it is becoming more common to have one officer handle both probationers and parolees.

The probation officer oversees a correctional plan outside detention. The parole agent helps offenders prepare for eventual discharge from the system. Today, however, more and more jurisdictions are using the same officer to perform in both a probation officer and a parole officer capacity.

Most states require at least a bachelor's degree for probation and parole officers. Careers in the correctional field are quite different from those in law enforcement, but probation officers can take defendants from the crisis point at which they enter the criminal justice system and work with them to help them alter their lives. This long-term payoff makes probation and parole work rewarding.

At the beginning of January 1997, 68,491 individuals were employed in the fields of probation and parole: 32,036 (47 percent) strictly as probation officers, 10,401 (15 percent) strictly as parole officers and 26,054 (38 percent) as both probation and parole officers (Camp and Camp, p. 174). This area is expected to expand considerably over the next decade, making it a career option worth thinking about.

> Probation and parole officers are professionals with vital roles in our corrections system. The job outlook for those interested in becoming probation and/or parole officers is positive, as the entire area of corrections is expected to expand through the year 2005.

Electronic Monitoring and Home Detention

Because of increasing jail populations, both the adult and juvenile systems are being forced to examine *home detention* as a practical alternative to incarceration. By keeping offenders at home, this technology provides a way to ease overcrowded jails and prisons. *Electronic monitoring* (EM) is often used in conjunction with home detention, offering an effective, inexpensive method of supervising probationers. A typical electronic monitoring system (EMS) consists of a bracelet worn on the detainee's ankle. The bracelet contains a transmitter that emits a signal that is continuously monitored, enabling authorities to know the whereabouts of the detainee at all times. Lilly notes (1995, p. 112) that more than 70,000 offenders nationwide are currently supervised via electronic monitoring. The increasing use of home detention and electronic monitoring is creating new work opportunities for those who implement and manage these programs.

> As home detention and electronic monitoring gain popularity and grow in use, new job opportunities are created for those who implement and manage such programs.

Other Careers in Corrections

Although corrections officers make up the largest number of those with careers in corrections, numerous other careers are available, including administrative, clerical, educational, professional/technical and maintenance/food service positions. Table 3-2 shows the number of employees in the various occupational categories at midyear 1995. Bear in mind that as more correctional facilities are built, an increasing number of staff in *all* these categories must be hired to keep the institution operating effectively and constitutionally.

TABLE 3-2   Employees in State and Federal Correctional Facilities, by Occupational Category, June 30, 1995

Jurisdiction	All Employees	Administrative	Custody/ Security	Clerical	Educational	Professional/ Technical	Maintenance/ Food Service	Other Staff
State	321,941	7,980	210,544	25,117	9,856	40,687	20,591	7,166
Federal	25,379	1,529	10,348	2,266	1,164	4,604	3,014	2,454
United States, total	347,320	9,509	220,892	27,383	11,020	45,291	23,605	9,620

SOURCE: *Correctional Populations in the United States, 1995.* Washington, DC: U.S. Department of Justice, Bureau of Justice Statistics, 1997.

Kelly (pp. 135–136) provides the following summary of jobs in corrections (Reprinted by permission):

While correctional job titles and descriptions vary according to the structure and needs of each institution and agency, a few titles are commonly accepted. Occupations within corrections are as varied as those found outside the field. Some positions require a high degree of formal education and training; yet, there are opportunities for those with more modest education and experience. The education, training, and experience required for the following occupations differ from one place to another. Check with the Federal Bureau of Prisons, as well as your state or local correctional agency for specific job descriptions and requirements. Remember that advancement within the system is possible with continued education and training. The following is a sample of the types of opportunities available in the corrections field.

MANAGERIAL/ADMINISTRATIVE SUPPORT

Warden/Jail Manager: Oversees all operations and programs within the superintendent facility.

Personnel/Human Resources Manager: Responsible for recruiting, advising, hiring, and firing staff; implements the institution's policies and procedures; provides leadership and supervision; advises and assists staff with benefits.

Employee Development Specialist: Plans, supervises or leads programs designed to train and develop employees; consults with or guides management on employee training and development issues.

Budget Administrator: Plans and coordinates the use of resources for a facility.

Financial Manager: Maintains financial services such as auditing and credit analysis; coordinates financial policies and procedures.

Facility Manager: Manages and maintains buildings, grounds and other facilities. Requires managerial skills and a broad technical knowledge of operating capabilities and maintenance requirements of various kinds of physical plants and equipment.

Safety Manager: Offers technical advice on or manages occupational safety programs, regulations, and standards. Requires knowledge of the techniques of safety and pertinent aspects of engineering, psychology and other factors affecting safety.

Ombudsman: Acts as an unbiased liaison between inmates and facility administration; investigates inmate complaints, reports findings, and helps achieve equitable settlements of disputes between inmates and the correctional administration.

Librarian: Manages and cares for the facility's collection of books, recordings, films, and other materials.

Computer Specialist: Manages or designs use and maintenance of computer systems. This is an area of great need in the corrections field.

Researcher: Analyzes data for budgets and for projected needs and assists in the evaluation of programs.

Food Service Manager: Manages and supervises the operation of the institution's or department's food services, including the storeroom, kitchen, dining rooms, and procurement. Often requires certification as a registered dietician and familiarity with federal, state, and local health codes and sanitary standards.

Correctional Officer: Supervises the treatment and custody of offenders in correctional institutions.

Probation/Parole Officer: Advises and counsels individuals who are on probation or parole; enforces and monitors compliance with the rules imposed on the offender by either the court or parole board.

Juvenile Services Officer: Advises and counsels juveniles in aftercare; evaluates and initiates treatment plans for juveniles in aftercare and makes referrals to appropriate support agencies.

COUNSELING/TRAINING

Psychologist/Counselor: Works with inmates and corrections professionals. Provides counseling and testing. Generally requires professional training. Closely allied specialists may include art therapists and drama therapists. Certified drug and alcohol abuse counselors are in great demand.

Chaplain: Offers religious guidance and spiritual counseling to inmates. Requires ordination by a recognized ecclesiastical body; chaplains may be called upon to minister to inmates not of their faith.

Recreation Specialist: Plans, organizes, and administers programs that promote inmates' physical, creative, artistic and social development.

Vocational Counselor: Provides educational programs or career training for inmates; determines learning needs, abilities, and other facts about inmates. May participate in discussions with other staff professionals to aid in inmates rehabilitation.

Vocational Instructor: Provides both classroom and hands-on training in a variety of trades.

Industrial Specialist: Assists or manages a prison industry, such as printing, carpentry, agriculture, and sign-making programs.

Juvenile Caseworker: Supervises the treatment and custody of juvenile offenders in correctional or rehabilitation facilities. Often provides support and counseling to juvenile offenders and participates in the development and implementation of treatment plans.

Teacher: Leads classes on subjects for both juveniles and adult offenders. Requires a bachelor's degree plus certification by the state education authority in specific subject area. Teachers certified in special education are in great demand.

MEDICAL

Health System Administrator: Responsible for the administrative management of the health care delivery system and use of outside resources to provide patient care.

Medical Officer: Performs professional and scientific work in one or more fields of medicine. Requires, at a minimum, the degree of Doctor of Medicine and, in most states, a current license to practice medicine. Medical support staff may include physicians' assistants, nurses, nurses' assistants, and pharmacists.

CONCLUSION

Many career options exist for those seeking work in our nation's courts and corrections. One of the most popular career choices is that of law. A multitude of other alternatives exists for those wishing to work in a courtroom setting, including jobs as a legal assistant or paralegal, court reporter, bailiff, clerk, psychologist, social worker, case manager or a variety of counseling positions. The field of corrections is experiencing phenomenal growth. Possible career options for those seeking work in corrections include corrections officers, probation officers and parole officers. The job outlook for those interested in becoming corrections officers and probation and/or parole officers is positive, as the entire area of corrections is expected to expand through the year 2005.

While government agencies find their challenge "doing more with less" to appease the very vocal "no new taxes" constituency, the less traditional fields of employment will expand. Even if it's in the areas providing alternatives to more expensive imprisonment, including probation and parole work, the areas that can lessen the burden on taxpayers will flourish. Beyond government employment, all areas of the system will continue to take advantage of private responses. No doubt a "partnership" will develop, allowing people to move from one area to another, with new possibilities always on the horizon.

ADDITIONAL CONTACTS AND SOURCES OF INFORMATION

American Correctional Association (ACA)
4380 Forbes Boulevard
Lanham, MD 20706
(301) 918-1800

American Probation and Parole Association
c/o Council of State Governments
Iron Works Pike
PO Box 11910
Lexington, KY 40578
(606) 244-8203
E-mail: appa@csg.org

Federal Bureau of Prisons (BOP)
320 First Street NW, Room 460
Washington, DC 20534
(202) 307-1490
Web site: http://www.bop.gov

International Association of Correctional Officers
1333 South Wabash Avenue, Box 53
Chicago, IL 60605
(312) 996-5401

AN INSIDER'S VIEW

LAWYERS WEAR MANY HATS: WHICH ONE IS RIGHT FOR YOU?

Marsh J. Halberg
Attorney at Law
Edina, Minnesota

The dilemma most students face, whether in college or law school, is trying to envision a job they will enjoy when they enter the workforce. Each of you knows that the "real world" is far different from that which you learn about in books.

When I was going to law school, the most common question people would ask me was what type of law I intended to practice. My standard answer at that time was, "I don't know. It could be anything except criminal law." Reflecting back on that, for the past 20 years over 90 percent of my practice has involved criminal law. I laugh at my poor prediction of what lay ahead for future employment!

What I discovered, upon looking more closely at the practice of law, was that a great number of lawyers spend their days sitting behind a desk and pushing papers, whether it be drafting corporate documents, preparing real estate papers or drafting wills. I recognized that I was very much a "people person" and it would be a slow, agonizing death for me to sit behind a desk all day, staring at four walls.

This meant that I wanted to practice in an area of law that involved interacting with people and getting out of the office. Criminal law, more than any other area, allows an attorney to interact with many different people daily and to also spend a great deal of time in the courtroom.

While corporate or commercial legal battles can drag on for many years, a criminal case is typically charged soon after the alleged crime occurs. The defendant has a right to a speedy trial, which may occur within several months after the case is charged. As such, criminal law involves a high volume, fast turnover type of workload.

Because of the high volume of criminal cases, most matters (over 95 percent) never go to trial. As such, the attorneys involved for both the prosecution and defense become professional negotiators, required to make quick decisions and move on to the next case. This is necessitated by the pure volume of cases in the system. We have all heard the saying, "It's not *what* you know but *who* you know." To a certain extent this is true in the state criminal court system. Because so many case negotiations occur, the practice of criminal law is very relationship-oriented. Attorneys work together over and over on a weekly, if not daily, basis negotiating, if not trying, cases. A level of confidence, respect and friendship develops between lawyers when that much contact occurs. As such, a relatively small band of criminal defense attorneys practice the lion's share of the criminal work.

Where I live, most of the municipal communities contract with private law firms to represent them on city prosecution matters because it is more cost effective than hiring full-time government employees. The city attorneys prosecute all of the lesser crimes (that is, everything short of felony cases). This might involve DWI, forgery, assault, prostitution, etc. The "big cases" (murder, robbery, etc.) are handled by a full-time county attorney's office.

The same private lawyers who handle the city prosecution matters on a contract basis are free to practice criminal defense work outside of the communities for which they prosecute. Therefore, it is very common to see an attorney being a prosecutor in a courtroom one morning and, that afternoon, being a defense attorney in a separate courtroom. This is an ethical and recognized course of practice. Frankly, it allows attorneys who are both prosecutors and defense attorneys to better serve both of their clients. That is, prosecutors know all of the defense tricks and vice versa. I think it also prevents attorneys from becoming too jaded by working on only one side of the fence. Specifically, attorneys see that police officers are not always right, nor are defendants always falsely accused. It gives the attorney a far better perspective of the tough job on both sides.

I work as both a city prosecutor and do private defense work for cases occurring outside the city. I am currently a prosecutor for a suburb of Minneapolis. Although the city is relatively small, we generate in excess of 10,000 charges per year. Many of the minor traffic matters are simply handled by the violator paying the fine and never going to court. Many cases, however, whether traffic charges or criminal charges, involve the defendants making a required court appearance. Another part-time prosecutor and I handle thousands of criminal prosecution files each year. I typically spend approximately 50 percent of every day in the courtroom. It is not uncommon, on a typical day, to work through in excess of 100 separate cases.

When I am retained as a defense attorney, I tell my clients that much of what they are paying for are my relationships with others within the system—it is my ability to be a professional negotiator rather than Clarence Darrow in the courtroom. More deals are done over the water cooler than standing in front of the judge in the courtroom.

I would encourage you to do internships for various lawyers to get a better feel for what the practice of law is actually like before making the dive into law school.

———————

Marsh J. Halberg has been employed in the legal profession for 20 years, during which he has served as an assistant county attorney, a city prosecutor and a defense attorney. He currently works for the law firm of Thomsen & Nybeck, P.A. in Edina, Minnesota.

AN INSIDER'S VIEW

THE PATH TO A CAREER IN CORRECTIONS

John J. Maas
Deputy Chief
U.S. Probation/Pretrial Services Officer

If you are looking for a career in criminal justice, you may wish to consider the corrections field. Corrections is a branch of criminal justice that deals primarily with the prosecution, detention and supervision of offenders. An important part of the corrections branch is the probation/parole system. Probation and parole officers serve the courts and paroling authorities by protecting the community from charged, convicted or released offenders who remain a criminal threat. These officers also help those same offenders pull their lives together. Probation/parole officers have a multifaceted job that brings them into regular contact with many branches of the criminal justice system.

Most county, state or federal probation and parole agencies require at least a bachelor's degree and some related experience before they will consider you for employment. Few candidates are selected directly out of college; therefore, you must be willing to start in a related field and work your way into a probation/parole officer position. It is not necessary that the experience you obtain be directly in corrections or criminal justice. You can easily obtain the required experience by working in one of several fields that provide services to people in need. Social services, education, child development, mental health, family services and youth services are just a few areas that come to mind.

Many probation/parole officers start out as teachers, counselors, social workers or caseworkers in any number of juvenile or adult treatment facilities. By beginning your career in one of these related fields, you can demonstrate your ability to work and communicate with diverse groups of people and effect change in people who may not know how to, or even want to, change. Work experience in any job that involves helping people help themselves can be extremely valuable to a potential probation/parole officer. Obtaining such experience is not that difficult because many social service agencies are looking for entry-level employees who want to gain experience.

Along with this field experience, however, you must also demonstrate excellent verbal and written communication skills. The abilities to communicate verbally and in writing (reports, letters, legal documents) are very important parts of the probation/parole officer's duties. Officers are often required to prepare critical documents for the courts, lawyers and other professional people, and they must communicate verbally with a wide range of socially and economically diverse individuals. If you can effectively demonstrate these abilities, you will put yourself at the top of the applicant list.

The last suggestion I have for potential probation/parole officers is to learn something of the philosophy of the agency to which you are applying. All probation/parole offices are *not* the same. Some tend to be more law enforcement oriented, requiring strict enforcement of conditions imposed by the court or controlling agency (for example, a "zero tolerance" toward violation of curfew). Others tends to lean more toward a social work approach, emphasizing rehabilitation, redirection or treatment modalities over immediate incarceration for violations.

Some offices require officers to carry weapons while others do not. Some require their officers to be confrontal and direct with offenders while others emphasize showing support, understanding and the flexibility to make adjustments. You should make every effort to determine that the philosophy of the agency to which you have applied embraces your philosophy. You will not get far in an interview if philosophical differences become apparent. Even if they don't surface and you are hired, your job satisfaction may be low, perhaps intolerably so.

Probation and parole work is interesting, exciting and challenging, but you must put considerable effort into preparing yourself for the job. With a little foresight, planning and patience you can become part of a very rewarding profession.

John J. Maas is a Deputy Chief and U.S. Probation and Pretrial Services officer with the U.S. District Court, District of South Dakota. He has been employed in the criminal justice field for 25 years. Mr. Maas holds a B.A. in sociology and a B.S. in secondary education from Black Hills State University. He's been married for 33 years to Linda; they have five children. He enjoys sports and recreational activities.

? MIND STRETCHES

1.   What do most people think of when they think of a "correctional officer job"? Where did you acquire the information on which you base your answer?

2.   What benefits would you find in a job in corrections that may not exist in a street police job?

3.   What negatives would you want to be aware of in considering a job as a correctional officer?

4.   Can you think of unique vocational or avocational skills that could make a job candidate more attractive to a hiring agency?

5.   Is there a danger in pursuing a specific job that "really excites" you, to the point you do not believe any other job would be worthwhile?

6.   What corrections jobs do you think will become more necessary in the future? Less necessary?

7.   How do you predict corrections will change? Why?

REFERENCES

Camp, George M. and Camp, Camille Graham. *The Corrections Yearbook, 1997.* South Salem, NY: The Criminal Justice Institute, 1997.

Hill, Gary. "Correctional Officer Traits and Skills." *Corrections Compendium*, Vol. XXII, No. 8, August 1997, pp. 1–12.

Kaplan, Joel. "Dreams Really Do Come True." *ABA Journal*, September 1995, pp. 76–79.

Kelly, Michael. "Is a Career in Corrections for You?" *Corrections Today*, July 1996, pp. 134–136.

Lilly, J. Robert. "Electronic Monitoring in the U.S." In *Intermediate Sanctions in Overcrowded Times,* edited by Michael Tonry and Kate Hamilton. Boston: Northeastern University Press, 1995, pp. 112–116.

Occupational Outlook Handbook. 1998-1999 Edition. U.S. Department of Labor, Bureau of Labor Statistics, Washington, DC: U.S. Government Printing Office, 1999.

Schmalleger, Frank. *Criminal Justice Today: An Introductory Text for the Twenty-First Century*, 5th ed. Upper Saddle River, NJ: Prentice Hall, 1999.

Stephens, W. Richard, Jr. *Careers in Criminal Justice.* Boston: Allyn and Bacon, 1999.

The Top 100: The Fastest Growing Careers for the 21st Century. Chicago: Ferguson Publishing Company, 1998.

CHAPTER 4

CAREERS IN PRIVATE SECURITY

Private security is the invisible empire of criminal justice.

—*Christopher A. Hertig*

Do You Know:

➢ The difference between proprietary, contractual and hybrid security?
➢ The difference between public and private policing?
➢ How private security and public law enforcement compare in terms of employment and spending?
➢ Why cooperation between public law enforcement and private security is necessary and what some examples of such cooperation are?
➢ What areas of public justice are being affected by privatization?
➢ What trend is occurring in corrections and who the largest provider of such services currently is?
➢ Why many law enforcement officers desire jobs as private security directors?
➢ What typical entry-level positions exist in private security and what the duties are for these individuals?
➢ What mid-level and top-level positions exist in private security?
➢ Where job opportunities in private security are most likely? Least likely?
➢ How common licensing and registration requirements are for private security professionals? Where to obtain information about such requirements?
➢ What qualities employers seek in private security applicants?
➢ What the outlook is for jobs in private security?
➢ What kind of salary one might expect from a job in private security?
➢ How available promotions are in private security?

INTRODUCTION

No area in the criminal justice system is growing as rapidly as careers in private security. Why? *People want lower taxes*! This unquestionably means that the private sector will pick up where the government leaves off. Lower taxes mean fewer police; fewer police mean fewer programs; fewer programs mean the burden of paying for whatever additional protection people desire will fall on the specific populations requesting it. Here is where opportunities abound for private entrepreneurs. As noted in the chapter opening quote (Hertig, 1993, p. 96):

> Private security is the invisible empire of criminal justice, largely unseen by the public, whether from the perspective of protective services or career path. Private security is undervalued in criminal justice literature and seldom recognized for the growing importance it plays in society.

Despite this lack of recognition, private security *is* big business and a protective presence that continues to get bigger every year. The American Society for Industrial Security (ASIS) reports (n.d., p. 2): "The security industry in the US is a $100 billion a year business and growing." Furthermore:

> Security is one of the fastest growing professional careers worldwide. A career in the security field provides a multitude of opportunities. These opportunities range from entry level security officer positions to investigators specializing in specific areas and managers and directors of security at major corporations and organizations around the world. The demand for heightened security is being increased by theft of information, workplace violence, terrorism and white collar crime.

ASIS also notes that all businesses, regardless of size, have numerous security concerns relating to fraud, theft, computer hacking, industrial espionage and workplace violence (p. 2). Matison and Hess (1997, p. 4) add:

> Crime, violence and workplace safety are major concerns of businesses and organizations. They want to prevent crime, violence and accidents and when prevention fails, they want to be able to find out who is responsible and how to avoid future incidents. Industrial espionage and corporate theft are areas which plague some larger companies. Store security, shoplifting, vandalism and even arson are significant problems for other businesses. This is a very major market.

This chapter begins with a comparison of the private security officer and the public law enforcement officer. It then examines the relationship between these two fields and discusses the criticality of cooperation between them. This is followed by an up-close look at career opportunities within the security profession, including salaries and the potential for growth in this field.

PUBLIC VS. PRIVATE OFFICERS

Because public policing and private security are closely related, and because people employed in one field often become involved at some time in the other, let's start by looking at how the two fields basically differ.

A primary difference between public policing and private security, as the names imply, is who you work for. Who pays your salary? Individuals in public policing are paid with tax dollars and, consequently, are accountable to the tax-paying citizens, whether on a local, county, state or federal level. They are under constant scrutiny by both the public and the politicians charged with overseeing expenditures of public funds. Many people live complacently with the attitude that "serious crime could never happen in our town, so why spend increased tax dollars on policing?" Therefore, regardless of rank, no public peace officer will become rich from the job. Private security positions, in contrast, are funded by business, industry or any entity in the private sector wanting protection beyond what public law enforcement provides.

Another basic difference between public policing and private security is the essential goals of each. Public law enforcement is quite reactive, operating as a service to the jurisdiction that pays for it. Ideally, it serves everyone within its jurisdiction equally, without a profit motive. People call, and the police are expected to respond.

Private security is proactive, seeking to prevent problems and limit losses for a particular private employer. Whether a private security operation is *proprietary* (the security officers are actual employees of the company) or *contractual* (the security officers are hired from an independent security company), the private security profession is profit oriented and serves the employer paying for such service. The current trend is *hybrid security*, which combines contractual and proprietary security.

Proprietary security officers are actual employees of the company they guard. Contractual security officers work for an independent security company and are assigned to guard a company without its own internal security staff. The trend is toward using hybrid security, combining both proprietary and contractual security services.

A third basic difference between public and private policing is in the statutory power involved. Public police officers are an arm of the government and act with its full authority, including the authority of arrest. Although police powers of arrest are awesome, police may be denied access to private facilities that are accessible to those facilities' security officers. Without a warrant, public police could well be denied access to an industrial facility that relies on its own security department to deal with such concerns as industrial espionage.

Private security officers have no more power than that of private citizens. However, as citizens, they can carry weapons, conduct investigations, defend property and make arrests. And they may, in fact, *appear* to have more authority than regular citizens as a result of wearing a uniform, carrying a weapon and having the approval and support of the organization to defend the property.

Differences between public police and private security officers include:

1. Where the paycheck comes from (public tax dollars vs. private sector budgets)
2. Whether the response is reactive or proactive
3. The statutory power involved

Growth

According to Minot B. Dodson, CCP, executive vice president of operations and training for Pinkerton Security and Investigation Services, and a member of the ASIS Standing Committee on Physical Security: "Private security is now clearly the nation's primary protective resource, outspending public law enforcement by 73 percent . . . and employing nearly three times the people . . . . The annual growth rate will be 8 percent for private security, double that of public law enforcement" (Hess and Wrobleski, 1996, p. 716).

Private security is the nation's primary protective resource today, outspending public law enforcement by more than 73 percent and employing nearly three times the workforce.

Frequently public policing and private security are viewed as being competitors. Additionally, many people in public law enforcement look down on security officers, calling them "wanna-bes," that is, individuals who really want to be police officers but didn't make it. But this is simply no longer true.

PUBLIC/PRIVATE COOPERATION

Private security has become the major player in safeguarding Americans and their property. As our increasing elderly and business populations are likely to continue their inhabitation of high-rise condos and office buildings, their reliance on private security will also increase. The traditional police officer patrolling public roads or a beat officer on foot cannot practically be expected to patrol such structures. Unlike public police officers, private security officers can and do patrol specific buildings, even specific floors or rooms within buildings. It can be anticipated that the fields of public law enforcement and private security may tend to blend together as society recognizes the need for each and as these professions themselves learn how they can best work together—to the benefit of all.

Arbetter (1994, p. 52) states: "Private security professionals are perfectly positioned to share the burdens of law enforcement." Kolpacki (1994, pp. 47–49) suggests:

> Community policing is public law enforcement's way of mirroring the private security industry. Like private security, community policing is proactive crime prevention that is accountable to the customer. The similar goal creates the opportunity for a cooperative program between the private and public sectors that would benefit both sectors as well as the community . . . .
>
> Realizing that the need for cooperative programs between the public and private sectors exists is the first step toward improved crime prevention and control. Toward this end, community policing programs should be expanded to include the resources of private security. Once this is done, responsibilities such as alarm response, workplace drugs, theft prevention, and disaster preparedness can be put into the hands of private security professionals for more effective handling.

The need for cooperation is further emphasized by Patterson (1995, p. 33):

> The relationship between private security and law enforcement has experienced a radical evolution that has taken form in public and private security initiatives. It is striking how much the relationship has evolved, and instructive to note why the change has occurred. Private security and law enforcement have not gone unchallenged in this era of "Do More With Less." Parallel objectives, commonality of threat, and crossover of professional career tracks have paved the road for alliances between private security and law enforcement. These alliances, many started years ago, provide the basis for mutual support that is the foundation for today's initiatives.

Examples of cooperation between the public and private sector are numerous, including combined efforts at the sites of natural disasters, common initiatives in controlling and securing large public events and cooperation in preventing and handling neighborhood crime (Patterson, p. 34).

An obvious reason for cooperation is that individuals often move from one field to the other. Some individuals use private security as a stepping stone into public policing. Likewise, some individuals in public policing enter private security, sometimes as a consultant, sometimes after retiring from public policing and sometimes as a part-time job while working as a public police officer.

Cooperation between public law enforcement and private security can benefit both sides and is an important step toward enhanced safety for all. Examples of cooperation between the public and private sector include combined efforts at the sites of natural disasters, common initiatives in controlling and securing large public events and cooperation in preventing and handling neighborhood crime.

PRIVATIZATION OF PUBLIC JUSTICE

The privatization trend has extended to more than just officers. It is working its way into other areas of the justice system as well. According to Trojanowicz and Bucqueroux (1990, p. 131):

> An equally dramatic and far-reaching change, for good or ill, taking place during this past decade has been the continued and increasing privatization of public justice—a profound change that has so far been both little researched and little understood. Almost invisibly, private for-profit and nonprofit corporations have been assuming roles that were once almost exclusively the province of the public criminal justice system. We have also seen a dramatic rise in the number of joint efforts involving some combination of public and private initiatives. A few examples follow: . . .
>
> - U.S. companies now spend an estimated $250 million each year on private undercover drug investigations of their employees.
> - Litigants in civil suits can now choose to hire a private rent-a-judge-and-jury to settle claims, virtually bypassing the public courts.
> - The federal Trademark and Counterfeiting Act of 1984 gave businesses expanded powers to protect their property and profits, including the right to conduct independent investigations, obtain search warrants, seize evidence, arrest suspects and pursue private criminal justice prosecutions.

Privatization has gone beyond the officer to include investigators, judges and juries.

West (1993, p. 54) notes: "State and local law enforcement authorities, confronted with rising costs and declining revenues, are being forced to find less costly ways to provide the necessary public safety services. The silver lining to this dark cloud is a growing market niche for private sector security providers."

The trend toward private justice can also be found in the area of corrections.

Private Corrections

The privatization of corrections is a highly controversial area. Many critics fear the quality of inmate care will be compromised as private facilities focus on generating a profit. Others raise concerns about the degree of control the government will have over the nation's criminals if they are housed in privately operated facilities.

Nonetheless, the privatization of corrections has been slowly gaining ground since the 1980s. According to Thomas (1994, p. 19): "The best available evidence now suggests that the appeal of privatization is accelerating." Furthermore, jurisdictions in Arizona, California, Colorado, Florida, Louisiana, Mississippi, North Carolina, Texas and Virginia currently have adult correctional facilities being operated by private companies.

An article in *Security Concepts* entitled "Wackenhut Largest in Corrections Industry" (1995, p. 27) states:

> Wackenhut Corrections Corporation has been selected by the state of Florida's Correctional Privatization Commission to finance, design, build and subsequently manage a 1,318-inmate state correctional facility . . . establish[ing] Wackenhut Corrections as the industry leader in privatized corrections, with more correctional or detention facility beds under contract or award than any other private company. The company has been a pioneer in the correctional services industry since 1984, and is now contracted for the management of twenty-two facilities, located in the United States, Puerto Rico, Australia and England, with a total contracted capacity of 13,732 beds.

Dr. George C. Zoley, president and chief executive officer of Wackenhut Corrections, said, "Our 120 percent growth rate during 1994, from 6,234 beds at the end of 1993, is a result of our well-established reputation for providing the finest correctional programs and services available. . . .

Timothy P. Cole, chairman of the board of Wackenhut Corrections, said, "The construction and operation of prisons and jails has proven to be less expensive to government agencies when accomplished by the private sector. We look forward to being of further service to the state of Florida, and are in hopes that we can have a positive influence on the reduction of crime in the state as well as on the reduction of costs."

Numerous companies are capitalizing on the expanding niche for private corrections, with some of the largest companies being the Corrections Corporation of America; Concept, Inc.; U.S. Corrections Corporation; Mid-Tex Detention, Inc.; Esmor Correctional Services, Inc. and, of course, Wackenhut Corrections Corporation.

The privatization of corrections has been increasing since the 1980s. In 1995 Wackenhut Corrections Corporation became the largest company in the national private corrections industry.

PRIVATE SECURITY—UP CLOSE

Because private security is profit oriented, opportunities exist that are not available in the public sector. With corporate America recognizing that security and loss prevention are as critical to a successful business as management and marketing, an increasing number of very appealing job opportunities are developing.

The stereotype of the retiree sitting at a guard desk overnight is no longer an accurate portrayal of what has become a profession in every sense of the word. Like law enforcement, much of what happens in this profession is not common knowledge. Consequently, many people considering employment in private security may find themselves relying on inaccurate data. Unless you know someone in the field, you probably obtained what you know about security work where most people do: television or the newspaper.

Television may lead you to believe *security work* consists primarily of solving crimes the police cannot or will not deal with. Television shows about private detectives frequently do two injustices to the profession. First, they unrealistically glamorize it. Second, they fail to explain what a lucrative and necessary area of business it is.

For reasons already addressed, law enforcement officials are able to do only so much. Even then, their work may not cover all aspects necessary to other participants in the criminal justice system, such as lawyers. Remember, the role of the police is to investigate *crimes*. Once they have done this, their job is over. But what about the facts surrounding a civil, noncriminal negligence case such as a car accident, which falls short of criminal activity but which might spawn significant litigation? Even if it *is* a police matter, police don't always put as much emphasis on obtaining evidence as a defense attorney might like—evidence that could help the accused be exonerated. Furthermore, the police have little interest in personal matters such as infidelity investigations or even workers' compensation violations. Here are excellent opportunities for the private investigator.

When you consider that the private sector may provide more advancement potential and more overall control of one's professional and personal life, it is easy to see why many law enforcement officers set eventual goals to become private security directors.

> Employment in the private sector usually provides more advancement potential and greater control over one's professional and personal life, explaining why many law enforcement officers desire jobs as private security directors.

As Carey (1996, p. 37) notes:

> Despite its differences from police work, many former law enforcement officers have found satisfying, lucrative careers in the private sector. And while these differences are notable, there are many transferable skills that enable police officers to work successfully for private employers.
>
> The work, after all, is interesting. The focus is on investigations, surveillance, interviewing, computer systems, management and securing property. And the compensation is often superior to that of smaller police forces. Perhaps most importantly, you can go into private sector security at almost any time in your career. Not only is the field an option for retirees, disabled officers and officers wishing to make a career change, it can also provide a part-time income for those wishing to remain in police work.

While many individuals who have enjoyed a successful career in law enforcement will enjoy a "second career" in private security, many people successfully use work in the private sector as a "stepping stone" into the public sector. Law enforcement is a popular career, and jobs as police officers are difficult to come by. Having worked as a security officer at any level says a number of things about an applicant for a police job:

➢ The applicant has been successfully employed.
➢ The applicant has worked in a position of trust.
➢ Unusual hours do not present a problem.
➢ The uniform does not create a power-hungry person.
➢ The applicant can keep cool under stressful circumstances.

Types of Jobs Available

The continuously evolving complexity of our society is necessitating specially trained private security officers in all phases of life. Businesses need individuals who can effectively use highly technical surveillance equipment. They rely on private suppliers of search dogs and strike/civil disobedience response teams. Some businesses need 24-hour surveillance. Services commonly identified as candidates for privatization include animal control, court security, funeral escorts, parking enforcement, patrolling of public parks, prisoner transport, public building security, public housing development patrol and special event security.

With the enhanced function of private security has come the opportunity for specialization. According to Patterson (p. 33): "As private security's role has expanded, niche markets have developed. A particularly interesting one involves the provision of security teams to support major labor relations incidents. One private security company now specializes in plant and industrial strike forces." ASIS (p. 4) states:

> The security field is divided into a number of specialized disciplines. In a large organization, a security professional may work full-time in one of these disciplines. In smaller organizations, a security professional may need to have some proficiency in each of them . . .

Physical Security—focuses on the protection of people, property and facilities through the use of security forces, security systems and security procedures.

Information Security—involves safeguarding sensitive information.

Personnel Security—deals with ensuring the integrity and reliability of an organization's workforce.

Information Systems Security—involves maintaining the confidentiality, reliability and availability of data created, stored, processed and/or transmitted via automated information systems.

As the private security profession expands, so have the kinds of jobs available. ASIS lists the following (p. 18) as security specialties with career opportunities:

Construction Security	Pharmaceutical Security	Security Investigations
Corporate Security	Proprietary/Information Security	Special Event Security
Entertainment Security	Real Estate Management Security	Wholesaling and Warehousing Security
Government Operations Security	Residential Security	Contingency Planning
Hi-Tech Security	Security Consulting	Crisis Management
High-Rise/Office Building Security	Security Design and Engineering	Executive Protection
Insurance Security	Security Education and Training	Terrorism Counteraction
Nuclear Security		

Regardless of the specific security discipline or specialty, opportunities in the private sector are typically categorized as entry-level, mid-level and top-level positions.

Entry-Level Positions. Typical entry-level jobs include private security guards and private patrol officers. Private security guards control access to private property; protect against loss through theft, vandalism or fire; enforce rules; maintain order and lower risks of all kinds. The *Occupational Outlook Handbook* (1999, p. 343) states:

In office buildings, banks, hospitals, and department stores, guards protect people, records, merchandise, money, and equipment. In department stores, they often work with undercover detectives to watch for theft by customers or store employees.

At air, sea, and rail terminals, and other transportation facilities, guards protect people, merchandise being shipped, property, and equipment. They screen passengers and visitors for weapons, explosives, and other contraband, ensure nothing is stolen while being loaded or unloaded, and watch for fires and prowlers. They may direct traffic.

Guards who work in public buildings, such as museums or art galleries, protect paintings and exhibits by inspecting the people and packages entering and leaving the building. They answer routine questions from visitors and sometimes guide tours.

In factories, laboratories, government buildings, data processing centers, and military bases in which valuable property or information—such as information on new products, computer codes, or defense secrets—must be protected, guards check the credentials of persons and vehicles entering and leaving the premises. University, park, or recreation guards perform similar duties and also may issue parking permits and direct traffic. Golf course patrollers prevent unauthorized persons from using the facility and help keep play running smoothly.

At social affairs, sports events, conventions, and other public gatherings, guards provide information, assist in crowd control, and watch for persons who may cause trouble. Some guards patrol places of entertainment, such as nightclubs, to preserve order among customers and to protect property.

Armored car guards protect money and valuables during transit. Bodyguards protect individuals from bodily injury, kidnapping, or invasion of privacy.

Most guards wear a uniform and some carry a nightstick or other weapons, such as a gun. Security guards may work inside and/or outside, patrolling the interior of buildings or the exterior grounds. They may be stationed at a desk to monitor security cameras and to check the identification of persons coming and going. As with many other jobs, a typical guard shift lasts eight hours, although many guards work at night, and many work alone. Because of the flexible hours common in security positions, many are able to pursue work in this field and have another job.

Private patrol officers are similar to patrol units of the public police force. They move from one location to another, on foot or in a vehicle, protecting property and preventing losses. Some patrol officers work for a single employer; others have several employers.

> Typical entry-level jobs include private security guards and private patrol officers. Private security guards control access to private property; protect against loss through theft, vandalism or fire; enforce rules; maintain order and lower risks of all kinds. Private patrol officers, similar to patrol units of the public police force, move from one location to another, on foot or in a vehicle, protecting property and preventing losses.

According to the *Occupational Outlook Handbook* (p. 344):

> Guards held about 955,000 jobs in 1996. Industrial security firms and guard agencies employed 59 percent of all guards. These organizations provide security services on contract, assigning their guards to buildings and other sites as needed. The remainder were in-house guards, employed in many settings including banks, building management companies, hotels, hospitals, retail stores, restaurants, bars, schools, and government.

Mid-Level Positions. Mid-level jobs in private security include private investigators, detectives, armed couriers, central alarm respondents and consultants. Private investigators and detectives may "freelance" or may work for a specific employer. Often the work involves background checks for employment, insurance and credit applications, civil litigation and investigation of insurance or workers' compensation claims. Sometimes investigators are brought in to work undercover to detect employee dishonesty, shoplifting or illegal drug use. The *Occupational Outlook Handbook* (p. 348) reports:

> Private detectives and investigators assist attorneys, businesses, and the public with a variety of problems. Their services include protecting businesses and their employees, customers, and guests from theft, vandalism, and disorder as well as gathering evidence for trials, tracing debtors, or conducting background investigations. While detectives concentrate on providing protection and investigators specialize in gathering information, many do some of each.

Regarding the employment of such professionals, the *Occupational Outlook Handbook* (p. 349) states:

> Private detectives and investigators held about 58,000 jobs in 1996. About 17 percent were self-employed. About 36 percent of wage and salary workers worked for detective agencies and about 42 percent were employed as store detectives in department or clothing and accessories stores. Others worked for hotels and other lodging places, legal services firms, and in other industries.

Top-Level Positions. Top jobs in security include managing a private security company or heading up security for a private concern. Common titles include loss prevention specialist, security director and risk manager.

> Mid-level jobs in private security include private investigators, detectives, armed couriers, central alarm respondents and consultants. Top jobs in security include loss prevention specialists, security directors and risk managers.

While guard and other security positions are found throughout the country, it makes sense that most of the positions are in urban regions with higher populations. Furthermore, international jobs are also available in security, but obtaining them is not easy. Many businesses and establishments, such as hotels, are opening facilities in foreign countries. Often the security director of such businesses and establishments are sent to set up the security system.

> Job opportunities in private security are greater in metropolitan areas. Security jobs are more difficult to obtain in foreign countries and in less populated areas of the United States.

Those seeking careers in private security may also wish to consider public security positions as well as those of special deputies, code enforcement officers and others with limited law enforcement authority. Many government agencies hire "special deputies" who possess law enforcement authority while on duty. These special deputies perform many of the same functions carried out by private security forces but do so for the government. At the local level, special deputies may be under the direct authority of the sheriff, or they may constitute a security department within a government organization. In New York, for example, security officers working for local governments are called *peace officers* to distinguish them from their public police officer counterparts.

Special deputies are also found in the federal government. For example, the U.S. Marshals assign special deputy marshals to courthouses. Such deputies are often contract employees who possess law enforcement authority only while on duty and only at their assigned venue. The Department of Energy (DOE), through its contractors, employs hundreds of individuals to perform security and safeguard responsibilities related to classified documents and materials. While such individuals are not DOE inspectors and lack law enforcement authority, they do work closely with local police departments and the FBI to investigate all levels of security breaches, thefts of government property and other crimes impacting government property and issues. Furthermore, compensation in this area can be quite lucrative.

As technology advances, the types of jobs available to those in the security profession also expand. One of the newest arenas of security is fighting cyber-crime. Weinstein (1999, p. J1) notes:

> A few years ago, cyber-crime served only as the subject of sci-fi novels. Today, it is a serious problem affecting everyone. . . .
>
> According to the annual CSI/FBI Computer Crime and Security Survey conducted by the Computer Security Institute and the San Francisco FBI Computer Intrusion Squad, system penetration by outsiders increased for the third year in a row, along with unauthorized access by insiders and financial losses because of computer security breaches (amounting to losses of more than $100 million).
>
> That's not the half of it. Many cyber-thieves are becoming instant millionaires by bilking brokerages and, especially, the insurance industry, according to Jay Valentine, CEO of Austin, Texas-based InfoGlide, a company that makes fraud-busting software. . . .
>
> In the past 18 to 24 months, tracking down cyber-thieves has ascended to high priority. More companies are creating computer security departments manned by cyber-sleuths or computer security investigators. "They used to be former police officers with technical skills. Now they're mainly young techies, many of whom are recent college grads, with a knowledge of C++, Java and Internet applications," Valentine said.
>
> About 300 of the Fortune 500 companies are hiring cyber-sleuths, according to Valentine. It all adds up to yet another emerging field with undefined job titles and job tracks. Valentine estimated that six to 10 computer security jobs exist at any midsize to large company, and the pay scale ranges from $60,000 to $100,000-plus at the senior levels.
>
> Whether entry-level or management, it's anything but a dull career. "A security person, for example, may be investigating multiple attempts to log on, monitoring log-on procedures, passwords, tracing attempts to break into a network or trying to discover what type of computer it originated from," Valentine said.

Obviously, this type of security work requires a specialized skill and degree of technical knowledge. While such technical knowledge is not a prerequisite for most security positions, employment requirements in the growing field of private security are becoming increasingly "professionalized."

Employment Requirements

Because private security is both recognizing itself and being recognized as a profession, the field is joining the trend of others that stress the importance of maintaining certain basic professional requirements. Employers with proprietary forces usually set their own standards for security officers. Contractual security companies often are regulated by state law. Individuals who wish to provide security services on their own may need to be licensed by their state. Requirements vary, so it is important to check on your local situation.

While some states require few, if any, qualifications be met by those wishing to work in private security, some states are becoming very strict as to who may practice in this field, either as an individual or a company supplying security services. Of the three professional licenses I (J. Scott Harr) hold, my private detective license required more comprehensive qualifications and was more expensive to initially obtain than my licenses as a police officer or a lawyer. Minnesota statutes stipulate who needs to be licensed as a private investigator in the state, what the application consists of and what must accompany the application. Each application in Minnesota must be accompanied by:

➢ A surety bond for $5,000.
➢ Verified certificates of at least five citizens not related to the signer who have known the signer for more than five years, certifying that the signer is of "good moral character."
➢ Two photographs and a full set of fingerprints for each signer of the application.

While Minnesota has some of the most restrictive regulations, more states are recognizing that some controls have to be in place to ensure responsible involvement by those operating in this field. The *Occupation Outlook Handbook* (p. 344) states: "Most States require that guards be licensed. To be licensed as a guard, individuals must generally be 18 years old, pass a background examination, and complete classroom training in such subjects as property rights, emergency procedures, and detention of suspected criminals." Regarding private investigators and detectives, the *Occupational Outlook Handbook* notes (p. 349): "The majority of the States and the District of Columbia require private detectives and investigators to be licensed by the State or local authorities. Licensing requirements vary widely. Some States have very liberal requirements, or none at all, while others have stringent regulations."

Be sure to investigate the requirements of the state(s) in which you want to work. Some county and city governments also require certification or licensure of those working in private security positions within their jurisdiction. Because many duties of private security officers can have consequences as critical as those of the law enforcement officer—for example, using firearms, K-9s and other weapons, arresting people, rendering emergency medical assistance and the like—it makes sense to have basic requirements in place. Most common are regulations regarding background checks, certain minimal knowledge and posting some sort of bond. Some states have a residency requirement. Many states have policies on autos and uniforms.

Nearly every state now has licensing or registration requirements for guards who work for contract security agencies. Some states have a residency requirement, and many states have regulations concerning autos and uniforms. Be sure to investigate these employment requirements by contacting the appropriate regulatory agency.

Training requirements and other qualifications vary among different agencies; however, some applicant qualities are fairly common. Most employers prefer guards who are high school graduates. Some jobs require a driver's license. Some employers seek individuals who have had experience in the military police or in state and local police agencies. Furthermore: "Applicants are expected to have good character references, no serious police record, good health—especially in hearing and vision—and good personal habits such as neatness and dependability" (*Occupational Outlook Handbook,* p. 344).

Because competition for prime security positions in increasing, applicants should strive to increase their marketability by gaining knowledge of the field through education and other types of experiences. According to ASIS (p. 2): "Students seeking careers in security should pursue course work in security, computer science, electronics, business management, law, police science, personnel and information management." Carey (p. 37) reports: "According to experts, police officers wishing to pursue a private security career should obtain the widest variety of police experience possible, with a particular emphasis on investigations." She also notes (pp. 37–38) police officers may enhance their marketability by developing skills in such specialties as technical accident reconstruction, fire cause and document examination.

In addition, some individuals may want to be certified by the ASIS through their *Certified Protection Professional (CPP) program*. This program, organized in 1977, is designed to recognize individuals meeting specific criteria of professional protection knowledge and conduct. To be eligible to take the examination, candidates must either have 10 years of experience with no degree, eight years of experience and an associate's degree, five years of experience and a bachelor's degree, four years of experience and a master's degree or three years of experience and a doctoral degree. At least half the experience must be in "responsible charge" of a security function. The examination takes a full day, with the morning devoted to general security knowledge and the afternoon devoted to a choice of four specialty tests selected from a wide variety of areas.

Most employers seek security applicants with high school diplomas and some experience in the military police or in state or local level police work. Other important qualities include good character references, good health, good personal habits and no police record. A valid driver's license may also be required. Eligible individuals may benefit by becoming a Certified Protection Professional, or CPP.

Job Outlook

According to *The Top 100: The Fastest Growing Careers for the 21st Century* (1998, p. 345):

> Security services is one of the largest employment fields in the United States. . . .
>
> The demand for guards and other security personnel is expected to increase much faster than the average through the year 2005, as crime rates rise with the overall population growth. The highest estimates call for more than 1.25 million guards to be employed by the year 2005.

The private security field is expected to grow more rapidly through the year 2005 than the average for all occupations, requiring the hiring of many employees to meet the increasing security needs.

Certain areas within the security industry are also projected to grow more rapidly than others. Bias (1999, p. 1) reports on the results of an ASIS survey: "The fields where the most security management job growth is expected are computer security and information technology. Contract security and investigations also appear to be gaining job positions due to the swell in outsourcing, and companies looking for cost-effective technology that allows a reduction in officer staffing are creating jobs in electronics security and alarm system design and installation."

Salaries

It is difficult to provide an accurate listing of "average" pay in private security because the range is extreme. Entry-level jobs may start at the minimum wage, but the upper wage is virtually unlimited. Owners of successful private security or investigation firms and upper-level security directors can expect lucrative salaries, with perks like bonus plans and company cars. According to *The Top 100* (p. 345):

Earnings for security consultants vary greatly depending on the consultant's training and experience. Entry-level consultants with a bachelor's degree commonly start at $26,000 to $32,000 per year. Consultants with graduate degrees begin at $34,000 to $41,000 per year, and experienced consultants may earn $50,000 to $100,000 per year or more. Many consultants work on a per-project basis, with rates of up to $75 per hour.

The *Occupational Outlook Handbook* (pp. 344–345) reports: "Median annual earnings of guards who worked full time in 1996 were about $17,300. . . . Guards generally earn slightly more in urban areas. . . . Guards employed by the Federal Government averaged about $22,900 a year in 1997. These workers usually receive overtime pay as well as a wage differential for the second and third shifts." The *Handbook* also notes (p. 349):

> Earnings of private detectives and investigators vary greatly depending on their employer, specialty, and the geographic area in which they work. According to a study by Abbott, Langer & Associates, security/loss prevention directors and vice presidents earned an average of $67,700 a year in 1996, investigators about $37,800 a year, and store detectives about $19,100.
>
> Most private investigators bill their clients between $50 and $150 per hour to conduct investigations

The "1999 Salary Survey" conducted by *Access Control and Security Systems Integration* magazine (1999, p. SS3) revealed: "Riding on the wave of a strong and expanding economy, many security industry professionals are enjoying healthy career growth and prosperity." While some security practitioners were earning less than $25,000 per year in 1999, the bulk of professionals in this field were in the $40,000–$65,000 range. About two percent of those employed in corporate security management reported incomes of $200,000 or more. The average 1999 salaries for selected security professionals are shown in Table 4-1.

Table 4-1   1999 Salary Survey

Pay for Performance Average Salary by Title	
Corporate Security Manager	$82,785
Director of Security/Safety	$67,380
Manager of Security/Safety	$55,664
Facility Manager	$60,921
Average of all respondents	$62,891

SOURCE: "1999 Salary Survey." Supplement to *Access Control and Security Systems Integration*, 1999, p. SS3.

Salaries in the field of private security vary greatly, ranging from around $16,000 a year for security officers to $200,000 or more a year for corporate security managers.

Fringe Benefits

According to the "1999 Salary Survey" (p.SS5), a variety of fringe benefits are commonly made available to those employed in the field of security. Listed in order from most common to least common, fringe benefits for security professionals include vacation (94%), medical insurance (90%), holidays (88%), sick leave (82%), dental insurance (75%), 401(k) plan (67%), long-term disability plan (67%), pension plan (65%), personal time (64%), tuition reimbursement (62%), trade show expenses (58%), vision insurance (52%), short-term disability plan (51%), cellular airtime/usage (49%), association memberships (48%), company car or auto allowance (30%), stock purchase plan (29%) and a profit sharing plan (29%).

Promotions

Like law enforcement, security careers can meet a stumbling block not as prevalent in other careers. Promotions can come few and far between—if at all. The problem is that jobs in the security field tend to be at one end of the spectrum or the other. At the entry level, security jobs can be minimum wage jobs, with minimal raises. "Middle management" positions are usually few in number. The money is in top management jobs, either for a corporation or for one's own business. At these levels there is literally no upward limit.

Somerson (1995, p. 27) believes promotions in the security field depend on applicants' skills in the business world:

> The security profession has traditionally been dominated by persons with a law enforcement, investigative, or military intelligence background. In addition, corporate security has been reactive, concerned more with resolving crises than proactively addressing business needs. But private industry is changing and security practitioners will need to develop more business expertise. Law enforcement skills will still be strategic to security's mission, but most management positions in the security industry will go to highly skilled business executives.

As in law enforcement, promotions in private security may be scarcer than in other professions, particularly into middle management where positions are limited.

CONCLUSION

Private security is the nation's primary protective resource today, outspending public law enforcement by more than 73 percent and employing nearly three times the workforce. The private security field is expected to grow rapidly through the year 2005, requiring the hiring of a large number of employees to meet the increasing security needs. A security job can serve as a stepping stone to other employment or a chance to obtain supplemental income as a second job or while attending school. Whether you seek employment in private security as a chance to acquire valuable training to help gain future employment in law enforcement or because the security field has exceptional future potential, private security can provide satisfying work.

ADDITIONAL CONTACTS AND SOURCES OF INFORMATION

ASIS International Customer Service
1625 Prince Street
Alexandria, VA 22314
(703) 519-6200
Web site: http://www.asisonline.org

Professional Training Resources
PO Box 439
Shaftsbury, VT 05262
(802) 447-7832 or (800) 998-9400
Publishes: *Cashing In on Consulting for the Private Security Professional*, by
Jim R. Matison and Kären M. Hess, 1997.

AN INSIDER'S VIEW

CAREER OPPORTUNITIES IN PRIVATE SECURITY

Robert B. Iannone
Certified Protection Professional
President, Iannone Security Management, Inc.

Preparing yourself for employment in any field should include achieving competency through pursuing three factors: (1) training, (2) education and (3) experience. Training includes attending security seminars, conferences and on-the-job training. Education refers to achieving a college degree in the security field or a related field. Gaining experience, of course, requires working in your chosen field. These elements apply no matter what field you pursue.

In private security, formal education can be obtained from the numerous colleges and universities throughout the United States that offer Associate of Arts degrees, bachelor's degrees and graduate degrees in security. Core courses in these curricula may include such subjects as Introduction to Security, Physical Security, Information Security, Computer Security, Ethics, Legal Aspects of Security and Security Management and Administration. A degree in a related field might include a curriculum in business or management.

Following graduation, experience can be achieved by obtaining an entry-level position. To assist prospective security applicants obtain the entry-level experience necessary, colleges and universities may offer a core security internship. Internships allow students to be employed in the industry and to perform actual security-related functions while earning credits toward graduation. In many instances, employers have retained the intern following graduation.

Security-related training can be gained through professional security organizations such as the American Society for Industrial Security (ASIS) and the International Security Conference (ISC). Security-related training courses offered through the ASIS and the ISC include virtually all aspects of the security profession. In addition, numerous periodicals published by security organizations such as the ASIS and the ISC address a variety of security-related subjects. Full advantage of the services offered by professional security organizations such as ASIS can be gained through becoming a member. Service offered through membership includes receiving newsletters, periodicals and announcements to ASIS-sponsored seminars and conferences. There is no membership to ISC; however, there is an interest mailing list.

Employment opportunities in the security field have increased in recent years. Some factors causing this increase include (1) the doubling of personnel working in the field over the past 20 years, (2) a current shortage of qualified personnel, (3) technological advances, (4) higher salaries, (5) a shift from the law enforcement image and (6) the availability of two-year, four-year and graduate degrees.

Employment opportunities available in the security industry include government service (military and civilian), banking, retail, health care, airport/airline, campus, lodging, computer, aerospace and the security services. Although employment opportunities in the aerospace industry have decreased in recent years, the security services industry has increased significantly. The security services include providers of security-related hardware such as intrusion detection systems and devices, access control systems and devices, closed-circuit television, fire detection systems and devices, lock and key control, physical barriers and identification systems. Other security service providers include suppliers of contract security officers. With the increase in the use of personal computers, there are also suppliers of computer software for a variety of applications such as data management and material accountability systems.

Salaries in the security field vary, depending on the industry. In addition, salaries vary within specific industries depending on such factors as training, education and experience. Salaries also differ between geographic areas and policy making and non-policy making positions.

In summary, career development begins with each individual; therefore, individuals who prepare themselves by acquiring job-specific training, formal education and field-related experience will obtain the best positions. In addition, regardless of the security discipline, they will be assured of higher salaries.

Robert B. Iannone, *CPP, is president of Iannone Security Management, Inc., located in Fountain Valley, California. Mr. Iannone has over 40 years' experience as a security practitioner, manager, author, consultant, expert witness, lecturer, educator and advisor to security book publishers. He has worked as a security manager for Hughes Aircraft Company, manager of security and investigations for Rockwell International, security inspector for Douglas Aircraft Company and for the U.S. Army Security Agency.*

Mr. Iannone is past chairman of the Greater Los Angeles Chapter of the American Society for Industrial Security, past member of the Board of Directors of the Research Security Administrators, and past member of the National Classification Management Society. Security articles written by Mr. Iannone have appeared in Security Management, and he performs public speaking that addresses a variety of security subjects.

For over 20 years, Mr. Iannone has been an adjunct professor, teaching security-related courses at the university level. Mr. Iannone has a Bachelor of Science degree in Criminal Justice (Security Management) from California State University, Long Beach, and a Master of Science degree in Management from the University of LaVerne. He has been married 33 years to Theresa; they have one daughter. His hobbies include working with personal computers.

THE CHANGING FACE OF PRIVATE SECURITY

Marie Ohman
Executive Director
Minnesota Board of Private Investigators and Protective Agent Services

The security practitioner of the new millennium is faced with a challenging and continuously evolving new frontier. This new frontier manifests itself in tremendous changes in the existing service industry. Modern society needs to maintain an effective system to protect the public from wrong and also to deal with the multifaceted criminal justice system. Private security has become an integral part of our society's efforts to maintain a semblance of order.

A major change is the evolving "face" of public law enforcement. The ability of the general public and business communities to rely on public law enforcement for prevention services, and for acting when this prevention fails, has diminished. A key factor in that change is economic. Attempting to provide services for a growing population with fewer dollars creates problems for traditional law enforcement agencies. The demands placed on public service force law enforcement administrators into deciding *not* what they need or would like to do, but just how much they can do with their limited resources. The areas of need left unaddressed, or instances where a special need is perceived, have begun to be taken over by private client dollars spent for private security services.

In 1990, a study published by Hallcrest Systems, Inc., projected a ratio of 3 to 1 of private security officers to that of public law enforcement as we enter the new century.

Private security forces have been and will continue to be a viable employer in our country's workforce. The stereotypical view of an elderly, gun-carrying security guard is slowly being replaced with that of a modern security officer who deals with all facets of protection from the traditional "observe and report" role to intricate knowledge of alarm and computer systems, thorough knowledge of security concepts and expertise in safety and first aid.

Private security will continue to be essential in society. From a philosophical view, as long as generations are raised in an environment of economic difficulties, materialism and little accountability for actions, the necessity for maintaining order will be an absolute. A trend in government today is to look at the business world for answers to problems. Included in that trend is the reality that private security plays a vital role in protecting people and property in this country, traditionally public law enforcement's role. After many years of evolution, private security has gained long overdue respect as a profession.

***Marie Ohman** is the executive director for the Minnesota Board of Private Detective and Protective Agent Services. She has worked in the field of criminal justice for more than 20 years and has been employed by the Minnesota Bureau of Criminal Apprehension in the Criminal Justice Information Systems and Criminal Records divisions. Ms. Ohman's background includes a Technical College Degree in Law Enforcement (Administrative Positions) and some college courses in law enforcement and business. She is a writer, traveler and frequent enjoyer of the outdoors.*

MIND STRETCHES

1. Why do you think the entertainment field is obsessed with depicting private security? Do you think this obsession helps or hurts the profession? Why?

2. Do you personally know any security officers? Are they like the private investigators depicted on television?

3. What is your favorite private detective show? Why?

4. Do you think television and the movies have influenced your career choice?

5. Do you think security work will become more specialized or more generalized in the future? Why? How will your job goals be affected?

6. What stereotype do you think private security officers have? Why? Is it justified?

7. Why do you think the trend to license all professions exists? Do you think it is helpful?

8. Are security salaries more or less than you had anticipated? Does salary affect your decision as to what field of employment you will eventually pursue? Why or why not?

9. How do you predict the field of private security will change? Why?

REFERENCES

Arbetter, Lisa. "A Commitment to Cooperation: An Interview with 1994 ASIS President Ken Joseph." *Security Management,* January 1994, pp. 52–54.

ASIS International. *Career Opportunities in Security.* Alexandria, VA: ASIS International, no date.

Bias, Bronson S. "Bright Employment Future." *ASIS Dynamics*, January/February 1999, pp. 1, 9.

Carey, Carol. "Private Eyes." *Police*, May 1996, pp. 36–38, 76–78.

Hertig, Christopher A. "Who Are the Forgotten Soldiers?" *Security Management*, February 1993, pp. 95–96.

Hess, Kären M. and Wrobleski, Henry M. *Introduction to Private Security*, 4th ed. St. Paul, MN: West Publishing Company, 1996.

Kolpacki, Thomas A. "Neighborhood Watch." *Security Management,* November 1994, pp. 47–49.

Matison, Jim R. and Hess, Kären M. *Cashing In on Consulting for the Private Security Professional.* Shaftsbury, VT: Professional Training Resources, 1997.

"1999 Salary Survey." Supplement to *Access Control and Security Systems Integration*, 1999, pp. SS3–SS7.

Occupational Outlook Handbook. 1998-1999 Edition. U.S. Department of Labor, Bureau of Labor Statistics, Washington, DC: U.S. Government Printing Office, 1999.

Patterson, Julien. "Forging Creative Alliances." *Security Management,* January 1995, pp. 33–35.

Somerson, Ira S. "The Next Generation." *Security Management,* January 1995, pp. 27–30.

Thomas, Charles W. "Growth in Privatization Continues to Accelerate." *Corrections Compendium,* April 1994, pp. 5–6, 19.

The Top 100: The Fastest Growing Careers for the 21ˢᵗ Century. Chicago: Ferguson Publishing Company, 1998.

Trojanowicz, Robert and Bucqueroux, Bonnie. "The Privatization of Public Justice: What Will It Mean to Police?" *The Police Chief,* October 1990, pp. 131–135.

"Wackenhut Largest in Corrections Industry." *Security Concepts,* May 1995, p. 27.

Weinstein, Bob. "Investigate the Job Prospects in Cyber-Crimefighting." (Minneapolis/St. Paul) *Star Tribune*, May 9, 1999, p. J1.

West, Marty L. "Get a Piece of the Privatization Pie." *Security Management,* March 1993, pp. 54–59.

CHAPTER 5

ON CHOOSING A CAREER:
KNOWING THE JOB AND YOURSELF

People are always blaming their circumstances for what they are. I don't believe in circumstances. The people who get on in this world are the people who get up and look for the circumstances they want, and if they can't find them—make them.

—George Bernard Shaw

Do You Know:

➢ Why job satisfaction is so important?
➢ The best way to avoid job dissatisfaction?
➢ What the four steps of the career development process are?
➢ What specific requirements and limitations you should consider when choosing a career?
➢ How your background could prevent employment in the criminal justice or security fields?
➢ What an *inventurer* is? If you are one?
➢ What five essential parts of a dream job must be considered before it can become a reality?
➢ The importance of taking risks?

INTRODUCTION

Previous chapters discussed some realities of careers in criminal justice and security. As you consider these professions, understand what they are—and what they are *not*. Also, take a serious inventory of your abilities and interests to determine if your career goals are realistic.

In this chapter you'll combine knowledge about your chosen field with an honest look at yourself, to make certain you are, indeed, on a road that will take you where you want to be. How often would you get into your car and just drive with no thought of where you want to go? Yet many people launch themselves toward a career with very limited forethought—or with unrealistic dreams. Many job seekers have dreams—dreams of a successful career and a carefree, pleasurable lifestyle. However, as Leider and Shapiro (1996, p. 94) state:

> The "perfect job" isn't really about enjoyment. Instead, it's one that mirrors perfectly the person who holds it. And people do find, or invent, or create these jobs. They do it by working a process—a surprisingly simple one. It's a process that links who you are with what you do. The process involves developing a clarity about your talents, passions, and values—looking inside yourself to discover what you do best, what you're interested in, and the type of working environment that supports what you care about most. And then combining all three to develop a clear vision of the kind of work that links who you are with what you do. . . .
>
> The perfect job isn't a standard of living. It's a state of mind and state of being. In the perfect job, you're applying the talents you enjoy most to an interest you're passionate about, in an environment that fits who you are and what you value.

The romanticized dream of a successful career becomes even more problematic when it involves the fields within criminal justice. Many people are intrigued with such employment because they want to be like the TV undercover police officer or private investigator they watch week after week. You must enter your career search with a much more open mind. Realistically, what *is* the job you are seeking?

SELECTING A CAREER

Carelessly pursuing a career can be costly. First, selecting a career is extremely important because the vast majority of your waking hours will be spent working. So who wants to be unhappy? Perhaps even worse is that job frustrations have a way of manifesting themselves in unpleasant, if not dangerous, ways. People who dislike their work show it. For people employed by the criminal justice system, job dissatisfaction could seriously affect job performance. At best, they may appear as unfeeling individuals, expressing little concern for anyone, including victims. At worst, inappropriate physical force, even brutality, could be evidence of something going on "inside." Such behavior can result in nationwide anti-police publicity as seen in the beating of Rodney King.

Career dissatisfaction can lead to unhappiness, negativity and cynicism in the individual and to a decrease in productivity and morale for the unit in which the individual works. The impact may be felt by co-workers and may affect their work attitude as well.

The best way to prevent career dissatisfaction is to research the field carefully before applying for employment, asking questions of those already in the field and carefully evaluating all the positive and negative aspects of the occupation *as they apply to your values and expectations*. There is a story about a woman who loved everything about being an engine mechanic—except getting dirty. Absolutely nothing could prevent her from leaving work each night grimy and greasy, and it was causing her to consider a career change. The simple fact was that an inherent part of her work was to get dirty. Determining whether getting dirty was worth it was an issue that had to be addressed.

Similarly, some facts about working in criminal justice and private security must be faced. The relatively mediocre pay, the difficult hours, the odd days off, the public's perception of the job and the inherent danger are all issues that may make the job unacceptable to some.

Take a realistic look at these issues now. Many people are trapped in jobs they dislike—even hate. How they got trapped like this may be hard for younger job seekers to understand, especially those who are single. But as you get older, changing jobs becomes less attractive. The benefits associated with seniority—acquired sick time, vacation time, and preferential scheduling—can make it difficult to consider leaving an "old" job.

Rather than jumping into a career you know little about, including how well suited to it *you* are, look objectively at the whole picture. Consider the job. Consider yourself. Is it a "match"? Or is it the frustrating pursuit of a fantasy?

> The best way to avoid career dissatisfaction is to thoroughly research the field you are interested in and to carefully and realistically address issues concerning the nature of the work, the hours, the pay—any and all positives *and* negatives. Go in with your eyes wide open.

DIRECTING YOURSELF

While this text is specifically directed at helping you develop your own job-seeking strategy, there is much more to the process than merely learning to write a resume. If you are not heading in a direction that will really work for you, your work will not be fulfilling.

We have a concern for those who are seeking employment in criminal justice. We know of no other field that is attractive to job seekers for reasons that go far beyond the motivations for other fields of work. Whether these reasons include wishing to play a helping role in society, having a career that can be really exciting or wishing for a job with significant power over others (good or bad), the call to the fields of criminal justice and private security can be dangerous. It is for this reason that you *must* examine *why* you want to work there and what your true expectations are.

Career counselors stress the importance of people developing the ability to examine their motivations. This applies to people who are seeking to enter a certain career and those considering getting out. Nathan and Hill (1992, p. 2) stress the importance of other issues in career counseling beyond just talking about jobs. They view career counseling as a process that enables clients to become more aware of their own resources to lead a more satisfying life as well as to "take into account the interdependence of career and non-career considerations" (p. 3). They cite the approach advocated by Parsons (1909) over 90 years ago:

> In the wise choice of vocation, there are three factors:
> 1. A clear understanding of yourself
> 2. A knowledge of the requirements and prospects in different lines of work
> 3. True reasoning on the relations of these two groups of facts

In Figure 5-1, Krannich (1995, p. 100) illustrates how the first two factors are critical to career development. The next section of this book focuses on steps 3 and 4.

> Krannich identifies the four steps of the career development process as (1) self-assessment, (2) career exploration, (3) job search skill development and (4) implementation of the job search steps.

Interesting changes have occurred in what motivates job seekers. It is important to carefully consider what jobs will be fulfilling. But this also requires people to be realistic about what work can provide. There is a danger in having unrealistic expectations about work. It is likely that as the baby boomers have become well-entrenched in the workforce, they have brought with them a degree of their "me-generation" mentality that has included a certain self-centeredness that results in an expectation that everything should be perfect. . . at least for them! The question is, then, can work be . . . perfect?

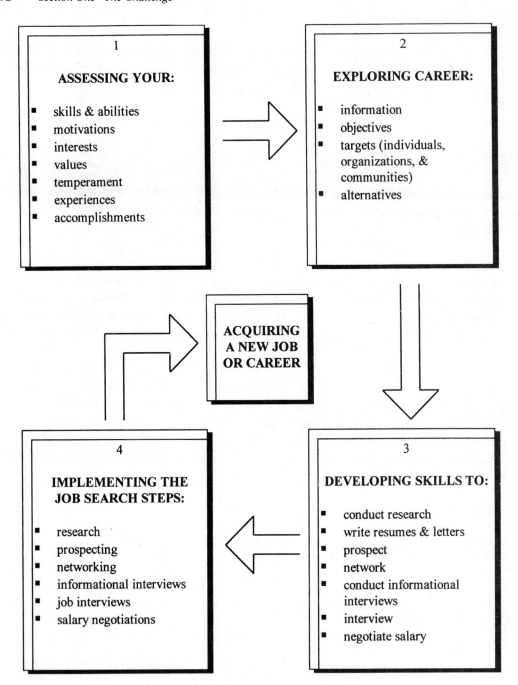

FIGURE 5-1   The Career Development Process

SOURCE: Ronald L. Krannich. *Change Your Job, Change Your Life.* 5th ed. Manassas Park, VA: Impact Publications, 1995, p. 100. Reprinted by permission.

Many Americans become encumbered by an ideal of the perfect job. But as Leider and Shapiro (p. 93) note: "Every job has its good parts and its bad parts. It's hard to imagine any kind of work that would be enjoyable 100 percent of the time. Even sports heroes and movie stars have their bad days."

Unrealistic expectations of work may be a natural evolution of American society. Post-Depression work, followed by post–World War II work, really did help satisfy the American dream. The economy was strong and growing; opportunities were everywhere, and work itself provided so much to so many.

Even as people expected more and more, the workplace was able to keep up . . . at least for a while. Increasing salaries, benefits and new types of jobs seemed limitless. But they weren't, and as a result, jobs became more scarce, upward mobility more challenging and the time of unlimited potential became limited.

The world of work, including why people seek the jobs they do, has come back to where it arguably began: to provide for our more basic needs. Personal, perhaps selfish, needs take precedence over the broader things that work provides. The importance of the "whole person" in society has emerged as more important than the individual. The benefits a job directly provides is only one aspect of how satisfying a job can be. Now the important question that needs to be asked is whether a job provides the leisure time for individuals to achieve their goals beyond just being successful on the job.

Charting Your Future Course

It's difficult to consider the future without becoming philosophical. No one *knows* what the future will bring, so all you can do is speculate about what might occur. Of course, you can make some pretty darned good guesses based on what has occurred in the past combined with what is happening right now.

Here's what is known for sure: technology demands that successful job candidates have certain skill levels, and work affects your life to the degree that careful thought must be invested in future job considerations. The future of *your* work will be dictated by the decisions you make about it. Even if you make no decision and let yourself be blown about the job market like a tumbleweed, you have, indeed, made that decision.

Not only is the rapid development of technology influencing the working world, but so are the reasons people pursue certain jobs. The job you seek *does* influence how you feel about yourself and those around you. You must have a balance of interests and activities, a sense of identity, a realistic sense of your capabilities and reasonable goals for your life. It is also important to feel in control of your destiny.

Surely, to ensure a lifetime working career (or, more probably, careers), you must be able to do far more than submit a quality resume. You must know *why* you are submitting that resume for that job. By examining yourself and your goals, together with a realistic idea of what expectations are truly important to you, you place yourself in control of your future. This chapter presents exercises that will help you learn about yourself and relate this insight to the careers you are considering. You need to recognize that many areas within criminal justice and its related fields are like the mythological Sirens, beckoning victims on to destruction. Take this opportunity to consider what is right for you and vice versa. It could save you and others considerable frustration and difficulties in the future.

One way to find out your true career interests *before* committing to a particular line of work is to volunteer with a potential employer, request a ride-along, or interview some officers or other employees. Visit agencies you think you'd like to work for and see what a typical workday is like. Alderman, a director of placement, notes: "The best approach to job hunting is a multiple one" (1995, p. 173). Job-search strategies include checking out job posting boards at colleges, reading the help-wanted ads in newspapers and trade publications, seeking assistance from career groups and accessing the on-line bulletin boards servicing your field(s) of interest. Alderman (p. 173) also suggests: "Your alumni office can supply the names of recent grads working in your field. Call them to find out industry news and names. You might even snag an interview."

Career Counselors

A variety of tools exist to help you better understand your own aptitudes and interests. You are encouraged to take such interest inventories and aptitude tests to help highlight career areas that might satisfy your many needs. There may even be job options you have never heard about or considered. A great place to start is the counseling department at your school.

With so many counselors available to help people deal with so many issues, it is surprising that more people don't consider this resource. Whether school counselors or those in the private sector, it helps to get advice from the pros. According to Messmer (1995, p. 40):

> Career counselors specialize in helping people get a better fix on which specific career options they should be pursuing. They don't find you jobs in the way that recruiters do . . . . Rather, they help you figure out for yourself . . . which career paths and jobs make the most sense. . . .
>
> Fees can run anywhere from $40 to $100 an hour, depending on the region and the reputation of the counselor.

Messmer (p. 41) offers advice on selecting a counselor, beginning with the suggestion that "the most reliable way to choose a career counselor is to get a personal recommendation from someone whose opinion you trust." Other starting places include local schools and community organizations, where you may receive recommendations on qualified counselors. Once you've chosen a counselor, you should take the following steps to ensure you have picked the right person (p. 41):

1. Interview the counselor—Get a feel for how the counselor works. Don't be embarrassed to ask about fees and what you can reasonably expect. Trust your instincts. If anything about the counselor gives you the creeps (for example, a boa constrictor is sleeping on one of the office chairs), find someone else.

2. Ask about the counselor's general approach—Find out how the counselor likes to work: whether the approach he or she uses relies heavily on testing or one-on-one interviewing and so forth. Don't be shy about asking what you can reasonably expect to derive from the overall experience. Ask for a description of the counselor's program—preferably in writing.

3. Ask for references—There's nothing wrong with asking a career counselor to supply you with the names of people with whom he or she has worked. If the counselor balks, find someone else.

Finally, Messmer cautions (p. 41):

Steer clear of counselors who

✓ Guarantee or promise that they can find you a job.
✓ Charge a high up-front fee.
✓ Subject you to a high-powered sales pitch.

For more information about career counselors or a list of certified counselors in your area, contact one of the agencies listed at the end of this chapter.

The steps to understanding yourself and your career goals have a beginning but never an end! Here's the beginning.

BRAINSTORMING POSSIBILITIES

Even if you are fairly certain about what you want to do with your life, it is worthwhile to consider other alternatives. These may be similar jobs, or they may be different altogether. Choices are what life is about, so start developing some.

Of all the exercises you will complete, this will be one of the easiest. Sit down with a clear mind and list in your journal the jobs that appeal to you. Don't analyze what you think you will or won't be qualified for. Simply write down the jobs that intrigue you. Do any general patterns emerge? Are the jobs you listed more in the service fields? The academic fields? Are they jobs which stress physical skills? Mental ability? Both equally? Do they stress working with people or alone? Indoors or outdoors? Why do you think you picked these jobs?

"JUST THE FACTS"

Having generated some career choices, next determine the facts about these alternatives. Areas to consider are:

➢ Age requirements.
➢ Physical requirements.
➢ Educational requirements.
➢ Background limitations.
➢ Experience requirements.

In deciding which career is best suited to you and your needs, you must consider age requirements, physical requirements, educational requirements, background limitations and experience requirements.

Age

Some jobs are better suited for young adults; others are ideal for retired adults. Some jobs, including certain law enforcement and security jobs, have age limitations. For example, in most states, you must be at least 21 years old to be a police officer. While the majority of policing jobs do not have an upward age limit for applicants, the federal system usually will not accept applicants older than 35. Some departments want very young recruits, while others may want more mature people.

Corrections and private security are open to an even greater variety of ages. On the one hand, either field is exceptional for entry-level people seeking to gain experience to help them on their way to becoming police officers. On the other hand, corrections and security work can be great fields in their own right or an ideal job for retired police officers or others.

Physical Requirements

It is likely that the jobs you are interested in have physical requirements. Most agencies or companies have minimum vision and hearing requirements. One young man went through law school to be an FBI agent, only to learn too late that his vision would not allow him to even take the entrance test. Check with the agencies to find out what they require.

Most agencies want height and weight to be proportionate, even if they do not follow a specific chart. If you need to lose weight, start an exercise program now, preferably one you can continue throughout your career. An increasing number of agencies are requiring physical "stress tests" to assess candidates' vascular health. You can prepare for this by participating in a regular exercise program.

Most departments or companies will ask if you have any physical restrictions that will interfere with job performance. Be realistic with yourself and honest with the employer. While occasional back pain may not be a problem, an inability to lift heavy items probably would be.

Various medical conditions will not necessarily eliminate you either. For instance, controllable diabetes should not be a problem for most jobs. Again, be honest with yourself and the employer regarding any health problems you may have.

Education

Different states have different requirements regarding what schooling is needed. Similarly, different employers have different standards. Employers in either the private or public sectors may require at least a high school diploma or general equivalency diploma (GED). Some states, Minnesota for example, require at least two years of college. Some agencies, particularly in the federal system, may require graduate credits or even a graduate degree, such as a law degree.

The more education you have, the better. This can include specialized training such as first-aid courses, first-responder courses, CPR and the like. Knowing a foreign language, knowing how to "sign" to hearing-impaired people, having skills in photography—any specialized knowledge is likely to be a plus as you pursue your career. As one hiring agent for a law enforcement agency notes:

> When I receive job applications I place them into three piles: those with a high school education (minimum requirements); those with some college; and those with a bachelor's, master's or JD degree. I seldom, if ever, reach down into the pile of applications where the minimum requirement was the standard. Even if a person can get hired on just a high school diploma, the chances of advancement without at least some college are negligible. Yes, there are police departments out there that will hire a person with a high school diploma, but I don't think most people who are thinking in terms of a professional career want to work there.

According to the FBI's web page, the agency is interested in people with the following backgrounds: law, accounting, foreign language and "generalist." Many believe getting a degree in a field besides criminal justice might "set them apart" from other applicants, since they will eventually learn what they need to know about being an officer by attending a police academy. However, the previously quoted hiring agent asserts:

> I believe there is a strong argument to be made for going ahead and getting that degree in criminal justice. First, not everybody going into criminal justice is going to be a cop and, therefore, will not go through an academy. Second, the training received at the academy is different than the education received at a college or university. Academies teach "how," whereas colleges teach "why." Both are needed to make a well-rounded criminal justice practitioner. Third, many students are going to end up in the private sector where they will need a criminal justice background in order to interface with the criminal justice system. Fourth, and finally, . . . would [you] go to an engineer if [you] needed brain surgery? As much as we are trying to make generalists out of our police officers these days, the skills, knowledge and abilities they need to do the job are not going to be picked up in a business college. Without a doubt, students in criminal justice need a strong background in liberal arts. . . , but a good solid core of criminal justice courses needs to be included in the student's/prospective employee's education.

It is further noted that a recent trend regarding hiring practices of the FBI and some other federal law enforcement agencies is to *not* hire students directly out of college, but rather to seek college graduates with two or three years of local law enforcement experience.

Background

Most private security companies, corrections facilities and certainly all law enforcement agencies will thoroughly investigate applicants' backgrounds. You should know what facts about your past will and won't affect your employment potential.

Most police departments and security agencies will not accept an applicant with a felony conviction on their adult record. Depending on the nature of the crime, a misdemeanor may not automatically eliminate you. Be prepared to honestly explain the situation to the employer.

While it will be difficult to deal with any criminal record, it is much easier to explain a petty shoplifting charge when you were 18 than a conviction when you were 28. Unfortunately, some students make serious errors in judgment while studying to become police or security officers—errors that ruin their chances at a career in criminal justice. For example, one night on a drunken excursion, a student slashed 40 tires, resulting in a felony conviction. While such behavior is wrong at any time, it's inexcusable while preparing to be a police, corrections or security officer. Act responsibly.

Traffic records, like lesser criminal records, may or may not be a hindrance. While they generally won't be grounds for automatic elimination from the application process, they will be strikes against you. Be up-front and honest about the circumstances. Many applicants make the mistake of saying they have no traffic record when, in fact, they do. It is easier to explain why you got a ticket 10 years ago than why you lied on your application. Lying is justification to eliminate an applicant. A traffic record may not be.

Juvenile records may also be a factor. Although the record may be sealed, an agency may likely find out about it during a background check. When police do a neighborhood check during the course of a background check, a neighbor may recall an incident involving the applicant and the police, where the applicant ended up leaving in the back seat of a patrol car.

Other situations need to be thought out honestly. Past counseling, or even institutionalization, may not be sufficient grounds for eliminating you from the running, but lying about it would be. Some agencies may be more likely to consider applicants who helped themselves by going through Alcoholics Anonymous or other self-help programs.

Most police departments and security agencies will not accept an applicant with a felony conviction on their adult record. A misdemeanor may not automatically eliminate you. Traffic records, like lesser criminal records, may or may not be a hindrance. Past counseling, or even institutionalization, may not be sufficient grounds for eliminating you from the running, but lying about it would be. Always be honest about such background circumstances.

Experience

Some agencies, such as the U.S. Bureau of Prisons and state probation and parole agencies, require previous experience in some related field. You should be aware of these requirements before applying for positions in these agencies.

Develop a Positive Attitude

As Kennedy (1994, p. 1E) advises:

> Recognize the things you cannot change. These include such things as you are out of work and need a job, and that you may be several inches shorter than you want to be. . . . Then recognize the things you can change. These include your attitude, your renewed vigor and your willingness to take a fresh look at what you really want to do.

Seeking employment can be frustrating. Be certain your attitude is not contributing to this frustration. Nathan and Hill (p. 69) list several attitudes and beliefs that are often unconsciously held and may be self-defeating:

- I don't need anyone's help.
- "X" will sort it all out for me.
- I can't live on less than I earn now.
- It's undignified to have to promote yourself.
- Somewhere there's the perfect job.
- There's no point planning ahead when there's so much change afoot.
- Nobody will take me seriously.
- Life is so unfair to me.
- Everyone else is better off than me.
- I won't be good enough.
- It's safer not to try than to risk failure.
- If I do well enough, Mum/Dad will love me.
- I'll fail.
- It's so competitive, I'd never get in.
- Everything will be okay when I get a new job.
- I can't change anything—I don't have any power.
- It's too late.
- If I wait long enough, things will change.
- I'm too old/young/overqualified/underqualified.
- I can't help the way I am—it's just the way I'm made.

(Reproduced from Robert Nathan and Linda Hill, *Career Counseling*, p. 69, copyright © 1992 by Sage Publications. Reprinted by permission of Sage Publications, Inc.)

WHAT DO YOU WANT FROM A CAREER?

A career is different from a job. A job is a short-term means to an end: money. High school and college students have jobs during the summer. People get jobs between careers to pay their bills.

A career is more long-term, with more serious implications. Too many people find their jobs dull, laborious and repetitive—a necessity of life, like death and taxes. Most people are afraid to make changes—to take risks—and yet this is what is needed to be happy. One who risks nothing usually gains nothing.

A primary reason people find themselves in a rut is that they fell into it. The deeper the rut, the easier it is to feel trapped. Rather than allowing yourself to fall into the job rut and become trapped, plan what you want out of life and then go after it. Nathan and Hill (p. 129) describe several "career drivers" you may wish to consider:

- Material rewards—seeking possession, wealth and a high standard of living.
- Power and influence—seeking to be in control of people and resources.
- Search for meaning—seeking to do things believed to be valuable for their own sake.
- Expertise—seeking a high level of accomplishment in a specialised field.
- Creativity—seeking to innovate and be identified with original input.
- Affiliation—seeking nourishing relationships with others at work.
- Autonomy—seeking to be independent and make key decisions for oneself.
- Status—seeking to be recognised, admired and respected by the community at large.
- Security—seeking a solid and predictable future.

(Reproduced from Robert Nathan and Linda Hill, *Career Counseling*, p. 129, copyright © 1992 by Sage Publications. Reprinted by permission of Sage Publications, Inc.)

In *The Inventurers*, Hagberg and Leider (1982) provide a map to help people identify what is important to them and how to get there. "The Excursion Map" (p. 6) helps people plan their own destiny rather than falling prey to a rut. They encourage readers to examine five important career issues (p. 106).

   Take time to do so now. In your journal, record your answers to the following career issues:

> ➢   What are my present skills?
> ➢   What values are important to me?
> ➢   What lifestyle do I wish to lead?
> ➢   What work conditions are important to me?
> ➢   What interests do I have?

Take an introspective look at yourself and honestly apply the information learned to answer the question, "Will this job allow me to get what I want from life?" By doing so, you are being an "inventurer, one of those special breed of people who take charge and create your own challenges to get yourself moving" (Hagberg and Leider). They note (pp. 3–4):

> You are an inventurer if you are willing to take a long look at yourself and consider new options, venture inward, and explore. You are an inventurer if you see life as a series of changes, changes as growth experiences, and growth as positive. You are inventuring on life's *excursions* and learning about yourself as a result. You may feel lonely at times, and get discouraged for a while. But you are willing to risk some disappointments and take some knocks in your quest because you are committed to a balanced lifestyle and to more than just making a living. You are part of a unique group of people who want to make a living at work. If you have these qualities, you are an inventurer.

> Inventurers are people who choose to take a fresh look in the mirror to renew and perhaps recycle their lifestyle and careers. Some inventurers, seemingly snug in life and career patterns, are exploring their "greener pasture" or "South Seas island" dreams in search of their own personal Declaration of Independence: the pursuit of happiness. Other inventurers are planning second careers or early retirements. Some are underemployed and seeking careers more integrated with their abilities and lifestyle. They are female and male, old and young, and in between.

According to Hagberg and Leider (p. 6): "These inventurers prove what wise teachers have said for ages: '*The knowledge is right in us—all we have to do is clear our minds and open ourselves to see the obvious.*'"

Inventurers are people who take charge and create their own challenges to get themselves moving. They are willing to take a long look at themselves and consider new options, venture inward and explore. They see life as a series of changes, changes as growth experiences and growth as positive.

One important step is to look at what you love to do. As Mackay (1993, p. 37) notes:

> Time and again I've observed that the people who stay happy and stimulated in careers for a lifetime are people who do what they love to do. George Allen was such a man. After retiring from coaching professional football for the Washington Redskins and the Los Angeles Rams, he became head coach for Long Beach State College. Was this a comedown from his glory days in the limelight? Hardly. George did it because he loved the young people and he loved coaching. When he died at the age of 72, the *Los Angeles Times* reported that he left several notes by his telephone. One note read:
>
> > 1) Win a championship.
> > 2) Have everybody graduate.
> > 3) Build a stadium.
> > 4) Then take a tough job.
>
> Do what you love and you'll never have to work a day in your life.

In *The Right Job*, Snelling (1987, p. 33) suggests you keep a "values journal" to help identify what is personally important and what is not. Write down how you spend your time. What problems do you encounter? What makes you happy, angry, sad, up, down? After keeping the journal for a while, review it, looking for patterns to such issues as the following:

➢ How do I, on an average day, generally spend my time?
➢ What are five or ten things that really interest me?
➢ What conflicts or problems do I have? Which ones did I create for myself, and which ones stemmed from outside factors?
➢ What short-range and long-range goals can I identify?
➢ What, ultimately, do I want to accomplish?

Snelling (p. 44) also encourages you to look at "the human equation" to answer the question, "What kind of life do I want with my family?" An involved family life may not be compatible with a career requiring exceptionally long hours, a lot of traveling and hectic scheduling. Consider also where you want to live. Is climate important to you?

At this point in your self-inquiry, look at yourself and the world around you in relatively general terms. As you develop a sense of what is important to you, apply these ideas to the specific job choices that came out of the earlier brainstorming exercise. Ask: are my needs compatible with that particular job? Don't fool yourself. No one is watching to make certain you are honest. You will have only yourself to blame if you kid yourself now. Begin to apply some of your answers to the previous questions to the overall requirements of the jobs listed at the start of this chapter. Can you get what you need from the jobs that interest you? Consider the following:

➢ Am I old enough? Too old?
➢ Do I have a background that will prohibit me from any certain work?
➢ Am I healthy enough for such work?
➢ Does the job coincide with my personal values?
➢ Do I have the skills for this work?
➢ Will I be able to achieve my long-term goals (including financial and promotional) through such work?
➢ Can my family goals be achieved with this job (considering such issues as travel and time commitments)?

Bolles (1999) encourages people to pursue their dream jobs, but realistically. According to Bolles, dreams about your "ideal work" have certain "essential parts" if they are to become realities.

 Consider each of these "essential parts" for your "ideal work" and record your responses:

- ➢ **Tasks**—What kinds of tasks, using what kinds of skills, do you see yourself doing? With what kind of style?
- ➢ **Tools or Means**—What do you need by way of information, things, or other people to be doing your ideal life's work?
- ➢ **Outcome**—What do you see your work producing, as its result? Immediately? Long-range?
- ➢ **Setting**—In what kind of setting do you see yourself working? "Setting" means both physical setting and also the invisible stuff: values and the like.
- ➢ **Compensation**—What kind of salary or other types of compensation do you want to have? What rewards do you hope your work will bring you?

Five essential parts for your ideal work are tasks, tools or means, outcome, setting and compensation. These parts must be considered if your dream job is to become a reality.

You might also consider taking an occupational preference test such as "Discovery II" to see how your interests and preferences match up with different occupations. Such tests are programmed so that computers can match your answers with answers given by representatives of different occupations. The computer compares your answers and indicates which occupational fields best match your interests.

MOVING TOWARD YOUR CAREER GOAL

Perhaps some jobs you considered in the brainstorming exercise were eliminated when you considered what you need from a career to be fulfilled in life. Perhaps you are still considering whether the career field or a specific career is right for you.

Be honest in considering a career because, as stressed, the very nature of the work in many areas of criminal justice and security is disruptive to what many consider a "normal work routine." Scheduling; having days off in the middle of the week; working nights, holidays and weekends; seeing people at their worst; having your professionalism and honesty challenged in court—all are realities of the criminal justice and security fields.

Also be aware of the areas on which the various levels of government are spending their resources. If you know you want to work in corrections but are unsure about where the majority of jobs are or how the payrolls compare, research the current available data.

In the final equation, do your goals, needs and desires balance with the realities of the job? Only you can make this determination. For example, if you were to enroll in an introductory course in law enforcement, where do you fit among the three groups of "typical" students enrolled in such classes?

> Students who have known since they were very young that they were destined to be police officers.
> Students who are considering the career, but have yet to make the commitment.
> Students who are fascinated by the subject, not the career.

If you have the chance to take an introductory course in law enforcement, corrections, private security or criminal justice, consider doing it. It's one good way to better understand what the careers involve and if they are right for you.

Acquire What You Need

As you continue to assess whether your career goals are compatible with your needs and interests, you will also learn what else is required to get into the field. If you need college, register. If you need a physical fitness regime, begin one. If you need experience, get it.

As mentioned earlier, do some investigative research by visiting agencies and interviewing those currently working in the field(s) you are considering. Volunteer and get involved in short-term experiences with potential employers—step into the shoes and walk around in them for awhile to make sure they fit *before* you commit to buying them. Plodding along an uncharted path will get you, at best, nowhere, and at worst, somewhere you don't want to be. *NOW* is the time to develop your own realistic, exciting career map.

Internships

Internships are an excellent way to discover if a specific area of criminal justice is a good fit for you. An internship is an opportunity to receive supervised, practical, on-the-job training in a specific area. Physicians, for example, undergo a one-year internship during which they apply to real life what they have learned in medical school. Many law enforcement agencies and correctional institutions are now offering internships, usually without pay, for those interested in learning about a specific area of employment while acquiring skills that make them more employable in that area. Often individuals who complete an internship with a specific police department are hired by that department when they have completed their formal education. Or, conversely, the intern or the department may find that the fit is not good and both are spared a difficult situation.

ALTERNATIVES

Look around and contemplate the almost infinite number of jobs that make up the criminal justice system and its related fields. It is truly amazing. Even if one job is not for you, another will be. Don't be afraid to change your mind, to take some risks. For many people, taking risks is more frightening than facing a gun. Facing a gun lasts only an instant—a wrong career choice lasts much longer!

Our culture does not encourage risk-taking. Even during the 1960s and 1970s, when a different cultural climate prevailed, a conservative work-ethic encouraged people to stay where they were and be glad they had any sort of job. This attitude was held over from the Great Depression when people truly were lucky to have a job.

Today's culture emphasizes a satisfying career, rather than "just a job." Certainly as you grow older and family responsibilities require more job security, you are not as likely to change jobs as frequently as when you were young. Still, you are living and working in an era that allows, if not encourages, people to chase their dreams.

Think about it. What's the worst thing that would happen to you if your choice of a job didn't work out? You find something else, right? People do it all the time—and grow and develop as a result.

Change *is* intimidating. But stagnation is even more frightening. The greatest hazard in life is to risk nothing. It has often been said: "Those who risk nothing, do nothing, have nothing, are nothing." Don't let it be engraved on your headstone, *Here lies John Doe, his potential fully intact.*

Over a dozen years ago I had a chance to shift careers from being a social worker to becoming a police dispatcher. I remember wondering *why* I ever said yes. It wasn't something I had trained for. It wasn't something I had planned on. But even then I knew it would be a challenge, one I could leave if it wasn't what I had wanted. It terrifies me sometimes to wonder what I would be doing today if I had not risked taking that step toward the unknown. As the saying goes, "Don't be afraid to go out on a limb. That's where the fruit is."

Risk-taking is important because it exposes you to challenges and prevents you from getting stuck in a rut. Ruts lead to stagnation, which leads to job dissatisfaction and other adverse effects, as discussed at the beginning of the chapter.

JUST DO IT!

An effective exercise for motivating yourself to change is the "last day of my life" test. Bolles suggests that you consider the statement "Before I die, I want to . . . ." and then list the things you would like to do before you die. Or write on the topic: "On the last day of my life, what must I have done or been so that my life will have been satisfying to me?"

    As the concluding exercise in this chapter, take time to write your feelings on one of these two topics.

Picking Daisies

If I had my life to live all over again, I would pick more Daisies.
If I had my life to live over, I would try to make more mistakes next time.
I would be sillier than I have been this trip.
I would relax. I would limber up.

I know very few things I would take seriously. I would be crazier,
I would be less hygienic; I would take more chances;
I would take more trips, I would climb more mountains,
Swim more rivers, and watch more sunsets.
I would burn more gasoline. I would eat more ice cream and less meals.

I would have more actual troubles, and fewer imaginary ones.
You see, I am one of those people who lives prophylactically
and sensibly and sanely, hour after hour, day after day.
Oh, I have had my mad moments, and if I had it to do all over again,
I would have more of them; in fact, I'd try to have nothing else,
just moments, one after another, instead of living so many years ahead.

I have been one of those people who never go anywhere without a thermometer,
a hot-water bottle, a gargle, a raincoat and a parachute.
If I had it to live all over again I would go places and travel lighter than I have.
If I had my life to live over again, I would start barefoot earlier in the spring,
and stay that way later in the fall. I would play hookey more,
I would ride on more merry-go-rounds. I'd pick more Daisies.

(Reproduced from *Mindstyles/Lifestyles*, by Nathaniel Lande, published by Price Stern Sloan, Inc., Los Angeles, California. Copyright 1976 by Price Stern Sloan, Inc. Reprinted by permission.)

Decide to take some risks. Chase your dreams. Have some fun. Really learn to *be*.

CONCLUSION

It is important to think carefully about what career you'd like to pursue *before* you jump into it. A hasty decision, or one based on rumor or television portrayals, will likely lead to disappointment and dissatisfaction. The four steps that comprise the career development process are (1) self-assessment, (2) career exploration, (3) job search skill development and (4) implementation of the job search steps. The first two steps are very important. In deciding which career is best suited to you and your needs, you *must* assess yourself and how your abilities and needs compare to the demands of the job.

Risk-taking is important because it exposes you to challenges and prevents you from getting stuck in a rut, which could lead to stagnation and job dissatisfaction. Become an *inventurer*, someone who takes charge and creates their own challenges to get themselves moving. Be willing to take a long look at yourself and consider new options. Venture inward and explore. See life as a series of changes, changes as growth experiences and growth as positive.

ADDITIONAL CONTACTS AND SOURCES OF INFORMATION

National Board of Certified Counselors (NBCC)
3 Terrace Way, Suite D
Greensboro, NC 27403
(910) 547-0607

National Career Development Association (NCDA)
5999 Stevenson Avenue
Alexandria, VA 22304
(703) 823-9800

AN INSIDER'S VIEW

THE PRIVATE SECURITY ALTERNATIVE

Bill B. Green
Manager, Security Services
Rosemount, Inc.

My exposure to the security profession started during my sophomore year in college. While attending the university, I also worked full time as a sales clerk for a large retailer. My declared major was criminal justice, and I became good friends with the store's detective and also its security manager. I increasingly found their daily work more interesting than what I was doing. Attending school full time and working 50 hours a week caused my class work to suffer. Something had to give. I was persuaded to enter a company management training program and dropped out of college. The management program, however, proved unsatisfying. I was drawn back to the two mentors from my brief retail career. The store detective, who also owned a small contract security firm, offered me a job. I went to work for him, first as a night shift security officer at an industrial complex, then as an account supervisor. I also again pursued college (this time much more successfully).

Another avenue I was drawn to was the military. Both mentors were retired military, and their stories piqued my interest. A year later, I enlisted in the Army. For a young man whose world had been confined within the boundaries of Arkansas, my specialty of Military Intelligence was a real eye-opener. Those three years in Military Intelligence proved extremely illuminating, both in terms of knowledge of the world as well as a career direction. After my three years in the military, I planned to return to civilian life, probably in law enforcement or something in the criminal justice system, gain experience, and eventually return to the private sector. I began networking nine months before ending my tour of duty and was offered a parole officer position by the Department of Corrections in Arkansas. Three weeks before my release, however, an Army acquaintance called from Texas with another alternative. I interviewed for a security consulting position in Texas, withdrew from the parole officer position and was on my way into the field of private security.

That position opened my eyes wider, offering the chance to do in the private sector what I had just spent three years doing in the military sector—learning a lot by working with senior-level professionals and advising clients on how to improve their security posture. While this was a dream position for a young man at such an early career stage, changes in the company led me only a year later to consider other employment opportunities. A consulting assignment with a precious metals distributor led to my next job—security director for that small company. That position provided a rare opportunity to "do it my way." The young entrepreneurial firm hired me to build a security department from the ground up. A start-up department is a tremendous, but extremely rewarding, challenge.

Two years later I found myself seeking bigger and better things. Note, however, that you cannot change jobs every couple of years (as I had been) without eventually paying a price, being labeled a *job hopper*. Few employers are interested in hiring someone who will stay only 12 to 24 months. Most positions take six months to a year to absorb the company's standards, culture, products and mode of operation. It simply does not pay employers to invest that time in you and then see you leave.

I knew my next position needed to be long term. Pursuing a local newspaper ad, I applied for a position with a high-tech manufacturing firm and found myself in the interviewing process, then in the second interview, then the third, followed by a battery of psychological exams and eventual selection as a member of their management team. Again I had the good fortune, and great challenge, to be in another start-up department—the first security professional ever hired by this firm of 1,900 employees.

Today that company has grown to a world leadership position in its market. Almost 14 years later I have assumed a variety of responsibilities along the way while remaining in charge of the overall security effort. You might sum up a career by looking at the titles held. Mine are as follows: security officer; security supervisor; intelligence analyst; parole officer (almost!); security analyst; security coordinator; director of security; security administrator; safety, security, and environmental manager; and manager of security services. Today I manage a security department of both proprietary and contract employees, providing protective, investigative and customer services.

I'd like to offer some thoughts on developing your career, particularly if you decide on a career in corporate security:

- Join the American Society for Industrial Security (ASIS) as soon as you qualify. There are memberships for students as well as for those already in the field.

- All security is not the same. Many of the principles apply from one segment of business to another, but different facets of private security have significant, noteworthy differences—contract security services, investigations, consulting and training, financial services, manufacturing, retail and so on.

- Volunteer for an internship. It's good exposure for you and looks good on your resume. *EVERYONE you meet is a potential employer or a potential lead to an employer*. A few personal examples include the mentor who gave me direction and eventually pointed me to the military to gain further experience, the good Army friend who recommended me for the Texas job and the client who saw my work and subsequently offered me a position. Show them all your very best—you never know which one may recommend you for your next position or promotion.

- Plan to pay your dues. If you decide to become a police officer, you won't start with the best shift or as a sergeant or lieutenant. In the military, private security or any other endeavor, you start at the bottom.

- In a smaller corporation, be prepared to do it all. Security managers are responsible for the physical security of the facility, protecting employees, staffing, scheduling, investigating, budgeting and always selling, selling, selling—themselves, their department and their security program.

- In a larger corporation, the security manager is likely to have more staff and more specialists to get the job done. In this capacity, you become more of a manager as opposed to the multitalented specialist of a smaller organization.

- Corporate security professionals are not "company cops." They are one of many specialists necessary to successfully operate a business. Their job is not to enforce laws (that's why you call the police). Instead, they protect corporate assets, which include people, property and information.

- Be honest with yourself about your likes, dislikes, and emotional and physical makeup. Are you well suited for law enforcement work? Is your eyesight good enough? Do you have any other physical limitations that may hinder a particular career pursuit? Do you have any criminal history (including even "youthful" mistakes such as a DWI)? Talk to some police officers and security managers. Find out what they think about their work. Conduct your own surveys. Forget what you've seen on television or at the movies—find out what the jobs are really all about.

- For law enforcement jobs in most parts of the country, a two- or four-year college degree is or will soon be required. While you are working on that degree, get some experience. Get a job at least related to the field you are thinking of pursuing. A stable work history as a security officer at a reputable firm will look better on that fresh graduate resume than some other totally unrelated experience.

As you settle on a career path, keep in mind that numerous opportunities will permit you to achieve the same honorable goal—"to protect and to serve."

Bill B. Green has been employed in the profession of criminal justice and security for 19 years. Past jobs include the director of security at Investment Rarities, Inc. and security analyst at International Security Group, Inc. Mr. Green holds a B.A. in Public Administration (Criminal Justice).

AN INSIDER'S VIEW

SEARCHING OUTSIDE THE "BOX"

Kenneth S. Trump

Assistant Director, Tri-City Task Force Comprehensive Gang Initiative;
Director of Safety and Security, Parma (Ohio) City School District;
National School Safety Consultant

The three job titles, combined with the heading of this section, should quickly indicate my main message: The only employment limits in the safety field today are self-imposed. Individuals searching for employment in this area should step outside the traditional "box," i.e., a local, state or federal law enforcement agency, to discover less publicized options that are increasingly available to talented professionals.

First, what is the history behind those titles? As a high school student, I developed an interest in school safety and security after spending an inordinate amount of study hall and lunch time in the school's security office where, initially by accident, I learned how the office operated and what strategies were needed to effectively keep schools safe. Graduating as valedictorian (a.k.a.: bookworm), my teachers and peers all knew I would head off to college for preparation in a career that would lead to great success: lawyer, doctor or possibly politician. My thoughts on working in the school security arena were simply, from their perspective, an unacceptable lowering of expectations and a disregard for my abilities (so they thought).

First volunteering, then getting paid part-time for four years and working retail security, I was later hired as a full-time Cleveland schools security officer while working on my undergraduate degree in social service/criminal justice and then my graduate degree in public administration. During this time, similar to how I began my interest in school security overall, I stumbled into a secondary interest while working in high schools and junior high schools—youth gangs. The gang problems emerged in the schools and in the city of Cleveland, and I happened to be on the front lines as this occurred.

The stages of increasing gang activity and school safety concerns are easily the subjects of two books in themselves. In short, each issue grew significantly in terms of public concern and attention over a five-year period, during which I intensified my personal interest, academic studies and professional activity in both areas (on the job and during most of my free time). Since both subjects were (and still are) surrounded by a significant amount of politics and image concerns, it was unpopular for a long time to publicly speak out about them. So I remained politically incorrect for an extended number of years while only a few others would dare aggressively pursue these subjects as a professional interest.

About five years after my initial hiring in the school security field, and with my graduate degree in hand, I was appointed to design and supervise what turned out to be a nationally recognized Youth Gang Unit in the Cleveland Public School system's Division of Safety and Security. Three years into that venture, with the record of a 39 percent reduction in school gang crime and disruptions, I was lured into the southwest Cleveland suburbs of Parma, Parma Heights and Seven Hills to assist in directing one of four federally funded anti-gang initiatives and to direct the school system's newly created Office of Safety and Security.

Ten years after stumbling into the fields of school safety and gang activity, it has become somewhat politically correct to be a specialist in these areas. Everyone who previously avoided the subjects like they were diseases is now seeking training and program development for these problems. Thus, another opportunity was created: consulting. In addition to my regular employment, I spend my vacation and compensatory time traveling regionally and nationally to conduct training, school safety assessments and related projects for schools, police, community agencies, professional conferences and any other organization seeking assistance.

What are the lessons from my unusual experiences? They include:

1. **Do not be afraid to step out of the "box."** Opportunities are increasing in the criminal justice arena. Potential places of public safety employment beyond traditional law enforcement agencies include public school systems, colleges and universities, public and private agencies needing investigative and protection services, independent consulting on specialty areas and many other potential employers. Limited exploration breeds limited potential for success.

2. **Risks exist with new opportunities.** The positive side of being "ahead of the curve" in recognizing a new issue and developing an expertise in that area is that you can literally define a new profession. Defining a new profession can also bring the frustrations of battling politics and the personal agendas of jealous competitors, inconsistent financial resources, possible financial failures and many other risks associated with new frontiers. On the flip side, it can also bring intellectual challenges, financial reward and personal satisfaction that traditional options may never provide.

3. **Plan for the future.** Regardless of whether you pursue traditional or nontraditional arenas, have a vision of where you want to be three to five years in the future. Although I approach each new position in terms of my job performance as though I will retire from that job, I also immediately ask myself, "Where do I wish to eventually go from here?" Remember, your primary responsibility is to do your best in your current position. Doing your best where you are now will take you where you want to be next in your career.

4. **Have a backup plan.** No matter how prepared or how good you are in doing your job, many factors out of your control can impact your employment. These include budgetary cuts and financial constraints, lower pay than other professions where there is less personal risk, politics, etc. Therefore, you should have a well-defined backup plan in case your present position is pulled out from under you.

5. **Do not limit your expectations.** Even with lower pay scales than most people desire for their full-time employment, the safety field has many opportunities to be promoted "horizontally" instead of "vertically." If you cannot move up in an organization, expand your opportunities by developing an expertise in a particular part of your field and grow outward with your own part-time business. Write professional articles, speak to community groups and work your way to national conferences, and provide your services (for a reasonable fee, of course) to agencies needing your expertise.

In conclusion, there are many ways to beat the career development frustrations often presented in the criminal justice field. Sometimes opportunities fall into your lap or you stumble into them. Most times, you have to go searching. Best wishes for success with your search!

———————

Kenneth S. Trump *is the director of safety and security for the Parma City School District and the Assistant Director of the Tri-City Task Force Comprehensive Gang Initiative for Parma, Parma Heights and Seven Hills, Ohio. He is an adjunct assistant professor of criminal justice at Ashland University. Prior to his current positions, Mr. Trump served over seven years with the Division of Safety and Security of the Cleveland Public Schools, where he designed and supervised the Division's Youth Gang Unit. Since 1989, he has consulted and trained nationally on youth violence, gang, school safety and security assessments.*

Mr. Trump received his Master of Public Administration degree from Cleveland State University, where he also completed a B.A. in Social Service with a criminal justice concentration. He has received special certification in School Safety Leadership by the National School Safety Center (U.S. Departments of Education and Justice, and Pepperdine University). He has also completed the state-certified private police training and over 1,300 hours of specialized training in gang, drug and school safety topics.

In addition to being co-founder, vice president and executive board member of the Ohio Chapter of the Midwest Gang Investigators Association, Mr. Trump is director of training and staff development, chairman of the Youth Gangs Special Interest Group and a member of the Board of Directors of the National Association of School Safety and Law Enforcement Officers. He is also a member of the International Association of School Safety Professionals, California Gang Investigators Association and American Society of Law Enforcement Trainers.

 MIND STRETCHES

1.   What is your strategy for identifying a career path? Do you know anyone who just "floated along" whichever way the current carried them? Are they happy? Why or why not?

2.   Do you think American workers are cynical? Why?

3.   How important is job security to you? Can you see it changing in five years? Ten years?

4.   How important is money to you? Will you be satisfied with an officer's pay? Can you see this need changing for you?

5.   Have you ever worked nights, holidays or weekends? What can you imagine would be good about such a schedule? Bad?

6.   What prevents people from accepting change? What keeps people from taking risks? Why do you think many people stick with a less-than-satisfactory job?

7.   What five jobs within the criminal justice field interest you? Why? What jobs in the field do not appeal to you? Why?

8.   What elements of your personal history might be negative factors in pursuing your career goals? How can you deal with these at the interview?

9.   Why do you think more people don't take an active role in their career choices?

10.   What are the five most important things you will consider when selecting a job? Are these under your control?

REFERENCES

Alderman, Lesley. "How to Land a Job Now, Whether You Are Starting Out or Starting Over." *Money,* June 1995, pp. 173–175.

Bolles, Richard Nelson. *The 1999 What Color Is Your Parachute? A Practical Manual for Job-Hunters & Career-Changers.* Berkeley, CA: Ten Speed Press, 1999.

Hagberg, Janet and Leider, Richard. *The Inventurers: Excursions in Life and Career Renewal.* Reading, MA: Addison-Wesley Publishing Company, 1982.

Kennedy, Joyce Lain. "Going Back to the Basics Can Help Job Seekers of Any Age." (Minneapolis/St. Paul) *Star Tribune,* November 13, 1994, p. 1E.

Krannich, Ronald L. *Change Your Job, Change Your Life,* 5th ed. Manassas Park, VA: Impact Publications, 1995.

Lande, Nathaniel. "Picking Daisies." *Mindstyles/Lifestyles*. Los Angeles: Price Stern Sloan, Inc., 1976.

Leider, Richard J. and Shapiro, David A. *Repacking Your Bags: Lighten Your Load for the Rest of Your Life*. San Francisco: Berrett-Koehler Publishers, 1996.

Mackay, Harvey. "Perfectly Positioned." *Successful Meetings,* February 1993, p. 37.

Messmer, Max. *Job Hunting for Dummies*. Foster City, CA: IDG Books Worldwide, Inc., 1995.

Nathan, Robert and Hill, Linda. *Career Counseling*. Newbury Park, CA: Sage Publications, 1992.

Parsons, F. *Choosing a Vocation*. Boston, MA: Houghton-Mifflin, 1909.

Snelling, Robert O., Sr. *The Right Job*. New York: Penguin Books, 1987.

SECTION TWO

MEETING THE CHALLENGE: PREPARING

Even if you are on the right track, you'll still get run over if you just sit there.

—Will Rogers

Most people don't plan to fail—they fail to plan.

—Anonymous

Before everything else, getting ready is the secret of success.

—Henry Ford

For every officer who is hired, there are 250 applicants who are not. The secret to accomplishing your dream comes down to one objective—preparation.

—Larry R. Frerkes

The normal process in seeking a job is to find where job openings exist, apply, submit a resume, undergo various kinds of testing, be interviewed and be hired! This section does not follow that order. Rather, it asks you to continue doing what you began in Chapter 5—looking at your own qualities, experiences and preferences and seeing how they fit with what criminal justice agencies and security departments are looking for. It also suggests ways to overcome any shortcomings you might find as you consider yourself in relation to the requirements of the job. This should be done *before* you actually begin looking for specific jobs. This section is written as though you were already actively engaged in testing and interviewing.

You'll begin by looking at the physical requirements of these fields and what tests you might have to pass (Chapter 6). One of the most important attributes of successful candidates is physical fitness—which doesn't happen overnight. Next you'll look at the educational and psychological requirements that might be considered and how they might be tested (Chapter 7).

This is followed by a discussion of the "beneficial attributes" of successful candidates in these fields, that is, who is most likely to be hired (Chapter 8), giving you a chance to realistically assess what attributes *you* have and how you might fare. The next chapter discusses how you can assemble the information you have collected about yourself thus far into that all-important document—your resume (Chapter 9). The section concludes with a critical part of the job hunting process—being prepared for rejection (Chapter 10). Each rejection must be seen as a learning situation, a chance to become better at presenting yourself and as being one step closer to that job you *will* eventually get.

These chapters should be reread at appropriate times during your actual job hunt. For example, if you are scheduled for a physical fitness test, reread Chapter 6 a few days before. If you don't even make it to the testing stage, reread Chapter 10. When you're ready, move on to Section Three, which presents specific job-seeking strategies to enhance your chances of getting a job in your chosen field.

CHAPTER 6

PHYSICAL FITNESS AND TESTING

Good physical condition not only adds years to your life, but life to your years.

—Anonymous

Do You Know:

➢ Why physical fitness is crucial for police, corrections or security officers?

➢ Why it is difficult for people in these fields to stay in shape?

➢ What five parameters are generally considered in evaluating physical fitness?

➢ What four things most physical fitness tests seek to measure?

➢ What three areas are of critical importance during the medical examination and what other tests might be conducted?

➢ What impact the ADA has had on medical examinations and inquiries about disabilities?

➢ How fitness and stress interrelate?

➢ How personality and stress interrelate?

➢ Why proper nutrition is important?

➢ What proportion of deaths in this country each year are due to an unhealthy lifestyle?

INTRODUCTION

One of the most critical criteria for obtaining a job in criminal justice, security and related areas is physical fitness. The importance of having physically fit personnel goes without saying. The job demands that those who pursue employment in these fields enter such work in shape and *remain* in shape.

Fitness can become a legal issue too. The people and property you are paid to protect will depend on your being able to do your job. If you cannot, you could be sued. In 1988, in *Parker v. The District of Columbia*, the jury awarded $425,046 to a man shot by a police officer who was arresting him. As part of the case, the court noted: "Officer Hayes simply was not in adequate physical shape. This condition posed a foreseeable risk of harm to others." According to Heiskell (1996, p. 33):

> Law enforcement requires a high degree of physical and mental fitness. The demands of a busy shift can be both mentally and physically exhausting. Physical fitness requires planning and regular exercise. Being physically fit means that you will not only be prepared for your busy shift, but will look and feel better, too.

Your future, your very life, may depend on your level of fitness. As noted by Slahor (1990, p. 55): "The FBI emphasizes that physical fitness is 'often the factor that spells the difference between success and failure—even life and death.'" How much more important can it be?

> Your future in criminal justice or security, your very life and the lives of the civilians you've sworn to protect depend on your physical fitness. Being "out of shape" can even become a legal issue.

As noted before, these professions, while appearing to be full of exciting chases and confrontations, are more likely to consist of extended periods of idle waiting, punctuated with demands for extreme activity. A shift, or maybe even an entire week, may go by without anything exciting occurring. Suddenly, you may be called on to exercise almost super-human strength—to drag a victim from a burning car, to carry a heart-attack victim from an upper-level apartment, to assist in carrying fire-fighting equipment up the stairs of a high-rise, or to fight for your life with a physically fit, drug-crazed criminal.

What is particularly critical about physical fitness for criminal justice and security personnel is that the nature of their jobs can actually contribute to keeping them *out* of shape. Most of these jobs involve a significant amount of inactivity. For example, sitting at a desk or driving all day provides little exercise. Combine this with odd working hours—often when only fast-food restaurants are open—and it becomes easy to understand why the stereotype of police, corrections and security officers is that of being overweight and out of shape. As noted by Noble (1989, pp. 38–39):

> Very few of us [police officers] die in shoot-outs and high-speed chases. In truth, police work takes its toll in more insidious ways. Instead of going out in a blaze of glory, the average officer dies by inches. It is the daily stresses, often compounded by poor eating, irregular sleep and a general lack of fitness, which erode our bodies and minds before helping us into early graves.

Commenting on how the nature of police work often contributes to lack of fitness, Hoffman and Collingwood (1996, p. 17) report: "Mortality statistics suggest that police officers have increased risk of premature death and may have a special vulnerability for certain diseases. Most studies indicate that officers die at earlier ages than expected for the general population for all causes of death, and in particular for diabetes, colon cancer, and cardiovascular disease." Strandberg (1997, p. 38) adds: "There is a great disparity between the longevity in civilian population and in law enforcement. The average American male lives to be 72 years old, while the average law enforcement officer lives to be 59.5."

> The very nature of police and security jobs can contribute a great deal to officers being out of shape. The often-sedentary duties, such as driving a car or sitting at a desk, and the need to eat quick meals on the go—often fast food high in calories and fat—all contribute to the deterioration of physical fitness.

Ignoring physical fitness is little different than carrying a malfunctioning gun or driving a defective squad car. It could kill you. Employers know it is a challenge to keep their officers in shape. It is difficult for everyone to keep in shape as the years pass. This is good reason for employers to seek applicants who are physically fit.

Think about what being physically fit says about you to an employer. It says you are concerned about yourself. It also says you can project a positive image of the agency or institution you represent. For obvious reasons, employers do not want employees who would make their agency or institution look bad.

WHAT IS FITNESS?

Fitness refers to a person's physical well-being or, to use the popular phrase, to being "in shape." Frerkes (1998, p. 54) defines physical fitness as: "The ability to carry out daily tasks with vigor and alertness, without undue fatigue, and with ample energy to engage in leisure time pursuits and to tolerate the above average stresses encountered in emergency situations." He cites five specific elements needed to make a well-balanced, comprehensive testing program:

➢ Cardiorespiratory endurance or aerobic capacity, measured by a 1.5-mile run
➢ Abdominal and lower back strength, measured by sit-ups
➢ Muscular strength and endurance, measured by push-ups
➢ Flexibility, measured by a controlled sit and reach test
➢ Body composition, or percentage of body fat

Physical fitness is being "in shape" and is often evaluated using five general parameters: cardiorespiratory endurance or aerobic capacity, abdominal and lower back strength, muscular strength and endurance, flexibility and body composition.

The trend is to look at the amount of body fat rather than weight as compared to height. The generally accepted percentage of fat for males is 14 to 16 percent of total body weight; for females, between 23 and 26 percent of body weight. Body fat standards for males ages 20 to 29 established by the internationally known Institute for Aerobics Research in Dallas, Texas, and used by many police departments are (Noble, p. 44):

8.3% or less, superior;
8.4–10.6%, excellent;
10.5–14.1%, good;
14.2–15.9%, average;
16.0–22.4%, below average; and
22.5% or more, poor.

PHYSICAL FITNESS TESTING

Most candidates may undergo some sort of physical fitness testing. The test may take the form of maneuvering through an obstacle course within a set time limit. Marlowe (1995, p. 14) notes the growing use of physical ability testing programs in applicant selection, such as the content-valid physical ability test developed by Stanard and Associates, Inc. (S&A), a nationwide public safety testing firm. According to Marlowe: "The job analysis process determined that the physical ability test should include such critical activities as crawling under low obstacles such as a porch, dragging an unconscious or uncooperative person a short distance, climbing through a window, sprinting to chase a suspect, and climbing stairs such as those commonly found in office and apartment buildings."

Pilant (1995, p. 87) explains the significance of *content validity* in such tests: "The content of the test is the same as that specified by the job. For example, if an officer typically has to climb a 6-foot fence during foot pursuits, then the test would measure the officer's ability to climb a 6-foot fence." According to Pilant (p. 88):

Fitness-standard testing, which has been found to be predictive of an officer's ability to perform [basic officer tasks], includes the following:

- Aerobic power/endurance (1.5-mile or 12-minute run): Pursuit tasks, use of force lasting one to two minutes.
- Anaerobic power (300-meter run): Sprints, use of force, any short intense burst of effort lasting less than 30 seconds to one minute.
- Absolute strength (1RM bench and leg press): Lifting, carrying, pushing and dragging heavy objects.
- Dynamic strength (one-minute sit-up and push-up): Use of force, lifting, carrying, dragging, pushing.
- Body composition (percentage of fat): Short and long pursuits, use of force, lifting, carrying. (. . . this test is not a strong predictor of fitness for duty. It has more recently been used as an appearance issue, not for making hiring or firing judgements.)
- Flexibility (sit and reach): Lifting, carrying, bending, pursuit with obstacles.

The Criminal Justice Institute at Broward Community College in Ft. Lauderdale, Florida, for example, uses the following physical agility obstacle course:

Start—Climb a 6' wall.
Climb a ladder.
Clear a hurdle.
Climb a chain-link fence.
Climb through a window.
Open and go through a wooden gate.
Climb a higher hurdle.
Run through a maze.
Crawl through a tunnel.
Complete a hand bar walk.
Run through a high stepper course.
Walk across a log.
Complete a horizontal hand walk.
Jump up and over a short wall.
Final run around two poles.

The Institute also tests strength and endurance using the following tests:

Trigger pull (strong hand 18, weak hand 12).
10 push-ups.
Standing jump.
3 pull-ups (from dead hang, palms facing away).
Vehicle push (20 feet, push from rear of vehicle).
½-mile run (5 minutes maximum time).

Another example of physical fitness testing is that of the United States Air Force Academy, whose admissions test requires the following:

Test	Minimum	Maximum	Average
Pull-ups			
Males	3	22	10
Females	1	12	2
Sit-ups			
Males	39	99	73
Females	36	94	70
Push-ups			
Males	11	85	40
Females	4	50	25
Shuttle Run (in seconds)			
Males	64.7	51.4	60.2
Females	78.6	55.4	68.3

The *pull-ups* must be done with the palms facing away from the face, arms fully extended. No swinging, kicking or stopping once the count has begun. Untimed.

The *sit-ups* are done lying flat on the back, legs flexed, hands placed behind the head with fingers interlocked. Sit-ups are done touching the elbow to the opposite knee, alternating knees each sit-up. Time allowed is two minutes, with no resting.

The *push-ups* are done with the body straight from shoulders to heels, with the weight of the body resting on hands and toes. Time allowed is two minutes, with no resting.

The *shuttle run* is 300 yards long. You must run six round-trip 25-yard laps (12 complete laps) between two turning lanes. Turns are made by pivoting on one foot; hands may touch the floor on the turns.

Candidates who cannot perform up to the minimum standards are disqualified. The goal of most candidates is to "max out," giving them an edge over less physically fit candidates.

Another approach used by some departments is having candidates perform "events." Simpson (1995, p.16) explains: "Four 'events' were determined to be appropriate for job-related physical fitness measuring. They were the Back Yard Pursuit, Stretcher Carry, Body Drag and 300-Yard Sprint."

Whatever tests are used, they are likely to measure endurance, agility, flexibility and strength.

A wide variety of physical fitness tests may be administered, but they are all likely to measure the same things: endurance, agility, flexibility and strength.

Most police departments, correctional institutions or businesses hiring security personnel require that job applicants have a medical examination as well as a physical test of some sort to be certain they are physically fit.

THE MEDICAL EXAMINATION

Three areas of critical importance during the medical examination are vision, hearing and the condition of the cardiovascular-respiratory system. The vision test may include a test for colorblindness. Most agencies will accept applicants who have *corrected* vision and hearing problems. If you think you may have problems in any of these areas, get checked out before you apply for a position.

The cardiovascular and respiratory systems play a critical role in fitness. To a large extent endurance, the ability to continue exertion over a prolonged time, is directly related to the ability of the cardiovascular-respiratory system to deliver oxygen to the muscles.

The medical exam may also include tests for determining blood pressure, smoking status, drug use, blood sugar level (for diabetes) and the ratio of total cholesterol to HDL cholesterol (to identify cardiovascular risk factors). If a physician finds that you have a functional or organic disorder, the recommendation may be made to disqualify you.

Three areas of critical importance during the medical examination are vision, hearing and the condition of the cardiovascular-respiratory system. The medical exam may also include a cholesterol check, blood pressure check, inquiries about smoking status or lung capacity checks, drug tests and blood sugar level check for diabetes.

It should be noted that the use of medical examinations in hiring is governed by the Americans with Disabilities Act (ADA). According to Rubin (1995, p. 114):

> The Americans with Disabilities Act (ADA) is the most sweeping civil rights legislation enacted in the past 30 years. Inspired by a desire to integrate more than 43 million individuals with disabilities into the mainstream, this law affects virtually every segment of society. . . . The ADA has significant consequences on how corrections hires personnel. The ADA prohibits administering medical exams or conducting any disability-related inquiries *prior to extending a conditional offer of employment* [italics added].

In addition, as noted by Arnold and Thiemann (1994, p. 45):

> Along with its prohibition of requiring medical examinations prior to the job offer, the act also prohibits inquiries regarding disabilities at the applicant stage. Test questions regarding mental and physical problems, such as whether a person becomes ill easily or has spent time in therapy, mandate that a test must be conducted only after tendering a conditional offer of employment.

The Americans with Disabilities Act (ADA) prohibits medical examinations or inquiries regarding disabilities *before* a conditional offer of employment has been made.

THE PREVALENCE OF PHYSICAL FITNESS AND MEDICAL TESTS

Most candidates for criminal justice or security positions will encounter some form of physical fitness and medical examination. However, as noted by Hogue et al. (1994, p. 120), some tests are used more often than others. Their findings are presented in Table 6-1.

TABLE 6-1   Reported Use of Selected Screening Techniques

Technique	Presently Used	Would Use if Budget Permitted	Not Worth the Time and Cost
Physical exam	79.3%	18.8%	1.9%
Medical records check	67.2	27.5	5.3
Vision exam	65.8	28.3	5.9
Diabetes	53.1	37.4	9.5
Epilepsy	52.0	39.0	9.0
Physical agility test	36.3	56.1	7.6
Drug screening	27.4	68.6	4.0

SOURCE: Adapted from Mark C. Hogue, Tommie Black and Robert T. Sigler. "The Differential Use of Screening Techniques in the Recruitment of Police Officers." *American Journal of Police,* Vol. 13, No. 2, 1994, p. 120.

SELF-ASSESSMENT

It is important that you know how physically fit you really are. Just because you feel good does not necessarily mean that you are "in shape." The FBI's publication *Physical Fitness for Law Enforcement Officers* recommends the following:

Feel your arms, shoulders, stomach, buttocks and legs. Are your muscles well-toned or are you soft and flabby?

Give yourself the pinch test. Take hold of the skin just above your belt. Are your fingers separated by more than one-half inch?

This publication describes cardiovascular, balance, flexibility, agility, strength and power tests to assess your physical fitness. Their descriptions follow.

Cardiovascular Tests

Cureton's Breath-Holding Test. One simple way to test your respiratory capacity is to step onto and off a chair, bench or stool (approximately 17 inches high) for a period of one minute and then see how long you can hold your breath. You should be able to hold it for at least 30 seconds. If you can't, it's an indication that your cardiovascular function has deteriorated below a desirable level.

Kasch Pulse Recovery Test (3 min.). This test can be performed at almost any age. Only the infirm or the extremely unfit would find it too strenuous. You should not smoke for one hour or eat for two hours before taking the test. Also, rest for five minutes before taking the test.

EQUIPMENT
12" bench or stool
Clock or watch with a sweep second hand

PROCEDURE
a) Start stepping onto and off the bench when sweep second hand is at 11.
b) Step 24 times per minute, total 72.
c) Duration is three minutes.
d) Stop stepping when sweep second hand is again at 11, after three revolutions, and sit down.
e) Start counting the pulse rate when sweep second hand reaches 12 on the clock, using either the artery located inside the wrist or the carotid artery in the throat. Count every 10 seconds and record for one minute.
f) Total the six pulse counts for one minute and compare with the following scale:

Classification	0–1 Minute Pulse Rate After Exercise
Excellent	71–78
Very Good	79–83
Average	84–99
Below Average	100–107
Poor	108–118

Cooper's 12-Minute Walk/Run Test. NOTE: People over age 30 should not take this test until they have had a complete medical examination and have completed approximately six weeks in a "starter physical fitness program."

Find a place where you can run/walk a measured distance of up to two miles. A quarter-mile track at a local school would be ideal; however, a nearby park, field or quiet stretch of road can be used. The test is quite simple—see how much of the two miles you can comfortably cover in 12 minutes. Try to run the entire time at a pace you can maintain without excessive strain. If your breath becomes short, walk until it returns to normal, then run again. Keep going for a full 12 minutes; then check your performance on the following scale:

Fitness Category (under age 30)	Distance Covered in 12 Minutes (in miles)
Very Poor	less than 1.0
Poor	1.00–1.24
Fair	1.25–1.49
Good	1.50–1.74
Excellent	1.75 +

Balance Test

Stand on your toes, heels together, eyes closed, and your arms stretched forward at shoulder level. Maintain this position for 20 seconds without shifting your feet or opening your eyes.

Flexibility Tests

Trunk Flexion. Keep your legs together, your knees locked, bend at the waist and touch the floor with your fingers.

Trunk Extension. Lie flat on your stomach, face down, fingers laced behind your neck and your feet anchored to the floor. Now raise your chin until it is 18 inches off the floor. (Note: Average for male students at the University of Illinois is 12.5 inches.)

Agility Test

Squat Thrusts. Standing, drop down to squatting position, palms flat against floor, arms straight. Next, with weight supported on the hands, kick backward so that your legs are extended fully. Immediately kick forward to the squatting position and stand up. You should be able to perform four in eight seconds.

Strength Tests

Pull-ups. Hang from a bar, hands slightly wider than shoulders, palms turned away, arms fully extended. Pull up until your chin is over the bar. Lower yourself until your arms are fully extended and repeat. You should be able to perform four pull-ups.

Push-ups. From the front leaning rest position, hands slightly wider than the shoulders with fingers pointed straight ahead, lower your body until your chest barely touches the floor. Push up to the front leaning rest position, keeping your body straight. Standards from the Institute for Aerobics Research for push-ups done in one minute are:

60 and up, superior;
50–59, excellent;
35–49, good;
25–34, average;
18–24, below average; and
17 or less, poor.

Sit-ups. Lie on your back with your hands behind your neck, with your legs straight and free. Flex the trunk and sit up, and then return to the starting position. Standards from the Institute for Aerobics Research for sit-ups done in one minute are:

49 and up, superior;
46–48, excellent;
42–45, good;
40–41, average;
33–39, below average; and
32 or less, poor.

Power Tests

Standing Broad Jump. From a standing position, jump as far forward as you can, landing on both feet. Do not take a running start. The length of your jump should equal your height.

Vertical Jump. Stand facing a wall, feet and chin touching the wall, arms extended over your head. Using chalk, mark the height of your hands on the wall. Now jump up and touch the wall as high as you can with one hand. (Again, use chalk.) Note the difference between the two marks on the wall. You should be able to perform a vertical jump of 18 inches or more.

Even if you successfully pass all these tests, be sure you remain in good physical shape. Your lifestyle may be such that you do not require a formal physical fitness program. Many people who are active in sports such as swimming, tennis, jogging or running do not need to do much more to keep in shape. If, however, you have a relatively sedentary lifestyle, you may want to start a basic physical fitness program.

A BASIC PHYSICAL FITNESS PROGRAM

As noted by Hoffman (1993, p. 25): "The majority of police work is done with a pad, pencil and radio, until the lid comes off and hell breaks loose, at which time the officer may need the physical attributes of an athlete to survive." Fay, a certified public safety physical fitness specialist and the program coordinator of the New York City Police Department's Cardiovascular Fitness Unit (1994, p. 22), suggests this plan:

An exercise regimen which is time efficient, job specific, and physically sound can be completed in less than one hour.

Begin with a two to three minute *warm-up* of mild walking, jogging or biking to prepare the heart and skeletal muscles for more vigorous activity. Three to five minutes of stretching exercises, emphasizing the lower back and hamstring regions will promote maintenance of good flexibility.

Twenty to 30 minutes of *aerobic training* using either treadmill, stair stepper, rowing and cross-country ski machines will reduce stress, improve body composition (weight loss), and strengthen the cardiovascular system. This should be followed by 15 to 20 minutes of *weight training and/or calisthenics* to develop upper body muscular strength and endurance. The abdomen and lower back regions are particular areas of concern and should not be neglected. Conclude with a five-minute *cool down* period of exercise of diminishing intensity, light stretching, adequate hydration and general relaxation.

Regular program adherence (three to five times per week) can have a significant impact on an officer's physical and emotional health as well as job performance.

An exercise program should start gradually and then build up. You should exercise at least three times a week. As you progress into your fitness program, you can increase the number of times a week you work out.

Tips

The following tips on exercising might be considered:

➢ Exercise to music.
➢ Vary your exercises to give yourself some variety.
➢ Drink water during your breaks.
➢ Plan your program to easily fit your daily routine. Exercise at the same time each day.
➢ Start small and work up to a full regime gradually to reduce your chance of injury.
➢ Record your efforts.
➢ Do not expect immediate benefits. It takes regular, long-term effort.
➢ Wait 10 minutes after your cool-down to take a warm shower. *A hot or cold shower can dangerously affect your blood pressure.*
➢ If you stop exercising for a while—even a week or two—start at a lower level and gradually work your way up again.

(*NOTE:* Never pursue an exercise program without consulting with your physician.)

Exercise is a powerful tool in managing stress, a common element of employment in the criminal justice and security fields.

FITNESS AND STRESS

Careers in criminal justice and security can be highly stressful—and so can seeking employment in these fields. An important part of being physically and mentally fit is managing stress.

> Physically fit bodies are better able to cope with stress, and stress is abundant in the professions of criminal justice and private security. Keep fit to ward off stress.

Some personality types tend to be more susceptible to stress, particularly those identified as *Type A*. Hawks et al. (1989, p. 49) describe such people:

> Individuals with a Type A personality typically speak and move rapidly, hold feelings in, have few outside interests, are precise and numbers-oriented, find it difficult to relax, are excessively time conscious, seek approval from others, are usually engaged in multiple tasks with impossible deadlines and are continually hurried and overscheduled. Due to the release of artery-damaging stress hormones associated with Type A behavior, the greatest health risk of having a Type A personality is heart disease. . . .
>
> Current research indicates that the Type A personality traits most responsible for increased heart disease risk may be hostility and anger.

If you are a Type A personality, which many people drawn to criminal justice and security are, be aware of these risks. Exercise and relaxation techniques can help reduce them.

> People with Type A personalities are more susceptible to stress and are at increased risk for heart disease. It is vital for such people to learn and use exercise and relaxation techniques.

In addition, three personality traits, called the *3 C's*, provide protection against the negative stress everyone experiences as part of living in our fast-moving, complex society: control, commitment and challenge. *Control* means taking charge of your life, being confident in your ability to direct your own life rather than letting it be directed by outside forces. *Commitment* means being actively involved and caring about your family, friends, job, hobbies and the like. *Challenge* means you accept setbacks as something to be overcome and change as something to be adapted to.

The Upside of Stress

Not all stress is negative. Most people need a certain amount of stress to keep them sharp. Think of the last time you had a deadline to meet. It was the stress of the deadline that probably finally got you moving. As noted by Hanson (1985, p. xviii):

> Stress can be *fantastic.* Or it can be *fatal.* It's all up to you. As well as respecting the dangers of stress, you can learn to harness its benefits.
>
> Olympic records are not set on the quiet training tracks, but only with the stress of competition—in front of huge crowds. . . .
>
> Serious poker players will play only if significant amounts of money are bet on each hand . . . . Many people with sedate working lives actively seek stress in the form of parachuting, cliff climbing, downhill skiing, horror movies, or simply riding a roller coaster. Such stresses bring more joy into their lives.

The key is to keep stress from becoming *distress*.

FITNESS AND NUTRITION

The U.S. Army's total fitness program emphasizes nutrition. Among the concepts it stresses are the following:

➢ Drink 6 to 8 glasses of water a day.
➢ Avoid too much sugar.
➢ Avoid too much sodium (salt).
➢ Include fiber in your daily diet.
➢ Cut down on protein and fats.

Obesity

Many police officers are obese. Recall that the average life span of officers in the United States is 59 years, compared to 73 years for the general population. Obesity may be an important risk factor in this death rate. High blood pressure, common among police officers, is also related to obesity.

The same is true for the related professions. The key to losing weight is a sensible diet and exercise. Physicians and health club consultants can suggest what diet might be best for you if you have a weight problem.

> Proper nutrition is an important part of fitness and avoiding obesity, believed to increase the risk of certain diseases and to shorten the life span.

SMOKING, ALCOHOL AND OTHER DRUGS

These substances are harmful to your health and your career. Keep in mind that an increasing number of both public and private agencies are limiting candidates to those who are nonsmokers. So if you smoke, quit. If you use controlled substances, stop. And if you drink alcoholic beverages, do so in moderation. Other people's lives, not to mention your own, depend on you having a clear head and quick reflexes.

To understand how drug use could seriously affect your employment potential, consider this scenario:

A few months ago, Grace was in the middle of looking for a security job. She had been on over a dozen interviews, but no job offers had been made and she was beginning to lose hope. One weekend, her friends suggested going to an outdoor concert to help lift her spirits, and she agreed it might help take her mind off her unemployment.

Early into the concert, Grace noticed one of her friends take something from her jacket pocket, light it, take a hit off it and pass it to the friend next to her. When it got to Grace, she hesitated. Her best friend leaned over and whispered, "C'mon, Gracie. You need to lighten up a little. It won't kill you."

A second later, Grace felt her lungs filling with smoke, and as she held it in she thought, "Yeah, I do need to relax." After a second hit, she passed the joint on to her friend. The rest of the evening was spent swaying to the music and getting high.

On Monday, Grace got a phone call from one of the security firms, wanting her to come in for a second interview. At first she was thrilled . . . then panic set in when she realized there might be a drug test.

Increasingly, companies are conducting random drug tests on current and prospective employees. As noted by Martin and DeGrange (1993, p. 39):

> An average of 10% to 20% of all employees abuse alcohol or use illicit drugs. Organizations lose an estimated $100 billion per year due to alcohol and drug abuse, resulting from poor performance, illness, absenteeism, injury, theft and product damage. One way to reduce losses is to avoid hiring individuals whose job performance will be negatively affected by substance abuse.

This certainly includes criminal justice and private security. A study by Hogue et al. (p. 119) reveals how negatively employers of law enforcement officers feel about social drug and alcohol use by their personnel (See Table 6-2).

TABLE 6-2   Desirability of Selected Characteristics For Police Officers

	Essential	Desirable	Not Desirable	Not Acceptable
Social alcohol use	3.9%	7.8%	73.7%	14.6%
Social drug use	1.4	1.9	11.7	85.0

SOURCE: Mark C. Hogue, Tommie Black and Robert T. Sigler. "The Differential Use of Screening Techniques in the Recruitment of Police Officers." *American Journal of Police,* Vol. 13, No. 2, 1994, p. 119.

FITNESS AND LIFESTYLE

According to the Centers for Disease Control's "Ten Leading Causes of Death in the United States" (1980), approximately 50 percent of U.S. deaths each year result from an unhealthy lifestyle. Hawks et al. (p. 51) suggest that the following simple lifestyle habits can add significantly to longevity:

- Sleeping for seven to eight hours each night.
- Eating breakfast every day.
- Not eating between meals.
- Maintaining an ideal weight.
- Exercising regularly.
- Drinking only moderate amounts of alcohol (or none at all).
- Not smoking cigarettes.

About half of the deaths in the United States every year occur because of an unhealthy lifestyle.

Hawks et al. (p. 48) suggest that individuals assess their lifestyle and general fitness in terms of risk factors they can control:

> The three most significant risk factors that can be controlled include hypertension (above 140/90), elevated blood cholesterol (over 220) and smoking. Additional contributing factors include obesity, lack of exercise, diet, stress, diabetes, and personality type. All of these factors are interrelated and have a multiplying effect when two or more are present.

BENEFITS OF BEING PHYSICALLY FIT

Dr. Kenneth H. Cooper (1982, p. 12), from the Institute for Aerobics Research in Dallas, Texas, says:

> Here are some of the benefits of total well-being that data from our research have shown us can be yours for the asking:
> - More personal energy;
> - More enjoyable and active leisure time;
> - Greater ability to handle domestic and job-related stress;
> - Less depression, less hypochondria, and less "free-floating" anxiety;
> - Fewer physical complaints;
> - More efficient digestion and fewer problems with constipation;
> - A better self-image and more self-confidence;
> - A more attractive, streamlined body, including more effective personal weight control;
> - Bones of greater strength;
> - Slowing of the aging process;
> - Easier pregnancy and childbirth;
> - More restful sleep;
> - Better concentration at work, and greater perseverance in all daily tasks;
> - Fewer aches and pains, including back pains.

Several of the preceding benefits would also be advantageous to the job seeker.

CONCLUSION

Your future in criminal justice or security, your very life and the lives of the civilians you're sworn to protect depend on your physical fitness. Being "out of shape" can even become a legal issue. Fortunately, fitness is one area you *can* control. Once you get in shape, *stay there*. This may not be easy because the very nature of criminal justice and security jobs can contribute a great deal to being out of shape. However physically fit bodies are better able to cope with stress, and stress is abundant in the professions of criminal justice and private security.

AN INSIDER'S VIEW

PRE-EMPLOYMENT PHYSICAL FITNESS

Richard W. Stanek
Captain, Criminal Investigation Division
Minneapolis (Minnesota) Police Department

A well-conditioned and physically fit police applicant has an edge in today's competitive job market. You will learn through daily contacts that initial impressions are usually the first and only means of evaluating people.

The administrators who will be hiring you look for all those credentials listed on your resume, but during a tense oral interview, your physical stature and appearance also are graded. Aesthetically speaking, a grossly overweight or out-of-shape applicant is not the type of officer a police department is looking for. Further, such officers are statistical liabilities in terms of coronary heart disease, stress and injury proneness. No department wants to inherit and deal with such risks during the officer's career.

Police work involves grave physical dangers. Violent encounters are always possible, but are not the only threat to officers' safety and well-being. Long hours, an occupational tendency toward poor diet and nutritional habits, inadequate exercise, insufficient sleep (often interrupted by court appearances and call-backs), can take their toll on officers' health.

Enhancing police officers' physical condition results in better crime-fighting and service to the public; a sharper, more professional image; increased esprit de corps and officer self-confidence; and a very substantial reduction in personnel costs. The benefits of a working fitness program for the employing agency includes fewer medical retirements, reduced annual sick leave and reduced health care costs.

Increasingly, employers are setting standards for fitness levels as a condition of employment both before and during employment with their agency. A recent national study of law enforcement agencies found that over 75 departments currently have mandatory fitness standards and annual testing to ensure their officers are physically fit. An even greater number of agencies require pre-employment physicals and passage of mandatory fitness tests.

Employing agencies and the citizens they have sworn to protect can reasonably expect police applicants to be in "better than average" physical shape. Nationwide research (U.S. Army standards, Cooper Institute) has determined that your fitness level should be in the top 60% of your age category. Failure to meet these standards prior to employment resulted in no job offers. In addition, failure to maintain fitness standards during employment was dealt with from progressive discipline to termination.

Physical fitness encompasses everything from strength training and cardiovascular endurance (aerobics) to smoking cessation, drug and alcohol substance abstinence and obesity reduction. Physical conditioning helps relieve stress and keeps the mind free from worries that could compromise an officer's safety when at work. A successful fitness program should include conditioning in strength, flexibility, cardiovascular endurance and body composition. The standard protocol that agencies measure against are:

- ➢ Cardiovascular
  - Timed one and one-half mile run or three-mile walk
- ➢ Strength
  - Push-ups: upper body
  - Sit-ups: abdominal
- ➢ Flexibility
  - Sit and reach
- ➢ Body composition
  - Percent body fat by skin fold caliper
- ➢ Blood pressure and cholesterol screening
- ➢ Proportionate weight and height measurements

Each fitness test has a minimum standard based on national averages and standards collected from research performed with thousands of individuals in all age categories.

You should prepare for a career in law enforcement/security by starting and maintaining a stringent workout program while progressing through the academic requirements of licensing.

———————

Richard W. Stanek *is a detective and captain with the Minneapolis (Minnesota) Police Department and has been employed in the field of criminal justice for 15 years. Prior to his employment as a public service officer, he was employed in the private sector. Capt. Stanek holds a B.A. in Criminal Justice from the University of Minnesota and an MA in Public Administration from Hamline University in St. Paul, Minnesota. He is a graduate of the 1992 AOC Southern Police Institute and has a Human Resources Certificate from the University of Minnesota. Capt. Stanek is also a state legislator in the Minnesota House of Representatives, District 33B and is the former chair for the Minnesota POST Board. He has been married 14 years to Sally; they have two children.*

AN INSIDER'S VIEW

WHAT PHYSICAL FITNESS REALLY MEANS: EVERYONE TALKS ABOUT IT, BUT NOT MANY UNDERSTAND

Sheldon T. Hess, M.D.
General Internist
Health Partners

In my profession as a general internist, I see daily the importance of physical fitness and its relationship to my patients' physical *and* mental well-being. Physical fitness implies that only the body is involved, but, in reality, the mind and emotions are equally involved. This is what so many people fail to realize.

Lack of fitness can manifest itself in objective (physical) findings, the most common being hypertension (high blood pressure). It can also manifest itself in subjective (mental) symptoms, including fatigue, stress, burnout and depression. Such conditions are commonly associated with the criminal justice and security professions.

So what are the components of fitness?…Four components are key to fitness: decreased alcohol intake, cessation of smoking, proper diet and adequate physical activity (not necessarily exercise).

The first two components are self-explanatory. As far as proper diet is concerned, the main things to be aware of are the amount of fat and sodium you take in, as well as the quantity of food you consume. You want to eat foods that are low in fat and cholesterol and low in salt. Avoid adding lots of extra salt to those french fries. And limit the proportions you eat if you have a weight problem.

Just a word of explanation on cholesterol, which is a mysterious entity to many. Cholesterol is the ingredient that causes coronary artery disease and leads to heart attacks. It comes in two forms:

> Low Density Lipoprotein (LDL)—the bad stuff
> High Density Lipoprotein (HDL)—the good stuff

When I treat a patient with hypertension, my goal is to lower the LDL and raise the HDL. A vast array of drugs are available to lower the LDL, but only exercise seems able to raise the HDL. An interesting sidenote: In a controlled study of people who were so severely depressed they had to be institutionalized, 50 percent were treated with antidepressant drugs and 50 percent were turned over to a marine-type drill sergeant who took them through regimented physical exercises daily. The results: no difference in the two groups. Exercise proved to be as effective as the antidepressant drugs in treating severe depression.

The value of being fit is not to make you into a muscle builder but to make you physically and mentally prepared to carry out your job and to do what you enjoy in your leisure time. Some jobs such as construction work require physical strength. People in these jobs are less likely to be under stress than those in jobs not requiring physical strength, for example, chiefs of police, wardens or security directors. These positions are likely to lead to severe stress unless the individuals holding them are physically active.

You don't have to be a marathon runner or eat a caveman diet (nuts, berries, rocks and twigs—no cholesterol, no salt, no saturated fat—unless they happen to luck out and bring down a woolly mammoth). You *do* need to use common sense.

The patients I treat for hypertension may have some hereditary disposition to the problem, but most are the result of poor diet and/or lack of exercise. I have overweight, out-of-shape patients who are 50 years old who have the physical and mental appearance of an 80 year old. Conversely, I have 70-year-old patients who were competitive in athletics such as soccer or tennis and who are still active in their sport, whose bodies and minds are that of a 50 year old.

Another indication of the importance of fitness that I have seen in my years of practice is the outcome of the patients I recommend for coronary artery bypass graft. These patients are given a new lease on life. Those who follow the recommendations regarding alcohol, tobacco, diet and exercise are much less likely to reclog their arteries than those who do not follow the recommendations.

It's difficult to generalize on any one individual. What works for one person won't work for another, but the suggestions I've presented should serve as general guidelines. Here's where your personal physician comes into play. He or she can assess your fitness and suggest what you might do to improve it—if it needs improving.

One final note. I am not a proponent of artificial exercise, such as that performed on equipment in a gym (rowing machines, stationary bikes, treadmills, and the like). Sports such as tennis, swimming, bicycling and cross-country skiing are a much more natural way of being physically active, from my perspective. I recommend you find a sport you enjoy and make/take time for it regularly—and watch your diet, quit smoking and drink alcohol only in moderation. This will help you get fit and keep fit—physically and mentally.

———————

Sheldon T. Hess, *M.D., is a general internist practicing with Health Partners, a large health maintenance organization (HMO) in the Minneapolis/St. Paul metropolitan area. He has been a physician for 34 years and an internist for 27 years. He received his B.S. from the University of Minnesota in 1961 and his M.D. from the University of Minnesota in 1965.*

  MIND STRETCHES

1.   How would you judge your current level of physical fitness?

2.   Are you currently working out? What is your fitness program?

3.   Why do you imagine the stereotype of the overweight, donut-eating cop exists?

4.   How do law enforcement and security careers tend to prevent fitness?

5.   Is being overweight and out of shape possibly part of the "macho" image of being a cop or security guard? If so, is this changing?

6.   What does an out-of-shape officer communicate to the public by appearance alone?

7.   Why do you think so few Americans exercise regularly?

8.   Recognizing that perhaps working night shift would make keeping in shape difficult, in what creative ways could an officer working such a shift exercise?

9.   Are criminal justice and private security more stressful than other careers? Why or why not?

10.   How would you define *physically fit*?

REFERENCES

Arnold, David W. and Thiemann, Alan J. "Psychological Testing in ADA's Wake." *Security Management,* January 1994, pp. 43–45.

Cooper, Kenneth H. *The Aerobics Program for Total Well-Being.* New York: M. Evans and Company, Inc., 1982.

Fay, Michael. "Sedentary Lifestyle: Putting Officers at Risk." *Law and Order,* June 1994, p. 22.

Frerkes, Larry R. *Becoming a Police Officer: A Guide to Successful Entry Level Testing.* Incline Village, NV: Copperhouse Publishing Company, 1998.

Hanson, Peter G. *The Joy of Stress.* Kansas City, MO: Universal Press Syndicate Company, 1985.

Hawks, Steven R.; Hafen, Brent Q. and Karren, Keith J. "How Does Your Health Rate?" *Journal of Emergency Medical Services,* March 1989, pp. 46–51.

Heiskell, Lawrence E. "The Road to Wellness." *Police*, November 1996, pp. 32–35, 71, 74.

Hoffman, Art. "Add Muscle to Your Fitness Programs." *Law Enforcement Technology,* August 1993, pp. 24–27.

Hoffman, Robert and Collingwood, Thomas R. "Fit for Duty." *Law and Order*, July 1996, pp. 17–18.

Hogue, Mark C.; Black, Tommie and Sigler, Robert T. "The Differential Use of Screening Techniques in the Recruitment of Police Officers." *American Journal of Police,* Vol. 13, No. 2, 1994, pp. 113–124.

Marlowe, Carolyn. "Ongoing Physical Ability Testing." *Law and Order*, August 1995, pp. 14–15.

Martin, Scott L. and DeGrange, Donna J. "How Effective Are Physical and Psychological Drug Tests?" *Security Technology & Design,* May/June 1993.

Noble, Thomas R. "Let's Get Physical." *Police,* May 1989, pp. 38–41, 44.

Physical Fitness for Law Enforcement Officers. Washington, DC: Federal Bureau of Investigation, U.S. Department of Justice.

Pilant, Lois. "Physical Fitness." *The Police Chief*, August 1995, pp. 85–90.

Rubin, Paula. "The Americans with Disabilities Act's Impact on Corrections." *Corrections Today,* April 1995, pp. 114–116.

Simpson, Leslie D. "A Struggle to Achieve Fitness." *Law and Order,* January 1995, p. 16.

Slahor, Stephenie. "Focus on Fitness: The FBI Way." *Law and Order,* May 1990, pp. 52–55.

Strandberg, Keith W. "Health and Fitness for Law Enforcement." *Law Enforcement Technology*, August 1997, pp. 34–40.

"Ten Leading Causes of Death in the United States." Atlanta: Centers for Disease Control, July 1980.

United States Air Force Academy. *The Air Force Academy Instructions to Applicants.* Washington, DC: U.S. Government Printing Office.

CHAPTER 7

OTHER FORMS OF TESTING

―――――――――――――――――――――――――――――――――――

Experience is not what happens to you; it is what you do with what happens to you.

—*Aldous Huxley*

Do You Know:

➢ What test anxiety is and how common it is?
➢ How you can improve your test-taking performance?
➢ What areas of general knowledge you might be tested on?
➢ What other kind of knowledge you might be tested on?
➢ What the most common kinds of tests are and what you should know about each?
➢ What assessment centers are and what purpose they serve?
➢ What psychological tests measure and if you can prepare for such tests?
➢ What integrity tests try to determine?
➢ What polygraph tests try to determine, how accurate they are and what law governs their use in pre-employment screening?

INTRODUCTION

The tests used in the hiring process are likely to include the following:

➢ Knowledge
➢ Psychological
➢ Polygraph

This chapter reviews areas commonly tested to help you understand what the tests are and what purpose they serve. You will not be given "suggested" answers. In fact, for some tests, preparing for or trying to "out-psych" them can be a mistake. It's important to know what to expect and what aspects of the testing you can prepare for. Before considering the specific areas, however, take a few minutes to look at a very common phenomenon: *test anxiety*.

TEST ANXIETY

Test anxiety is a general uneasiness or dread characterized by heightened self-awareness and perceived helplessness that frequently leads to diminished performance on tests. It includes the psychological, physiological and behavioral responses to stimuli associated with the experience of testing. In other words, it is the worry, concern and stress commonly associated with any circumstance in which individuals find themselves being evaluated.

Test anxiety is a reality for most people. Recognize its existence and take control of it. How? First, be as prepared as possible. The fewer surprises a test-taker encounters, the less anxiety is experienced. You probably can recall walking into a test and being pleasantly surprised to find an essay question you knew the answer to "cold." Conversely, you can also probably recall walking into a test and being confronted with a question that was indecipherable.

Test anxiety is the worry, concern and stress commonly associated with any circumstance in which individuals find themselves being evaluated. It is a reality for most people.

Frerkes (1998, p. 42) notes that most written pre-police service tests are made up of multiple-choice questions and that it is possible for applicants to prepare for such tests, and consequently improve their scores, by *practicing*. Numerous books are available that contain hundreds of practice multiple-choice questions typical of those found in many written police tests. Arco and Monarch publish general intelligence study references that can also be used to help you prepare for the written tests used by many criminal justice agencies and departments. Two specific books are listed at the end of the chapter as additional sources to help officer applicants prepare for such exams. Frerkes concludes (p. 42): "Successful test taking is often determined by repetition. The more opportunities you have to take written tests, the better you will do." Furthermore, as you gain confidence in your test-taking abilities, you will also likely notice a decrease in test anxiety.

Test performance can be improved through practice and repetition. The more practice you have with such written tests, the better you are likely to do.

In addition to being as prepared as possible, the following will help reduce test anxiety:

➤ Get a good night's sleep before the test.
➤ Eat.
➤ Take at least two pens, two #2 pencils and a large eraser.
➤ Know exactly where the test is to be given and how to get there. (You might make a practice run to the site.)
➤ Arrive with time to spare so parking or other hassles do not make you anxious.

TESTING KNOWLEDGE

It is hard to imagine that only a few years ago a person could become a law enforcement officer by merely responding to an advertisement. In fact, many fine officers today applied for their jobs rather spontaneously one day and were handed a gun and badge the next. Even today, many security jobs, some involving immense responsibility, require little, if any, knowledge of the applicant.

As appealing as this may sound at this stage of your job search, it is easy to see the many problems associated with what is quickly becoming a practice of the past. As these fields strive to become recognized professions and respond to the increasing demands and potential liability created by our complex society, employing agencies are having to take their hiring practices much more seriously. Whether the job for which you are applying requires certification or licensure or just requires applicants to be responsible individuals, almost all employers will want to determine what the applicant knows.

General Knowledge

Some tests are designed to assess certain basic levels of ability in areas such as math, English, composition and grammar. Because communication skills are so vitally important, employers should be assured that the people they are considering hiring (for *any* level job) can express themselves well. According to Rafilson (1997, p. 100): "Basic skills tests measure ability. This can be broken down into things like problem-solving (cognitive ability), interpersonal communications and specific skills. These ability tests will all be predictive of what an employee is capable of doing on the job. It is the 'can do' component of testing."

Many large departments, particularly those sensitive to minorities, focus more on general knowledge, such as reading comprehension, vocabulary, analogies and general math. Computer literacy is also becoming more important.

> General knowledge that is commonly tested includes reading comprehension, vocabulary, analogies and general math—basic reading, writing and arithmetic. Computer literacy is also becoming more important.

While different tests can be used to examine these basic areas, they will all look at the same basic abilities. Ask yourself if you possess the necessary reading, writing and math skills required of any employee (usually a college freshman level). If you are not at this level, immediately start a plan to improve your skills. Many community colleges have a policy of open admission. As part of the process, the student is tested in reading, writing and math skills. The college offers remedial courses for the underprepared student.

Lack of basic reading, writing and math skills cannot be hidden from an employer for very long on the job. To avoid wasting everyone's time, many job applications include some basic questions to let the hiring agency know if you have these basic academic abilities. For example, an increasing number of application forms have a section that requires a brief essay to test your writing, spelling, grammar and organizational abilities.

If you need remedial help, get it *now*. Many opportunities exist to improve yourself. Often the only thing stopping someone from improving themselves is that they feel too embarrassed to ask for help. The help you need may be in a review book available from a library or bookstore, or you may want to enroll in a class at a community college or in an adult learning program.

Specific Knowledge

Applicants may be required to know specific information for certain jobs. In states requiring certification or licensure, successful completion of requisite levels of training or education will be evidence of such knowledge.

Certainly such required knowledge will indicate the areas of specific knowledge you will be expected to know. For example, in Minnesota, which requires a minimum of two years of college to be eligible to be licensed as a police officer, areas of required knowledge include:

- Administration of justice
- Criminal investigation
- Criminal procedure
- Cultural awareness
- Defensive tactics
- Firearms
- Human behavior

- Juvenile justice
- Patrol functions
- Police operations and procedures
- Report writing
- Statutes
- Testifying in court
- Traffic law enforcement

Less specific knowledge is required to be a private investigator in Minnesota, but in addition to passing a strict background investigation, a minimum of three years' experience in security work is required.

Even if the areas of specific knowledge are not set forth clearly, you should be able to foresee what may be asked during an oral interview. Basic statutes that apply to public or private officers would be likely questions. Frequently, such questions are intertwined with the "What would you do if . . . ?" question. This allows employers to test not only specific knowledge, but the application of it using problem-solving techniques and communications skills.

Applicants should expect to be tested on some specific knowledge in areas pertaining to the field, such as relevant statutes and procedures.

It's your responsibility to be prepared to the best of your ability. If you do not know what you might be tested on, it does no harm to call ahead to ask. The worst that could happen is that they won't say. But it is much more likely you will be told. That will put you a giant step ahead of applicants who haven't a clue as to what will be asked.

Do what you can to learn and review what you think will be asked. Remember, no one can know everything. All you can be expected to do is your best. Sometimes you will be able to immediately give the exact answer, maybe even amazing yourself. Sometimes you may give a wrong answer. Sometimes you may draw a complete mental blank. You are likely to experience all these reactions at one time or another during testing.

It's also a good idea to learn as much as possible about the department or agency you are applying to. If it is a law enforcement position, perhaps you can arrange for a ride-along. This would provide an opportunity to ask questions about the department. If it is a corrections position, arrange to visit the institution if possible. If it is a private security position, perhaps you can visit the facility and talk with a security officer.

Keep in mind the purpose of the testing process. If the only thing employers wanted were accurate answers, they would replace their employees with computers. Employers want someone who can think and act human. Part of being human is to *not* know it all and yet to keep functioning. In fact, tests might include an "off-the-wall" question just to see how you respond. In all probability, you will look a lot better admitting you are nervous and forgot or don't know the answer (but know where to find it), than to fake it. In short:

> ➢ Be as prepared as you can be.
> ➢ Seek remedial help if necessary.
> ➢ Know as much as you can.
> ➢ Know how to find what you don't know.
> ➢ Don't be afraid to admit what you don't know.
> ➢ Don't make up answers.

Memory and Observation Tests

Many police departments use tests to determine applicants' ability to recall information. For example, pictures of several "bad guys" may be flashed on a screen and personal information given about each of the individuals, such as names, ages, criminal activity, etc. The test then continues by flashing a picture on the screen and requiring the applicant to recall all the information about the subject, or recall a nickname, or match a crime with a face.

STRATEGIES FOR TAKING TESTS

No matter whether the tests cover general information, specific knowledge, memory and observation skills, or a combination, the successful candidate knows how to approach the specific type of test given.

The most common tests are multiple choice, true/false and essay, and each type of test has its own guidelines and strategies to follow.

Olson (1990, pp. S-17–19) offers practical advice for approaching such tests.

Taking the Test[1]

When you are given the test, look it over so you can plan how to allocate your time. Answer the questions you know best first. Then come back to the harder questions. Always read directions very carefully. *The number one cause of errors on tests is the failure to read and follow directions.*

For *MULTIPLE-CHOICE TESTS*, follow these guidelines:

- If you are asked to read long passages and answer questions about the material, read the question stems before you read the material. This will help you find what you are looking for faster and easier.

---

[1] From *Study Skills: The Parent Connection*, 2nd ed. by Patricia S. Olson. © 1990 by Reading Consulting, Inc., Burnsville, MN. All rights reserved. Reprinted by permission.

- Do not be afraid to change your answer if you have a good reason. It's a myth that you should stick to your original choice. Research studies show that most students are at least twice as likely to change an incorrect answer to a correct one.
- Read the stem of the question. Try to answer the question before you read the possible answers. Then skim all the answer choices and select the one most like your initial answer.
- Absolute words such as *a, none, always, constantly, never, entirely, every, only* and *best* often make the answer false and can usually be eliminated as possible answers.
- Make a complete sentence from the stem and each choice and ask yourself, "Is the statement I made true or false?" A true statement is probably the correct answer.
- Think logically. If the options are dates or numbers, you can usually eliminate the lowest and highest numbers. The option "all of the above" is usually the correct answer. And the longest statement is usually the correct answer.
- Don't spend too much time on questions you can't answer. Leave them and come back later if you have time.

For *TRUE/FALSE QUESTIONS*, follow these suggestions:

- Assume the question is true unless you can establish that it's false.
- It is usually easier to write a true question than a false one.
- A statement is false if any part of it is false.
- Absolute statements tend to be false. Be aware of the words *never, always, none, all, best, invariably, entirely, every*. These statements are usually false. However, words such as *many, most, generally, frequently, sometimes* and *often* are most often used in true statements.
- The word *not* completely changes the meaning of a statement. Be careful in answering a question containing *not*.
- If you are not sure what the question is asking, ask your teacher to explain it.
- It is all right to guess on a true/false question. You have a 50-50 chance of guessing the right answer.

For *ESSAY QUESTIONS*, follow these steps:

- Read over the essay question and jot down in the margin any ideas that immediately come to mind.
- Briefly outline your main points in the margin before you begin to write. This will help you stay on track.
- Restate and answer the question in the first sentence of the essay. This serves as your introduction. For example, the question is, "Discuss the three main causes for the Revolutionary War." Your answer should begin: "The three main causes for the Revolutionary War were _____, _____ and _____."
- Support each main point with specific examples. Show your reader why you think your answer is valid.
- Don't forget to write a conclusion. ("In summary, _____, _____ and _____ were the three main causes of the Revolutionary War.")
- Proofread your essay before turning it in. Composition errors make a poor impression on the reader and may affect your grade.

GENERAL RULE: Never skip an item or leave an answer blank *unless* it is stated that mistakes count against you.

ASSESSMENT CENTERS

According to Garner (1998, p. 77): "Assessment Center Testing has been around for the last 60 or 70 years. Both the Allies and the Axis used it during World War II to train their spies. The technique involved putting the candidates in a situation where they must role-play the position they are seeking." Hogue et al. (1994, p. 114) note that assessment centers use psychological assessment as well as a broad range of techniques, including situational tests. These tests present candidates "with unusual situations which, although encountered rarely in the field, require quick and intelligent responses under stress." Rachlin (1995, p. 29) states:

> The assessment center is a process (not a facility) that uses a variety of techniques to evaluate performance skills. . . . [It] is usually administered near the end of the selection process—after the resume and applications have been reviewed, the candidates screened and interviewed, preliminary background checks have been conducted, and possibly a battery of psychological tests have been given. . . . It is used to identify candidates' strengths and weaknesses in areas critical to successful performance of the job. . . . The essential elements of an assessment center include a job analysis which identifies the dimensions (abilities) needed for the position; multiple assessment techniques which must include simulation-type exercises; multiple assessors who must be properly trained; and scores that must be derived by using a consensus process.

Assessment centers are processes that identify a candidate's strengths and weaknesses to evaluate how well that candidate is likely to perform on the job. Situational tests are a common part of such assessment centers.

Rachlin also notes (p. 30): "A typical selection process may include other exercises or tests that are not simulations, such as paper and pencil tests, multiple choice tests, intelligence tests, personality inventories, and management type indicators."

PSYCHOLOGICAL TESTING

Psychological testing is a cause of anxiety for applicants because so much of it is out of their control. What should I say? How should I answer? What are they looking for? Psychological testing is an immense and complex subject about which hundreds of texts have been written. So what do you need to know?

First, such tests should not and probably could not be prepared for through such traditional means as memorization. It is better to understand what these tests are meant to do, how they are administered and what they can show.

Purposes of Psychological Testing

Although psychological testing is a relatively new practice, no doubt you have taken some form of psychological test, probably at some point in your school career. Most people would agree that law enforcement officers should be mentally and emotionally stable. But defining and assessing what this consists of is a complex, challenging task.

> Most psychological tests measure differences between individuals or between the reactions of the same individual on different occasions. Preparing for such tests is very different from preparing for more traditional "knowledge-based" tests, but you *can* prepare for them.

Sgt. Dennis Conroy, St. Paul (Minnesota) Police Department, also a clinical psychologist, gives the following advice concerning psychological tests administered to police/security candidates:

> To prepare for a psychological evaluation, applicants must begin to get psychologically "fit" several months before the examination. Preparation for a psychological evaluation *cannot* be rushed.
>
> Applicants must begin preparation early enough so they can make changes to assure that they are as psychologically healthy as possible. This includes looking at relationships, mature behavior and ways to deal with tension.
>
> Frequently applicants take psychological evaluations just after finishing school. Their lives have been hectic. They have not taken time to relax for months. They are wound tighter than a $2.00 watch. This stress affects their entire being. It determines how they see the world. It is crucial for applicants to take time to relax before a psychological examination. This requires more than a 15-minute process the day before the evaluation. Some practical suggestions after you have taken time for yourself are as follows:
>
> - Don't fight with your wife or husband, boyfriend or girlfriend or parents the night before the evaluation.
> - Get plenty of sleep the night before. Make sure you are at your best.
> - Get up early the morning of the evaluation so you have time for yourself. Take a walk and relax.
> - Leave early for the evaluation. Get there with about 15 minutes to spare. Take time to relax when you get there. Read the paper or something.
> - During the exam, *be honest*. You have honestly worked toward entering this profession for a long time. Don't change now. Copy from the person next to you only if you are *absolutely sure* you want his or her personality and are willing to bet your career on it.

According to Frerkes (p. 87): "Research data indicates that psychological testing disqualifies 40 to 60 percent of applicants." Nonetheless, honesty cannot be stressed enough. Champion (1994, p. 3) states:

> Attempting to outwit the testers is one of the worst mistakes job applicants can make. I have had more students come to me and say, "How should I answer this or that scenario?" My answer is, "Use your best judgment." If they say, "How should I respond to personal questions—masturbation, thoughts best kept to one's self, etc., what should I say?" I always advise them to tell the truth, no matter what.

Testing Methods

Methods vary greatly from test to test. Personality tests are of two main types: objective and projective. Objective personality tests, such as the Minnesota Multiphasic Personality Inventory (MMPI), ask true/false or multiple-choice questions that are objectively scored. These questions are then grouped into scales to measure different aspects of personality. Projective tests involve ambiguous stimuli that the subject must interpret by "projecting" into the interpretation aspects of his or her own personality. Common projective tests are the Rorschach Inkblot Test and the Thematic Apperception Test (TAT).

Specific Psychological Tests

In attempting to look into the future to anticipate how an applicant might perform, evaluators look at both the past (for example, job references, grades, traffic and police records, etc.) and at the present. Psychological tests are a tool employers use to learn about the applicant's present state of mind, what is important to that person and how that person is likely to respond to certain stimuli.

These tests do not ask for yes/no or black/white answers. Rather, the answers form patterns that can be evaluated. Psychologists can compare the patterns with past studies to determine a psychological profile of the applicant. Tests frequently given include the following:

➢ Minnesota Multiphasic Personality Inventory (MMPI)
➢ California Psychological Inventory
➢ Myers-Briggs Type Indicator™
➢ Wonderlic Personnel Test
➢ Watson-Glaser Critical Thinking Appraisal
➢ Strong Interest Inventory
➢ Behavioral Personal Assessment Device (B-PAD)
➢ Rorschach Inkblot Test
➢ Thematic Apperception Test (TAT)

The *Minnesota Multiphasic Personality Inventory (MMPI)* is frequently used for entry-level psychological screening. It is used primarily for emotional stability screening. This self-report questionnaire is *the* most widely used paper-and-pencil personality test being used (in all fields). Respondents are asked to indicate "true," "false," or "cannot say" to 680 statements. Test items include a variety of psychological characteristics such as health, political, sexual, social and religious values; attitudes about family, education and occupation; emotional moods; and typical neurotic or psychotic displays such as obsessive-compulsive behavior, phobias, delusions and hallucinations.

According to Conroy, the MMPI is virtually impossible to study for. Its validity scales have cross-indexed questions and, in most cases, applicants who try to "fool" the test "fool" themselves out of a job instead. The MMPI has numerous sufficiently similar items so that it is difficult to lie consistently. The best advice here, again, is to tell the truth. One candidate tried to beat the MMPI and was denied a federal job. When the same candidate took the test again a year later and told the truth, he got the job.

The *California Psychological Inventory (CPI)* is the second most popular personality test. The test is a "multi-level self-administering questionnaire designed to identify the status of highly important factors in personality and social adjustment. Each scale forecasts what a person will say or do under defined conditions. The test identifies individuals who will be described in characteristic ways by others who know them well. Gough (1988, p. 45) describes the CPI as a multipurpose questionnaire designed to assess normal personality characteristics important to everyday life.

The *Myers-Briggs Type Indicator*™ is a widely used measure of people's disposition and preferences. Millions of people in a wide variety of occupations have taken the Myers-Briggs. The test describes 16 easily understood personality types based on individuals' stated preferences on four indexes:

➤   Extroversion-Introversion
➤   Sensing-Intuition
➤   Thinking-Feeling
➤   Judgment-Perception

The *Wonderlic Personnel Test* is a timed (12 minutes), 50-item paper-and-pencil test that can be taken individually or in groups. This test predicts success in learning situations and is a very accurate estimate of intelligence that serves as a quick assessment of cognitive skills or as a screening device to determine the need for more detailed evaluations.

The *Watson-Glaser Critical Thinking Appraisal* has five subtests:

➤   Inference
➤   Recognition of Assumptions
➤   Deduction
➤   Interpretation
➤   Evaluation of Arguments

The test has 80 items and is to be completed within 40 minutes. The test includes problems, statements, arguments and interpretations of data like those encountered daily at work and in the classroom.

The *Strong Interest Inventory* has 325 items covering a wide range of occupations, occupational activities, hobbies, leisure activities, school subjects and types of people. It compares a person's interests with the interests of people happily employed in a wide variety of occupations. It measures *interests,* not aptitude or intelligence.

The *Behavioral Personal Assessment Device (B-PAD)* is one of the more progressive testing instruments in police recruiting, and is used to measure problem-solving ability, judgment under pressure, decisiveness, diplomacy and an applicant's genuine interest in people. The test is presented in video format. The applicant views numerous video screens and must respond as if he or she was the officer at the scene. B-PAD was designed not as a test of police procedure but rather to assess an applicant's ability to effectively evaluate a variety of situations typically encountered by police officers (Frerkes, p. 89).

The *Rorschach Inkblot Test* consists of 10 inkblot patterns of various shades and colors. The applicant is shown a pattern and asked what it might be. Frerkes (p. 92) states: "The test is effective in assessing an applicant's objectivity, values, and emotional tendencies as well as revealing neuroses, psychosis, character disorders, addictions, and psychosomatic disorders."

The *Thematic Apperception Test (TAT)* is a projective instrument similar in context to the Rorschach Test but with no quantitative scoring technique. The test consists of 10 picture cards for women, 10 for men and 10 for both sexes. The purpose of the TAT is to provide insight into an applicant's self-image, relative strengths and various needs by inducing thoughts, attitudes and feelings about a subject depicted on the picture cards.

Integrity Tests

One type of psychological test commonly used by employers is the paper-and-pencil honesty questionnaire. The first test of this type was developed in 1951 by John E. Reid and was called the Reid Report. This test, described by Inbau (1994, p. 34), consists of:

> . . . a questionnaire with approximately eighty questions that are answered by a yes or no response, accompanied by biographical data questions, and by a list of thefts or theft-related acts that the candidate may have committed.

The questionnaire has four parts. Part 1 determines trustworthiness by asking a series of questions, such as, "Do you believe a person should be fired by a company if it is found that he helped another employee take a little merchandise from the company?" Part 2 is a criminal admissions questionnaire. Part 3 elicits information about recent drug use, and Part 4 examines work history.

> Integrity tests are psychological tests commonly used by employers to determine trustworthiness. The test asks questions about the candidate's ethics, criminal record, recent drug use and work history.

COMPUTERIZED SCREENING

You should also be prepared to be assessed by computer. As Clede (1995, p. 16) describes:

> Candidate Officer Preliminary Screen ("COPS") is a psychological test that candidates can take by keyboard-selecting best answers to multiple-choice questions on the computer monitor. Designed by two psychologists with more than 15 years' experience of police candidate testing, "COPS" evaluates basic honesty, domination desire, ability to handle stress, and also looks at basic personality features.

POLYGRAPH TESTING

In 1892 Dr. James MacKensie invented the "Ink Polygraph," which recorded heartbeat, venous pulse and arterial pulse. A clock spring mechanism drove a paper ribbon with time markers every fifth of a second. Three decades later the Larson Polygraph, credited as the original "lie detector," was built for Berkeley Police Chief August Vollmer. Bulky and complicated, the device took half an hour to set up.

The modern polygraph is much more compact, about the size of a briefcase. It measures changes in

➤ Relative blood pressure and pulse rate with a standard medical blood-pressure cuff
➤ Galvanic skin resistance (GSR), or perspiration, by means of two electrodes attached to the fingertips
➤ Stomach and chest breathing patterns with hollow, corrugated-rubber tubes, one placed around the abdomen and one around the upper thorax

Activity in each of these physiological measurements is monitored by either electronic or mechanical means and is permanently recorded on a paper chart by a pen-and-ink system. Dees (1995, p. 53) states:

> The most recent innovations in polygraph technology occurred in the last few years with the advent of computerized polygraphy. In computerized polygraphy, much of the mechanical equipment (streaming graph paper, mechanical pens, wet ink) that led to many glitches during the process of the exam is done away with in favor of a "virtual" graph on the computer monitor.

According to Clede (1998, p. 91): "Computerized models use the POLYSCORE mathematical algorithm developed at Johns Hopkins University by the Applied Physics Lab (APL) . . . [which] claims an interpretation accuracy of over 95%." Yet despite such claims of high accuracy, the Supreme Court has held there is simply no consensus that polygraph evidence is reliable. An opinion written by Justice Clarence Thomas in "Supreme Court Finds No Violation in Ban on Polygraph Evidence" (1998, p. 3) states:

> To this day, the scientific community remains extremely polarized about the reliability of polygraph techniques . . . . There is simply no way to know in a particular case whether a polygraph examiner's conclusion is accurate, because certain doubts and uncertainties plague even the best polygraph exams.

Use of the polygraph in pre-employment is so controversial that it has become strictly regulated through the Employee Polygraph Protection Act (EPPA), signed into law by President Reagan in 1988. This law prohibits the use of all mechanical lie detector tests in the workplace, including polygraphs, deceptographs, psychological stress evaluators and voice stress analyzers. The EPPA does, however, allow for the polygraph to be used by private sector employers for certain types of pre-employment screening, such as companies who provide certain types of security services. Furthermore, the EPPA does not apply when the particular employer is the United States government or any state or local government. Government employers may use any lie detector test without complying with any of EPPA's procedures or restrictions.

In other words, although using the polygraph during pre-employment is prohibited in most fields, it is *not* prohibited in law enforcement or in many private security jobs. Therefore, make no objections if you are asked to take such an exam. The employer probably has the right to request this. Just be yourself. Relax, and tell the truth.

Polygraph tests are used to determine a candidate's honesty and, according to field practitioners, are 90 to 95 percent accurate. Use of the polygraph during pre-employment screening is *not* prohibited in government jobs, including law enforcement.

The primary use of the polygraph is to substantiate the information gathered during the background investigation.

BACKGROUND CHECKS

Another type of test candidates must pass is the background check, also referred to as pre-employment screening. Chiaramonte (1995, p. 72) notes: "The use of pre-employment screening programs has become more important in recent years as companies are increasingly being held liable by the courts for the actions of employees. Liability is often based on the employer's failure to perform reference checks or to verify past employment."

The background check typically includes checking with past employers and references listed on your application form. It may also include checking your credit history, driving record, academic background, criminal record and whether you possess any and all required professional licenses.

According to Odom (1995, p. 70): "Pre-employment screening is the key to a quality work force for the [department or agency] that wants to survive into the twenty-first century."

THE PREVALENCE OF OTHER TESTS AND SCREENING TECHNIQUES

Recall Table 6-1, which shows how common medical and physical tests are used with law enforcement candidates. Hogue et al. (p. 120) also collected data regarding how common other screening procedures were, including those discussed in this chapter. The results are shown in Table 7-1.

TABLE 7-1   Reported Use of Selected Screening Techniques

Technique	Presently Used	Would Use if Budget Permitted	Not Worth the Time and Cost
References	96.7%	2.8%	0.5%
Arrest records check	96.4	2.7	0.9
Driving record check	96.4	3.2	0.5
Educational record check	89.6	8.0	2.4
Fingerprint check	87.6	10.9	1.5
Oral board review	78.2	13.0	7.8
Field investigation (background)	76.7	19.8	3.5
Screening interview	70.4	13.0	6.0
Military records check	69.5	23.5	7.0
Financial records check	49.7	34.1	16.2
Mental health records check	49.4	44.3	6.3
Psychological evaluation:			
intelligence/ability	41.7	52.9	5.3
emotional stability	37.6	56.6	5.8
Written exam	29.6	56.2	13.0
Polygraph examination	12.6	67.1	19.8

SOURCE: Mark C. Hogue, Tommie Black and Robert T. Sigler. "The Differential Use of Screening Techniques in the Recruitment of Police Officers." *American Journal of Police*, Vol. 13, No. 2, 1994, p. 120.

CONCLUSION

The testing process is another opportunity to prove to a prospective employer that *you* are the one to hire. Present yourself as you are. If you do not feel you would test well now, improve yourself by developing a rigorous plan to increase both your fitness level and your knowledge. Take some practice tests. Be *realistic* about who you are and what you can be. Be honest with yourself. Because work greatly influences *all* aspects of your life, you do not want to pursue any career that will be a dead end. View the testing phase of the application process as a positive experience for both the employer and you, to both determine if there is a match. If not, it is best for everyone to learn this while there is time for you to find a different niche in the world of work.

ADDITIONAL CONTACTS AND SOURCES OF INFORMATION

Two recommended test preparation books:

How to Prepare for the Police Officer Examination,
   by Donald J. Schroeder and Frank A. Lombardo,
   Barron's

Police Officer
   ARCO Publishing, MacMillan General Reference,
   A Prentice Hall MacMillan Company

AN INSIDER'S VIEW

GETTING SET

Dennis L. Conroy, Ph.D.
Director of the Employee Assistance Program
St. Paul (Minnesota) Police Department

In preparing for tests to become a police or security officer, it is crucial that you properly prepare for the various tests. There are likely to be tests in the areas of knowledge, physical fitness, psychological preparedness and perhaps even a polygraph.

You *can* study for knowledge tests. You must be able to not only understand the police/security function, but to articulate that function, specify ways in which that function can be fulfilled and how you will fit into the system to fulfill the function. In other words, expect more than just a multiple-choice or true/false test of knowledge. You must be able to state what police/security officers do (protect and serve), how that can best be accomplished (specific methods of protecting and serving) and what role you see for yourself in that system (how you see yourself functioning as a police or security officer).

Tests of physical fitness require significant prior preparation. There will often be tests of stamina (cardiovascular fitness), strength (muscle tone) and agility (mobility). Almost any fitness center can help you with programs to prepare for such tests. It is best to find the specifics of the department you are applying for and train to meet those standards.

To study for a psychological test is much like studying for a urine test. There *is* important preparation, but it cannot be done the night before the exam, or even a week before.

"I'm gonna' ace this baby."

You must begin to prepare for the psychological exam *at least* several months before the actual test itself. You must present yourself as psychologically fit to do police or security work, and such preparation takes time. It should be more a reaffirmation process than change. You should not be afraid of psychological examinations. Just be honest. If the assessment indicates that you may not be suitable for police work or security work, it is just as often indicating that police or security work will not be good for you.

––––––––––

Dennis L. Conroy is a sergeant with the St. Paul (Minnesota) Police Department. He has been a police officer for over 23 years. He has worked as a patrol officer, patrol supervisor, vice-narcotics investigator, juvenile investigator, trainer and Employee Assistance Program director.

Dr. Conroy has a Ph.D. in Clinical Psychology and conducts a psychology practice and consulting business. He is the lead author of Officers at Risk: How to Identify and Cope With Stress.

AN INSIDER'S VIEW

LEARNING SHOULD NEVER STOP

Russell M. Anderson
Field Supervisor and Investigator
Wisconsin Alliance for Fair Contracting

The criminal justice major has vast areas of opportunities and agencies to choose from, and you must be willing to become diversified once you are employed. A good applicant will have the motivation to attend training programs offered by the employing agency, while pursuing the educational and other training opportunities on their own.

Because criminal activity is not limited to the boundaries of traditional police work, different agencies, departments and organizations have been created to assist, enforce and monitor the ever-increasing problem of nontraditional criminal activity (white-collar crime, computer crime, environmental crime).

Once hired, some people are content with a position of generalized responsibility, while others want to specialize in a certain area or field. If given the opportunity to become specialized, by all means, take advantage of it. The learning process should never stop. Once you have acquired a position, the next step should be the pursuit of professionalism and expertise for that position. A highly trained and educated person not only feels less job stress but, more importantly, so do their supervisors.

Training, education and position knowledge are the three most important factors in lowering job stress—and there's always more to learn. You also have control over how you approach your job. Three approaches you can follow when dealing with your job are proactive, reactive and corrective. The proactive approach is being sure you are knowledgeable, educated and trained to perform your job as effectively as possible. The reactive approach is using the knowledge, education and training as needed to effectively deal with situations you must respond to. The corrective approach is evaluating the overall outcome of the performance of the proactive and reactive approaches and correcting any difficulties encountered. This might be done through more training, education and feedback from others who have the knowledge to raise performance.

Russell M. Anderson currently works as a field supervisor and investigator for the Wisconsin Alliance for Fair Contracting. He is responsible for conducting investigations for violations of federal and state prevailing wage laws throughout a 45+ county region in Wisconsin.

Mr. Anderson was formerly a director of surveillance and investigations enforcement with the Wisconsin Winnebago/HoChunk Nation. He also worked as a full-time temporary tax examiner for the Internal Revenue Service and served in the U.S. Army from 1982 to 1986. He holds a B.S. in Criminal Justice from Winona State University in Winona, Minnesota.

MIND STRETCHES

1.   Does your field require proof of certain levels of knowledge? How will you prepare for this?

2.   What do you anticipate a battery of psychological tests will say about you? Are there factors in your life that need to be attended to before you pursue your chosen career?

3.   How do you feel about taking a polygraph examination? Are there skeletons in your closet that you need to honestly confront?

4.   As part of your job search strategy, have you taken into account what you can and cannot prepare yourself for?

5.   What areas of the hiring process do you have such limited control over that you can't prepare for them? Is there any area of the hiring process that you have absolutely *no* control over, or is there always something you can do to give yourself an edge over the competition?

6.   Is what you have done in the past a realistic indicator of how you will perform in the future?

7.   Have you ever taken a psychological test? If so, how did you feel: positive, neutral or negative? If negative, what can you do to reduce these feelings?

8.   If you suffer from test anxiety, what can you do to reduce it?

REFERENCES

Champion, Dean J. Review of *Seeking Employment in Law Enforcement, Private Security, and Related Fields*, 1st ed. October 11, 1994, p. 3.

Chiaramonte, Joe. "Background Checks: Past as Prologue." *Security Management,* May 1995, pp. 72–77.

Clede, Bill. "Screening Officer Candidates." *Law and Order,* March 1995, p. 16.

Clede, Bill. "Technology—It Helps Find the Truth." *Law and Order*, July 1998, pp. 91–93.

Dees, Timothy M. "Polygraph Technology." *Law Enforcement Technology*, July 1995, pp. 52–54.

Frerkes, Larry R. *Becoming a Police Officer: A Guide to Successful Entry Level Testing.* Incline Village, NV: Copperhouse Publishing Company, 1998.

Garner, Kenneth. "Assessment Center Testing." *Law and Order,* November 1998, pp. 77–82.

Gough, Harrison G. "California Psychological Inventory: Proven Measure of Normal Personality." *1988 CPP Catalog.* Palo Alto, CA: Consulting Psychologists Press, Inc., 1988, pp. 45–47.

Hogue, Mark C.; Black, Tommie and Sigler, Robert T. "The Differential Use of Screening Techniques in the Recruitment of Police Officers." *American Journal of Police,* Vol. 13, No. 2, 1994, pp. 113–124.

Inbau, Fred E. "Integrity Tests and the Law." *Security Management,* January 1994, pp. 34–41.

Odom, R. Carl. "Candid Candidates: What's Behind the Resume?" *Security Management,* May, 1995, pp. 66–70.

Olson, Patricia S. *Study Skills: The Parent Connection*, 2nd ed. Burnsville, MN: Reading Consulting, Inc., 1990.

Rachlin, Harvey. "Assessment Centers." Part of "The Hiring of a Police Chief." *Law and Order,* March 1995, pp. 29–31.

Rafilson, Fred M. "Everything You Always Wanted to Know About Written Exams . . . but Were Afraid (Really) to Ask!" *Law and Order*, September 1997, pp. 100–102.

"Supreme Court Finds No Violation in Ban on Polygraph Evidence." *Criminal Justice Newsletter*, Vol. 29, No. 5, March 3, 1998, p. 3.

CHAPTER 8

ATTRIBUTES OF SUCCESSFUL CANDIDATES

It's not your aptitude, it's your attitude that determines your altitude.

Anonymous

Do You Know:

➢ If a lack of law-related experiences seriously hurts one's chances of obtaining employment in the fields of criminal justice or private security?

➢ What your past is a good predictor of?

➢ What past employment says about you?

➢ What the benefits of volunteering are?

➢ Where you might look to gain some work-related experience in criminal justice or security?

➢ If military experience is beneficial or detrimental to one seeking a job as a police, corrections or security officer?

➢ What advanced education says about an applicant?

➢ How important communication skills are?

➢ What the benefits of internships are?

➢ How you should handle past mistakes when applying for a new job?

➢ What role ethics plays in law enforcement and security?

INTRODUCTION

 Imagine yourself as an employer responsible for selecting the best candidate from a number of applicants. What criteria would you use to make this decision, which is sure to have important consequences? What positive attributes or characteristics would you, as an employer, look for? List these in your journal.

 What negative attributes would influence you *not* to hire a candidate? Again, write them down.

Employers are not just selecting employees; they are selecting people who will often directly influence other people's lives and who will also be representing their department or agency.

Police officers routinely deal with the most private business of the public for whom they work. Officers bandage wounds, intervene in disputes, guard property, search homes and offices and educate children. Officers may bring victims back to life or have to watch them die. They uphold the law, which not only benefits the public, but also holds the guilty responsible by drawing them into the criminal justice system in a way that will alter that defendant's life forever. Being a police officer is an *awesome* responsibility.

Correctional officers perform a vital function in guarding those sentenced to any of the variety of corrections facilities throughout our country. They deal with our nation's offenders daily and have the power to make positive changes in those offenders' lives. Correctional officers also bear the burden of protecting society from these offenders by making sure those they are assigned to guard do not escape. Some correctional positions involve counseling inmates, while others are limited to an armed position in a watchtower.

Security officers also have great responsibility. Most security directors have complete access to every part of a company's assets—its secrets, its property, its cash—all are literally under the protection of the security manager and the security officers. As noted by one security manager, it is ironic that companies "pay them $7 an hour and expose them to millions. Imagine opening a bank vault with millions and paying a guard $4 an hour to guard it" (Remesch, 1989, p. 35).

Yet other professionals in criminal justice fields are equally entrusted with important issues. Whether social workers, psychologists or other people in the helping professions, *all* employees in criminal justice are truly professionals.

What criteria are used when hiring criminal justice and security personnel? These criteria range from how you present yourself to who you really are.

HOW DO YOU APPEAR ON PAPER?

Impressions are important. Initial contacts, resumes and follow-ups are critical. Employers *will* look at both what you have done and how you have done it. If you are determined to get the job, take control of your future by establishing a solid background of knowledge and experience. Many opportunities are available to acquire those attributes employees seek in candidates.

PERSONAL ATTRIBUTES

What kind of background will help you get that entry-level job? Recognize that employers are often as interested in non-law-related experience and attributes as they are in law-related ones.

Most employers are more interested in the type of a person you are than in what you know about law enforcement, corrections or security work. A more general background helps anyone broaden their perspective of the world in which they live. Those doing the hiring want to know how you can relate your past experience to law enforcement, even if all you've done is flip burgers. Did you deal with customers? Did you have to solve problems? Did you do public relations? Did you have to communicate with people? These are things that will help the candidate get the job even if there has been no "police experience."

A lack of law-related experience by no means disqualifies you as a candidate for work in criminal justice or security. In fact, most employers are more interested in the type of a person you are than in what you know about law enforcement, corrections or security work.

Hogue et al. (1994, p. 121) state: "There appears to be considerable agreement among those who make screening decisions in law enforcement about the characteristics that are desirable for police officers. The candidate should be honest, reliable, emotionally stable, patient, and of good character." The desired characteristics for law enforcement officers are summarized in Table 8-1.

TABLE 8-1   Desirability of Selected Characteristics for Police Officers

Characteristic	Essential	Desirable	Not Desirable	Not Acceptable
Honest	96.8%	3.2%	--	--
Truthful	94.1	5.9	--	--
Emotionally stable	92.8	7.2	--	--
Good character	90.1	9.5	0.5%	--
Reliable	88.6	11.4	--	--
U.S. citizen	88.4	10.6	0.9	--
Law abiding	87.7	11.9	0.5	--
GED certificate	75.5	15.1	8.5	0.9%
Loyal	73.4	26.6	--	--
Fair	70.4	29.2	0.5	--
High school diploma	60.7	37.9	1.4	--
Careful	60.2	38.7	0.5	--
Skillful driver	49.5	48.6	1.9	--
Slow to anger	48.6	50.9	--	--
Patient	47.8	50.5	--	--
Firm	43.1	55.6	1.4	--
Past job performance	41.7	58.3	--	--
Consistent	41.1	57.5	0.5	--
Good physical appearance	35.6	63.5	0.9	--
Ambitious	28.4	68.4	3.3	--
Assertive	24.9	73.2	1.9	--
Authoritarian	19.5	55.7	23.3	1.4
High intelligence	16.2	81.0	2.8	--
Aggressive	16.1	66.4	15.6	1.9
Rigid	13.0	38.6	45.4	2.9
Good financial management	12.3	79.2	4.7	3.8
Vision without glasses	10.2	77.7	11.6	0.5
Appearance of strength	9.2	78.8	12.0	--
College education	4.7	80.5	14.4	--
Social alcohol use	3.9	7.8	73.7	14.6
Social drug use	1.4	1.9	11.7	85.0

SOURCE: Adapted from Mark C. Hogue, Tommie Black and Robert T. Sigler. "The Differential Use of Screening Techniques in the Recruitment of Police Officers." *American Journal of Police,* Vol. 13, No. 2, 1994, p. 119.

In examining how one department selects the best-qualified candidates for police work, Slahor (1998, p. 60) found:

> The department . . . [makes] sure it finds people who are problem solvers and who can make judgments under pressure. Willingness to confront problems, devise solutions and work not only with colleagues, but with the community are also key to the selection process.

> Successful candidates must have an interest in people and be sensitive to the best steps to take in a situation. Integrity and dependability are essential . . . not only for the daily work and for testifying in court but also in the wider scope of the officer's role in the neighborhood and community.

Weiss and Dresser (1998, p. 48) add: "The two most important abilities required of a police officer are communication skills and common sense." Furthermore (p. 50): "Departments are looking for people who are flexible but also determined and able to assume control under pressure." Desirable characteristics include maturity, openness, emotional stability, flexibility, cheerfulness, judgment, congeniality, the ability to handle social situations, the ability to deal with people at their worst, and tolerance for other opinions.

These same traits are vital if you're considering a career in the corrections or private security fields. These traits are not genetic. They are learned. The more general life experiences you have had, the better your chance to have acquired these traits. Broad experience also helps you better understand human behavior, a much-needed attribute.

Two other important attributes are ego strength and anger control. Ego strength is essential and comes from having good self-esteem and a good self-valuing system. Anger control is especially important because of the nature of the work. An empathetic attitude toward those who come to your attention because they are violating the law or a company policy is highly desirable. True professionals do not take client behaviors personally. They try to keep emotion out of decisions that affect other's lives through a process called *intellectualization.* That is, they think before they act.

In addition to possessing the preceding characteristics, successful candidates have also performed well in the past. It is generally agreed that a good predictor of how candidates will perform in the future is how they performed in the past. Experiences that can reflect positively on a candidate include the following:

➢   Past general employment
➢   Volunteer community experience
➢   Work-related experience
➢   Military service
➢   Education
➢   Communication skills/experience
➢   Computer, typing and word processing skills
➢   Interning

It is generally agreed that a good predictor of how candidates will perform in the future is how they performed in the past.

Past General Employment

While some employers may be looking for specific experience, those hiring entry-level personnel are usually more interested in a person's general background. Past employment says a lot about a person.

The simple fact that a person was successfully employed says that someone wanted to hire that person and that they were responsible enough to stay on the job. Keeping a job says that the person could operate on a schedule, complete assigned tasks, not take advantage of the basic trust placed in all employees and get along with others.

It might also be said that the more remote a person's past jobs were from the position being applied for, the more favorable the experience would be viewed. Many employers would rather hire entry-level personnel and train them "from scratch." Also, more general backgrounds provide a broader view of the world and opportunities to have developed varied experiences.

Don't worry if the only work experience you have is flipping burgers or stocking shelves. It says you chose to work. The more and varied experiences you have, the better you'll look—at least on paper.

> Past employment, regardless of the setting, says a lot about a person, such as the person was responsible enough to stay on the job, could operate on a schedule, complete assigned tasks, not take advantage of the basic trust placed in all employees and get along with others.

Volunteer Community Service

Volunteering speaks highly of the way we view our neighbors, reaching out to help when needed. Those who give of themselves make a statement—that they are willing to help. Because criminal justice and security are heavily into interacting with and helping people, any experience in doing so will reflect positively on you.

Many people looking for work, especially younger people, become frustrated that most employers want some experience. How do you get experience without a job? Volunteering in any way in your community is an exceptional opportunity to gain experience.

> Volunteering is an exceptional opportunity to gain experience and reflects positively on you by telling a prospective employer you are willing to help your community.

Work-Related Experience

While experience not directly related to your career goals has many benefits associated with it, you may be eager to become involved in your chosen field. Opportunities for such experiences are abundant and provide a strong base from which to seek employment.

Explorer posts, for example, provide opportunities to combine social and learning experiences. Similar to Boy Scouts and Girl Scouts, law enforcement explorer groups have a great deal of fun while learning about the profession. Generally sponsored by a community law enforcement agency, explorers learn such skills as shooting, first aid, defensive tactics and crime scene investigation. Good-hearted competition helps to hone these valuable skills.

Police reserve units also serve several valuable functions. Not only do such units provide backup to the paid officers in such situations as crowd control and crime scene searches, but it is yet another chance to gain experience in the field while serving the community. Participating in a reserve unit says you can work as part of a team and not abuse this association.

Volunteer fire departments offer another opportunity to do more than "get your feet wet" (literally). Fire fighting, recognized as an extraordinarily dangerous activity, demands the same attributes required of police, corrections and security officers: a cool head, the ability to work on a team and the ability to confront dangerous obstacles. Because police officers may answer fire calls, too, it helps to know how to respond.

Other agencies have opportunities that provide valuable experience. For example, some sheriffs' departments have special rescue squads, water patrol units and even mounted posses—all staffed by volunteers. Some departments have opportunities available for qualified individuals to provide patrol services to supplement their paid officers. In addition, some colleges have security departments staffed by students, another excellent opportunity to acquire experience in private "policing."

> Work-related experience may be gained by becoming involved in an explorer post, police reserve unit, volunteer fire department, special rescue squad, water patrol unit or mounted posse.

Military Service

Military service has many advantages for people considering work in the fields of security and criminal justice. First, military service provides an opportunity to enter an admirable field of work with absolutely no previous experience. It allows you to gain valuable experience while enhancing your reputation and developing maturity— not to mention drawing a paycheck.

Military service is a great chance to spend some time serving your country, even if you aren't sure about what your final career goals will be. Rather than wasting the time after high school or college by drifting, you could demonstrate your ability to develop in a professional field by joining the service.

Employers recognize that law enforcement, corrections and security are paramilitary and that successful military service is a very good indication of potential success in such civilian service. If you know early enough that you seek involvement in security or criminal justice, getting into a military policing unit can give you valuable experience.

On the other hand, the trend is toward a more humanistic, less authoritarian style of policing in both the public and private sectors. Because the military trains its officers to follow military law rather than the U.S. Constitution, such training may be a detriment to civilian policing. According to one employer, those who had been in the military drew more citizen complaints than their non-veteran counterparts. Furthermore, military veterans tended to be less flexible and less problem-solving oriented than their non-military comrades in police work. Veterans tended to look for "by-the-book" answers. Rigidity and by-the-book responses are out of sync with the current objectives of community policing and problem solving. Additionally, bear in mind that the military teaches interdependence and teamwork, and while both are important parts of policing, the majority of police work is done by the officer acting alone.

One benefit this employer did see from military experience was discipline. He also noted that those officers who combined military experience with advanced education were his best-prepared officers.

Keep a balanced, realistic view of the value of military experience.

Military experience can be beneficial to those seeking employment in police, corrections or security work because it develops discipline and allows maturity of the individual. However, military training may also be a detriment because civilian policing strives for a more humanistic, less authoritarian approach and reversing the military training may be difficult.

Education

Education is more important today than ever in many fields, including criminal justice and private security. If these fields are to be considered professions, which they are striving to do, then education plays an important role.

New focus has been placed on how well our schools are preparing young adults for life in the working world. To examine this issue, the U.S. Department of Labor has formed a commission known as the Secretary's Commission on Achieving Necessary Skills, or SCANS. According to a 1992 SCANS report titled "Learning a Living: A Blueprint for High Performance" (1992, p. ix): "[SCANS] was asked to define the know-how needed in the workplace and to consider how this know-how is best assessed." The Commission's first report, issued in 1991 and titled "What Work Requires of Schools," identified the need for schools to help students develop a foundation of basic academic skills, thinking skills and personal qualities necessary to achieve competency in the workplace, as shown in Figure 8-1. See Appendix A for more detailed definitions of these competencies and skills.

The 1992 report (p. xiv) also revealed:

> The time when a high school diploma was a sure ticket to a job is within the memory of workers who have not yet retired; yet in many places today a high school diploma is little more than a certificate of attendance. As a result, employers discount the value of all diplomas, and many students do not work hard in high school.

Education says something about those who obtain it. It says the person can identify, pursue and accomplish important goals. It shows patience, drive and self-determination. It shows the ability to commit to both short- and long-range goals. It says those seeking education are interested in both themselves and the world in which they live.

The know-how identified by SCANS is made up of five competencies and a three-part foundation of skills and personal qualities that are needed for solid job performance. These are:

WORKPLACE COMPETENCIES: Effective workers can productively use:

- **Resources**—They know how to allocate time, money, materials, space and staff.

- **Interpersonal Skills**—They can work on teams, teach others, serve customers, lead, negotiate and work well with people from culturally diverse backgrounds.

- **Information**—They can acquire and evaluate data, organize and maintain files, interpret and communicate and use computers to process information.

- **Systems**—They understand social, organizational and technological systems; they can monitor and correct performance and they can design or improve systems.

- **Technology**—They can select equipment and tools, apply technology to specific tasks and maintain and troubleshoot equipment.

FOUNDATION SKILLS: Competent workers in the high-performance workplace need:

- **Basic Skills**—reading, writing, arithmetic and mathematics, speaking and listening.

- **Thinking Skills**—the ability to learn, to reason, to think creatively, to make decisions and to solve problems.

- **Personal Qualities**—individual responsibility, self-esteem and self-management, sociability and integrity.

FIGURE 8-1 Workplace Know-How

SOURCE: "Learning a Living: A Blueprint for High Performance. A SCANS Report for America 2000." The Secretary's Commission on Achieving Necessary Skills, U.S. Department of Labor, April 1992, p. xiv.

Education *does* make you view the world differently. Education expands horizons, helping you better understand the differences that make our heterogeneous society not a threat, but a challenge. In addition, many agencies now *require* some college. According to Sharp (1997, p. 27):

> Some 69% of the respondents to a recent poll acknowledged a trend in law enforcement work that requires college degrees as a condition of employment. Only 14% did not see the trend. (The rest were not sure.)
>
> And 53% answered that college degrees should be required for police officers as conditions of new or continued employment for *all* departments. Significantly, 91% stated that college degrees were important in departments of all sizes.

For the past three decades, every national commission on violence and crime in America has concluded that college education can improve police performance. Over 25 years ago the National Advisory Committee on Criminal Justice Standards and Goals warned: "There are few professions today that do not require a college degree. Police, in their quest for greater professionalism should take notice." Vodicka (1994, p. 91) asserts:

> In this highly technical age, police officers must be able to perform a myriad of duties with skill and success—information processor, community organizer, crime analyst, counselor, street corner politician, arresting officer, school liaison, and community lead. Any of these actions, taken individually, would generally warrant a higher education requirement. Yet, the idea of college for police officers evokes much emotion and debate.

Mahan (1991, pp. 285–286) likewise urges that departments establish a policy regarding educational requirements and that several arguments support a requirement for college credits for those pursuing employment in law enforcement:

- It develops a broader base of information for decision making;
- It allows for additional years and experiences for maturity;
- Course requirements . . . [instill] responsibility in the individual;
- It permits the individual to learn more about the history of the country, the democratic process and an appreciation for constitutional rights, values and the democratic form of government;
- College education engenders the ability to flexibly handle difficult or ambiguous situations with greater creativity or innovation;
- It permits a better view of the "big picture" of the criminal justice system and both a better understanding and appreciation for the prosecutorial, courts and correctional roles;
- Higher education develops a greater empathy for minorities and their discriminatory experiences through both course work and interaction within the academic environment;
- It permits a greater understanding and tolerance for persons with differing lifestyles and ideologies, which can translate into more efficient communications;
- The college-educated officer is assumed to be less rigid in decision-making . . . with a greater tendency to wisely use discretion to deal with the individual case;
- The college experience will help officers communicate and respond to crime and service needs of the public in a competent manner with civility and humanity.

These same arguments apply to other positions within criminal justice and security.

No longer do legal barriers stand in the way of police departments requiring college education. In *Davis v. Dallas* (1986), a U.S. Court of Appeals upheld a requirement by the City of Dallas that entry-level police recruits have completed 45 college credits with a C average.

Advanced education is valuable to anyone seeking employment in criminal justice or private security not only because of the actual knowledge gained but also because of what pursuing such education says about you to a prospective employer—that you can identify, pursue and accomplish important goals; that you have patience, drive and self-determination; that you possess the ability to commit to both short- and long-range goals and that you are interested in both yourself and the world in which you live.

It is recommended that you keep a personal training log or journal documenting any training or educational programs in which you participate. Such a journal may be useful in preparing your resume or in answering any questions prospective employers may ask about your training and/or education.

Communication Skills

Communication skills are critical for public and private officers, for they communicate orally and in writing every day. How well you communicate will, to a great extent, determine how far you advance. Writing skills are especially important because once something is in writing, it is *permanent*. In addition:

➤ The police reports are often the first impression a judge or defense attorney has of an officer's competence, both generally and in regard to the specific elements of the offense charged.
➤ The decision to charge someone with a crime is based upon the police reports, usually alone.
➤ Complete and well-written police reports help to speed up the entire system. Delays in prosecution often occur because of incomplete reports.
➤ A well-written report alone can settle a case.

Unfortunately, most schools do not teach what the workplace requires. Any experiences you can have that enhance your ability to communicate, both orally and in writing, are extremely important.

> Communication skills—oral and written—are critically important for public and private officers and may determine how far you will advance in your career.

Computer, Typing and Word Processing Skills

You may be thinking, "I'm not applying for a secretarial job. Why do I need to know how to type?" But let's face it—we've gone techno. With today's reliance on the computer to generate reports and manage casework, typing, keyboarding and computer skills are essential for entering the fields of criminal justice and security. For example, it is estimated that probation and parole officers spend approximately 75 percent of their workday *typing* presentence investigation reports. Clearly, knowing your way around the keyboard is a must for this job.

You will be expected, to one degree or another, to be comfortable with computers. Your first sign of this to a prospective employer is the appearance of your application materials. There is no question which comes off an old manual typewriter and which comes off a word processor.

Bear in mind, too, that many agencies (private and public) are going to computerized report writing and making an effort toward the "paperless office." More and more police departments are giving their officers laptop computers in their squad cars, expecting them to write their reports, possibly at the scene, and send them via radio to the office computer. The old-fashioned "hunt and peck" typist isn't going to be as strong at the job, or in applying for it, as one who is even moderately proficient in typing and computers.

A practical example of how such skills are required to perform the everyday duties of police work is given by Pilant (1999). An officer responding to an accident scene involving six vehicles and multiple injuries needed to, among other things, write several DWI tickets and send seven people to three different hospitals. Pilant (p. 12) states: "The paperwork alone would have generated at least 35 forms, all of which required filling in the same information—for example, name, date of birth, and driver's license number." Instead of doing this all "by hand," however, the officer was able to use the Advanced Law Enforcement Response Technology, or ALERT, to enter the basic information once and assign it to as many forms as needed. ALERT is an on-board computer that performs numerous vital functions, including controlling patrol car devices (lights, sirens, radar) and enabling officers to write and transmit reports.

Strandberg (1998, p. 82) notes:

> Writing is a constant fact of life for law enforcement. Reports, memos, updates, evaluations—all of these and more have to be written to drive the information machine that is law enforcement.
>
> Unfortunately, a great deal of law enforcement writing is mired in stilted language, unclear reporting, inconsistencies and mistakes, jargon and inappropriate word choice. This directly impacts how the justice system works.

Hess (1999, p. 44) offers the following caution regarding the accuracy of spelling in reports:

> A misspelled name, for example, might cause serious problems for the reporting officer. And although spell-checkers are great—you can't rely on them completely. Consider the following examples—all of which would get past a spell-check:
>
> - He was arrested for a mister meaner.
> - He was a drug attic.
> - The victim was over rot.
> - After the accident he went into a comma.

Interning

A great way to break into the real world of work while still learning is by participating in an internship. As an intern, you get to work on the job as an educational experience. Many criminal justice programs across the nation are implementing internship programs and courses to help prepare their students for future careers. And while internships are seldom paid positions, the experience itself is priceless.

Interning serves a number of purposes. Some will be to the agency's benefit, but most will be to yours. Not only will you get an opportunity to see if this type of work, in general, suits you, but you will get a view of the profession that only an insider can attain. You may be expected to merely observe or to take a very active part in all aspects of the job. Be it helping to investigate a homicide at the crime scene or helping a probation officer interview a client, interning provides an excellent chance to combine experiential learning with academic learning—a true educational experience. It also provides a means to determine if this is the profession for you.

Internships provide a unique opportunity to look into a field to determine if it's the right profession for you while allowing you to gain some valuable experience.

Taylor (1999, p. 3) asserts:

> Internships will help [students] determine the most desirable areas for their future careers or indeed, decide whether they want to remain in the discipline at all. . . . Furthermore, student interactions with agency supervisors, clients, and the agency staff constitute a comprehensive instructional experience that will prove invaluable and will aid in cultivating alliances that may be beneficial in obtaining employment in the future. In some instances, students may be employed by the agencies after the internships end.

Taylor (p. 95) also notes interns are expected to follow certain ethical guidelines for the benefit and protection of themselves, as well as for that of clients, internship supervisors and agencies, and the internship coordinator and educational institution. Ethical standards interns must adhere to involve confidentiality, competency, avoidance of corruption and building interpersonal relationships.

A word of caution to those considering taking advantage of internship opportunities: be careful! If you behave in a manner that causes you to be asked to leave, this will *not* look good for you in the future. If you anticipate scheduling problems or any other issues that might cause you to receive a less-than-favorable report on your internship, you are better off to wait until you can perform at your best. Being an intern is about as close to actually having the job as you can get. Naturally, a prospective employer will question whether you could do the job now, if you couldn't as an intern.

This may sound easy, but it isn't necessarily so. You will certainly have less training than those who are actually employed in the profession. And you may not be provided with absolutely clear expectations or guidelines. You are going to have to use excellent judgment; they will be watching how you perform. More and more agencies use their interns as a pool from which to consider actual job applicants, so you simply can't afford to blow it here. You can be sure that when the background investigator checks on your internship performance, he or she will be told how you did. So the most important advice for interns is: don't be a know-it-all. I actually witnessed an intern tell a senior officer how she could do her job better! Needless to say, that intern didn't even get considered for full-time employment. Keep quiet, ask appropriate questions, and don't expect to be accepted as "one of the gang," at least not at first. And don't take this personally. Again, your time will come . . .if you allow it to happen.

PAINTING A PICTURE

The job application process is an opportunity to present a picture of yourself to a prospective employer. The picture is made up of the experiences you have developed for yourself.

   What experiences do you have that make a statement, and what do they say about you? Write them in your journal.

MAKING THE BEST OF BAD SITUATIONS

How many people can honestly say they have absolutely no blemishes on their records? If you're like most people, you learn more by making mistakes than by doing it right the first time. Did you really believe your mother when she said the stove was hot? Honestly? Or did you have to see for yourself?

I used to keep a poster above my desk that read: *When life gives you lemons, make lemonade.* However you say it, if you have made a mistake—which everyone has—it does not mean you have forfeited your future in security or criminal justice. Granted, *some* mistakes will bar you from certain positions in these fields. For example, no state will permit you to be a police officer if you have a felony on your record. They may, however, allow a misdemeanor or traffic offense.

Know in advance how you will deal with past mistakes. Begin by accepting that they do not automatically make you an outcast from society or from your chosen profession. Most professions accept mistakes, but they do *not* accept people who cannot change their ways, nor do they accept dishonesty. To lie on an application says nothing less than that you can't be trusted—that you are a liar. It may even be a crime. For example, *to lie on a federal job application is a felony.*

How do you deal with blemishes such as traffic citations or misdemeanor criminal charges? First, approach them upfront and honestly. Since the best defense is often a good offense, you will usually want to confront these issues head on. It looks better if you bring them up rather than having the employer learn about them during the background check. If they dredge up one questionable issue from your past, they may wonder what else might be hidden.

Once you have admitted you have made a mistake (or two, or three), take it one step further. Share what you learned from the experience. If you have a less-than-perfect traffic record or a shoplifting charge from your youth, it would sound better to explain how that experience influenced you to want to become a police officer or a security officer.

Imagine how a hiring board would accept being told that you were so influenced by the professionalism exhibited by the police officers who gave you those tickets that you wanted to become a police officer and positively influence others in the same way. What about a DWI conviction? Rather than eliminating you from the running, it could result in your taking subsequent steps to get your life together. To admit any shortcoming and prove you took advantage of an opportunity to grow and change does not make you an undesirable person. It makes you exceptional.

You can't change the past. You *can* present it so it looks positive rather than negative. Imagine, for example, that you had a questionable driving record and were in competition with one other applicant. Other than the driving record, you have identical attributes. Would the hiring board use your driving record to decide against you? Or maybe even for you? They might if you accept that you are what you are. Present yourself in the best light—honestly. While you might have made some admittedly questionable decisions in the past, you want them to fully understand that that was then and you learned from it. To do otherwise makes you look, at best, on the defensive and, at worst, a liar.

Judge for yourself—which of the following sounds best in response to an interviewer's question: "How is your driving record?"

Candidate #1. Fine. (If this is true, great. But it will take about 10 seconds to verify this on the computer. If you lied, you're out.)

Candidate #2. Well, I've had a few tickets. But I was only a kid, and the cops in my town had it in for me because of that. I think they just had to meet their quotas and it was easier to do by picking on us kids.

Candidate #3. As a matter of fact, I got some traffic tickets when I was a teenager. I can't say I didn't deserve them because I did. I learned about obeying traffic regulations the hard way—having to work summer jobs to pay for the tickets and the increased car insurance premiums. But it taught me a valuable lesson. *I* was accountable for my actions. It wasn't the fault of the officers who gave me the tickets or my parents for not picking up the tab. It was my own fault. It worked for me. This is one reason I want to be a police officer—to help others learn.

You get the picture. Consider another situation, this time with candidates responding to an interviewer's question: "Have you ever used illegal substances?"

Candidate #1. No. I would never do anything illegal. (Again, if this is true, great. But if the background investigation proves you to be a liar, you are out.)

Candidate #2. To be honest, as a teenager I did experiment a few times with marijuana. Most of my friends did pot, and I gave in to their pressure. It didn't do a thing for me, and I was forced to think about who was running my life—my friends or me. I knew it was time to stand up for myself, and it was quite a learning experience. In fact, most of my friends quit too. We each thought the others expected it of us. What an eye-opener that was!

To take care of minor problems that would generally bar employment, consider interviewing with a mid-sized agency that has hired applicants with minor problems.

Although some mistakes will bar you from certain positions in these fields, most employers accept mistakes *if* you are open and up front about them during the pre-employment interview, share what you learned from the experience, and express honestly how you have changed your ways.

CRIMINAL JUSTICE, PRIVATE SECURITY AND ETHICS

Ethics has become a "buzzword" in almost every profession. Certainly criminal justice and private security demand the highest of ethics. You can anticipate eventually having to deal with this issue. In fact, ethics is a favorite topic of interview boards, so carefully consider your values and what you believe ethical behavior to be.

To develop and maintain a professional reputation, codes of ethics have been adopted in both law enforcement and private security. The Law Enforcement Code of Ethics is shown in Figure 8-2.

As a law enforcement officer, my fundamental duty is to serve the community; to safeguard lives and property; to protect the innocent against deception, the weak against oppression or intimidation, and the peaceful against violence or disorder; and to respect the constitutional rights of all to liberty, equality and justice.

I will keep my private life unsullied as an example to all and will behave in a manner that does not bring discredit to me or my agency. I will maintain courageous calm in the face of danger, scorn or ridicule; develop self-restraint; and be constantly mindful of the welfare of others. Honest in thought and deed both in my personal and official life, I will be exemplary in obeying the law and the regulations of my department. Whatever I see or hear of a confidential nature or that is confided to me in my official capacity will be kept ever secret unless revelation is necessary in the performance of my duty.

I will never act officiously or permit personal feelings, prejudices, political beliefs, aspirations, animosities or friendships to influence my decisions. With no compromise for crime and with relentless prosecution of criminals, I will enforce the law courteously and appropriately without fear or favor, malice or ill will, never employing unnecessary force or violence and never accepting gratuities.

I recognize the badge of my office as a symbol of public faith, and I accept it as a public trust to be held so long as I am true to the ethics of the police service. I will never engage in acts of corruption or bribery, nor will I condone such acts by other police officers. I will cooperate with all legally authorized agencies and their representatives in the pursuit of justice.

I know that I alone am responsible for my own standard of professional performance and will take every reasonable opportunity to enhance and improve my level of knowledge and competence.

I will constantly strive to achieve these objectives and ideals, dedicating myself before God to my chosen profession . . . law enforcement.

FIGURE 8-2   Law Enforcement Code of Ethics

SOURCE: Reprinted with permission from the International Association of Chiefs of Police, Alexandria, Virginia. Further reproduction without express written permission from IACP is strictly prohibited.

The International Association of Chiefs of Police (IACP) has also developed a Police Code of Conduct that covers primary responsibilities of a police officer, performance of the duties of a police officer, discretion, use of force, confidentiality, integrity, cooperation with other officers and agencies, personal/professional capabilities and private life. See Appendix B for the entire IACP Police Code of Conduct. The security profession has also developed a similar code of ethics, which is presented in Appendix C.

The ethics of police, corrections and security officers play a large role in whether these fields are viewed as true professions. In fact, ethics is a favorite topic of interview boards, so you should thoughtfully consider your values and what you consider to be ethical behavior.

According to Smotzer (1999, p. 32): "Ethics isn't a written code, it's about what we do." He cites "the six pillars of character" as trustworthiness; respect; responsibility; justice and fairness; caring; and civil virtue and citizenship. He also stresses five principles of ethical policing: fair access, public trust, safety and security, teamwork, and objectivity.

The importance of ethics is also emphasized by the Ethics Training Subcommittee of the IACP Ad Hoc Committee on Police Image and Ethics (1998, p. 14): "Ethics is our greatest training and leadership need today and into the next century." The IACP has recommended a Law Enforcement Oath of Honor as a symbolic statement to ethical behavior (p. 19):

> On my honor,
> I will never betray my badge,
> my integrity, my character,
> or the public trust.
> I will always have
> the courage to hold myself
> and others accountable for our actions.
> I will always uphold the constitution
> and community I serve.

CONCLUSION

Your life is like a painting being continuously worked on. It will be developed, refined, altered and improved. It is never completed. Although the canvas may occasionally be briefly set aside, the paint is never completely dried—unless you allow it to be. At every phase of your life, you will appear to others as you have developed yourself. How will you appear to prospective employers? How can you add to your "life's painting" to be as appealing as possible? If you need more substance to your picture, get it. You have the control, the opportunity. Do you have the ambition and foresight?

AN INSIDER'S VIEW

GETTING YOUR FOOT IN THE DOOR

Michael P. Stein
Chief of Police
Escondido (California) Police Department

In California it is estimated that only one applicant out of 100 successfully competes for a police officer position, from the initial application to the final interview. As overwhelming as those odds are, there are strategies that can help you be that one in 100.

As departments go to community-based policing, the requirements for police officers are changing from the traditional enforcement role to one that requires the officer to be a community activist and facilitator. Police agencies are looking for candidates with experience in problem-solving and working with various elements of the community. The successful candidate for the future is the one who has experience in working with community agencies that work to solve problems for the community good. Think about volunteering at your local Boys' and Girls' Clubs, your local school district or any other social agency in the community. This will give you hands-on experience in working with others and being a "team player."

It is never too early to begin planning to compete for that police officer position. When I was finishing high school, I knew that I wanted to join the police profession, but really didn't know how to go about it. After four years in the military, I was able to compete with just a high school diploma. This is no longer the case. Now an applicant will be competing with many who are currently working toward a degree at the community college level and many others who may have a bachelor's degree.

Our department has recognized the need for better-educated applicants, even at the high school level. In cooperation with the local high school district, we have started a program called the "Code 3 Academy," where police officers present classes, lectures, field trips and physical training to students interested in preparing for a law enforcement career. Students learn based on what is being taught at local police academies. English classes include studies in report writing, computer keyboarding, powers of observation and exercises in written and verbal communication with their peer group and members of other cultures. The program gives students an opportunity to form a mentorship with police professionals who can assist them in their future law enforcement career goals. Another opportunity for high school students is to join their local police department's Explorer Program. This gives the student the ability to see what police work is really about.

Any position that gets your foot in the door of a police agency is beneficial. Does your local department need volunteers? Does it have a police auxiliary or a Reserve Program? Establishing this type of personal relationship with a local department is one key thing you can do to increase the odds of being selected.

Once a year, our department holds a special recruitment for police officer trainee positions, when any of our active reserve officers can compete. The number then falls from one in 100 to something like one in 15 for a position. In the last 35 years, 49 of our reserve officers have been selected as police officer trainees with our department, and many others have been hired by other law enforcement agencies.

Does your local police academy allow you to attend without a department affiliation? In California a student can put himself/herself through any police academy in the state. Once you have your certificate of graduation from an academy, you then compete with only other academy graduates, not the at-large public. All departments are looking for experienced or previously trained candidates, and this is a real advantage as you compete for a position.

When applying for a police officer position, ask if any other positions are currently being recruited for in the department, such as community service officer, traffic control officer, dispatcher, etc. These are positions where the competition must not be as stringent as for police officer, but, if hired, this gives you an opportunity to show your work ethic to the department as you compete later for a police officer position. In our department, nine former community service officers now serve as police officers.

Does the agency that you aspire to join serve a large population of non-English speakers? In many southern border states, because of the influx of monolingual Spanish speakers, the ability to be bilingual in Spanish and English is an asset all police departments desire. Many departments do bilingual Spanish recruitments where applicants need to be proficient in both languages to apply. This has the effect of lowering the overall number of applicants, but again increases the chances of those who have this skill to be successfully recruited. The other benefit of these recruitments is that it allows the departments to be more reflective of the newly diverse communities they serve.

The preceding recommendations used individually or collectively will enhance your ability to secure a law enforcement position. Best of luck!

Michael P. Stein rose through the ranks of the Escondido (California) Police Department to become the chief of police. He has 33 years of experience in the field of law enforcement, holds a B.A. in Public Administration and a Master's degree in Human Behavior. Chief Stein is also a graduate of the 129th Session of the FBI National Academy.

AN INSIDER'S VIEW

OUT OF THE ORDINARY

Monte D. Zillinger
Special Agent in Charge
Burlington Northern Railroad

Since 1885 railroads have employed police officers to protect railroad property, personnel, passengers and cargo. Pennsylvania was the first state to appoint railroad police. There are now about 3,000 railroad police in the United States working with police authority in 48 states. In 1990 the federal government, recognizing the need for railroad police to travel across state lines while conducting investigations and protecting sensitive loads, enacted legislation authorizing railroad police to exercise police authority in all states the particular railroad operated in (except Hawaii and Minnesota).

Railroad police respond to emergencies involving derailments and criminal incidents. They provide protection against trespassing, vandalism, theft and sabotage. They protect military loads, hazardous materials, international shipments and high-value loads while in transit.

Railroad police are also business men and women involved in dealing with customers, suppliers and employers. Internal noncriminal investigations are often conducted to support or deny claims, to detect employee misconduct, to protect sensitive business information and to provide executive protection. Railroad police are commonly involved in business projects in their assigned areas.

Since the variety of work requires such a complex mix of skills, most railroad police are recruited from other police fields after they have already honed their police abilities for several years. Officers with quality college educational backgrounds are generally more competitive in the employment process and more successful in developing business abilities.

Railroad police positions are not normally advertised in standard police channels but through customary business employment methods, such as employment agencies and human resources departments. Most railroad police are employed by railroads because they met a railroad police officer and asked about employment opportunities.

Numerous large railroad police departments operate over large parts of the United States, and many regional railroads have smaller police agencies. The variety of assignments from one "road" to another is as interesting as the diversity provided by local, state and federal police agencies. Each railroad police department has its own particular character with different degrees of emphasis on policing and business applications. Police officers looking for new challenges and rewarding work need to look around to discover what private industry has to offer in law enforcement fields.

Monte D. Zillinger is a special agent in charge of the Assets Protection Department of Burlington Northern Railroad in Minneapolis, Minnesota. He has 22 years' experience in criminal justice and has previously worked as a police officer in Alliance, Nebraska; a deputy sheriff in Box Butte County, Nebraska; and as a patrolman, special agent and assistant division special agent for Burlington Northern in Nebraska and Alabama. Mr. Zillinger has an A.A. in Criminal Justice, a B.A. in Criminal Justice and a certification from the Nebraska Law Enforcement Center. He is also a former member of the BN System Pistol Team. Mr. Zillinger is a member of the Minnesota Chiefs of Police, Anoka County Chiefs of Police, and South Dakota Police and Peace Officer's Association. He is also a past member of the Tri-State Peace Officer's Association and the Nebraska Peace Officer's Association. He has been married 18 years to Dianne; they have three children.

 MIND STRETCHES

1.   Do you believe your past is an accurate assessment of your employment potential?

2.   Who would be a better risk as an employee: candidates who tested the system as juveniles, occasionally having run-ins with the law, or candidates who walked the "straight and narrow," never doing anything "wrong," but also never testing their own limitations?

3.   What are important benefits of attending college?

4.   What volunteer opportunities exist in your community?

5.   What do good writing skills say about you? How can you develop them?

6.   Name five important attributes an employer might seek from applicants, regardless of the job. How can you develop these attributes?

7.   Why is ethics of particular importance to criminal justice and private security?

8.   As you look at your past, are there facts that could hurt you as a job applicant? How will you address them to put them in the most positive light?

9.   What are your personal and professional strengths?

10.   Is it possible to be "overqualified"? Why or why not?

REFERENCES

Hess, Kären M. "The ABCs of Effective Reports: Observe the Basics." *Police*, March 1999, pp. 43–44.

Hogue, Mark C.; Black, Tommie and Sigler, Robert T. "The Differential Use of Screening Techniques in the Recruitment of Police Officers." *American Journal of Police,* Vol.13, No.2, 1994, pp. 113–124.

IACP Ad Hoc Committee on Police Image and Ethics, Ethics Training Subcommittee. "Ethics Training in Law Enforcement." *The Police Chief,* January 1998, pp. 14–24.

"Learning a Living: A Blueprint for High Performance. A SCANS Report for America 2000." The Secretary's Commission on Achieving Necessary Skills, U.S. Department of Labor, April 1992.

Mahan, R. "Personnel Selection in Police Agencies: Educational Requirements for Entry Level." *Law and Order,* January 1991, pp. 282–286.

Pilant, Lois. "Going Mobile in Law Enforcement Technology." *National Institute of Justice Journal*, January 1999, pp. 11–16.

Remesch, Kimberly A. "Shared Responsibility." *Police,* November 1989, pp. 32–35, 67.

Sharp, Arthur G. "The Forecast for Police Employment Is a Matter of Degrees." *Law and Order*, May 1997, pp. 27–32.

Slahor, Stephenie. "How One Department Gets the Best." *Law and Order*, May 1998, p. 60.

Smotzer, Andrew A. "Ethics Training for Law Enforcement." *Law and Order*, February 1999, p. 32.

Strandberg, Keith W. "Toward Better Report Writing." *Law Enforcement Technology*, June 1998, pp. 82–84.

Taylor, Dorothy. *Jumpstarting Your Career: An Internship Guide for Criminal Justice.* Upper Saddle River, NJ: Prentice Hall, Inc., 1999.

Vodicka, Alan T. "Educational Requirements for Police Recruits: Higher Education Benefits Officers, Agency." *Law and Order,* March 1994, pp. 91–94.

Weiss, Jim and Dresser, Mary. "Job Hunt Karate." *Law and Order*, May 1998, pp. 47–52.

CHAPTER 9

THE RESUME:
SELLING YOURSELF ON PAPER

Writing a Resume: Spend time on self-assessment first. Identify all the achievements of your past that illustrate skills. Describe them in active verbs and look for consistencies. That's the clue as to what you should emphasize. A resume is scanned, not read. It's a sales tool that should give someone a sampling, not details in full.

—*Jean Clarkson*

Do You Know:

➢ What a resume is?
➢ What purposes a resume serves?
➢ What seven steps are involved in creating a resume?
➢ What items to include in your resume?
➢ What is best left off your resume?
➢ What three basic types of resumes are commonly used and how they differ?
➢ What is important about the format of your resume?
➢ What the key to writing an effective resume is?
➢ What to keep in mind when printing your resume?
➢ When to send a cover letter and what elements are essential?
➢ The best way to deliver your resume and what to do after the delivery?
➢ How to make your resume computer compatible?

INTRODUCTION

You've spent a lot of time thinking about your goals and yourself, your fitness, education and attributes. Now it's time to pull all this information together into one of your most important job-seeking tools—the resume.

You probably know what a resume is. But that's a little like saying you know what surgery is. A vast amount of territory exists between recognizing a concept and grasping its true meaning. To have a working understanding of such a concept is even more involved. This chapter gives a working knowledge of the resume. *Resume* is a French word (pronounced *REZ-oo-may*) that means "summary." In French the two "e's" have accents over them, but since you're writing in English, it's all right to omit them.

What is a resume? Webster's defines *resume* as: "A short account of one's career and qualifications prepared typically by an applicant for a position." A resume is a capsulized account highlighting and describing *significant* aspects of your background and qualifications for a given job—a promotional tool designed to *sell* you.

A resume is a brief, well-documented account of your career achievements, which highlights significant aspects of your background and identifies your qualifications for a given job. Its purpose is to *sell* you to a prospective employer.

Dauten and Nelson (1997, p. D5) suggest that the "ticket to employability" is to document your achievements and to keep improving your resume by acquiring "braggables." Wendleton and Dauten (1999b, p. D4) state: "The average resume is looked at for only 10 seconds!" They also note: "Ten seconds is plenty of time, if you remember that your goal isn't to answer every possible question, but to arouse enough interest to make a manager want to interview you." They relate the story of an ad in *Variety*, the trade paper for show business, that read: "WANTED: Tamer lion by lion tamer." Dauten remarks: "There's a whole story in those five words. If you could capture that kind of efficiency in a resume, you could get yourself tossed into the 'Interview' pile and have eight seconds left over."

Kennedy (1995, p. J1) notes:

> A recent national meeting of the Professional Association of Resume Writers featured a panel of corporate human resource specialists on the topic of what employers really want in a resume. Here are highlights from that panel . . . They search for key words and phrases, they review accomplishments, and they are critical in assessing the quality of the written document.

Other suggestions were to print your resume on plain white paper to allow for better quality scanning and copying by the employer; use crisp, action-oriented power words in your writing; and *always* attach a cover letter (p. J1).

A good resume can be the determining factor in whether an employer calls you in for an interview. A well-prepared resume may get you a "foot in the door." Your resume will probably precede you in all your dealings with prospective employers, so it must be the best image you can project.

The competition to attract an employer's attention is keen, bitter and brutal. You need every tool you can get, and at the outset, your resume is the only one you have. Your resume may be your first contact with a potential employer. It may also be the last. The choice is yours.

In some instances, however, particularly in larger agencies and institutions, resumes are not used. Instead, the agency goes through a civil service commission. Applicants are asked to fill in only the civil service commission's paperwork and can add nothing to it. A resume can backfire if you include it and it is *not* asked for or wanted.

THE PURPOSES OF THE RESUME

The resume is important to the *employer* because it helps *weed out* unqualified candidates. For most employers, this is the most important function of a resume. Employers will use *any* flaw in a resume to cut down the number of individuals to be interviewed. Resumes also help employers cut through a lot of preliminary questioning about applicants' qualifications. They also help employers to structure their interviews.

The resume is important to *you* because it can help get you in the door for an interview. It serves other purposes as well. Preparing your resume will force you to take a good hard look at your skills, qualifications, past experiences and accomplishments. It will force you to recall (or look up) dates and addresses. It will force you to organize your past clearly and concisely. This will help you present yourself in an organized manner during the interview as well. In addition, you can approach the interview confident that you have the qualities and background the employer is looking for, or why would you be called in?

> Resumes serve a variety of purposes for both the employer and the applicant. A resume helps an employer by weeding out unqualified candidates, answering preliminary questions about an applicant's qualifications and structuring an interview. A resume helps applicants obtain interviews and organize their experiences, accomplishments, present skills and qualifications so they may be coherently discussed during an interview.

During the interview, the resume will save time by providing a common ground to start from. It will also keep you honest. The temptation to exaggerate your experience or accomplishments will be removed when you know the employer has seen your resume. Now that you know how important your resume is, look at the specific steps in creating one.

STEPS IN CREATING A RESUME

Creating a resume is like painting a picture of yourself. From the conception of the idea to the completion of the masterpiece, you need to take seven specific steps.

> The seven specific steps to creating a resume are:
>
> 1. Compile all relevant information.
> 2. Select the most appropriate type of resume.
> 3. Select a format.
> 4. Write the first draft.
> 5. Polish the first draft.
> 6. Evaluate the resume and revise if necessary.
> 7. Print the resume.

Creating an effective resume is *hard work*, but the results will be well worth it. Without an effective resume, you are wasting your time applying for most jobs. You won't get to first base. Even if an agency does not require a resume, they will expect you to be a "living resume" at the interview. Get yourself organized before that. Make up your mind to devote several hours to this important document.

COMPILE INFORMATION

Gather all the information that could possibly be included in your resume. Some will be used; some won't. Painters gather all of their brushes and paints before they begin to work so they aren't interrupted during the creative process. Likewise, you will want to gather all the information you *might* decide to include. You don't want to interrupt the creative flow of writing by having to look up a phone number or address.

 Use the worksheets in Appendix D to organize your resume information. Flip to the back of the book and place a paper clip at the top of Appendix D to help you locate it quickly while working through this section. Don't cut corners during this first step. Your background makes a great deal of difference. As you compile information, you may be amazed at how much data an employer will need to even consider you.

Don't guess at dates. Verify them. Don't guess at addresses. Check them out if it has been several years since you last worked or lived there.

You'll look at three kinds of information: (1) data you must include, (2) data you might include and (3) data you should probably not include but should be prepared to discuss.

Let's look first at what *MUST* be included: personal identifying information, your educational background and your work experience.

Personal Identifying Information

Name. Obvious? Yes. But believe it or not, some people actually forget to include their name. In addition, think carefully about how you want your name to appear. Do you want to include your middle name? An initial? A nickname? A title?

If you include a nickname, put it following your first name with quotation marks around it, like this: *Robert "Bob" T. Jones*. This lets the employer know what you prefer to be called. Avoid extreme or inappropriate nicknames such as "Killer."

 How do you want your name to appear in your resume? Write it on the worksheet.

Address. It is usually best to give only your home address. Put the street address on one line. Do not abbreviate. Put a comma between a street address and an apartment number. Put the city and state on the next line and separate them with a comma. Use the two-letter state abbreviation—both letters capitalized and NO period. Include your zip code. Do *not* put a comma between the state and zip code.

Example: 123 Third Avenue South, #401
                My Town, MN 55437

How should your address appear? Write it on the worksheet.

 If you move frequently, you may want to include a permanent address in addition to your present address.

Phone Number. *Always* include a phone number. Busy employers often prefer to call rather than write. Make it easy for them. Give the area code, followed by a hyphen and then your phone number. Indicate if it is a home or a work number. Many people prefer to *not* include a work phone to avoid being called at work. Would getting job-search-related phone calls at work cause you any problems? If so, do *not* include your work number.

Some people also include the hours they can be reached at a given number. Others put this information in their cover letter.

Example: Home Phone   612-555-8818 (6 to 10 p.m.)
               Work Phone   612-555-9929 (9 to 5)

 Enter your phone number(s) on the appropriate line on the worksheet.

Did you know there was so much to think about in simply giving your name, address and phone number?

Education

Information about your education is crucial to your resume.

 College. List each college attended, city and state, number of years completed, major/minor, unique areas of study and degree(s) earned. Start with the most recent and work backwards. Include any honors, awards or leadership positions. Include grade point average *if* outstanding.

 Professional Schools. Include the same information as for colleges. Include academies here also.

 Internships. Include the place and length of the internship.

 Certificates. Relevant certificates would include first aid, CPR and the like. Give the year the certificates were awarded and expiration dates, if relevant.

 Other Educational Experiences. Include any relevant seminars, workshops, correspondence courses and the like.

 High School. Include name, city and state, year of graduation, and grade point average if it is outstanding. Include your high school *only* if you graduated within the last 10 years or if you have no other education to include.

Work Experience

Recall from Chapter 8 that past general employment of any type is valuable in the job search, even if not related to your field. Volunteer experience, work-related or not, should also be included on your resume.

Of special importance are the qualifications and skills you bring to the job. You may want to refer to Chapter 8 for attributes most employers are looking for. Your resume should stress achievements more than education and experience.

 Begin with your present job, or your most recent job if you are not currently employed. Work back in time. Use the worksheet in Appendix D. Make a copy of this worksheet for each job you have had. Use the work experience section to describe your qualities and skills wherever and however you can. In fact, if applicable, you might also demonstrate these qualities and skills in the education portion of your resume as well.

Several other areas of information might also be included in your resume, depending on your specific background. Even if you decide *not* to include much or most of the following information, it is important for you to think about it and have it clear in your mind because it could come up during the interview.

Position Desired or Employment Objective

What specific job do you have in mind? Are you open to *any* position in your chosen field? This information can be very helpful to busy employers as they skim through stacks of resumes. "An attractive job candidate is one who knows what he wants to do," according to Barkley at New York City's Crystal Barkley career advisory service (Alderman, 1995, p. 175).

 In Appendix D, write down the position desired and your employment objective. An example might be: *Position desired: Entry-level officer with opportunity for rapid advancement.*

Other Information

Other information that may be put in your resume includes the following:

 Birth date, height, weight, health, willingness to travel, willingness to relocate, military experience, professional memberships, knowledge of foreign language(s), foreign travel, awards, publications, community service or involvement, interests and hobbies. Also, list your accomplishments and don't be modest.

 Many job-search consultants suggest giving a glimpse of your personal side: marital status, spouse's occupation, ages of your children, family interests and hobbies. It gives a more well-rounded impression of you.

You might also want to include your availability—can you start immediately or do you need a certain amount of time to give notice to your present employer? Can your present employer be contacted?

Your resume should also include the statement: "References are available on request." And be sure they are.

References

If you get to the point in the hiring process where you are being considered, most employers will want to check your references.

 Choose references *now* and fill in that portion of the worksheet in Appendix D. Try to have business/professional/academic references and personal references.

Choose your references carefully. *Always* ask your references if they are willing to provide you with a *positive* reference. Most people do *not* include the references in their resumes. You can simply state: "References available on request," and prepare a separate sheet of references to make available to employers who request them. This also keeps your references confidential until a request is made for them.

Photograph

Some books on resumes suggest that a photograph should never be included with a resume. Other books highly recommend it. Those who are against it suggest that it violates anti-discrimination laws by providing information an employer cannot legally ask about. For example, race, sex and approximate age are revealed in a photograph. If you feel these factors may work in your favor, you may decide to include a photograph.

One advantage of including a photo is that it will probably make your resume stand out from the rest, always a primary goal. However, unless it represents you in a way the employer will appreciate, the photo could detract from your resume. If you do include a photo, be certain it is recent, professional and puts you in a favorable light. You should be neatly groomed and the reproduction should be clear and crisp.

Items you *must* include in your resume are personal identifying information (name, address and phone number), educational experience and work experience. You might also include the position you desire, your employment objectives, personal information (birth date, health status, marital status, etc.), your willingness to travel or relocate, military experience, professional memberships, knowledge of foreign language(s), awards, publications, any community service or involvement and your availability. You should include a statement that references are available upon request. Whether to include a photograph is debatable. Include a photograph only if it is recent, professional and presents you in a favorable light.

What *Not* to Include

What not to include is a matter of opinion. You obviously want to present yourself as positively as possible. While you will *never* lie on a resume, you will want to present yourself so that even negative occurrences look good for you. If you have to explain them in depth during an interview, that's fine, as long as you *get* to the interview. What *not* to include depends to a great extent on your particular circumstances.

Including too much data is the *number one* fault on resumes. Not only does it present a document that won't get read, but you can harm yourself by saying too much. For example, you will usually have no need to state in a resume why you left past jobs. If the reason was somewhat spectacular, for example a series of promotions, put it in. The presumption will be that you moved upward and onward to better positions.

Exceptionally personal data can also detract from the emphasis that should be on your skills and qualifications. If you want to state your family status, fine. But don't give the names and ages of everyone in your family. Does the employer really care? Could it work against you? What if you have very young children and the employer thinks you should be at home with them? What if the employer sees your children are all grown and concludes you are too old for the position? Don't include anything that could work against you. Individual circumstances will determine whether including children's ages allows a glimpse of your personal side or detracts from the more important elements of your resume.

The resume is not the place to explain difficulties you have experienced. It is a chance to provide a *brief* overview of yourself, to be expanded on once it has gotten you into the interview. Be certain everything you include is relevant and cannot in any way detract.

Including too much data is the *number one* fault on resumes. Don't overdo it. *Avoid including* these items in your resume:

- ➤ Reasons for leaving your current or previous job.
- ➤ Salary (previous or desired).
- ➤ Religious or church affiliations.
- ➤ Race, ethnic background, nationality.
- ➤ Political affiliations/preferences.
- ➤ Anything that negatively dates your resume.

SELECT THE TYPE OF RESUME

When you go fishing you select the bait that will best serve your purpose based on the specific conditions at that particular time and the fish you're after. Likewise, you should have all the "bait" you need to land an interview in the form of the data you have just put together. Now decide how to present it. Three basic types of resumes are commonly used:

- ➤ Historical or chronological
- ➤ Functional
- ➤ Analytical

Each type has a specific format, specific content and a specific purpose.

Historical/Chronological Resume

The historical/chronological resume is the most traditional and is often considered the most effective. As implied by the name, this style presents information in reverse chronological order, starting with your most recent work experience and moving back in time to your past work experience. The educational and employment information worksheets in Appendix D are organized this way. Both education and employment lend themselves to this style. Always include dates and explain any gaps in the chronology.

The historical/chronological resume is easy to read and gives busy employers a familiar form that can be quickly read. It is the best format to use when staying in the same field. It is not the best format if you have little related experience According to Corwen (1988, p. 24) you should use a chronological resume if:

➤ You have spent three or more years with previous employers and have not changed jobs frequently.
➤ You are seeking a position in the same field in which you have been employed during the course of your career.
➤ You have worked for well-known, prestigious companies.
➤ You can show steady growth in responsibilities.
➤ Your references are impeccable.

See Appendix E for a sample chronological resume.

Functional Resume

The functional resume emphasizes your qualifications and abilities as they relate to the job you are applying for. After each job you briefly describe your duties and expertise. Dates do not receive as much attention. This style is most applicable if you have had only a few jobs or have been with a particular company or department for a long time. Such a resume stresses experiences and abilities rather than a chronological listing of jobs. It minimizes irrelevant jobs, employment gaps and reversals while maximizing scant work experience. Corwen (p. 24) suggests you use a functional resume if:

➤ You are seeking a job in a new field not related to your present career.
➤ You are re-entering the job market after a long absence.
➤ You have been unemployed for more than three months.
➤ Your duties and responsibilities are complicated and require explanation.
➤ You can point to specific accomplishments while on your last two jobs.
➤ You have to compete with younger applicants for the same level position.

See Appendix E for a sample functional resume.

Analytical Resume

The analytical resume stresses your particular skills. It is especially helpful if you are changing career goals but you have obtained necessary skills and qualifications from your present and past jobs. It lets you stress those *skills* and *talents* instead of your work history. Dates are usually omitted, but past jobs and experiences are referred to at some point. Again, you must determine if this approach can best reflect your particular abilities.

See Appendix E for a sample analytical resume.

The three basic types of resumes commonly used are the historical or chronological resume, the functional resume and the analytical resume.

➢   The *historical/chronological resume*, the most traditional and often considered the most effective, presents information by beginning with the most recent experience and going backward in time.
➢   The *functional resume* emphasizes your qualifications and abilities; minimizes irrelevant jobs, employment gaps, and reversals; and maximizes scant work experience.
➢   The *analytical resume* is appropriate if you are changing career goals and stresses *skills* and *talents* instead of past jobs.

What About Creativity?

You may be wondering if these three styles are rather boring. You may want to be somewhat more creative. Think carefully about it. An imaginative or creative approach may be of great benefit, or it may burn you. The positive side of such an approach is that it may set your resume apart from the dozens, hundreds, even thousands of others, thus receiving the attention it deserves.

The negative side of a creative resume is that it might be the reason the employer is looking for to jettison your resume, along with any others that do not appear "normal." Remember that your potential employer is probably *conservative.* Most employers feel a resume is a business matter and should be presented in a businesslike manner.

If you decide to use an imaginative/creative resume, be sure to include all the information any other style would present. If you can do so, you just might be on to something. For example, what could possibly catch a police department's eye quicker than a resume that takes on the appearance of a "Wanted" poster? It might work, but give very serious consideration to such an idea at an entry-level position.

FORMAT THE RESUME

The format is the layout of the information. Decide what to put first, second and third. *Block* your material and use *headings* to guide the reader. If you have recently graduated, your educational background is probably most important and should come first. If you decide to include hobbies and other personal information about yourself, this is usually tucked in at the end.

Plan for margins around the resume, top and bottom as well as both sides. Use white space freely. The format you design should be attractive, businesslike and professional. Actually *design* your format on a sheet of paper. Will you center your identifying information? Have it flush left? Will you use one or two columns for the bulk of the information? Try to format it so all the information goes on *one* page.

The format of your resume should be attractive, businesslike and professional and should allow all the information to fit on *one* page.

WRITE THE RESUME

If possible, use a word processor to write your resume. This will make editing it much easier and will also make updating less painful. The key to writing an effective resume is to use short, action-packed *phrases*.

Short. Omit all unnecessary words. This includes:

  ➢ Personal pronouns: *I, me* and *my.*
  ➢ Articles: *a, an* and *the.*

Action-Packed. Write with *verbs,* not with *nouns.* For example, don't say *conducted an investigation*, say *investigated.* Writing with verbs is also shorter than writing with nouns. Look at the following:

> I conducted an analysis of all the incoming calls to the dispatcher, and I compiled detailed analytical reports based on my analysis.

Twenty-two words. Eliminate the pronouns (*I, my*) and articles (*an, the*) and use verbs instead of nouns. What you'll get is something like the following:

> Analyzed all incoming calls and wrote detailed reports.

Which statement would you rather read? Which conveys an image of the writer as forceful and authoritative?

Phrases. Phrase your writing. Watch where lines end. Avoid hyphenating words at the end of the line. For example, read the following:

> It was a difficult job because my boss was a rat-
> her rigid person.

The key to writing an effective resume is to use short, action-packed *phrases.*

Get the idea? Pay attention to effective ads on television and in print. Notice how the words are strung together for maximum effect. You can do the same in your resume. Try using short "bullet" phrases that begin with active verbs. Strive for variety in your verbs. Here are some that might fit your experience:

achieved	decided	invented	represented
adapted	delegated	investigated	researched
administered	designed	led	reviewed
analyzed	developed	managed	revised
applied	edited	modified	scheduled
approved	educated	monitored	selected
arranged	encouraged	operated	served
assessed	established	organized	set up
assisted	evaluated	planned	solved
built	examined	presented	spoke
chaired	guided	produced	supervised
completed	hired	proved	surveyed
conducted	identified	provided	taught
consulted	improved	published	trained
controlled	increased	recorded	updated
coordinated	inspected	re-designed	wrote

A final suggestion: tailor your resume to fit the job. Dauten and Nelson (1996, p. D3) recommend: "Have at least three or four [resume] versions, each with a different length and emphasis. Then . . . match the version with the preferences of the reader. There is one rule: 'The reader rules.'" They explain how a simple phone call to the company can help you find out which style the reader prefers:

> Picking up a copy of the employment ads from our local newspaper, Mark took the first ad he came to—a job for an accounting clerk. He got human resources and asked for the person who screens resumes. A pleasant, young-sounding man named Glen took the call. He explained that he usually is the one who looks at resumes but that for this job they would be screened by the company's accountant, Karin.
>
> "What kind of resume does Karin like to see?" my partner asked. "Oh, she likes them really short. No baloney. Crisp." Before long, Glen recommended that Mark send a resume directly to Karin and say Glen suggested it.
>
> So, in less than a quarter of an hour, Mark was in a position to send a custom resume directly to the person doing the hiring. He could say in a cover letter that her coworker asked him to do so and mention that his resume is short because that's what he heard she likes.

Once you have written your first draft, let it sit, at least overnight. You will then be ready to edit and polish it.

EDIT AND POLISH YOUR FIRST DRAFT

First drafts simply don't cut it. Continue to work with it until it has the punch you want. Because employers are busy, say as much as you can with as few words as possible. Spend time refining each phrase. Work at developing brief statements that explain clearly and strongly what your education and experience are, what opportunities you've taken advantage of and what qualifications and skills you would bring to the job.

You might consider hiring a professional editor or even a professional resume writer at this point. Using such services will be less expensive if you have completed all the background research, designed a format and written the first draft.

Proofread your draft. Check the spelling of every word. Check every capital letter, every punctuation mark. Then check it again. Better yet, have a friend whose writing skills you respect check it for you. It is very hard to see your own writing errors. Some people find it helpful to proofread by going from right to left in each line, looking at each word. Other people find it helpful to read it backwards, concentrating on each word.

EVALUATE AND REVISE

 Use the form in Appendix D to evaluate your resume. Consider both appearance and content. Grade each category as Excellent, Average or Poor. If a category is poor, decide how to improve it.

A note: Formatting your resume to be sent online and other computer compatibility issues are discussed later in the chapter.

PRINT YOUR RESUME

You are at the final step. Don't blow it now. Have your resume professionally printed or use a high-quality laser printer. Consider the following:

➢ Use 8½-by-11-inch white bond paper and print only on one side.
➢ Buy a quantity of blank paper and matching 9 x 12 envelopes.
➢ Have it printed using black ink.
➢ If necessary, have it slightly reduced in size to assure adequate margins.
➢ Use a type that is easy to read, at least 10-point size.
➢ Do NOT use all capital letters, script, bold or italic print. Use such graphics sparingly or, better yet, not at all.
➢ Most people prefer a *serif* typestyle. Serifs are the little curves or feet added to the edges of letters to make them more readable. This book uses a serif typestyle. *Sans serif* typestyles do give a crisp, clean appearance, but are much harder to read. (Example: Arial Typeface—compare p and p, or A and A.)

Have your resume professionally printed in black ink, on 8½ x 11 inch white bond paper. If necessary, reduce it slightly to assure adequate margins, and use capital letters, script, bold and italic print sparingly.

MAKING IT A "10"

Your resume is a direct reflection of you on paper. Make certain it depicts you as you want—a professional for a professional job. Everything about your resume will say something about *you*. Because employers have to start cutting back the number of finalists, they look for reasons *not* to pursue you as a candidate. For example, typos on a resume have served as a legitimate reason for disregarding an application for any number of positions.

Sometimes, when there are a lot of very good applicants, reasons for getting rid of one resume and keeping another become, at best, arbitrary. What will top off an otherwise excellent resume? It may boil down to the final presentation. Just like a fine meal is made all the better in how it is served, so is a good resume.

Take time to put your resume in an attractive binder or enclose it in an attractive envelope with the name and address of the prospective employer typed. This may say that this particular applicant put that extra effort into the process and should, therefore, be given consideration—an interview. Think about it. Do not, however, use anything slippery or difficult to file. You do not want your resume to stand out from the rest because it is hard to handle.

Rachlin (1995, p. 31) offers the following advice:

> [The] first impression is very important . . . [and] with oftentimes more than 100 application cover letters and resumes awaiting consideration, screeners narrow the pile down quickly in the first step of the process. . . . 'A sloppy resume, or one that's not understandable . . . will just summarily be taken off the stack.' Indeed, the cover letter and resume, the only elements by which screeners initially know you, should be as exemplary as possible.

"I hope they accept a resume written on an apron."

THE COVER LETTER

Never send a resume without a cover letter, even if the employer has asked you to send a resume. Cover letters should be individually typed, addressed to a specific person and company or department, and signed. Anything less will be ineffective.

Keep your cover letter short and to the point. It is a brief personal introduction of the "you" embodied in your resume. Don't repeat resume information. Entice the reader to want to find out more about you. Make clear in your opening paragraph the type of resume submission:

➢ Unsolicited. If so, give a reason for selecting this particular employer.
➢ Written as a referral or from personal contact, for example, "My mechanic told me your department was looking for qualified security officers."
➢ Written in response to a job advertisement.

Send the letter to a specific person and use that individual's title. You can usually get this information by calling the agency or department, asking who is in charge of hiring and asking for the spelling of that person's name and official title. The little time this takes can pay big dividends. Kaplan (1994, p. 3) states:

> Hiring managers use cover letters to screen likely candidates from the unlikely. An enticing letter encourages them to review your resume. Your resume should be very striking, but if your cover letter doesn't tempt the reader, your resume may not get a glance.

As noted by Wilbers (1994, p. D2):

> [The] most personal and crucial of documents: [is] the letter of application. The application letter is your opportunity to breathe some life and personality into the cut-and-dry outline format of your resume. To treat it as nothing more than a cursory note or transmittal letter is to miss an important opportunity to make a statement that sets you apart from the crowd. . . .

- Open by clearly identifying the job you are applying for and stating where you learned about it.
- Highlight especially pertinent qualifications.
- Anticipate and address questions raised by your resume.
- Convey a sense of your personality.
- Offer a positive reason for leaving your present position.
- Consider using an attention-getting opening.
- Make your letter an example of your professionalism and competence.
- Close by asking for an interview and stating where you can be reached. . . . don't say you'll call to schedule [an interview]
- Avoid gimmicks or clumsy attempts at humor.

Always send a resume with a cover letter. Cover letters should be individually typed, short and to the point, addressed to a specific person (including his or her title) and a specific company or department and signed.

An effective format for a cover letter is the full-block style—everything begins at the left margin. The parts of the letter should be as follows:

Your name
Your address (street number, street name, and apartment number, if applicable)
Your city, state and zip code

The date you are writing

The name of the person you are writing to
That person's title
The name of the company/department
The address of the employer

Salutation (Dear . . .):

Opening paragraph—why you are writing.

Second paragraph—provide some intriguing fact about yourself as a lead into your resume.

Concluding paragraph—suggest that you will be calling to arrange an interview or, as Wilbers (p. D2) suggests: "Close by asking for an interview and stating where you can be reached."

Complimentary closing (Sincerely, or Yours truly),

(Skip four lines—sign in this space)

Typed name

Encl: Resume

Notice the spacing between the various sections. Notice the capitalization and the colon following the salutation and the comma following the complimentary closing.

Avoid starting every sentence with "I." *Never* start with: "I am writing this letter to apply for the job I saw advertised in the paper." BORING! Focus on the reader. More effective would be something like this: "Your opening for a police officer advertised in the *Gazette* is of great interest to me." Keep your letter short—one page. Be direct in requesting an interview.

SENDING YOUR RESUME

Mail your cover letter and resume unfolded in a 9x12 envelope. Everybody else's is going to be folded and unfolded and crinkled. Resumes that travel flat are going to look better than all the others. As one employer commented: "When I looked for resumes, the easy ones to find are the ones that are flat. They stand out in the pile of folded resumes." Also, mail your letter and resume to arrive in the employer's office on a Tuesday, Wednesday or Thursday.

One final suggestion—consider using certified mail, with a return receipt requested. Not only will you eliminate those nagging doubts about if it got delivered, but again, it says something to the employer about the kind of person you are. Here is a candidate concerned enough to make *sure* it arrived. That's the kind of a detail a lot of employers are looking for. See Appendix F for a sample cover letter.

HAND DELIVERING YOUR RESUME

It's always a good idea to hand deliver a resume if possible because it allows the employer to associate your name with a face. Dress well and look professional when you deliver your resume. Even if you don't get to the boss, you will make a good impression on the staff person accepting it. These people can have a great deal of influence on their bosses. Don't let your guard down because you aren't dealing directly with upper management. When you drop your material off, it is another opportunity for you to emphasize that you really want the job.

FOLLOW UP

Be sure to follow up. The follow up is another opportunity to prove what kind of person you are—the kind they should hire! A day or two after you have mailed or hand delivered your resume, write a brief letter to the employer. Recognize that the employer will be busy and only a short letter stands a chance of being read.

Confirm that you delivered your resume and thank the employer for the chance to participate in the hiring process. Even if this merely gets stapled to your resume without getting read initially by the employer, or gets forgotten by the employer who might read it, it is something that just might catch the attention of the interview committee when your resume surfaces. If they are looking for reasons to keep some and get rid of others, this could be the reason yours stays in the running. See Appendix F for a sample follow-up letter.

Wendleton and Dauten (1999a, p. J1) assert: "A follow-up letter should sell you, separate you from your competition and state a next step—such as 'I have a few ideas for the job I'd like to discuss with you.'. . . The goal is to keep the dialogue going. . . . Follow-up is one way that employees 'self-select' themselves into jobs."

Hand deliver your resume if possible to enable the employer to match your name with a face. Dress well and look professional when you deliver your resume. A day or two after you have delivered your resume, be sure to follow up by writing a brief letter to the employer confirming the delivery of your resume and thanking the employer for the chance to participate in the hiring process.

But *don't* become a pest. Too many letters or calls can just as easily land you in the "no" pile, identified as overly eager or unable to exercise enough common sense to known when it's "too much."

PREPARING YOUR RESUME FOR CYBERSPACE

Mullins (1994, p. 12) advises:

> Prepare a resume that is compatible with electronic data bases. Many firms rely on computerized resume data bases to generate potential job applicants. Instead of being screened by a person, your resume may be scanned into an electronic data base. The data base uses applicant-tracking software to match key words from a job description with key words in the resume.
>
> To make your resume compatible, you should use a common typeface, such as Courier, which is readily recognized by optical scanning programs. Since some scanning programs have trouble reading italic and boldface type, use these sparingly.

As more companies go online, newer and more immediate ways of submitting resumes are becoming available. "Please e-mail your resume in ASCII format" is becoming an increasingly common statement in job listings. As noted in one article titled "Launching Your Resume into Cyberspace" (1998, p. 30): "ASCII text (pronounced "askee") is the standard, common text language that allows different word-processing applications to read and display the same text information. . . . To create an ASCII resume, type your resume using any word-processing application and then save it as a text-only document." ASCII files or text-only documents do not retain special formatting commands, so to make your resume easy to follow by the recruiter, you need to follow several guidelines (p. 30):

➢ Do not use special characters such as mathematical symbols.
➢ Use your spacebar rather than tabs.
➢ To indent a character or center a heading, use the spacebar.
➢ Use hard carriage returns to insert line breaks, not the word-wrap feature.
➢ Fonts will become whatever your computer uses as its default face and size, so boldface, italics and various sizes will not appear in the ASCII version.
➢ Always run a spell check on your document before you save it as a text-only file.
➢ Instead of bullets, use asterisks or plus signs at the beginning of lines.
➢ Instead of lines, use a series of dashes to separate sections. Don't try to underline text.

A basic rule of thumb is to keep it simple, as if you were using an ancient typewriter with no function keys or fancy formatting devices.

> Make your resume computer compatible by using a common typeface, avoiding use of italic and boldface type and saving the document as a "text only" file.

It is common practice in many companies to scan resumes received via regular mail so they may easily search for keywords and transmit the document to any and all interested parties. Fancy graphics, complicated formatting and general clutter typically do not scan readily, and the resume that will appear on the recruiter's monitor may simply look too messy and unappealing to even warrant a read-through. Potter (1996, p. 22) cautions:

There is an acronym from the computer industry that is worth considering when you are developing your resume: "GIGO." It stands for "garbage in = garbage out." If your resume is disorganized, difficult to read, filled with misspellings, or just plain unimpressive, it won't get any better (or any more impressive) when it is scanned into a computer! If your resume doesn't represent you well on paper, it won't represent you well on a computer screen.

Faxing Your Resume

In the search for ways to get your resume to prospective employers faster, it may be tempting to use a fax machine. And while fax and e-mail submissions are routine and acceptable for many employers, do not assume it is acceptable for all of them. You must ask first before you submit your resume via fax machine. Here is a tip from a human resources specialist concerning this:

> *Don't fax your resume.* Since you know that there is a chance, with almost any available job, that your resume will be scanned and stored in a computer, don't take chances. If you have ever received a fax, you know how bad the printing can be. There are many reasons why a fax can be degraded during transmission, but the point is that a faxed copy is never as good as the original (Potter, p. 20).

FOR MORE HELP

Bookstores and libraries have dozens of texts on resume writing, each with its own particular advice. Other sources of information and assistance may be found online—search under the keyword "resume." The references at the end of this chapter provide a start if you want to go into this topic in more detail or from other perspectives.

CONCLUSION

One of your most important job-seeking tools is the resume. A resume is a brief, well-documented account of your career achievements, which highlights significant aspects of your background and identifies your qualifications for a given job. Its main purpose is to *sell* you to a prospective employer. But don't overdo it. Including too much data is the *number one* fault on resumes. And remember, *always* include a cover letter with your resume, even when delivering the resume in person.

AN INSIDER'S VIEW

THREE KEY OPPORTUNITIES

Jim Clark
Chief
Eden Prairie (Minnesota) Police Department

The hiring process generally affords you a minimum of three opportunities to "catch the eye" of those responsible for hiring:

➢ The resume and application
➢ The written test
➢ The interview

The Resume and Application

The resume and application provide the first, and most lasting, opportunity to present information about yourself. In some cases applicants are eliminated through a resume-screening process. Therefore, take great care in preparing your resume and completing the application.

The best resumes are short, truthful and powerful. Carefully consider the qualifications before beginning to prepare your resume. Most applicants tend to "underinform" or to "overinform." For instance, if the position requires you to be licensed by the state, document your license. Generally you need not provide details of your schooling related to that license.

If, however, the hiring does not specifically require a certain qualification but you know that, after employment, the agency will train you in a specific skill you already have expertise in, make that known. For example, a police department may require only first-aid training meeting the state requirement, but provides Emergency Medical Technician training for all officers after employment. If you are already trained to that level, make it known in your resume. Make certain the information you provide is pertinent to the position. This demonstrates that you investigated the job requirements.

A cover letter lets you show interest also. It should be short (one page), but powerful. It gives you a chance to share something you know about the position that someone else who didn't do their "homework" would not know.

When submitting a resume or application, avoid distractions, for example, letterhead with personal graphics. Another common mistake is including pictures. Often applicants who submit pictures do more harm than good. I once reviewed an application that had a picture attached of the applicant holding a gun.

Simply stated, resumes should be clear, professional in appearance, show a strong interest, be short and focus on the position you are applying for.

The Written Test

The second chance to "catch the eye" of those responsible for hiring is the written test. Unfortunately, being noticed in this environment without being perceived as a "pest" requires some creativity and common sense. In the police written test setting, it is common to test hundreds of applicants at the same time. The written test is most often used as a screening device. Consequently most applicants do not try to "put their best foot forward," believing the only important part is their test score.

That belief is only partially true. In fact, in most departments, police officers and supervisors attend solely to spot and track good applicants. Even though the testing environment appears very hectic, opportunities exist to impress people. The most common mistake I have observed at a written test relates to dress. Apparently most applicants do not believe it is important to look "sharp." Remember, you may not get to talk to someone; consequently, our only memory of you may be what we see. I have memories of people attending a written test without shoes, or wearing torn pants and T-shirts. To me this is unacceptable and demonstrates lack of concern which may spill over to work habits.

My most vivid memory of an applicant goes back approximately eight years when a young man appeared for the testing and was the only applicant in the room with a suit and tie. Needless to say, he was watched. When he was finished and was handing in the test, he made a point to thank our staff at the table for the opportunity to test, and on the way out the door he again thanked the chief of police. His choice of clothing and a simple thank-you on the way out left a very positive impression. It showed his common sense and a very positive personality. Although he did not test extremely high, he tested high enough to be granted an interview and was later hired. The decision to hire him began in earnest when he took that written test.

The Interview

The third and most important opportunity you will have to "catch our eye" is at the interview. If you are among the small group of applicants fortunate enough to earn an interview, approach it like you may never have another chance. The interview process is very difficult for the *interviewers* as well as those being interviewed. The interviewers are subjected to listening to responses to the same questions asked over and over. Consequently, how you look and present yourself may be as important as your answers.

Again dress is very important. However, applicants sometimes make serious mistakes when selecting appropriate clothing. If it is not normal for you to "dress up," consult with someone who knows what it takes to look "sharp." Consultants are available who will work with you, or you may consider a friend employed in a position requiring a professional appearance to help you. Either way, spend some time and money preparing for this very important interview.

Be personally comfortable with your appearance. Try some "dry runs" if time allows. Applicants often spend a lot of time tugging at a tie or simply looking uncomfortable. Also be certain to get several "opinions" from friends or associates regarding your choice of clothing. Tell them to be honest. Your career may depend on it.

Avoid bright colors and unnecessary jewelry that may distract the panel. In a male-dominated profession, women applicants tend to wear more masculine clothing in an attempt to gain an advantage. It is much more appropriate to be yourself.

As you prepare for the interview, learn as much as possible about the city and agency. Visit city hall, the school district offices, the chamber of commerce. Visit with people who live in the city or are clients. Locate and read any books, annual reports or other documents. Talk to current employees. Talk to the personnel department about benefits and salary.

The police officer who wore a suit to his written test and did an outstanding job did the same at the interview. Even though his raw interview skills would not have carried him through, he had outstanding answers. He clearly had researched the city. His answer to why he wanted to work here was that he had a strong interest in working with children and knew our department had a commitment in that area. In fact, he told us, "I talked with several people who were very impressed with your program that allows police officers to go on camping trips with school groups." Clearly he had done his homework and discovered this little-known fact. Today he is one of our school-liaison officers and accompanies children on these trips. I later learned his research was not an accident. It was well planned and required commitment. He actually walked through neighborhoods on a Sunday afternoon and visited with anyone willing to talk to him.

On the other hand, applicants arrive at the interview totally unprepared. One recent applicant, when asked if he knew anything about our city, responded that he knew the population was 29,000. The actual population is nearly 40,000. He obviously got the 29,000 figure from the outdated sign displayed as you enter the city on the interstate freeway. He clearly had made no commitment.

Arrive for the interview at least 15 minutes early if possible, but never arrive late. As you wait your turn, employees may pass in the lobby. I would strongly suggest a simple smile and hello. They may be on the interview panel, and this may give you an edge. Opinions differ on what time slot you should pick—near the beginning, the middle or end. I am not certain there is a perfect time; however, avoid being first or in the first third. If you can select, pick a time in the early morning. Most panels are more alert and, consequently, better listeners then.

As you are introduced to the panel, try to remember names and greet each with a handshake. A simple handshake generally tells something about you. I would suggest a firm, but not overpowering, handshake. Remember, we expect you to be nervous, but control your nerves so you don't lose control. Most questions are simple, designed to help us learn about you, the "person." Most interviews do not get into your education or experience. Most of that is on your resume. You may, however, be asked questions to judge the accuracy of your resume.

Some thoughtfulness, without long delay, is very appropriate. Asking to have a question repeated is also appropriate. If you ask for repetition very often, however, your listening skills may be questioned. Avoid asking inappropriate questions. In one case an applicant asked before the interview began what type of guns we carried. I can honestly say, I did not listen to the remainder of that interview.

The panel wants to know about the real you—a challenge to accomplish in one-half hour. Take advantage of questions and "feed" us more information without being overly obvious. Most questions are not designed with a right or wrong answer. Also, do not bring any materials with you unless requested. All too often a notebook becomes something to fidget with and, thus, a distraction.

Remember during an interview, time is generally a premium; consequently, use it well. Applicants, given the opportunity, ask questions about pay, benefits, uniforms and the like that could best be asked at another time or before the interview by calling the personnel department. And as you leave the interview, a parting handshake and thank-you can be very important memories for the panel.

In Conclusion

Employment in this job market takes work. You must do research, spend some money and invest some time. Be powerful, but to the point, short and truthful. Most important, learn everything you can about the position, the hiring agency and the clients served. It is not always what you learn, but the fact that you are willing to make an investment in your career that demonstrates character.

———————

Jim Clark is the chief of police for the City of Eden Prairie, Minnesota. With 24 years' experience, Chief Clark has worked his way up through the ranks, taking full advantage of opportunities to prepare himself for the position of chief of police with one of Minnesota's most rapidly developing suburbs.

AN INSIDER'S VIEW

THE RESUME: A BALANCE OF MODESTY AND SELF-CONFIDENCE

Gil Kerlikowske
Police Commissioner
Buffalo (New York) Police Department

The law enforcement field offers a wide variety of employment opportunities. Police agencies operate with a number of specialists in areas such as finance, computer technology, planning and education as well as enforcement officers. Having hired individuals for these positions has given me an opportunity to review thousands of resumes. I have also served on search committees for CEOs. Nothing can be of more importance than the quality of the application and resume submitted.

The cover letter should be specific to the individual job you are interested in. Photocopies and generic cover letters are an automatic turn-off to reviewers. The letter should be addressed to an individual, not "Personnel Department" or another title. Match your qualifications to those requested in the advertisement and keep the letter to one page. A balance between modesty and self-confidence is what you are striving for. If the letter shouts out how outstanding you are, the reviewer might question your sincerity to be a team member. On the other hand, you want to stand out from the hundreds of other applicants.

There are several types of resumes and numerous books to guide you in developing your individual resume. If you have experience in the criminal justice field and are interested in a more senior position, I would recommend a style that illustrates experience and accomplishments. An applicant who is new to the field and is looking for an entry-level position should opt for a style that emphasizes their interest, education and dedication.

The resume should also *fit the specific qualifications* the job requires. *Length* depends upon your experience and age. One to two pages is sufficient for entry-level positions and no more than four to five pages for management and executive positions. Education and specialized training (dates, course titles and degrees, of course) in an easily read style are a must. Where they are included is another style question; however, large type headings for Education, Experience, Training, etc. make it easy to scan the resume and check off important qualifications.

If you do not meet minimum qualifications, it is *generally* not worth your effort to apply for the position. Individual jobs just have too many applicants who *do* meet the requirements. However, if you know other positions you may be qualified for are going to become open, I suggest you *meet with someone* in that division to discuss your interest. Having someone in the department know your name and interest may be the extra push that helps you land the job you want in the future.

One automatic disqualifier for me has always been information that is not completely accurate. Most employers are careful to make sure individuals have the degrees and experience they claim. Areas of experience are more subjective. The rule of thumb is to be cautious in stating your qualifications. For example, if you once filled in for a crime prevention officer at a community meeting, do not cite experience as a crime prevention specialist.

Finally, photographs, copies of diplomas and other material are not necessary in an initial application. After you make the cut, those items may be requested. My personal feeling is that newspaper and magazine articles about you are self-serving. In the second or third phase of the employment process these materials, if they are focused on a program or unit you worked in or managed, are acceptable.

The employment process is different in every locality and can be frustrating and time-consuming. Professionalism and perseverance will be your greatest allies in finding the job you desire. And remember, nothing can be of more importance than the quality of the application and resume submitted.

Gil Kerlikowske is the police commissioner for the Buffalo (New York) Police Department and has 26 years' experience in criminal justice. Prior to working in New York, Commissioner Kerlikowske was the chief of police in Fort Pierce, Florida, for four years. He holds an M.A. in Criminal Justice.

MIND STRETCHES

1. Imagine you have been assigned the task of reducing an extremely large pile of resumes to a more workable number. Regardless of the position, what are five reasons you can think of to get rid of applications right away?

2. What are three things you might look for that would make a resume stand out as being worth taking time to look at further?

3. Paint with words the picture you want your resume to make. Use three words. Use six words.

4. How can you liven up your resume?

5. What might be dangerous about preparing a resume that is too creative? What benefits might result?

6. What attributes do you have that will impress an employer?

7. What concerns do you have about your qualifications that you will need to consider in preparing your resume?

8. What are five power verbs you associate with yourself?

9. Which resume style could work best for you? Why?

10. What unique ways can you present your resume?

REFERENCES

Alderman, Lesley. "How to Land a Job Now, Whether You Are Starting Out or Starting Over." *Money,* June 1995, pp. 173–175.

Corwen, Leonard. *Your Resume: Key to a Better Job.* New York: Arco, 1988.

Dauten, Dale and Nelson, Mark. "A Little Research by Phone May Reveal How to Tailor Your Resume to the Job." (Minneapolis/St. Paul) *Star Tribune,* July 14, 1996, p. D3.

Dauten, Dale and Nelson, Mark. "To Keep (or to Get) a Job, Try Thinking, Acting Young." (Minneapolis/St. Paul) *Star Tribune,* December 28, 1997, p. D5.

Kaplan, Robbie Miller. *Sure-Hire Cover Letters.* New York: American Management Association, 1994.

Kennedy, Joyce Lain. "Tips From the Pros on Writing Resumes." (Minneapolis/St. Paul) *Star Tribune,* February 5, 1995, p. J1.

"Launching Your Resume into Cyberspace." *Successful Meetings,* July 1998, pp. 30–31.

Mullins, Terry. "Search Skills: How to Land a Job." *Psychology Today,* September/October 1994, pp. 12–13.

Potter, Ray. *Electronic Resumes That Get Jobs.* New York: MacMillan, 1996.

Rachlin, Harvey. "Cover Letters and Resumes." Part of "The Hiring of a Police Chief." *Law and Order,* March 1995, pp. 31–33.

Wendleton, Kate and Dauten, Dale. "Good Follow-Up Ensures a Successful Hunt." (Minneapolis/St. Paul) *Star Tribune*, April 18, 1999a, p. J1.

Wendleton, Kate and Dauten, Dale. "Tailor Resume to Highlight Skills You Want Noticed, Not Red Flags." (Minneapolis/St. Paul) *Star Tribune*, January 31, 1999b, p. D4.

Wilbers, Stephen. "Effective Writing: Well-Written Letter Can Open Door to Interview." (Minneapolis/St. Paul) *Star Tribune,* September 23, 1994, p. D2.

CHAPTER 10

PREPARING FOR NOT GETTING THE JOB

Accept that some days you're the pigeon and some days you're the statue.

—Roger C. Anderson

Do You Know

➤ What you can do to prepare for and effectively handle rejection in your job search?
➤ Why a support system is beneficial?
➤ The importance of maintaining a positive attitude?
➤ What feelings follow the sequential reaction to loss and change?
➤ What feelings follow the transition curve?

INTRODUCTION

It's hard to get a job in these fields! It is most unusual for a person to get the first job they apply for. And because the job market today is changing so rapidly and downsizing is more prevalent than ever, you will find an increasing number of people competing for work. You should gain comfort in knowing that the vast majority of successful applicants were eventually successful because they had a lot of experience in the application process. Many people, in any negative situation, fail to take advantage of a great opportunity to gain from it. Energy *is* present, albeit uncomfortable, and can be rechanneled in a positive direction.

While the majority of this book deals with how to get a job, this brief but important chapter deals with *not* getting a job—a realistic part of any job search. You need to know how to deal with failure in order to continue on. You may want to reread this chapter when you get that first, almost inevitable, rejection. It should assure you to know that your feelings are normal and that you need to go forward.

HANDLING REJECTION

Consider the following adages:

> *Failure is not falling down; it is remaining there when you have fallen.*
> *Our greatest glory is not in never falling, but rising every time we fall. —Confucius*
> *He who dares nothing need hope for nothing.*
> *The only time you mustn't fall is the last time you try. —Charles F. Kettering*

You may hear similar sentiments following a less-than-successful interview:

> There must be something better around the corner.
> They didn't deserve you. Besides, they're probably all jerks anyway.
> You can do better than that place.

These statements may be true, and you will no doubt hear them from your friends and family. After all, they want to support you. You will agree, of course, but inside you may be thinking things like:

> I knew I could never get that job.
> I'm no good.
> Everyone else is better than me.
> I'll never get a job.
> I should never have gone into this profession.
> Etc., etc., etc., etc.

If you are not careful, this negative "self-talk" can become overwhelming, acting as a self-fulfilling prophecy. If you get to the point that *you* don't believe in yourself, why should a *potential employer* believe in you? Remember, success comes in "cans"—failure comes in "can'ts."

Tell yourself everyone must take their share of rejection. Sure, some take a little more, some take a little less, but everyone takes it. It's simply part of the package of looking for a job. If you understand ahead of time the reality of rejection and are prepared for it, when the first one hits you, it's not likely to knock you down so hard. And if you're one of those fortunate few who hears "yes" on the first try, way to go! You beat the odds on this one. For the rest of us, each "no" we hear brings us one step closer to that "yes". . . as long as we don't give up. Keep in mind: It takes an average of two years to land an entry-level job in law enforcement.

It has been said the average job seeker must send out ten resumes to get one interview, and that it takes an average of ten interviews to get one job offer. If you do the math, you'll see that it takes the average person a hundred resumes to receive one job offer. That's 99 "nos" for every one "yes"! So don't get discouraged—the "yes" will come.

 Try this exercise: Take a deck of standard playing cards and shuffle them well. Pretend every face card is a job interview and that one of them, say the queen of hearts, is a job *offer* following a dynamite interview. The rest of the deck (aces through tens) are flat-out "nos." With the deck facedown and starting with the top card, flip over cards until you get an interview. How many flips did it take? Flip again until your next interview. Try this several times and you'll get the picture. Sometimes you get an interview on the first flip; sometimes it takes seventeen flips and then you get four interviews in a row—and the queen of hearts is one of them! Or she could be at the bottom of the deck, under 51 rejections. But she's there. If you stop flipping after the fourth, fourteenth or even forty-fourth "no," you'll never get to her.

No one ever said job hunting was easy. For all practical purposes, job hunting will have to be a full-time job itself, at least for a while. If it isn't full-time timewise, it will be energywise. But, in the beginning, you'll probably believe rejection could never happen to you.

It's similar to the "It Can Never Happen to Me" syndrome frequently heard in discussions of officer safety. The idea is that an officer's daily existence would be too difficult if he or she thought that harm or perhaps death was lurking around every corner. Officers instinctively develop the "It Can Never Happen to Me" attitude in order to continue on with their day-to-day lives. To a certain degree it helps prevent them from becoming hopelessly paranoid. Problems arise, however, when all caution is thrown to the wind. Police, corrections and security officers must accept the natural risks associated with their jobs, but they must also be prepared. They must be realistic. Similarly, job applicants must balance the risks. If you know you're going to be rejected, why even try? This is what happens to some job seekers who start out feeling they will never be rejected. Two or three rejections turn them into defeatists who simply go through the motions.

Part of life is competing for what you want. No one can always be number one. The top doesn't have that much room. Accept this and decide that doing your best is what it's all about. Eventually this *will* pay off. You will get where you want to be. Accepting the facts of job seeking from the start will keep you from getting overwhelmed when rejections are received. Goulston and Goldberg (1998, p. 45) suggest: "Take things seriously, not personally."

Consider the applicant who had become so defeated after several "thanks but no thanks" letters that when he woke up on the morning of an interview and found that it was raining, the weather became the last straw. He decided to stay in bed. This would-be police officer made it easy for the employer to weed out one more applicant. Who does this applicant really have to blame for this failure?

Success is getting up one more time than you fall down. Make up your mind right now to accept the facts of job seeking.

- ➢ Fact #1: Criminal justice and security are *very* popular, sought-after, competitive jobs.
- ➢ Fact #2: You're up against many, many applicants.
- ➢ Fact #3: Eventually you will get hired IF you're right for the job.

The benefit of having to repeat the application process is that you will improve each time. The downside is that it can get you down. The choice is *yours*.

> To prepare for and effectively handle rejection in your job search, be aware that it does happen to just about everyone and that the only ones who fail are the ones who stop trying. Avoid negative self-talk and never lose faith in yourself. Each "no" brings you closer to a "yes."

REMAINING POSITIVE

You can and, in fact, must turn the negative energy from rejection into positive momentum. Rather than giving up, become determined to strive that much harder, knowing you are stronger and more polished. How does that saying go? *That which doesn't kill me makes me stronger.* It's what makes a boxer or any other professional athlete more determined—what's often referred to as "having the heart of a champion." No one likes to be turned down, especially for a desperately wanted job. But it is bound to happen, and it is going to sting. It does not get any easier the second, third or sixth time. In fact, the more you are turned down, the heavier it may weigh on you.

Maintain a positive attitude. To deal most effectively with that most common part of job hunting—the rejection—keep the following basics in mind:

➤   Go into the process understanding you probably will have to try for several jobs. With so many applicants, the odds are against you.

➤   Not getting this job does not mean you deserve to be banished from planet Earth. It simply means you did not get this one job.

➤   Another job is just around the corner (trite, but true). Avoid the temptation to believe that a particular job is your one-and-only dream job.

➤   If you need help, *ask for it!* No law says you must go it alone. If you are not confident about your job-seeking skills, seek help. If you get depressed, seek help. Just ask—not always easy for officer-types!

➤   Most important—keep trying. You've come this far. It is no time to give up. *Listen* when everyone tells you that you can get a job. You can. Just give yourself time. As it has been said: "You just have to cast your net real wide and kiss a lot of frogs before the prince shows up."

Take advantage of everyone else's understanding of rejection and build a support system from the start. It really helps to talk, and you might be surprised by how many people have experienced similar rejection. Besides, there *is* strength in numbers.

> Support systems are valuable because they allow you to talk out your frustrations and realize you are not the only one who has ever felt rejection—everyone else has experienced it too. People in your support system may be able to share what worked for them in getting past their rejection.

Do not be afraid to get support and help if you need it—professional or otherwise. To get frustrated and disheartened is normal. Do not let it get the best of you. Negative feelings can become overwhelming, and they can also be self-perpetuating. Feeling depressed and gloomy often leads to deeper feelings of depression and gloominess. Besides not feeling good, they can sap so much of your energy that your interview skills become less than adequate, and you will not perform as you need to.

Employers are very aware of how much competition you have—they have to sit through all those interviews! What would happen if you went into your tenth interview all worn out and depressed and the next person after you was upbeat and positive because it was only their first interview? Presenting the same energy and freshness during your tenth interview that you possessed at your first one will not only leave a positive impression on the interviewer but will help fuel positive feelings in yourself. You have a choice: You can come out of the interview feeling even worse because you *knew* you were mopey and unenthusiastic, or you can come out feeling great because you gave it your best shot. In short, if you do not deal with the uncomfortable feelings that go along with rejection, you will eventually come to believe that you do not deserve to be hired, and it will show. Pick up and press on.

> Remaining positive is crucial to a successful job search. A positive attitude leaves a favorable impression on an employer, and it helps fuel positive feelings in yourself.

LEARNING FROM THE PROCESS

Ask prospective employers who turned you down what could have made a difference. If approached in a non-threatening way, people will usually be honest and open. As one employer states: "I was impressed several times by young applicants who, after being turned down for a job, called and made an appointment to visit with me to discuss their job-hunting strategies. I even ended up hiring a couple of them."

NORMAL REACTION TO LOSS

The fear of the unknown is always the worst. Since it helps to know what to expect, here's a brief explanation of what many people experience when they lose something (such as a death in the family, a ruined relationship or a lost job opportunity). Called the *sequential reaction to loss and change*, it describes how many people *normally* act when they lose something important. If you get a rejection, you may feel the following, in roughly this order:

➢ Denial
➢ Anger
➢ Sadness
➢ Hopelessness
➢ Disorganization
➢ Withdrawal
➢ Reorganization

This sequential reaction to loss and change is illustrated in Figure 10-1.

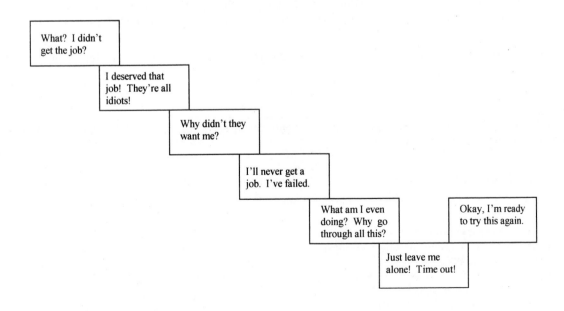

FIGURE 10-1   Sequential Reaction to Loss and Change

Denial. This is the "It can never happen to me" phase. It hasn't quite sunk in yet that you didn't get the job. Denial helps because it keeps you from getting too hurt from rejection(s). It can be harmful, however, if you don't move on or get too hung up on that rejection (possibly thinking that this is the only job in the world for you).

Anger. Once you have accepted the rejection, the understandable response is anger. "I wanted that job! I deserved that job! They aren't going to get away with this! The process is unfair!" These things may be true, but the fact is you did not get the job. Staying angry too long will, at best, depress you and, at worst, drive you to do something you may later regret, like writing a nasty letter, making a nasty phone call or paying a hostile visit to the employer.

Sadness. After the anger subsides, you may feel sad. Sadness can run from a mild case of the blues to a bout with deep depression. It depends on many factors and reflects the absolute need of a strong support system as you seek work. Don't beat up on yourself too much if you feel down. Who doesn't after rejection? Rather than fight it, accept it, draw some energy from it, and move on. If it becomes overwhelming to the point of your being unable to continue the job search, or if it begins to seriously affect other areas of your life, get help.

Hopelessness. Hopelessness may occur as the feelings of anger and depression subside. The hopelessness may seem overwhelming, but it is a normal part of adapting to rejection. The natural assumption after one or more employers reject you is that you are unemployable. No one wants you. This is not true. It simply means those jobs did not work out. You have to keep going, which isn't always easy because of the natural progression of feelings.

Disorganization. At this point you may want to continue on, but nothing seems to fit anymore. You find it difficult to organize your time or your thoughts. You spend time haphazardly reading help-wanted ads and making futile attempts to schedule a productive day. Frustration may set in, and you may simply give up.

Withdrawal. Wanting to give up or withdraw is also natural. It is understandable that you are frustrated, uncomfortable and wanting to simply quit. This is how your psyche lets you rest, regroup and get ready to jump into the battle again. Rather than fight the desire to withdraw, help it along. Get away from job hunting for a while. Go to a movie, take a long walk or even go on a vacation. Retreat and regroup. Do not, however, withdraw by skipping scheduled interviews or by showing up and not putting forth your best effort. If you need a break, take it.

Reorganization. At last! You have worked through the normal feelings associated with being rejected. You're now ready to get back out there and get that job.

The progression of feelings involved in the sequential reaction to loss and change are denial, anger, sadness, hopelessness, disorganization, withdrawal and, finally, reorganization.

According to Nathan and Hill (1992, p. 30), many other people go through a somewhat different set of feelings, a pattern they refer to as *the transition curve,* which is characterized by the following chain of reactions:

Shock, denial: Unable to believe that it has happened. 'You're joking!' A feeling of emptiness, perhaps numbness.
Euphoria: Making the best of it, and minimising the reality of the change. 'Now I've got time to . . . paint the house, take a holiday . . .—I didn't like the job anyway.'
Pining: Hoping that the job will come back—an unrealistic expectation that the next job will be exactly the same.
Anger: Blaming someone—'I never could work with him (my boss) anyway.' 'They should have . . .'
Guilt: Self-blame—'They chose me because I wasn't up to it/did something wrong.'
Apathy: A sense of powerlessness and hopelessness as the reality sinks in.
Acceptance: Letting go of the past, and the emergence of a new energy.

Nathan and Hill's transition curve is illustrated in Figure 10-2.

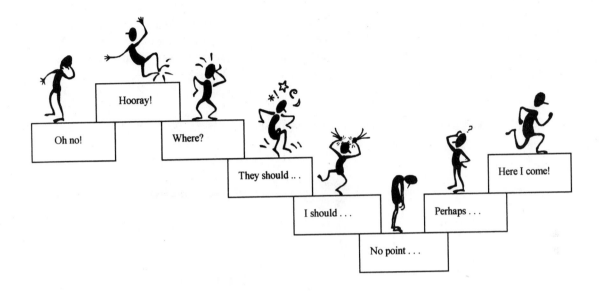

FIGURE 10-2   **The Transition Curve**

SOURCE: Robert Nathan and Linda Hill. *Career Counseling,* p. 30, © 1992 by Sage Publications, Inc. Reprinted by permission of Sage Publications, Inc.

Another common progression of feelings following rejection are those of the transition curve, namely, shock or denial, euphoria, pining, anger, guilt, apathy and acceptance.

No matter what feelings you experience following rejection, how long it takes you to work through the negative feelings depends on how serious the rejection is. The first rejection is not as bad as the second. The more rejections, or the more important a job is to you, the more extreme your reactions may be. Remember: Accept the inevitable and understand that this is how it is going to feel. There is strength in self-awareness. As George Bernard Shaw says: "Better keep yourself clean and bright; you are the window through which you must see the world."

Mullins (1994, p. 13) offers this good advice:

> **Don't give up.** Job hunting is psychologically challenging. You will face obstacles, setbacks, and rejections. Some people you encounter in your search will be unfeeling; a few will be cruel. You will get discouraged and you will be tempted to quit looking. However, the economy is creating hundreds of thousands of new jobs every month. . . . Many jobs being created are challenging and pay well. One can be yours, but only if you didn't give up wanting it.

CONCLUSION

The knowledgeable, prepared applicant understands and accepts that *everybody* experiences these negative feelings when they lose something they want. To prepare for and effectively handle rejection in your job search, be aware that it does happen to just about everyone and that the only ones who fail are the ones who stop trying. Avoid negative self-talk and never lose faith in yourself. Each "no" brings you closer to a "yes." But whatever setbacks you may experience, "nos" you may hear or rejection you may feel, DO NOT GIVE UP!

You may be disappointed if you fail, but you are doomed if you don't try.

—*Beverly Sills*

AN INSIDER'S VIEW

EACH FAILURE IS ONE STEP CLOSER TO SUCCESS

Timothy J. Thompson
Director of Public Safety and Parking Services
University of St. Thomas, St. Paul, Minnesota

Accomplishing your employment objective is often not in your control. Any decision to hire involves many factors. Since you're looking at the situation of *not* getting the job offer, let's analyze the hiring process to understand why you sometimes don't have control. As discussed in previous chapters, the hiring process involves three main areas:

➤ Education—what you've been taught.
➤ Work history—what you've done.
➤ The interview—how you appear.

Additionally, one other component of the hiring process is a vital factor in the employment selection: *who* is doing the hiring. If you know someone involved in the hiring process or are related to the president of the company, your chances of getting the job are obviously many times better than those without such connections.

How the hiring is done and by whom often differs greatly from agency to agency and firm to firm, making it hard for applicants. To be properly prepared, you must research the hiring process as well as the position. The process may involve a simple application to a company president or personnel manager or may be much more complex, involving panels and boards. Because the process is not uniform, the people doing the hiring are not always proficient at employee selection. Many do not have practical experience to adequately evaluate the ability and qualifications of applicants. Police commissions and selection boards are good examples of such lack of practical experience. All too often the groups doing the hiring are made up largely of community lay people, lacking professional credentials in the field for which applicants are applying. Even city managers and personnel directors have not always had enough experience in hiring to make good choices.

So where does this leave you? Well, when the candidates appear on paper to be equally qualified, that is, their educational credentials and work history are very similar, the selection comes down to an interview and personalities. With so many variables operating, no one can pick a favorite. But if you have an outstanding resume, you can make yourself appear more qualified than the rest. How? Consider these guidelines.

Your resume should reflect information pertinent to the position for which you are applying. Entry-level positions should generally be a page or two, tops, but should contain information necessary to qualify for the position. Employers have neither the time nor the interest to read lengthy resumes for entry-level positions. In these cases, the cover letter will help sell your qualifications.

For nonentry-level positions where prior experience is desired or required, additional information can be added to the resume and cover letter. This information should include specific experiences and accomplishments but, again, should be brief. If you are applying for a management position, your resume can, and in some cases should, include as much information as possible regarding your background, education, experiences and achievements. However, this information should be compiled in an easy-to-read format with appropriate headings and short paragraphs. Employers seeking managers want to know as much about the applicant as possible before the interview. This is why telephone interviews are becoming more popular with personnel recruiters. It is better to have the information already prepared on your resume than to have to think about it when someone calls. And your chance of getting that call improves the more the recruiter is impressed with your submitted credentials.

I have discovered that my ability to conduct interviews and effectively examine applicants' backgrounds to determine job suitability has dramatically increased with experience. Unfortunately, many management people, selection boards, firms and the like lack adequate experience to hire effectively. It is no wonder many people are performing jobs for which they are unsuited. It is also no wonder that perhaps you and your talent are being overlooked. Even when you have done all your homework, researched each position, individualized your application and resume for the job, looked for inside people to help and prepared for each interview separately, you still may not get the position.

It is easy to become frustrated, bitter and resentful when you have worked so hard to prepare and you feel so confident in your ability to perform the job—given the chance. Remember, you are seeking employment in extremely popular fields, and you have plenty of competition. You do not have to give up, however. You *will* get a job that is right for you. And it may come when you least expect it. I know how frustrating it is to get rejection letters. I have a file full of them. I want to share from my experience some do's and don'ts related to the feelings of frustration and hopelessness involved in being rejected for a job.

DO

➢ Do develop a support system. It is important to have an avenue to vent your feelings. Find an understanding friend who will listen while you express these feelings.

➢ Keep networking. The more people you know, the better your chances of learning about job openings. Often when you least expect it, a job will appear. Just ask some friends and acquaintances how they got their jobs.

➢ Look for alternatives. Often people get tunnel vision when looking for jobs, limiting themselves to one particular area when in fact they have abilities in many areas. You may want to be a police officer, but what about other possibilities such as being a U.S. Marshal, a state fraud enforcement officer, a postal inspector, an FAA enforcement officer, an FBI secret service agent and on and on.

➢ Consider relocating as an option if possible.

➢ Use the Internet for your job search.

DON'T

> ➤ Don't spend every minute worrying about your job situation. Take time for other things, especially recreation. Remember, jobs often appear when you least expect.
>
> ➤ Don't give up. Talk with friends. Acquaint yourself with other people in your chosen field. Join associations.
>
> ➤ Don't make compulsive decisions. This is no time to make major changes in either your employment situation or your lifestyle. Do not, for example, pack up and move to Florida because you believe more job opportunities exist there, unless you really want to live in Florida. Nor should you buy a house or new car because you think it will make you feel better.

Hang in there. Press on. You *can* and *will* land that job.

Timothy J. Thompson is the associate director of administration and auxiliary services and the director of public safety and parking services for the University of St. Thomas in St. Paul, Minnesota. He is also a Minnesota manager and investigative consultant with Verifications Incorporated in Minneapolis, Minnesota. Prior employment includes the director of human resources and corporate relations and arena manager for the Minnesota Timberwolves professional basketball team; the director of security and risk manager for Canterbury Downs Racetrack in Shakopee, Minnesota; special agent with the Thoroughbred Racing Protective Bureau in Fairhill, Maryland; director of public safety and chief of police for St. Bonifacius and Minnesota Department of Public Safety; chief of police and emergency preparedness director for the City of Winsted, Minnesota; police officer and investigator for the City of Deephaven, Minnesota and a police officer at the Minneapolis/St. Paul International Airport Police Department.

Mr. Thompson's educational background includes the Metropolitan State University in Minneapolis, Minnesota; Normandale Community College, Bloomington, Minnesota; Northwestern Electronics Institute, St. Paul, Minnesota and the Emergency Management Institute, Emmitsbury, Maryland. He has also completed FBI Academy Training in instructor development. His past and present certifications include State of Minnesota licensed police officer, licensed private detective and certified emergency management official; certified police classroom instructor and certified police firearms instructor. Mr. Thompson is also a member of numerous associations and councils, including the International Association of Chiefs of Police, the American Society for Industrial Security, the Minnesota Emergency Management Association and the International Association of Campus Law Enforcement Administrators.

AN INSIDER'S VIEW

LIFE'S GREATEST REWARDS CAN'T BE MEASURED IN DOLLARS AND CENTS

Penny A. Parrish

Public Information Officer, Minneapolis (Minnesota) Police Department
Parrish Institute of Law Enforcement and Media

Seven years ago I was a journalist. I was in charge of a television newsroom in a major market. Today, I am a member of the Minneapolis Police Department (MPD). It was quite a career change. It came about as the result of a ride-along. I went out with an officer who provided a first-hand look at modern policing. By the end of the shift, I was hooked. I knew I wanted to be a part of the law enforcement community.

I went back to college and took law enforcement classes while continuing my TV career. I even did an internship with the MPD. After three years of night school, I received my degree. The big question: what was I going to do with it? I was 40-something years old—not the typical age of a rookie cop. The idea of chasing criminals up and down alleys was beyond what my body and mind could fathom. But I'd worked hard for that degree. There had to be some way to be part of this interesting and exciting new world I'd discovered.

Time, or the lack of it, became a big factor in my career decision. I needed time to search for a position, but my current job was very demanding. After much soul-searching, I decided to leave TV news and open up my own business to assist law enforcement on media issues. It was the first time in my life that I'd walked away from a paycheck. It was a *nice* paycheck and, believe me, it wasn't easy. But I bought a home computer, had stationery and business cards printed and began contacting law enforcement agencies. I got a couple of nibbles and did a few seminars, but overall I was rejected. On paper, I had great credentials. In reality, I had no policing experience. The savings account dwindled.

I was rescued by a phone call. The MPD, which had never had a public information officer (PIO), was in the process of creating that position. The department wanted a civilian with a media background who also had an education in law enforcement. I applied, and after months of applications and interviews, I got the job. It's what I'm doing now.

Every day I talk to reporters doing their beat checks and I also touch base with every unit and precinct looking for stories. I do the usual press releases on murders and mayhem, but I also try to get the "good police work" stories out. It's important for the citizens to know that the MPD is made up of outstanding officers who strive to make this city safe.

My private business continues to grow. With the duties I fulfill at the MPD, I now have that "police experience" I was lacking before. I have done several workshops and seminars on local, state and national levels. I also continue to work with the FBI on several projects.

Law enforcement can be an exciting and fulfilling career, but you don't have to be a sworn officer to reap the rewards. The MPD is "civilianizing" more and more positions, from media specialists to firearms examiners to computer technicians. These positions are no less crucial to a department than those performed by people wearing a badge.

Sometimes you have to take a chance to get where you want to go. And sometimes you have to work in a job that bridges where you came from and where you want to end up. The important thing is that with every job change, you gain experience that can be applied to your final destination. I took my rejection to heart. I learned from it and listened to what people told me: you don't have the law enforcement tie-in. I found a way to fill that gap. I not only got the experience I needed, I found a position with an incredible police department.

As to that savings account, it's no longer dwindling, but it's not growing either. There was a *lot* more money in TV news, but sometimes life's greatest rewards can't be measured in dollars and cents. I'm living proof of that.

Penny A. Parrish is a public information officer with the Minneapolis (Minnesota) Police Department and runs her own business, the Parrish Institute of Law Enforcement and Media. She has held her current position for six years after spending a decade working in television news. Ms. Parrish holds a BA in Speech and Theater from North Central College, an MEd in Education and the Media from the University of South Florida and an AAS in Law Enforcement from Normandale Community College. She likes to spend her spare time gardening, reading and doing photography.

⟨?⟩ MIND STRETCHES

1.   What benefits can come from *not* getting a job?

2.   Why is it helpful to understand the sequential reaction to loss and change and the transition curve?

3.   Why is it harmful to ignore negative feelings arising from a rejection to an application?

4.   Why would someone ignore these feelings?

5.   Do you think applicants for criminal justice or security jobs are less likely to deal with their feelings? Why?

6.   Why do you think unsuccessful candidates might lash out at an employer who didn't hire them? Could this ever be successful?

7.   Is there ever one perfect job?

8.   Is there danger in believing there *is* one perfect job?

9.   Who is included in your support system? How can you best use them?

10.   Can you think of "failures" or "losses" in your life that actually benefited you?

REFERENCES

Goulston, Mark and Goldberg, Phillip. *Get Out of Your Own Way*. Perigree, 1998.

Mullins, Terry. "Search Skills: How to Land a Job." *Psychology Today,* September/October 1994, pp. 12–13.

Nathan, Robert and Hill, Linda. *Career Counseling.* Newbury Park, CA: Sage Publications, 1992.

SECTION THREE

JOB-SEEKING STRATEGIES

A wise man will make more opportunities than he finds.

—*Francis Bacon*

You've decided what you're looking for in a career. You've also closely examined your personal characteristics and have found a fit. You've created an impressive resume to demonstrate that fit to potential employers. And you're prepared to handle rejections. You're ready. Where to find jobs and how to get them is the focus of this section. Chapter 11 looks at the application process. It takes you through various strategies for locating job openings and making your availability and interest known. It discusses the importance of the application form and the role of your resume, it and reviews the testing process.

If all goes well to this point, you will be invited for a personal interview. The basics of presenting yourself for an interview are the focus of Chapter 12—how to dress, communicate and follow up. Chapter 13 takes a closer look at the all-important interview process and what to expect from it.

Figure S3 illustrates the steps you've already completed and what lies ahead.

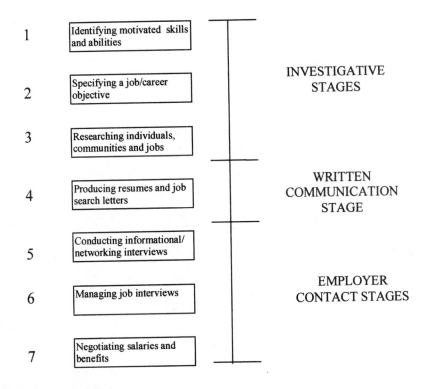

FIGURE S3   Job-search Steps

SOURCE: Ronald L. Krannich. *Change Your Job, Change Your Life*, 5th ed. Manassas Park, VA: Impact Publications, 1995, p. 101. Reprinted by permission.

CHAPTER 11

THE APPLICATION PROCESS:
FINDING AND APPLYING FOR JOBS

(1) Regard job hunting as a real job—and expect that it, like any other job, demands time, persistence, and discipline. (2) Recognize that while you can get a good job through ads or employment agencies, competition for jobs that are advertised tends to be fierce. (3) Apply directly to an employer even without any hint there is a job opening. Positions constantly become available and it's wise to be on a good list. (4) Try to get as many job interviews as you can and concentrate on smaller firms. (5) If you can see a layoff coming, start looking for a job while you are still working. (6) Expect to be discouraged. Guard against anger, apathy, or feeling defeated.

—Sylvia Porter

Do You Know

➢ What you must identify before beginning your job search and how many hours you should spend each week looking for work?
➢ Which ads to read in the classified section of the paper and which papers to look in?
➢ What specialized periodicals to review?
➢ How the Internet can help?
➢ The variety of other places to check for leads on job openings in your field?
➢ The importance of looking and acting your best during any contact with a potential employer?
➢ What to keep in mind when making contact with a prospective employer by mail?
➢ If using fax machines in your job search is a good or bad idea?
➢ What networking is and how important it is to your job search? Who you should talk to?
➢ Why it is important to never "burn your bridges"?
➢ What the entire application process usually involves?
➢ What information the application form usually asks for and what impact the Equal Employment Opportunity (EEO) guidelines have had on these application forms?
➢ The importance of follow-up?

INTRODUCTION

Although waiting to hear about a job opening may work once in a great while, you usually must *look* for work. More accurately, you have to *work at finding work*. Serious job searchers find that pursuing employment requires as much, if not more, effort than a full-time job and that a thought-out strategy is essential. A well-developed search demands action. No one who creeps or shuffles along a career path can expect success in this competitive world. They will be trampled over by people who really want to work and to advance. Unmotivated, unenthusiastic, undirected individuals are easily identified and weeded out by employers. *You've got to be a tiger!*

Employers are looking for that *special* applicant who exudes drive, energy and genuine enthusiasm. Develop your strategy so you not only maintain the energy necessary to pursue your career goals, but so your energy *shines brightly* to employers.

Don't just plan to look for work. Chase it! Hustle! Scramble! Be creative! Have fun! Turn what can be a frustrating experience into a personal challenge. Each disappointment, each new challenge, is part of the training that will let you succeed. *Get what you want!* Let the process feed you, not defeat you.

If this all sounds a bit too "rah! rah!"—the opposite of the stoic, macho attitude police officers, corrections officers, security personnel and those in related fields are "supposed" to exhibit—think again. Employers are looking for *real* people who truly want the job and will, in turn, do a great job for them. Job hunting is frustrating at times, so you *need* to keep yourself charged up for the process.

DEVELOPING YOUR JOB-SEARCH STRATEGY

To keep on track—physically, emotionally and intellectually—you have to develop a strategy. The first step is to determine *what* you are looking for. Even the smaller newspapers have an incredible number of employment want ads. The unemployed are frequently asked, "How can you not have a job? Hundreds (thousands) are advertised for!" True, but take a closer look. You are not going to apply for every job advertised. Somewhere between *actuarial* and *zookeeper* are the jobs you will consider.

Begin with the questions: "What do I want? How do I get it?" If nothing short of police officer will satisfy you, do not apply for private security positions. On the other hand, might a position as an armored-truck driver, for instance, be a good stepping-stone to lead to your end goal? Unless you are desperate for money, taking a full-time position of no interest or value to your career goals could result in several problems. For example, say you start applying randomly, get a job in an unrelated field and eventually quit for a job you probably should have waited for in the first place. This could make you look like a "job jumper," create hard feelings with that employer when you leave and maybe result in a negative reference.

This doesn't mean you should sit at home unemployed until you get your "dream" job. For a variety of reasons, including financial and emotional, it is frequently much easier to get a job when you have a job. What is important is to identify what you want before going after it.

Mullins (1994, p. 12) notes: "Most job seekers suffer more from poor job-hunting skills than from lack of opportunity." Among his suggestions for improving your chances of finding a job quickly is: "Make job hunting a full-time commitment. . . . If you are unemployed, you should spend a minimum of 40 hours a week actively searching for work. As a full-time job seeker, your goal should be at least one interview a day with someone who has the power to hire you."

Richard Koonce, an accomplished human resource consultant, has written a book entitled *Career Power! 12 Winning Habits to Help You Get from Where You Are to Where You Want to Be* (Kennedy, 1995, p. 1J). Among his suggestions to "upgrade your life": (1) take responsibility for managing your career, (2) commit yourself to continuous learning, (3) learn to "suitcase" your skills and leverage your experience, (4) help others find jobs and (5) keep your resume up-to-date.

Don't overlook federal jobs. According to Krannich and Krannich (1995, p. 23): "Government agencies always hire, even during the worst of times. They have an average annual turnover rate of 10–14 percent. Furthermore, federal agencies hire nearly 1,000 people each day, or 300,000 to 400,000 each year."

It is important to identify what you want before going after it. Then you must make job hunting a full-time commitment, spending a minimum of 40 hours a week actively searching for work if you are currently unemployed.

WHERE TO LOOK

Begin with the most obvious place to look for employment—newspaper want ads. After watching the local papers daily for several weeks, you will identify the generally accepted procedure employers in various fields use to advertise for employees. Ads for law enforcement positions, for instance, are usually placed in the Sunday paper, under the heading of "police." Private security positions generally appear under the heading of "security." Is this how it is always done? Of course not.

Think creatively. Ads for police officers could appear under such headings as "law enforcement," "public safety" or "officer." Corrections positions may appear under "prisons," "jails," "guards" and the like. Security jobs may appear under the title of "risk management" or "loss control." Take time to familiarize yourself with all the possible headings your job could fall under and continue to scan the entire listing.

Perhaps a clerk or a secretary placed the ad without knowing anything about the actual job and thought "safety officer" or even "city employee" or "state employee" would be the best spot. Maybe the ad will appear, accidentally or purposely, on a Tuesday only. Do not let yourself get lazy just because such ads are usually in the Sunday paper under a specific section.

 Under what other headings might a police position appear? List them in your journal.

 Under what other headings might a private security position appear? List them in your journal.

 If considering a related field, under what headings might it appear? Note these in your journal.

Job openings are usually placed in the classified ads that appear in columns, row after row. Take time, however, to also check the display (box) ads used most frequently by corporations. These bigger ads are more expensive, but occasionally a city or private employer that wants to state specific needs or is particularly in need of people will use this approach. Scan ALL the newspaper want ads.

Also consider the possibility of ads appearing in papers other than those published in your particular city. A Minneapolis job seeker, for instance, should check the St. Paul newspaper. The Oakland job seeker should check a San Francisco paper. The Seattle job seeker should be looking in a Tacoma paper. Read the local and neighborhood papers as well as those of surrounding cities.

Begin your job search with the most obvious place to look for employment—newspaper want ads. Think creatively and scan ALL the ads. In addition to your local and neighborhood papers, check the papers of surrounding cities.

Specialty Periodicals

Every field has trade publications. Law enforcement, corrections and private security have many magazines, frequently with ads appearing in them. Such periodicals as *The Police Chief, Law and Order, Corrections Today, The Prison Journal, Corrections Compendium* and *Security Management* may not only contain position openings at the higher levels, they also contain current information beneficial to individuals applying in these fields.

Other publications deal with more general topics and could contain an ad for your job. For example, magazines that deal with municipal government could contain such ads. Become familiar with a variety of specialty periodicals. Also become familiar with periodicals that list only jobs. One such publication of particular interest to those seeking employment in law enforcement and private security is the *National Employment Listing Service,* which contains only related employment opportunities.

Other specific publications only address federal jobs, state jobs, county jobs or city jobs. If not contained in such specialized publications, they will usually be posted. If you are interested in a federal job, the *Federal Jobs Register* is a valuable resource. Another source for federal positions or for positions out of the country is the U.S. Civil Service Commission, the address for which is given at the end of the chapter.

> Every field has trade publications. Check the specialty periodicals associated with your chosen field, whether it's police work, corrections, private security or a related criminal justice field.

Using the Internet

Newspapers from across the country can be accessed over the Internet, making it much easier to search the want ads in a variety of papers. And when you find yourself interested in a position, the Internet offers a spectacular opportunity to learn about the company, organization, agency, or even community by accessing the ever-increasing number of web sites.

Computer bulletin boards are becoming a popular means of interacting with others having similar interests and for finding information about a particular topic. A computerized job network system—*America's Job Bank*—is run by the U.S. Department of Labor and lists approximately 50,000 job openings a week. Frerkes (1998, p. 129) notes: "The vast amount of information that is available on the world wide web has opened the doors for job seekers to monitor daily those agencies that are in the process of hiring." Several relevant and potentially helpful Internet addresses are listed at the end of the chapter.

> The Internet has become an increasingly valuable resource, not only for job listings but also for information about specific agencies and communities where career opportunities are available.

Other Places to Look

The serious job hunter routinely stops at the federal, state, county and municipal offices every week or two to check job postings and to ask what job openings are available or anticipated. For law enforcement employment, one of the best sources of information at the local level is the city or county personnel office.

You may be able to subscribe to job listings used by government agencies as well as the privately published services. These are often quite expensive, so become familiar with what your local libraries have. Regularly review these sources.

Placement offices of educational institutions that offer programs in law enforcement, corrections, criminal justice or private security often post job notices and have excellent employment listing services. Know where to look and what to look for, and regularly watch postings and other resources. Appendix G includes a list of such resources.

Another place to look is in your local telephone directory. Check listings under government agencies (federal, state and local) for personnel departments. Employment services and organizations can also help you find jobs, as can universities with job placement services and employment information resources.

Several helpful publications also exist. *Tips for Finding the Right Job* is a U.S. Department of Labor pamphlet offering advice on determining job skills, organizing the job search, writing a resume and interviewing. *Job Search Guide: Strategies for Professionals* is a U.S. Department of Labor publication that discusses specific steps job seekers should follow to identify employment opportunities.

Many Jobs Aren't Advertised

It is essential to know that many jobs are either not advertised or are actually filled before an ad is placed. How could that be? Probably because an aggressive job seeker with an effective strategy found a way in (long before you ever became aware of the job opening), either by having established a relationship with the employer (perhaps as an intern) or by making the employer aware of their interest before the job opening existed. Frequently, in such cases, an ad is run because of department policy or to meet a legal obligation. Your strategy, then, is to learn about these jobs before these probabilities occur. Just because an employer doesn't yet know a job will open up doesn't mean you should not be trying for it.

Telephone Inquiries

Active job seekers put considerably more effort into their pursuit than just browsing through newspaper ads. You've got to get out there and investigate. An easy, quick, relatively nonthreatening way is to telephone and ask if a certain department, agency or company has, or expects, any openings. Ask if they send out a mailer for job openings or if you could get on a specific list to be notified for a particular job. With a little polite interaction, you may be able to get an individual notice from the contact person you impressed while inquiring. Even if the contact you made proves fruitless, never hang up without asking if they know of anyone *else* who is hiring. Kenning (1998, p. 1) suggests: "Warm up to the idea of cold calling by remembering: You are skilled in the art of information gathering and problem solving. It's just a matter of assigning your skills to a new set of challenges: The Job Search!"

When making such calls, begin by asking whoever answers whom you should talk with about possible job openings. Then ask if you should contact anyone else at that particular place or elsewhere. Your goal is to develop an ever-expanding list of resources and contacts.

Personal Inquiries

Another approach to inquiring about a position is to stop in. This can be risky. First, most employers are extremely busy and usually do not have or take time to visit with someone who has no appointment. This could result in closed doors or in aggravating a potential employer. On the other hand, it shows real interest on your part, as well as a willingness to take risks. You will also have the chance to let them see you as a person they would possibly want on their team. If you use this approach, don't take up too much of their time. Get in, deliver your message, and get out in a few minutes.

Never go empty-handed. Have a resume to leave even if you are not able to see anyone. Follow up with a letter, especially if someone took time to talk with you.

Other places to check during your job search include the federal, state, county and municipal personnel offices; your local library for job listing mailers used by government agencies and privately published services; placement offices and employment information resources at local educational institutions and universities; your local telephone directory; employment services and organizations; computer bulletin boards; and government pamphlets and publications. You might also consider making telephone or personal inquiries at companies or agencies that interest you, requesting information about current or anticipated job openings.

ON BEING YOUR BEST

An absolutely essential part of your strategy is to be your best at *every* phase of the job-search process. Because of the natural frustrations of the process, this is sometimes difficult. If you are making phone inquiries, be away from crying babies, barking dogs and other noises that could be distractions for both you and the person you're calling. Also, when making phone inquiries, consider dressing as you would for a personal interview. If you look sharp, you will feel sharp, and will then act sharp, making a better impression than if you were calling while lounging in your bathrobe at 11 o'clock in the morning. Besides, you never know if the prospective employer might say something like, "Can you come down right now?" It happens.

When making personal contacts, coming across well is equally important. Applicants who drop off resumes while wearing extremely casual attire or something bizarre, take a possibly fatal risk. There is always a chance you could meet with someone, even if you meant to only leave your resume and ask about possible openings. Perhaps the person responsible for hiring will walk by or has told the person at the front desk to send any applicants to see him/her. Maybe a new receptionist or a temporary employee will mistakenly send you into the employer's office. If you are wearing cut-up jeans and lizard-skin cowboy boots, you have damaged what should have been a spectacular opportunity. The prepared job seeker is always ready for the unexpected.

Finally, be courteous to every person you have contact with. You may not think the receptionist, secretary or person who casually strolls up and asks if they can help you is important. They are. You never know who you are talking with. The boss may be covering the phone or sitting up front while that person is taking a break. This, too, happens.

As is more likely, the first contact person delivers your message or resume *with* an editorial comment. It had better be something like:

➢   This applicant sure was polite.
➢   This person dressed well.
➢   This one seemed like she would fit in.
➢   This is the one who called and was so courteous.

You don't want something like:

➢   Wait till you see this slob.
➢   This guy was really rude just now.
➢   This is the gal who hung up on me last week.

Not only does niceness go a long way, you will likely be talked about after you leave, so make sure the talk is positive. You may also get something more from being nice—the person taking your call or greeting you at the front desk may be willing to give you advice, a tip on future openings and perhaps even a little encouragement. It is also possible they may go back and tell the boss, "There is someone here you may just want to meet," or even contact you with information about a new opening. Because you never know, always be prepared. Even if you feel frustrated, frazzled and tired, look like this is *the* most important contact you are making.

An essential part of your strategy is to be your best at *every* phase of the job-search process. During phone contacts and especially during personal contacts, dress and act professionally. Expect the unexpected. You may be talking to the boss and not know it.

CONTACTS BY MAIL

The importance of appearance in making a good impression also applies to written material. Such material is a direct reflection of you. While you may not actually see the person doing the hiring, if you supply a resume, chances are it will at least get looked at. Provide that person with something that interests them, not something that gives them a reason to throw it away.

Contacting prospective employers by mail is perfectly acceptable. Like telephoning, it is quick, easy and even more nonthreatening. It may, however, be less effective. While it may be hard to say "no" to someone in person, it is easier over the phone, and easiest with a letter (usually by promptly depositing it in the circular file). But letter writing is a viable strategy.

Note here the recommendation is *not* "resume mailing," but "letter writing." It makes little sense to send an agency or company only a resume. The receiver will have little idea why it was sent, and even if a position is open, a bare resume shows lack of common sense by the applicant. A cover letter makes the process more personal and sincere.

Whether responding to an ad or merely inquiring about what might be available, include both a cover letter *and* resume. The cover letter, as you may recall, introduces you and tells why you are writing. It tells about you not only through words, but also by showing a command of English and that you are neat, to the point and courteous.

Writing skills are exceptionally important, and here is a chance to shine. To make a favorable impression when you write, consider the following:

➢ Don't provide a letter without a resume or a resume without a letter.
➢ Don't submit anything in pencil (and write neatly in ink only if you are absolutely unable to locate anyone within the free world who can type it for you).
➢ Don't use sheets torn out of a spiral notebook or lined, three-hole notebook paper.
➢ Don't use the back of a used piece of paper or an old invoice or receipt.
➢ Don't send form letters, especially when they were designed for another job area.
➢ Don't send copies of letters or resumes that have been copied so many times they are faded and hard to read.
➢ Don't fold your material into strange shapes. Enclose it unfolded in a 9 x 12 white envelope.

As difficult as it may be to believe, all of the preceding have been submitted, and all have been thrown away without ever allowing the applicant to recover from the negative impression he or she made.

Employers are busy, especially if they are shorthanded and need to hire more personnel. They will not have time to go through all the applications, so they will look for reasons to throw out most of them. Foolish applicants provide plenty of justifiable reasons to jettison their letters and resumes. When providing a prospective employer with *anything* in writing:

➢ Make sure it is neat.
➢ Make sure it is typed.
➢ Make sure it is personalized for *that* contact. (Call to find out who to address it to and the proper spelling.)
➢ Proofread it; proofread it again; and proofread it again. Have another person proofread it. Then proofread it one last time. Improper grammar and typos provide an excellent reason for a resume to be thrown away.

When providing a prospective employer with *anything* in writing, make sure it is neatly typed on good-quality paper, personalized and free of errors. Never send a resume without a cover letter or a letter without a resume.

FAX

While fax machines are popular, the jury is still out on how effective they are in a job search. You should view a fax machine as a tool to work with in some situations. You may make yourself stand out from the crowd of applicants by faxing a letter and resume. If you don't own a fax machine, you can pay for this service at major hotels, large secretarial services or many office supply stores.

For many employers, faxes are a perfectly acceptable means of sending in your resume. While many ads will state that application by fax is acceptable, if you don't know this for sure, ask first. Even then, it may be advisable to mail or hand deliver a hard copy of the material.

You may view a fax machine as a tool to work with in some situations, yet uncertainty remains as to how effective they are in a job search.

NETWORKING

Because the vast majority of job seekers make several applications, you will want to constantly seek new contacts and new possibilities. After being hired, you may eventually change jobs (maybe several times), so you will need to continue to expand your contacts. This process, called *networking*, is being relied upon more and more.

According to Lankford (1997, p. 84): "Networking is the most important step in your career search." It is further noted in an article entitled "Networking 101" (1997, p. 10): "Approximately 70 percent of job openings are filled by people who heard about the job through word of mouth. The more contacts you have . . . , the greater your odds are to be considered for a position. A side benefit of networking is that you also increase your base of friends—many of whom share your same interests." Mullins (p. 12) suggests: "Create a network of friendly contacts who can hire you or recommend you to others who can. Developing a network of contacts is the single most important task of a job seeker."

Salespeople have effectively used this networking concept for years, only they call it "developing leads." You are a salesperson, selling yourself. The process involves setting up a network of resources who you will not forget and who will not forget you. It begins with making whatever contacts you already have and taking every opportunity to add to this list. You then use each contact to make more contacts, and more contacts, etc., etc., etc. For instance, you make a contact at a particular company or city. You then ask if you should check with anyone or anywhere else. Imagine if each contact gave you two or three other employers' names. You could quickly develop literally hundreds of possible contacts.

What becomes difficult and complex is *how* you develop your networking strategy and to what extreme you should take it. Because networking can, and in fact should, mushroom into many contacts, proceed in an orderly way. This is best done in writing, with a plan in mind. Here's how:

1. Make an initial contact.
2. Document that step.
3. Acquire additional contacts.
4. Document them.
5. Take action.
6. Follow up.

It's easy until you start to develop more than about five contacts. Then you will want to record your efforts on something more workable than scraps of paper. You can buy networking workbooks, but it may benefit you to make up your own networking book. You can design it for your own particular needs, and you will feel like you are really working at developing your own strategy. It will make the entire process more personal, not to mention more gratifying by accomplishing something concrete.

 In your journal, or in a separate networking notebook, list the important information you need to keep track of and organize it so it is workable. Data to be maintained should include:

> ➢ Company, agency, department name, address, phone.
> ➢ Names and titles of contacts (spelled correctly).
> ➢ What you did.
> ➢ What you will do.

Also have a separate calendar to set up dates you will contact or recontact sources. The first recontact should be a week or two after the initial contact. Follow up every month thereafter, but be sure to recognize the fine line between an assertive applicant sure to be remembered and a pest they want to forget. Strive for a balance.

Unlike the process of actually applying for specific jobs, the networking process should have no limits. You have no way to know where job information is lurking. Effective networking includes not only professional contacts (both individuals and agencies or companies), but also your acquaintances, friends and family. Someone may know someone who knows someone who knows someone in the field who may be looking for someone just like you. This is how you get a jump on your competition—by finding out about job openings before they are advertised or even before they become openings. The thing is, you never know who has this information, so let the world know that you are available.

Professional networks are a growing piece of the career industry. According to Lancaster (1995, p. J1):

> The three biggest services are Exec-U-Net, with about 3,000 members; the Search Bulletin in Great Falls, Va., with 2,000 members,; and Net-Share in Novato, Calif., with nearly 1,300.
>
> To get into the . . . networking-swim, you subscribe and receive mailings (most are twice monthly) that have several hundred job listings. These give title, job description, salary, hiring contact and other details. . . .
>
> Finally, this bit of cogent perspective from George Crosby of the Human Resources Network: "People get too reliant on these things. If you think just sending out your resume will get you a job, you're crazy. [These services are] just a supplement to a core strategy of networking your buns off."

Pursue your job search positively and energetically. Develop every opportunity to show yourself off in your best light. Be creative and learn from each experience. Even the contacts that appear to be unproductive give you a chance to learn more about the market and yourself. If nothing else, you come away from the experience knowing you are tough enough to accept a setback and survive. As noted by Bolles (1998): "You only need one YES—and the more NOs you get out of the way, the closer you are to that YES."

Networking is the process of connecting and interacting with the individuals who can be helpful to you in your job search and is a crucial element in an effective job search. Place no limits on your network—talk to anyone and everyone.

ON BURNING BRIDGES

No matter what approach to contacting prospective employers you take, be it responding to an ad, phoning, sending a letter with a resume, sending a fax, stopping in, or for that matter, sending smoke signals, *never* leave a door permanently closed behind you. Don't burn any bridges that may eventually lead to a great job.

You will find that people can be terribly insensitive, unfeeling and downright rude. You are bound to get tense yourself because job seeking is difficult. But never show any negative feelings to anyone who may affect your future professional life. Don't be rude or vent your frustrations on anyone where you are applying for work, no matter how they treat you. If they treat you badly, it's probably not *you* they are upset with. They are probably having a bad day. You may well return, *if* you have kept the door open. If you have sworn at someone, had a temper tantrum or otherwise behaved unprofessionally, you might as well cross that resource out of your networking notebook. The following personal experiences illustrate that bridges must never be burned.

While attending law school, I replied to an ad for a police investigator with a local public safety department. Although I was a finalist, both the employer and I determined this was not a good time for me to consider the job. I let the sergeant I was dealing with know I appreciated the opportunity, and then I called the chief. I had not had contact with him, but I thanked him and let him know his sergeant was great to deal with and that everyone involved was the type of person I would love to work with. I certainly did not have to call the chief. The likelihood of me ever coming into contact with him again was almost zero. Years later I did have contact with him. Not only did he remember me, he said he was impressed that I had bothered to call him and that no one had ever done that before. He also offered me a job—which I accepted. It was one of the best jobs I ever had. We have since become friends. I am sure none of the subsequent benefits would have come to me had I just "blown off" that job.

Similarly, my public safety director job could easily have never been. It turned out my former boss and I were the two finalists for the position. As the result of a number of factors, some of which I perceived as being unfair, Jim got the job. I was devastated and still recall that day as one of the biggest disappointments I have ever had. I *really* wanted that job and couldn't figure out why I didn't get it. In fact, I am embarrassed to say that on several occasions I actually started driving out to tell the city manager, the mayor and Jim just what I thought of them and how they had "ruined" my entire life. Fortunately, I always came to my senses and retreated. When Jim and I finally did meet, we hit it off so well, he offered me a job as his assistant. That gave me the chance to learn from him, an unanticipated opportunity that I could have ruined. He was hired away to head up security at Walt Disney Pictures and Television, and I got his job. It turned out perfectly, although I never would have believed it at the time. Things do happen for a reason, so don't mess it up.

The moral: Accept reality as it presents itself and make the best of apparently bad situations. Things do have a way of working out for the best.

Never burn any bridges. Doing so only removes any opportunities the future may have held for you.

IF NOTHING SEEMS TO WORK—CONSIDER BEING CREATIVE

Perhaps something other than the ordinary could make you stand out among the masses applying for that job you want. Again, particularly in a field of work that is quite conservative, anything "too far out" could immediately land your application in the circular file (or shredder). On the other hand, desperate times call for desperate measures. The ideas can be as extensive as your imagination. Different colored paper, a unique cover design, or the way you approach the hiring authorities. Don't over do it, but show you can be different than every other applicant in line for the same job.

Dauten and Nelson (1996c, p. D3) advocate trying an offbeat approach when all else seems to fail: "The problem with doing 'all the right things' is that it comes down to doing what everyone else is doing. . . . Most people don't realize that trying harder usually doesn't help either." They also state (1996b, p. D4): "It would be better to send out two resumes a week than 200, as long as [you] back up those two a week with networking and plenty of research on potential employers." Finally, they note finding a job takes ingenuity, time and determination (1996a, p. D3): "A good job detective will find job openings before the companies themselves know they exist. . . . When Thomas Edison made that remark about genius being 'one percent inspiration and 99 percent perspiration,' he wasn't doing a Right Guard commercial; he was offering a practical guide to how you turn ideas into reality."

YOU'VE FOUND AN OPENING AND THEY'VE ASKED YOU TO APPLY

Once you've found an opening and have been asked to apply for the position, you can expect to go through several steps, illustrated in Figure 11-1. The order in which these steps occur may vary, but in almost all instances, the first step will be to complete an application form.

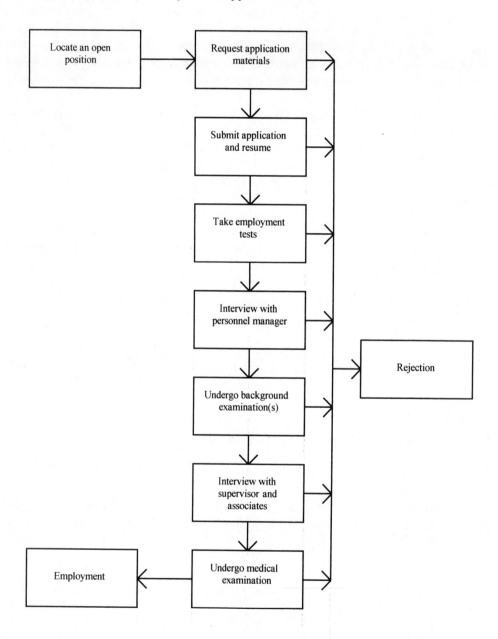

FIGURE 11-1   Typical Employment Process

SOURCE: Adapted from *Supervision*, 2nd ed., by Stan Kossen, p. 205; copyright © 1991 by West Publishing Co. Reprinted by permission.

> The application process usually involves completing an application form, taking a series of written tests, having a preliminary interview, undergoing a background check, having a final interview and taking a medical exam.

The Application

Some application forms are very simple. Others are extremely complex. If you have done a thorough job on your resume and have a copy of it along, you should have all the information you need at your fingertips. If they will allow you to take the application home to type it, do so. If not, complete it neatly using *black ink*—it copies much better. Use your best printing. Think before you write so you do not have to erase or cross out information. Be complete. If you do not understand something on the form, ask.

Many forms have optional sections to complete. Such sections ask for information that is not legal for employers to insist on because of Equal Employment Opportunity (EEO) guidelines, for example, ethnic background, religious preference and marital status. It is usually in your best interest to complete these sections. One job candidate who knew employers were interested in this information but could not legally ask for it attached a second sheet to his job application entitled: "Everything my Equal Opportunity Employer would like to know about me, but cannot ask."

> Application forms vary greatly in their complexity and depth, but they usually ask for the same information you gathered in preparing your resume, so always have a copy of it with you. Although the Equal Employment Opportunity (EEO) guidelines make mandatory responses to questions about ethnic background, religious preference and marital status illegal, it is usually in your best interest to complete these optional sections.

Appendix H contains a sample application form. Appendix I contains Equal Employment Opportunity guidelines.

Armstrong and Schmalleger (1994, pp. 23–27) present helpful hints for completing and submitting an application for federal employment:

> ➤ Make your [application] nice to look at and easy to follow. Make sure entries in each block are in the block, not crowding over the lines, . . . Vertically align repetitive data in sequential blocks.
> ➤ Consider hiring professionals to do your form.
> ➤ Say you'll accept a job anywhere. If you don't want to take an offered job, you can always decline.
> ➤ DO NOT LEAVE <u>ANY</u> BLOCK ON THE SF-171 BLANK! . . . No matter what the block asks for, give 'em an answer, even if it's just "N/A."
> ➤ Collect everything you'll need to complete the form. . . . past work descriptions, high school diploma, GED certificate, college transcripts, certificates [and] any special licenses or qualifications.
> ➤ If your work history includes managerial experience, tell them how well you <u>managed</u>, not how you did the work yourself!
> ➤ Do not spend your time and money hand-carrying your [application] to the servicing Federal Office of Personnel Management or the personnel department of the agency to which you are applying.
> ➤ Mail [it] via Certified Mail and get a return receipt, or send it via Federal Express. Why? Because bureaucracies tend to swallow things whole.
> ➤ Do not leave gaps in documentation of employment dates.
> ➤ Do not give up! T-E-N-A-C-I-T-Y is the name of this game. Don't get discouraged because you send in lots of applications but get no calls. Be patient. Try to understand that there's not a lot of "hurry" in the hiring end of the government.

Many departments and agencies are including a written essay as part of the application process, requesting candidates to write two or three pages on a specific topic, such as "Why are you interested in this field?" or "Why are you interested in being hired by this particular agency?"

  Take time *before* you apply for a job to write two- to three-page answers to the following questions:

1. Why have you selected this particular field?
2. Why have you selected this particular agency?
3. Who are YOU? (Write a brief autobiography.)

REMEMBER THE MAGIC WORDS—THANK YOU

One absolute: *never* leave a contact without following up with a thank-you. Not only is this good manners in a world sorely lacking in this area, but it also is another chance to present yourself positively. The more you can get your name in front of employers, the more they will remember you at hiring time.

You can phone or write your thank-you for the opportunity to interview or to submit your resume. If you can't decide which way is better, do both. Don't express your thanks to *only* the chief of police or the president of the security company who took time to see you. Also thank the secretary who took time to set up the meeting or greeted you for your appointment. Show them you are thoughtful and courteous, the kind of person they would like working with them.

Always follow up a contact with a thank-you. It demonstrates your good manners and gets your name in front of the employer one more time.

WARNING

If you think job hunting sounds like a lot of work, you are absolutely correct. Every aspect of the process is emotionally and physically taxing and time-consuming. You will be approaching other people trying to sell yourself, knowing the chances of immediate success are slim.

None of us likes to hear the word *no*. It becomes increasingly difficult to dial the phone, knock on the door or send the next letter. It is risk-taking at the most critical level. You are setting yourself up for a certain number of rejections. It is difficult, if not impossible, to keep from taking the entire process too personally. A rejection does not have to be a failure. Indeed, it can merely be the elimination of another job on your quest to find the job you are looking for.

Rejection can come for a number of reasons. Primarily, there needs to be a match between the candidate and the department. What may be inappropriate for one agency will be a gold mine for another. Rejection may simply mean it wasn't the best match for the department or for *you*.

Take care of yourself. If the whole thing starts to get the best of you, treat it like you would any other job. Set hours, including breaks. Plan your days. Take an occasional vacation. Finally, recognize the very real need for a support system. Plan time with people who accept you. You can do this informally with family or friends, or more formally by organizing a support group with others in the same position. Such groups work extremely well for sharing support, ideas and helpful hints. Most important, be sure your strategy allows you to keep at it. The next contact could have your job for you.

TESTING YOUR CAREERING COMPETENCIES*

INSTRUCTIONS: Respond to each statement by circling the number at the right that best represents your situation.

SCALE: 1 = strongly agree
           2 = agree
           3 = maybe, not certain
           4 = disagree
           5 = strongly disagree

1.	I know what motivates me to excel at work.	1 2 3 4 5
2.	I can identify my strongest abilities and skills.	1 2 3 4 5
3.	I have seven major achievements that clarify a pattern of interests and abilities that are relevant to my job and career.	1 2 3 4 5
4.	I know what both I like and dislike in work.	1 2 3 4 5
5.	I know what I want to do during the next 10 years.	1 2 3 4 5
6.	I have a well-defined career objective that focuses my job search on particular organizations and employers.	1 2 3 4 5
7.	I know what skills I can offer employers in different occupations.	1 2 3 4 5
8.	I know what skills employers most seek in candidates.	1 2 3 4 5
9.	I can clearly explain to employers what I do well and enjoy doing.	1 2 3 4 5
10.	I can specify why employers should hire me.	1 2 3 4 5
11.	I can gain the support of family and friends for making a job or career change.	1 2 3 4 5
12.	I can find 10 to 20 hours a week to conduct a part-time job search.	1 2 3 4 5
13.	I have financial ability to sustain a three-month job search.	1 2 3 4 5

* SOURCE: Ronald L. Krannich. *Re-Careering in Turbulent Times: Skills and Strategies for Success in Today's Job Market*. Manassas, VA: Impact Publications, 1995, pp. 103–105. Reprinted by permission.

14. I can conduct library and interview research on different occupations, employers, organizations, and communities.   1 2 3 4 5

15. I can write different types of effective resumes and job search/thank you letters.   1 2 3 4 5

16. I can produce and distribute resumes and letters to the right people.   1 2 3 4 5

17. I can list my major accomplishments in action terms.   1 2 3 4 5

18. I can identify and target employers I want to interview.   1 2 3 4 5

19. I can develop a job referral network.   1 2 3 4 5

20. I can persuade others to join in forming a job search support group.   1 2 3 4 5

21. I can prospect for job leads.   1 2 3 4 5

22. I can use the telephone to develop prospects and get referrals and interviews.   1 2 3 4 5

23. I can plan and implement an effective direct-mail job-search campaign.   1 2 3 4 5

24. I can generate one job interview for every 10 job search contacts I make.   1 2 3 4 5

25. I can follow-up on job interviews.   1 2 3 4 5

26. I can negotiate a salary 10-20% above what an employer initially offers.   1 2 3 4 5

27. I can persuade an employer to renegotiate my salary after six months on the job.   1 2 3 4 5

28. I can create a position for myself in an organization.   1 2 3 4 5

You can calculate your overall careering competencies by adding the numbers you circled for a composite score. If your score is more than 75 points, you need to work on developing your careering skills. How you scored each item will indicate to what degree you need to work on improving specific job-search skills. If your score is under 50 points, you are well on your way toward job-search success.

CONCLUSION

Although waiting to hear about a job opening may work once in a great while, you usually must work *at finding work*. It is important to identify what you want before going after it. Then you must make job hunting a full-time commitment, spending a minimum of 40 hours a week actively searching for work if you are currently unemployed. An essential part of your strategy is to be your best at *every* phase of the job-search process. *Always* follow up a contact with a thank-you.

ADDITIONAL CONTACTS AND SOURCES OF INFORMATION

Career Paths: A Guide to Jobs in Federal Law Enforcement
   by Gordon M. Armstrong and Frank Schmalleger,
   Regents/Prentice Hall Publishers, 1994.
      Lists all major federal agencies, criminal justice positions
      available, addresses and phone numbers

U.S. Civil Service Commission
1900 East Street, NW
Washington, DC 20006

<u>Web Sites:</u>

      Career Path—a leading site on the web for job seekers. After selecting a geographical location, the applicant can peruse the
        major newspapers' classified ads for current openings in that area.
      URL: www.careerpath.com

      The Police Officer's Internet Directory—over 1,500 individual home pages of information on law enforcement agencies across
        the country. Included is a state-by-state breakdown of agencies with current openings.
      URL: www.officer.com

      On Patrol—includes free postings of law enforcement opportunities on a state-by-state basis.
      URL: www.onpatrol.com

AN INSIDER'S VIEW

FROM BOTH SIDES OF THE PROCESS

Brian Beniek
Police Officer
Plymouth (Minnesota) Police Department

Way back in 1982 I made a very important decision. That decision—I wanted to be a police officer. So already one year into my college education, I checked out how to do it and how fast I could complete the courses. If you can believe it, one and a half years later I was pounding the pavement looking for a cop job.

I always could interview for a job and get it. I never had been turned down for a job in my life. . . . until I entered the world of law enforcement. No one ever told me it was going to be so hard. Let me tell you, it was a rude awakening. After some rejections I decided to enroll in a few job-seeking classes, and then I would *for sure* get a job. Unfortunately, they never taught me how to get a cop job. So now you're asking yourself, how did I get a job as a police officer?

The first thing I did was set a goal and made the goal happen. It took a lot of hard work and trial and error, and most of all determination. But the day came five years later when I got the call: "We would like to offer you a job as a police officer with the City of Plymouth." I will never forget those words.

Following are a few tips, tricks and ideas that helped me land that job. As a person who has sat (on the edge of my chair) not only in interviews, but who has also had the chance to interview candidates for police officer jobs, I have some valuable experience to pass on. These things worked for me. They should work for you.

YOUR BACKGROUND

Besides the interview, you will find your background can make or break you. Once you have decided law enforcement is what you want to do, stop all activities that can get you in trouble. Remember, a background check is standard on any applicant. An investigator's job is to do nothing but dig up any dirt on you. Now don't think these guys are that closed-minded. They realize we all have some skeletons in our closets. They're just trying to weed out those who have a whole cemetery!

Your *education* is very important. A four-year degree can make a big difference. Try to take additional law-enforcement-related classes. Grades are important. Make sure yours are solid and consistent. English and math are just as important as your law enforcement classes. (You should remember that from your parents.)

Probably your *current and past jobs* will speak the loudest about you. Try to get a job where you deal with conflict and make decisions. Remember, cops deal with conflict daily. Probably one of the best jobs I had that must show what a cop does on the street was working hotel security. This job dealt with some of the exact things I deal with out on the street. So if you can find a job in hotel security, take it. (Thank you, Radisson South.) If you can become active in a police reserve program, do it. Your foot will be in the door with that department.

The other things you have to consider are what your friends, family (remember sisters and brothers count too), neighbors, teachers, employers and "drinking buddies" are going to say about you. A good background investigator will look further than just those people listed on your application. Now is not the time to start burning bridges.

Just as a side note, when you *first* fill out that background form, usually no less than 27 pages, *copy it*. You will probably need it again. Be sure you are thorough and do not try to hide anything. Honesty goes a long way.

APPLICATIONS

As you enter the world of law enforcement, you may have to look a little to find out who is hiring. Not every department advertises in the Sunday paper. Make some friends in the law enforcement field. Believe me, cops know what's happening and who is hiring and when. It's always a topic of discussion at coffee [breaks]. Look in newspapers, watch job postings. And it doesn't hurt to call a few departments.

Never, never, turn in a handwritten resume or application. All correspondence with a department should be typed. Always enclose a cover letter. You want to sell yourself and bring out some of your major points. Keep it to one page. Make it sound like their department is the only one you are applying to.

THE RESUME

The resume is what can really bring out your strong points. Make it neat and include all those standard items resumes have plus one exception. Add extracurricular activities. Don't be afraid to get involved in such activities and to list them. Employers like to see involvement.

THE ALL-IMPORTANT INTERVIEW

The interview separates the men and women from the boys and girls! This is where you make your lasting and most critical impression. Besides all those things you have been taught about interviews, a few tips from my personal list are important. Remember, I have seen both sides of the process.

Some Do's and Don'ts

Do:
- Be on time.
- Be honest. The background check will reveal a lot.
- Conduct some research on the department and city. (Maybe even arrange for a ride-along.)
- Look sharp. Wear a suit. Shine your shoes.
- Shake hands firmly.
- Make good eye contact with all board members.
- Show interest and initiative.
- Be friendly. SMILE.
- Show compassion.
- Use common sense.

Don't:
- Come unprepared—expect the unexpected.
- Pass yourself off as a know-it-all or be cocky. Remember, board members have experience too.
- Try to hide how nervous you are. They understand that you're under a lot of pressure.
- Mumble.

The Situation Questions

Be prepared for situation questions. Practice with a friend or an officer. Know your deadly force statute. I guarantee you'll be asked about it. When you are asked about a situation, most people are looking for common sense and compassion, not just right or wrong responses. You do not have to know every policy to get through these questions, but hopefully *common sense* will prevail. Be flexible and have a good reason to back up your statement. If you do give an answer, don't change your mind. You don't want to be shown as someone who changes position just because someone questions your decision. Even if you're not correct, you will have a better chance with the board members if you can explain your decision and show common sense. It's from the old school, but it still applies.

THE FINAL TOUCH

This last hint will help you throughout every step. It's called a *thank you*. We sometimes forget these two little words, but it shows you care. I always (no exceptions) sent a thank-you letter (typed) after the test and interviews. Send it to the chief. He makes the final decision. You want him to remember your name. Don't send letters to every oral board member. By this time they have already made their decision. Even if you don't get the job, follow up with a thank-you letter. Remember, don't burn those bridges.

IN CONCLUSION

Hopefully these tips will give you an added advantage over the competition. Some day you will look back and say, "I'm glad I listened to those who have been through the process. They had some good ideas." Believe me, all this will be worth it when you have applied, interviewed, gotten the job, and completed your field training program. Your greatest day will come the first time you are on your own and you make your first traffic stop, write your first ticket or make your first red light and siren run. Good luck. I'll see you on the streets. And remember, be careful out there!

———————

Brian Beniek is a police officer with the Plymouth (Minnesota) Police Department and has worked in the field of criminal justice for 10 years. He is currently a field training officer, a reserve officer coordinator and a hostage negotiator. Mr. Beniek was recently appointed to be a school liaison officer at Wayzata Senior High School. He is also a member of the Critical Incident Stress Debriefing Team and an active member of the Community Policing Committee and peer counselor. He has been awarded every commendation award his department has to offer, including the Medal of Valor. Mr. Beniek holds a BS in Criminal Justice and is a licensed Minnesota police officer, a certified firefighter II and a first responder. He's a paid on-call firefighter for the City of Chanhassen, where he holds the position of captain. He is married to Chris and is president of Beniek Lawn Service (lawn care and snow plowing service). He enjoys jetskiing, traveling (cruising), landscaping, boating, fishing and computers.

AN INSIDER'S VIEW

LAW ENFORCEMENT JOBS: LEARNING HOW TO GET THEM
TAKES THE SAME SKILLS REQUIRED TO DO THEM

John Lombardi
Professor of Criminal Justice and Criminology
Albany State College

Students want to pursue law enforcement positions for a number of reasons. There are also a number of different things a person can do in his or her travels from a student "wannabe" to a real cop, and getting the job is but one of these "rights of passage." This is not a personality contest. It is serious business. I do not believe all students are cut out to be police officers, nor are all police officers meant to be students. However, a student does not have to study law enforcement, but a police officer who aspires to be a professional must become a student of multi-methods of gathering different kinds of information. Dealing with the public, particularly with "street people," is an "art form" more than a science. It is more a pursuit of professionalism through continual training and education than an initial profession after graduating from an academy.

Serving the public is a truly honorable way to make a living, but always place your individual standards higher than those of the public you serve while still regarding them as equals. This is a lot to comprehend. However, if you cannot, it is likely you will be unable to muster the patience to make it through the "gatekeepers" who separate the "wannabe" from the "is." Consider the educational transformation you will experience during the job quest going from student "wannabe" to the world of law enforcement.

TALKING TO POLICE OFFICERS

For me and my POST [Peace Officers Standards and Training] undergraduate students in Minnesota, the search for a job starts early, during their sophomore year. Approximately one of three or four students applies for academy training in Minnesota. Most of my students apply outside the state because it takes less time to find a law enforcement job. Part of their training in their employment search is to speak with various police officers. This offers many benefits.

Chief Scott Harr spent an hour with my criminal procedure class explaining procedures and answering questions from students, since we use his criminal procedures textbook. How does this work? I set up a call to the criminal justice professional, announce to the class who the speakerphone guest is and ask each student to make up at least one good question. The day of class I give the students several more minutes to look over their questions and collaborate with other students. The students are picked at random, come up to the speakerphone, ask their own questions and interact with the speaker. I have found that this opens up quiet students, gives them some confidence in speaking with authority figures and makes sense out of questions they have created from their own perspectives. It takes you away from book verbatim and familiarity of the professor while, at the same time, showing you overlap and consistency between the professor and what is learned in class and is supported by other criminal justice professionals with whom you speak and gather new information.

STATE APPLICATIONS

Students universally complain about filling out long applications. A simple solution to this for some positions is to request several state employment applications. Fill out one application, perfectly typed. The only spaces left open should be the date and job applied for. Copy this completed application, possibly 100 times. Also, ask that your name be placed on the state job mailing list or visit a state employment office weekly and file as many job applications as you wish. Most people who do this get a positive response relatively quickly. Remember, you will probably switch jobs a few times, according to research data. Consider "positioning" yourself for your second job as you contemplate your first. The first job *is* important but will likely be a stepping stone along your career path.

TRAINING IN ORAL INTERVIEWS

I have taught a senior seminar in criminal justice which considers oral interviews, what types of questions to consider, possible responses and why, and the impact of what students have studied in college. The students are told to anticipate obvious questions:

- ➤ "Why do you want to be a police officer?" (Give three reasons including that you want to help people.)
- ➤ "Why do you want to be a police officer in this department?" (I have heard that your mandatory training opportunities are excellent; your department pays for graduate courses in management; your field training officer program is well known, etc.)
- ➤ "What are your strong points?" (I have been trained to be a problem solver, not a problem creator.)
- ➤ And "stock" hypothetical questions such as "What would you do in a situation that is either impossible or is one in which you surely have not been, as yet, trained?" (Call your supervisor, follow policy and chain of command, etc.)

As you gather information, cast it into question form. This will get you in the mindset to think on your feet. You must learn to control situations and yourself. You should become sensitive, but sitting and crying for someone does not help that person and does not make you a problem solver. Finding solutions for the person in need is the beginning of helping him gain control.

If asked, "How has your education prepared you for a police officer position?" the hiring board does not want an academic, laborious listing of your criminal law or abnormal psychology courses. It is more practical and useful to respond with answers concerning an understanding of (1) mandatory training, (2) the difference between formal education and academy training, (3) factors involved in what being a "professional" means, (4) understanding the chain of command, (5) knowing what "1983 actions" are and not being afraid to ask the hiring board what type of 1983 actions their department has and is experiencing and how their academy is responding to the litigation,   (6) officer turnover and promotional list rates for similarly situated individuals in positions for which you are applying and (7) opportunities existing in areas for which you aspire (e.g., tactical teams, violent crimes units, task forces, etc.). Taking "a broader stroke" to responses shows you understand the "bigger picture" and are sensitive to the organization and the environmental impacts on the agency and its budgetary position.

Don't ask questions about salary. That can be found in job descriptions. And it is permissible to walk into an interview with a legal pad listing "solid" questions (e.g., education, mandatory retraining opportunities, outside "inner city" voluntary opportunities for off-duty officers through various service agencies, etc.). If the hiring board asks you if you have any questions, you will be prepared. You can raise your oral board scores by asking several penetrating questions that allow board members to respond. This shows that you have thought ahead, that you have researched the agency beyond color coordination of uniform and squad car and that you are career-oriented.

SUBSCRIBING TO MONTHLY JOB OPENING LISTS

Local and national job openings can be purchased for a nominal fee. Ask at your local police department for such listings. In addition, investigate the possibilities in states that have high crime rates, as well as police academies that train for particular police jurisdictions (e.g., Florida). In other words, the state will not only train you, but will also help place you once you graduate. It is possible to qualify for 20 police departments or more with one application and then have an agency pay your salary when going through the academy. Check on hiring versus training rates: how many people qualify each year in a particular state versus the number of persons actually hired.

BOOK LISTINGS OF LAW ENFORCEMENT AGENCIES

You can find annual listings of police agencies in the library or through local law enforcement agencies. You might pick agencies geographically and send a brief one-page request for an application, deadline dates, etc. Keep information on each mail out, whether the agency is accepting applications or not. Call the agency to see if the application was accepted or when applications might be accepted. Write down the name of the officer spoken with and, when calling back, make sure to ask for the same officer.

WORKING OUTSTATE

In Minnesota, people like to stay instate. However, students who really want to be police officers will travel to states that have jobs. As Dr. Darrell Krueger, President of Winona State University, says, "Prepare for your second job." It is prophetic since many of my students who have not found law enforcement jobs in Minnesota have gone to other states having reciprocity with Minnesota, that is, the student can work in another state as a fully sworn police officer for several years, then return to Minnesota and become a licensed police officer by counting the prior out-of-state police training accepted by POST. These officers need simply to pass a test to avoid the long waiting period of unemployment. This is good, smart business because it reduces loss and increases credentials.

THE MILITARY

The military can be a tremendous opportunity for immediate and future employment. If this is of interest, cultivate the recruiters starting in your junior year. The more a recruiter interacts with you, the more opportunity exists for that recruiter to see traits that would benefit the military occupational specialty for which you wish to contract.

NON-LAW ENFORCEMENT MAJORS

At a law enforcement training workshop, Dr. Jim O'Connor, at the time second in command of the FBI Academy in Quantico, Virginia, stated that within a few years many police departments will forgo the traditional street patrol requirement prior to becoming a detective and do direct hiring of business students into the detective ranks. Why? Because, according to Dr. O'Connor, traditional police training has failed to produce investigators capable of combating complex white-collar crimes that directly impact drug and violent crimes. You should know this as preparation for becoming a law enforcement professional.

EMPHASIS ON CRIME PREVENTION AND SECURITY

A major trend in law enforcement education and training is to include crime prevention and security functions. This is emphasized in many states, such as Minnesota, which has supported the Minnesota Crime Prevention Practitioners Association. This major movement blends the private sector with the public sector. The School of

Criminal Justice at Michigan State has blended programs with their business school. The Florida State University School of Criminology has a long tradition of multidimensional methodological interdisciplinary training.

Be prepared to confront more complex issues in the future as an interested "problem solver," not simply a standard criminal justice major or veteran of many police ride-alongs. Even Forrest Gump understood the private sector. You cannot major in criminal justice and not understand the private sector.

TIMING AND SALESMANSHIP

In an employment search, timing is important. So is salesmanship. Do what you love, not just what you like. If all else fails, take second best or whatever is available. This is where "positioning for future jobs" becomes important. Patience is important when you realize that the first job is not what you want, but is doable until the "right one" comes along.

It is easy to seek comfort when the rejection form letters come in. Good people get rejection letters, the same as all others. The difference is that those meant to be police officers are persistent. You have to sell yourself. You buy from salespeople who believe or want to believe in their product. For the same reason you want to help people, the public wants to believe in the concepts you have to sell . . . "serve and protect." These are intangibles until you make them concrete. Each department can function well only if the majority of their officers practice what they preach. And this can happen only if each officer has faith in their ability to sell themselves, to let the public "buy into" that particular offer.

THE PERFECT TRAINING PROGRAM

I am often asked what I would include in the "perfect training program." I would include philosophy, English literature, verbal and written communication, business management, salesmanship and marketing, problem definition, resource allocation, policy development and an evaluation of what you think you'd accomplished after all that. Why? For *awareness.* For prevention of loss and reduction of faulty risk-taking. For increasing accurate anticipation. *The same skills used to interpret a poem are used to write an accurate police report. And preventing loss is the same as increasing sales.*

In conclusion, do what you love and getting the job will be the easy part when you look back years later. And if you love what you do, the hard part will rarely surface unless you lose your sense of awareness, presence and problem definition. Love being a problem-solver for a simple reason: it takes less effort to sell an idea you love. You are about to go places where most of the public would not go, but do you have what it takes? Would you hire yourself?

———————

John Lombardi, Ph.D., CST, CPO, NAPS, IAPSC, is a professor of criminal justice and criminology at Albany State College in Albany, Georgia, where he teaches graduate and undergraduate courses in methodology, crime prevention and organizations. He earned his Ph.D. from the School of Criminology at Florida State University, has numerous national board certifications and is the former training director of the criminal justice training academy in Panama City, Florida and POST coordinator/professor at Minnesota State University in Winona, Minnesota.

MIND STRETCHES

1. List as many sources as you can in which employment ads might appear.

2. Why are many jobs filled without being advertised or filled before the ad appears?

3. List 10 contacts you have available right now through which you could begin networking.

4. If you were an employer deluged with applications, how would you eliminate 50% of them right away?

5. What errors could applicants make when contacting a prospective employer by mail?

6. Whether you contact an employer by phone, mail or in person, what three things would you want that person to remember about you?

7. What creative things can you do to get the attention of an employer? What possible benefits and detriments can you think of for each?

8. What strategies will you use to locate employment opportunities?

REFERENCES

Armstrong, Gordon M. and Schmalleger, Frank. *Career Paths: A Guide to Jobs in Federal Law Enforcement.* Englewood Cliffs, NJ: Regents/Prentice Hall, 1994.

Bolles, Richard Nelson. *What Color Is Your Parachute?* Berkeley, CA: Ten Speed Press, 1998.

Dauten, Dale and Nelson, Mark. "Finding a Job Takes Ingenuity, Time and Determination." (Minneapolis/St. Paul) *Star Tribune*, April 29, 1996a, p. D3.

Dauten, Dale and Nelson, Mark. "Job Hunt Requires More Than a Resume." (Minneapolis/St. Paul) *Star Tribune,* November 10, 1996b, p. D4.

Dauten, Dale and Nelson, Mark. "Trying an Offbeat Approach Sometimes Results in a Job." (Minneapolis/St. Paul) *Star Tribune*, June 23, 1996c, p. D3.

Frerkes, Larry R. *Becoming a Police Officer: A Guide to Successful Entry Level Testing.* Incline Village, NV: Copperhouse Publishing Company, 1998.

Kennedy, Joyce Lain. "Tips on Cautiously Moving Toward Getting the Job You Want." (Minneapolis/St. Paul) *Star Tribune,* February 26, 1995, p. J1.

Kenning, Linda. "Making Contact." In *Jobs*, a weekly publication of the (St. Paul) *Pioneer Press*, March 1, 1998, p. 1.

Krannich, Ronald L. and Krannich, Caryl Rae. *Find a Federal Job Fast! How to Cut the Red Tape and Get Hired*, 3rd ed. Manassas Park, VA: Impact Publications, 1995.

Lancaster, Hal. "Job-Lead Networks Growing in Popularity." (Minneapolis/St. Paul) *Star Tribune,* February 26, 1995, p. J1.

Lankford, Kimberly. "Help Wanted: Updating Your Search Skills." *Kiplinger's Personal Finance Magazine*, October 1997, pp. 83–85.

Mullins, Terry. "Search Skills: How to Land a Job." *Psychology Today,* September/October 1994, pp. 12–13.

"Networking 101." *Career Path Coach*, Vol. 1, 1997, p. 10.

CHAPTER 12

YOUR JOB-SEEKING UNIFORM:
PRESENTING YOURSELF AS THE ONE TO HIRE

You never get a second chance to make a good first impression.

—*Will Rogers*

Do You Know

➤ What the investment of the employer is in the hiring process?
➤ What the job-seeking uniform is and what elements it consists of?
➤ What the primacy effect is?
➤ What the four-minute barrier is?
➤ How you can find out how you come across to others and why this information may be useful?
➤ What the purpose of the interview is and how important knowledge is to this purpose?
➤ How what you are wearing influences people's perception of you?
➤ Why it is important to begin your job search in good physical condition?
➤ What your strategy will be for presenting yourself?
➤ The importance of follow-up?

INTRODUCTION

One critical aspect of how you present yourself is in the written material you submit. The importance of written materials was discussed in Chapter 9. It is emphasized again here because it is a vital part of how you will be viewed. Whatever you do, do it well. Don't submit insufficient, incomplete material or anything that doesn't look perfect. Just as "you are what you wear," so *you are what you write.*

Typos, misspellings, poor grammar, erasures and messy cross-outs tell an employer a lot. You cannot afford to look inept, uneducated, careless or sloppy. The weeding-out process becomes arbitrary at times, particularly with a number of equally qualified applicants. You may find yourself out of the running for something as simple as one misspelled word in your resume. This is not necessarily fair, but it is a fact. How you present yourself begins with your written materials. If you do an effective job, you are likely to get an interview. How should you appear at such an interview? What makes up your job-seeking uniform?

In a sense, we *all* wear uniforms, whether they have badges, patches and whistles, and whether we are actually on the job. A uniform is apparel that makes a statement. The police, corrections or security officer's duty uniform is designed to make a specific statement: *I am in charge!* Clothing worn by undercover officers also makes a statement, although quieter: I fit in (hopefully unobserved). Similarly, nurses have uniforms that meet their professional needs, as do bus drivers, waitresses, letter carriers, custodians, delivery people, orderlies, flight attendants, pilots and military personnel.

When matching clothing to a day's work, consider: What image do I want to project? What encounters will I have today? What does this sport coat say about me? This dress? This tie? This scarf? These shoes?

THE EMPLOYER'S INVESTMENT

Before getting into specifics of *how* to present yourself, look first at the situation from the employer's perspective. When hiring, employers are making a significant financial commitment. The typical medium-sized police agency will spend a few thousand dollars just on the hiring process alone. After an applicant is hired, it is expected they won't be truly productive for at least the first year of employment, so the agency is expending a year's salary just to cover training and administrative costs. Furthermore, that does not include the salaries of those who will be doing the training, guiding, etc. to bring the recruit "up to speed" so that he or she will become a productive member of the team.

During hiring, employers are also making an extremely important organizational decision. Employers are hiring someone to represent them to the public. In all areas of criminal justice and private security, public perception is critical. Employers can find themselves in serious trouble if they hire the wrong people for these jobs. In fact, employers may face civil lawsuits for "negligent hiring" (holding the employer responsible for hiring unsuitable employees who cause some sort of harm). Combine this with the fact that it is increasingly difficult to fire people, particularly in the public sector, and you can see the importance employers must place on the entire process.

> The employer has a significant investment in hiring the "right" people. In addition to the financial investment, those they hire represent the employer to the public. Also, hiring the wrong people can land an employer in legal trouble via "negligent hiring" lawsuits.

ELEMENTS OF YOUR JOB-SEEKING UNIFORM

Because employers have so much at stake when they hire personnel, and because their decisions must often be based on a few pieces of paper and 30 minutes of personal time with you, you *must* make the most of those pieces of paper and 30 minutes. How you present yourself during an interview is an important aspect of the overall getting-a-job process. Your strategy for presenting yourself must encompass the entire spectrum of how the prospective employer views you. Many factors come into play here. Employers will tell you that while someone may appear spectacular on paper, the interview provides an opportunity to eliminate many candidates.

Unwary applicants fall prey to this phase of the process for one of two basic reasons. First, they don't consider the importance of the various aspects of presenting themselves. Second, importance is placed on the wrong factors. Going into an interview with misunderstandings is like going into an exam only to find you have studied the wrong materials.

How you appear to the employer is obviously of critical importance. Appearance consists of the "whole person." The physical self, the emotional self and the spiritual/ethical self combine to create the balance that makes up "you." If one aspect outweighs the rest or is significantly lacking, you are out of balance. Something appears wrong. For instance, police officers may work odd schedules and perhaps compound things by attending school on the side. They may not have sufficient time to exercise regularly. Weight gain or a poor nutritional program could affect their health, making them feel run-down, irritable and out of sorts. Officers in this situation should re-examine their lifestyles to restore balance.

Employers will try to view the "whole" applicant during the hiring process. The obvious difficulty is that what employers get to see represents a small portion of your overall identity. After all, how long does it take for you to get to know another person, even yourself, before acquiring an accurate perception? Certainly more than the 30 minutes spent during the average interview.

Employers will look for high self-esteem, alertness, intelligence, critical thinking abilities and humanistic traits. They will also consciously watch for indications of sadistic, brutal, obsessive-compulsive personalities as well as those who might become victims of "groupthink" and "deindividualization" in the face of peer pressure, as in the case of the Los Angeles police incident involving the beating of Rodney King.

Most employers will examine the following elements during the hiring process to "get a feel" for the "whole" applicant:

- Initial contact
- Clothing/grooming
- Physical condition
- Grammar and speech
- Manners
- Personality
- Enthusiasm
- Knowledge
- Follow up

These elements make up your *job-seeking uniform*—what you put on to go out and get the job you want. Your uniform consists of more than just the clothes you wear; it's your total package. Wear it well.

> Your job-seeking uniform is how you present yourself during an interview. It consists of more than just the clothes you put on—your uniform includes how you come off during the initial contact, your grooming, physical condition, grammar and speech, manners, personality, enthusiasm, knowledge and follow up.

This is a lot of data to present to an employer, particularly in the short time you have. You have to develop a strategy to take advantage of the opportunities to sell yourself in each area. Properly pursued, you will have more than enough time to provide employers with an accurate picture of you. To best understand this, consider the dynamics of the interview process, that is, the mechanics of the system and the importance of the first few minutes.

THE PRIMACY EFFECT AND THE FOUR-MINUTE BARRIER

In *Effective Human Relations in Organizations*, Reece and Brandt (1987, p. 268) discuss the criticality of the first moments of any interaction among people: "When two people meet, their potential for building a relationship can be affected by many factors. Within a few moments, one person or the other may feel threatened, offended, or bored." This tendency to form impressions quickly is called the *primacy effect*. According to Reece and Brandt (p. 267): "The general principle is that first impressions establish the mental framework within which a person is viewed, and later evidence is either ignored or reinterpreted."

The primacy effect is the tendency to form impressions quickly, otherwise known as first impressions.

How long does it take for the primacy effect to occur? Leonard and Natalie Zunin give their opinion in the title of their book, *Contact—The First Four Minutes*. The Zunins introduce the concept of the *four-minute barrier* and suggest that within this short time, people in social settings will decide whether to continue the interaction. If you get through those first four minutes successfully, your interaction is likely to continue, and on a positive note.

The four-minute barrier refers to the length of time it typically takes for the primacy effect to occur. According to this concept, the first four minutes of a social interaction are crucial to the continuance of the interaction.

Reece and Brandt also suggest (p. 268): "The way you are treated in this world depends largely on the way you present yourself—the way you look, the way you speak, the way you behave. Although human contact is a challenge, you can learn to control the first impressions you make on others. The key is to become fully aware of the impression you communicate to other people." You can test the primacy effect theory by asking yourself some questions:

➢ Have you ever sat next to someone on a bus, train or plane and almost immediately wanted to talk with them? Or—decided to quickly get your nose into your book or magazine? Why?
➢ Have you ever had someone come to your door seeking contributions for some worthy cause and known almost immediately that you'd probably contribute? Or cut them short? Why?
➢ Have you ever had a teacher you just knew wasn't approachable to discuss a grade you received? Why?
➢ Have you ever gone into a job interview and known within minutes that you were a strong candidate? Why?

  In your journal, list what turns you off when you meet someone. What turns you on to a person?

It is natural to like some people and not others. How do you get to feel that way? How long does it usually take? How do you come across to others? Have you ever considered asking someone how you came across to them when you first met?

DIFFICULT INQUIRIES

It is important to understand *how* you come across to others because you can seldom judge this for yourself. How could you know how others perceive you? Do you dare ask? Most people seldom think of this. It's just too risky.

But it may be necessary, particularly if you are experiencing repeated rejections. We can all take constructive criticism. If that is what is needed to identify your weak points, take that risk.

For example, after leaving my initial law enforcement career path to go to law school, I returned to seek employment in the police field. Armed with experience, training and extensive education, I finished number two on almost every interview in which I participated. Why? I had to know. I called several individuals I had applied to and explained my motives for inquiring—not to criticize them, not to come back for another try at that job, but to understand how I could improve. I was stunned to learn I had not convinced them I did not want to practice law. They were all sure I would stay with them only until a "real" lawyer job was offered to me. Was this *their* fault? Of course not. It was mine for failing to anticipate this reaction and making false assumptions. My only regret was not taking this step earlier. In this case it worked. I got the next job I applied for.

Find out how you come across to others by asking. Although it may seem risky, the constructive criticism may help you identify and strengthen some of your weak points, particularly if you've been experiencing repeated rejections.

GETTING TO KNOW EACH OTHER

The goal of the preliminary process is really the same for both the prospective employer and for you: *getting to know each other*. It would be considerably more fair and accurate if time was unlimited. But it is not. For better or worse, you must deal with the brevity of the process and acknowledge the reality of the four-minute barrier. This is not all bad, however. If you recognize the elements of the interview, this is actually an ideal amount of time. Now take a more detailed look at each element of the job-seeking uniform, including what comes before and after the interview.

BEFORE THE INTERVIEW

One critical event before the interview might be a *phone call* to arrange the interview—or even a preliminary telephone interview. Yate (1998) discusses this important aspect of job seeking:

> Whatever circumstance creates this telephone interview, you must be prepared to handle the questioning and use every means at your disposal to win the real thing—the *face-to-face* meeting. The telephone interview is the trial run for the face-to-face, and is an opportunity not to be bumbled; your happiness and prosperity may hinge on it.

> Here are some tips:
> *Take a surprise call in stride.*
> *Beware of over-familiarity.*
> *Allow the company representative to do most of the talking, to ask the questions.*
> *Beware of giving yes/no answers.*
> *Be factual in your answers.*
> *Keep up your end of the conversation.*
> *Speak directly into the telephone.*
> *Take notes.*

The telephone interview has come to an end when you are asked whether you have any questions. Ask any more questions that will improve your understanding of the job requirements. If you haven't asked before, now is the time to establish what projects you would be working on in the first six months. By discovering them now, you will have time before the face-to-face meeting to package your skills to the needs at hand . . . .

And if you have not already asked or been invited to meet the interviewer, now is the time. Take the initiative. "It sounds like a very interesting opportunity, Ms./Mr. Smith, and a situation where I could definitely make a contribution. The most pressing question I have now is, when can we get together?"

INITIAL CONTACT

The interview itself is the brass ring you strive to get. When you get it, you *must* be on time. Before your interview date, it's important to know exactly where you're going so you can get there on time. Making excuses for a late arrival as an opener for your interview gets you off to a rocky start. So, when you are called for an interview, get clear directions on how to get to the interview. Make a trial run of the actual trip so you know how to get there and how long it takes. Plan to arrive 10 minutes early to allow yourself plenty of time in the event of traffic delays or parking problems.

CLOTHING AND GROOMING

Clothes make the person—and get (or lose) the job. Like so many other things, the "experts" have made a science of dressing for success. John T. Malloy, who coined the term *wardrobe engineering,* was among the first to stress publicly the link between professional accomplishments and wardrobe in his well-known book *Dress for Success.* His research indicates that your credibility and likability are immediately established by what you are wearing.

It cannot be overemphasized that those doing the hiring are likely to be older, conservative *men*. When a male applicant comes in with long hair, a studded earring and a tattoo, those doing the hiring will have already made up their minds before the first question has been asked. It isn't fair, and it probably isn't right, but employers are looking for people who will not cause problems by deviating from the norm all the time. Wharton (1997, pp. 59–60) asserts the path to a successful career begins with a great first impression:

> A job interview is a lot like a screen test: If you want to get hired, you'd better look the part. That means putting forth your sharpest image while avoiding small but potentially deadly gaffes, like a defiant clump of hair jutting from the back of your head. . . .
>
> When it comes to clothes, a little research goes a long way. Stroll through the lobby of your would-be workplace, or watch the parking lot at quitting time to see what employees are wearing. . . .
>
> Dark-blue and gray suits almost always work.

Wallach, in *Looks that Work* (1986, pp. 21–22), suggests: "Clothes talk. They say volumes about how we feel, how we want to be perceived, how we see others. We communicate through our appearance. The way we package ourselves sends out a particular message." Wallach (p. 20) explains that the wrong kind of clothing can make you feel awkward and out of place. Conversely, the right kind of clothing can make you feel confident and competent: "Most of us have also had the pleasure of wearing something that we feel makes us look attractive. That gives us confidence, and the confidence helps us to do a good job. All of these positive feelings become self-fulfilling. The better we feel about ourselves, the better the job we do."

Research indicates that your credibility and likability are immediately established by what you are wearing.

Few would argue with the research that tells us that people's appearance has a direct impact on how they come across to others and how they will be treated. Since clothing is extremely important, how should you dress for a job interview to make a favorable impression? You have dressed effectively if your interviewers do not even remember what you were wearing. You want them paying attention to you, not your clothing.

In planning an "appearance strategy," begin by identifying exactly what job is being interviewed for. An applicant for an executive position would dress differently than an applicant for a manual labor position. An interview for an officer position falls somewhere in between. Start with several givens:

➢ The jobs themselves are conservative.
➢ Extremists are generally not well accepted.
➢ The fields are viewed as important.
➢ They are seeking to be viewed as professions.
➢ You've got to look the part.

Begin by deciding on clothes that fall between the extremes, that is, *conservative*. A spangled three-piece suit and lots of gold jewelry is obviously inappropriate. So is a hopsack loincloth or a low-cut dress. Most agree that a smart looking, fresh, low-key appearance is called for.

Comfort is a factor. You will not perform up to your potential if you are dressed uncomfortably. If you do not feel good, it will show. Therefore, pick clothing you feel comfortable wearing. You can build on your interview outfit from this point.

A suit is traditional for an interview—for men and women. A suit conveys a statement: the person wearing it is businesslike, is capable of creating a positive image and is taking the interview and the interviewers seriously. The same can be said for a sharp sport coat with a nice pair of slacks, or a good-looking skirt with a neat blouse or sweater. The final decision is yours, but consider the following:

➢ Is your outfit conservative?
➢ Is your outfit comfortable?
➢ Could a suit work to your advantage or disadvantage? (Might a rural jurisdiction view a suit as "too much"? Might another jurisdiction view a tweed sport coat as "too little"?)
➢ What do you own now? Chances are you feel comfortable in clothing you own.
➢ Can you afford to buy new clothes for your interviews? Can you afford *not* to?
➢ How do you think you look?

Be aware that a dirty, stained or frayed item of clothing draws attention away from you. A new shirt does not cost that much, particularly considering that a worn collar looks just plain terrible. For women who chose a skirt instead of slacks, always wear hosiery and keep an extra pair handy in case you get a run.

The bottom line is: you are selling something—*you!* You need the tools to make that sale. If you do not have the proper clothing to make a good impression, buy some. Do so even if it means borrowing money or throwing yourself on the mercy of your family. You *must* appear like someone the interviewers would want representing their city, county, department, agency, institution or company.

A frequently overlooked area is that of accessories: socks, belt, tie, jewelry, shoes, etc. In addition to being conservative, you should use *common sense*. To review a few basics you probably already know:

➢　White socks? Absolutely NOT.
➢　Socks that are too short, or droop, or have runs or holes in them? Ridiculous.
➢　Hosiery that's more appropriate for evening or holidays? Hold off for the office party.
➢　An old, cracked, mismatched leather belt? Absurd.
➢　Too much jewelry? Leave it at home.
➢　Still using your father's old clip-on tie? Spend a few dollars for a new one.
➢　Worn-out heels or scuffs on the back of the heels from driving? Replace them.
➢　And don't forget to shine your shoes.

Avoid wearing pins or other jewelry identified with a particular fraternal, religious, athletic or other group or club. You risk offending someone participating in the interview. Even if such would not be the case, a lapel pin depicting a particular organization gives the interviewers something other than your face to focus on. Do not give them excuses to avoid eye contact. This reasoning also suggests that loud colors, wild patterns or any unusual apparel should be avoided. Colors and styles come and go. It is not a good idea to wear an obviously outdated style into an interview, no matter how well preserved that old lime green leisure suit is.

Since your perception of yourself is too subjective, solicit feedback from someone you trust. Ask them how you look. Hear the answer—good or bad. Make any necessary improvements. Also, seek help from clothing store clerks. Usually these people are fashion conscious. If you explain the purpose of the clothing you need, they can often offer very good suggestions. And remember the advice from an unknown source:

> *In clothes as well as speech, the man of sense*
> *will shun all the extremes that give offense,*
> *dress unaffectedly, and without haste,*
> *follow the changes in the current taste.*

Consider other resources when setting up your strategy for dressing. Many books and magazines deal with how to dress. Some go into great detail about what certain types of clothing and color. Such an approach may give you a slight advantage. Whatever works.

Another consideration is personal grooming. Although these things may seem obvious, before an interview evaluate such things as hair and nail care, makeup, antiperspirants, fragrance and breath freshness. Some things can be fixed relatively quickly; others may take more time.

One aspect of personal grooming that needs to be addressed before the day of the interview is your hair. Plan ahead to get a haircut so you are not panicking at the last minute. You don't want to walk into the interview looking like Shaggy the Wonder Mutt or with a perm so bad it looks like you just got struck by lightning. Maybe the interviewer won't even notice, but you will. The real danger is that you'll be uncomfortable and overly self-conscious, wasting valuable energy worrying about something that should have been taken care of earlier. Some applicants get a haircut a week or so before the interview to avoid that "freshly cropped" look, or leave enough time to fix a perm that didn't work. Women with long hair should consider putting it up or pulling it back so it doesn't fall in their face, creating a distraction for both the interviewer and the interviewee.

Also pay attention to your nails. Make sure they are clean and trimmed. Women should use discretion in how long they allow their nails to grow. You don't want your employer to wonder if you can type up a report or even pick a pen up off the floor without difficulty. If you choose to wear nail polish, select something subtle.

Women who wear makeup should choose a natural or professional look, as opposed to a dramatic look. Avoid heavy applications of eye shadow or cheek color, and select a lipstick that is flattering but doesn't scream "Read my lips!" Before the interview, make sure there is no lipstick on your teeth. If you're uncertain about how to achieve a professional look with makeup, consult a local department store cosmetics clerk.

Know if your antiperspirant works well in anxiety-producing situations. If it doesn't, find a new one! You'll likely be nervous enough without having the added worry about body odor. Conversely, don't overdo it on the fragrance. Go easy on the strong aftershave or perfume. While most people find body odor offensive, many people are just as offended by strong fragrances. Some people suffer allergic reactions from smelling such chemicals, and it will do you no good to have your interviewer in a sneezing fit throughout your entire interview.

Pay particular attention to your breath and oral hygiene. Nothing turns another person off more than *bad breath,* and many people don't even know when they have it. Believe me, your interviewer will know. Be sure to brush and floss your teeth before an interview, and avoid drinking liquor or eating exotic foods. These things can stay on your breath long after you've ingested them. The smell of garlic, for example, can remain in your system up to 72 hours after you eat it. Exotic foods, besides lingering on your breath, have the potential to cause other digestive complications. Save the exotic cuisine for the celebration dinner after you get the job.

One final note—never smoke or chew gum during an interview. Put it out or spit it out before you even enter the building. Check yourself in a mirror one final time before entering the interview room. And *smile.* A friendly smile can be key to the impression you make during those critical first four minutes. Make them feel good when they look at you.

PHYSICAL CONDITION

Closely related to clothing and grooming is your physical condition. Chapter 6 was devoted entirely to physical fitness and its importance. The fact is simple: Few other professions require you to be more physically fit than those of criminal justice and private security. You are not expected to be at your peak for only a few seasons or to compete in a once-in-a-lifetime event like the Olympics. You need to be in top physical condition every day you report for duty. The public depends on it. Your partners depend on it. *Your* life may depend on it. The very nature of the job is stressful. Many officers die, not only at the hands of criminals, but as victims of their own clogged arteries and unhealthy hearts.

Employers in these fields *will* notice your physical condition. Every police, corrections and security administrator knows it is hard to keep their officers in peak shape as the years tick by. They certainly do not want to start out with officers who are out of shape. It's not good for the employee, and it's not good for the department, practically or for appearance's sake.

Health factors aside, every organization is concerned about how the public perceives it. So much of criminal justice and security work is accomplished by easily identified officers. They are often uniformed and drive marked cars. No department wants overweight, out-of-shape officers representing them.

> Your job-search strategy should include being in good physical shape, not only because employers expect it, but because you will feel more confident about yourself. And confidence shows.

Finally, don't smoke. If you do—quit. An increasing number of police departments and private employers are including "nonsmoker" in their initial requirements. Public buildings are also quickly becoming totally smokefree. Besides the obvious health-related problems, smokers today look out of place, and many feel smokers present a bad image. Further, most smokers don't realize just how obvious the odor they have clinging to them is. An interview panel of nonsmokers will almost certainly be overwhelmed by the offensive odor of an applicant who smokes. It sends a message you don't want to send.

GRAMMAR AND SPEECH

Individuals employed in criminal justice and security are expected to present themselves like any other professional. As educational requirements for applicants increase, so do expectations about communication skills. Use of slang, obviously mispronounced words or limited vocabulary can embarrass an applicant.

Like physical fitness, communication skills take time to develop. Some people are better than others, and some simply need to brush up in this area. If you need to improve the way you speak, take some speech classes. Join Toastmasters. Volunteer in ways that require you to interact with the public. Feeling confident in how you sound will make you feel better because you will know you will be perceived better.

Be yourself. To try to come off too intellectually or too much like a seasoned professional will be perceived as phony. Don't address your interview panel as though you were giving a grand performance at Radio City Music Hall. Present yourself as you are.

MANNERS

Good manners make a great impression. They start with being on time for your appointment. If circumstances you cannot control dictate that you will be late, call to explain your delay. Shake hands with people at the beginning and end of each contact. Make your handshake an extension of yourself. It can communicate warmth, strength and confidence. Use a firm, full, deep grip and maintain eye contact. You might want to ask some friends how they feel about your handshake and, if need be, work to improve it. Reece and Brandt (pp. 281–282) offer seven "rules of etiquette" important in a business setting:

1. *When establishing new relationships, avoid calling people by their first names too soon* . . . . Informality should develop by invitation [call me Bob] rather than by presumption.
2. *Avoid obscenities and offensive comments or stories* . . . . Never assume that another person's value system is the same as your own.

3. *Do not express strong personal views regarding issues that may be quite controversial . . . .* There is seldom a "safe" position to take in the area of politics or religion.
4. *Never smoke in the presence of a fellow employee, customer, or client unless you are sure he or she will not be offended.*
5. *Avoid making business or professional visits unless you have an appointment . . . .* A good rule of thumb is always make an appointment in advance and arrive promptly.
6. *Express appreciation at appropriate times.* A simple thank you can mean a lot. Failure to express appreciation can be a serious human relations blunder.
7. *Be aware of personal habits that may be offensive to others . . . .* Chewing gum is a habit that bothers many people, particularly if you chew gum vigorously or "crack" it. Biting fingernails, cracking knuckles, scratching your head, and combing your hair in public are additional habits to be avoided.

Never let any contact with a prospective employer end without thanking the individual(s). Good manners go a long way toward impressing people.

PERSONALITY

Let the real you shine through! The stress associated with the job-search process makes it hard to appear as well as you need to. Stress and anxiety can intimidate you to the point that you sit rigidly upright during the interview, responding with short, one-word responses—the only goal being to live through the interview. Relax. Let them see *you*. You wouldn't buy a car or house based solely on how it looked from the outside. The same goes for hiring someone. Employers want to see who it is they are hiring, so let them.

ENTHUSIASM

Do you want the job, or do you *WANT* the job? Employers aren't interested in hiring someone who will pursue their work halfheartedly. They want people who greet each day as a unique challenge, make the most of every opportunity and do a *great job*. If you meander into the interview and respond casually to questions, why should they hire you? *You must show them* that you don't just want *a* job, you want *this job* with *this organization*. Let them know why. If you don't, someone else will.

It is amazing that so very few applicants, even when asked *why* they want the job, exclaim it is because they really want to work here, for *this* organization. When the interviewer asks if you have anything else you'd like to ask or say, you should make it absolutely clear that you really *do* want this particular job and that you will do a great job for them . . . and be enthusiastic about it!

KNOWLEDGE

The biggest error most applicants make when presenting themselves to prospective employers is misunderstanding what the employer is looking for. In the hiring process, this can be fatal. The purpose of the hiring process is for applicants to present themselves—the only thing the employer is interested in learning about is *you*. But most applicants go into the process thinking the employer wants to learn how much the applicant knows. If you concentrate entirely on memorizing facts, data, laws, rules and procedures, you have missed the point. They want to get to know *you*, not your capacity for memorizing. In fact, this is why the application process is so frightening for most applicants. They worry that they do not know enough. This is *not* what employers are looking for. This is not the police licensing exam. This is not the Certified Protection Professional licensing exam. *The interview is a chance for the employer to get to know you.*

Frerkes (1998, p. 63) states:

> The primary focus of the oral board process is to establish the applicant's command presence, integrity, initiative, interests, communication skills, tolerance for stress and judgement/decisiveness. It is their opportunity to assess the applicant's desire for professional growth, commitment to the community, whether he or she is people-oriented and has the potential to be a professional law enforcement officer.

The purpose of the interview is for the employer to have a chance to get to know *you,* not your capacity for memorizing or how much you know.

In reviewing the elements of your job-seeking uniform, you can see where an overemphasis on what you *know* could effectively prevent you from concentrating on the important factors—showing good manners, being enthusiastic about the job you're applying for and letting your true personality shine through. The incorrect assumption is that you will be hired for what you know instead of for who you are. If you get "hung up" thinking knowledge is all-important, you will waste an incredible amount of time before the interview trying to memorize reams of data that, for this particular purpose, are irrelevant. Concentrate on presenting yourself in the most positive way possible.

Knowledge *is* important. That is why it is included as part of your job-seeking uniform. Part of what the employer must know about you is what you know, but it is only one part, and a fairly small one. Depending on what field and position you are being interviewed for, there are certain things you will need to know. For example, in Minnesota, a person applying for any law enforcement position must know such elementary laws as the use of deadly force applicable and some basic Fourth Amendment search and seizure concepts. Such an applicant should be ready to answer questions about some basic procedures, for instance, situations dealing with Miranda, citizen safety or officer safety. You might want to take some criminal justice classes to help prepare. Ask people who have applied for similar jobs what questions they were asked.

You should also be able demonstrate how you would solve more complex legal issues. For example, if asked about fifth-degree assault, be able to tell the interviewer where you would go for that information. Or, given a hypothetical situation and asked how you would respond, be able to explain the process you would use to analyze the situation rather than just saying what you would do.

It is also important to know about the organization you're applying to. As Frerkes suggests (p. 64): "Be prepared to show a hiring authority that you care enough to know the particulars of that community. Educate yourself." For example, you should research and learn details about the follow specifics of a community:

➢ Population
➢ Racial climate
➢ "High profile" issues
➢ Size of the police force
➢ If community policing has been implemented
➢ Chief's name and how long he/she has held the position

> Type of government system in place
> Recent increases or decreases in crime statistics
> Unemployment rate

Much of this information can be obtained by doing an on-line search of a community's or agency's web site. The local chamber of commerce may also be able to provide up-to-date data.

If you were applying for a position as a brain surgeon or scientist, *what* you knew might be of primary importance. But for criminal justice and security jobs, particularly at an entry-level position or at the initial promotional stages, employers recognize that the right kind of person will be able to learn and grow with the job.

Take advantage of what you now know about what to expect during the interview and *plan your strategy* as to how you will present yourself.

"So what if you're not Einstein. Just go in there and be yourself."

Mullins (1994, p. 12) offers some advice on what to expect during an interview and how you should prepare for it. He refers to it as an "interview story" which typically consists of three scenes:

> Scene One: Lasting about three minutes, this scene consists of small talk and is really a compatibility contest. . . .
> Scene Two: Lasting about 15 minutes to an hour or more, this scene is mainly you telling your story. . . .
> Scene Three: Lasting only a minute or two, this scene closes the interview and sets up the next steps.

 In your journal, write down your plan for these three scenes.

1.   Scene One: What things will you do when you first enter the interview room? How can you show that you are polite, friendly and comfortable with yourself and the situation? Remember, this scene takes up most of the four-minute barrier time. What impression are you going to make and how? Write down your plan.

2.   Scene Two: This is your sales pitch scene—you must sell the interviewer on *you*. According to Mullins (p. 12), during this scene:

> You need to explain your skills, abilities, accomplishments, and ambitions. Emphasize your ability to add value to the employer. If you can claim credit for increasing sales, reducing costs, or improving quality, now is the time to do so. If you have any holes in your experience or blemishes on your record, handle them now. As you conclude this scene, stress your ability and willingness to perform at a high level.

Write your script for what you will say during this scene. Practice it. Get comfortable with it. Many people are uneasy talking about themselves or "tooting their own horn." That's what Scene Two is all about. Write down enough to keep you talking for at least 10 minutes (although realize it won't be 10 minutes *straight*—just have enough to say). Don't expect the interviewer to carry the conversation here—chances are you'll hear little from them during this scene.

3.   Scene Three: How will you end the interview? Mullins (p. 12) says:

> Do not allow the interviewer to close with the usual, "We'll be in touch with you when we decide something." This statement leaves you powerless to influence the decision. Instead, you should end the interview by saying, "I'll keep you posted about developments in my job search." This comment keeps you in control, allowing you to follow up with additional information that may improve your chance of being hired."

Write in your journal a closing comment similar to the one above, again, something you'd feel comfortable saying. Practice saying it. When the interview comes to a close, don't be caught off guard. You want your comment ready to roll off your tongue for the strongest possible conclusion to your interview story.

FOLLOW-UP

Follow-up refers to the extra steps taken after the interview, the time when most applicants sit and wait to hear from the employer. Just as you must never leave a contact with an employer without saying "thank you," you must not walk out of an interview never to be heard from again. A single follow-up thank-you letter can give you another chance to show off how well you wear your job-seeking uniform by reviewing such elements as:

> ➢ Grammar
> ➢ Manners
> ➢ Personality
> ➢ Enthusiasm
> ➢ Ability to follow up
> ➢ Knowledge

Six of the nine elements can be reinforced *after the interview*. You can also demonstrate again your proficiency with written material, and you provide the employer with one more reason to remember your name positively. Imagine the employer sitting with half a dozen or fewer resumes that all look good, pondering a decision. Suddenly you call to say thank you for the interview. This simple thank-you can tip the scales in your favor.

How you follow up is up to you. Some employers prefer not to be called while they are making a decision. While a phone call may not be a bad idea, it should not replace a letter. A letter is a necessity. Write to everyone who participated in your interview. Get their names, proper spellings and titles from the secretary on your way out or call the secretary later to get this information. Remember a thank-you for the secretary too.

Too much of a good thing is never good. Recognize the fine line between being remembered positively and becoming nothing more than a pest. Where that line is depends on your specific situation. You must decide. Remember, no one likes to be smothered, even by kindness.

Always follow up after the interview with a thank-you letter and possibly even a phone call. However, recognize the fine line between being remembered positively and becoming nothing more than a pest. Don't lay it on too thick.

CONCLUSION

Your job-seeking uniform is just that—how you present yourself during an interview. It consists of more than just the clothes you put on, however. Your uniform includes how you come off during the initial contact, your grooming, physical condition, grammar and speech, manners, personality, enthusiasm, knowledge and follow-up. Take advantage of what you now know about what to expect during the interview and *plan your strategy* as to how you will present yourself. Pick out your job-seeking uniform and put it on *before* your interview, just to make sure it fits and that you're comfortable in it. The more you wear it, the more natural it will feel. But you must practice putting it on and wearing it for it to be most effective. Plan how you will present yourself as *THE* one to hire.

AN INSIDER'S VIEW

BE PREPARED

Robert P. Meyerson
Minnesota State Trooper I

Most law enforcement departments look at many applicants before filling an available position. Successful candidates find a way to distinguish themselves. Working at each step of the job application process is vitally important. Successful candidates will impress the potential employer both with the substance of their abilities and background, *and* with their candidates' style that shows that they care enough to try a little harder than the rest of the field. If you follow the steps outlined below, you will land the job you want.

An initial job interview may last only 20 or 30 minutes. Successful candidates make every minute of the interview count. This requires preparation well before the interview takes place.

Before you ever get an interview, you will undoubtedly submit an application and a resume. Make a good first impression. If possible, type the application. If you submit a resume, make it look professional. It is money well spent to have your resume professionally typeset or prepared on a word processor.

Emphasize those matters on your resume that will impress your potential employer. Obviously, law enforcement-related activity is important (both past employment and education). But also remember other activities which show that you are a dependable team player who will work well in the department: community activities, participation in athletics and volunteer work are just some examples of activities you should include in your resume. Caution: include all-important information, but limit your resume to one or two pages. No one wants to read your autobiography.

If you are asked to appear for an interview, *get prepared.* Find out everything you can about the department that will interview you. How large is it? How is it organized? What are special projects or cases that have received attention within the department, in the community and the like? What will your starting pay be if you are hired? What will the job requirements be? What benefits are offered? What kind of person is this department looking for? Who will conduct the interview? What kind of person is he or she?

These questions are all-important to you, but why waste your valuable 20- or 30-minute interview getting the answers? You can learn much of this information by checking local newspapers, getting any community or departmental information pamphlets which describe the department, reading information given with the job posting and talking with people familiar with the agency.

If you know someone with connections in the department, do not be shy about letting that person know about your interest in the job. These contacts can be an invaluable source of information, and you never know when they may communicate a favorable impression of you to the department.

When you get to the interview, look your best. Wear a professional-looking suit. If you do not own one, now is a good time to buy one. Be well groomed. Remember: an interviewer will see many candidates. Everything you do to rise above the competition increases your chances of success.

During the interview, be *confident*. You should be. You have already put your best foot forward with a well-prepared application and resume. You have learned everything you can about the department and the interviewer who is interviewing you. Now be a salesperson. Let the interviewer know that you have done your homework by asking intelligent questions. (Example: "I know that the department has an active accident prevention program. How would a new officer have an opportunity to participate?")

Let the interviewer know that you truly believe you can contribute to the department by giving examples of how your experience has prepared you for the job. (Example: "I was a referee in Pop Warner football; I learned to maintain my authority when others lost their cool.") Be confident, but do not be cocky or full of hot air. A good interviewer or officer will spot B.S. immediately.

Remember that a department has many candidates applying for the same job. If you work at each step of the process to be a little better than the rest of the crowd, you *will* get the job you want.

Robert P. Meyerson is a Trooper I with the Minnesota State Patrol. He has 18 years' experience in criminal justice. Mr. Meyerson has also worked as a deputy sheriff for the Hennepin County Sheriff's Department and a police officer in both Lake Crystal, Minnesota, and Janesville, Minnesota. He holds a B.S. in Political Science and Law Enforcement from Mankato State University. Trooper Meyerson is married to Kammie; they have two children. His hobbies include hunting, fishing, singing and dog training. He is currently a canine handler for the Minnesota State Patrol.

AN INSIDER'S VIEW

PRESENTING YOURSELF AS *THE* ONE TO HIRE

Brenda P. Maples
Lieutenant
Memphis (Tennessee) Police Department

Whether you are applying for a position with a large law enforcement department or a small department, you will be required to complete a series of testing procedures. This allows the department to glean the best qualified from all the applicants. This battery of tests will probably consist of written, oral and physical agility tests. The testing procedure may vary from department to department; however, at some time during the hiring process you will be asked to come for an oral interview. This is your chance to sell yourself, to make a lasting and favorable impression.

First impressions do persist. Your initial appearance can go a long way toward impressing the interviewer, either positively or negatively. Take a long look in a full-length mirror. If you were running a business, would you hire someone who hadn't put on clean clothes or gotten a haircut in several weeks? Wear your "Sunday go to meetin'" clothes and get a fresh haircut or style so you appear neat. You will feel more poised when you know you look your best.

Don't go into the interview cold turkey. Prepare!! The purpose of the oral interview is to gather information and judge face-to-face interaction. This is an important element of law enforcement work because of the time spent dealing with the public, either as complainants, victims or suspects. You will be continually seeking information from others in order to make decisions.

An interviewee must be confident but not overly aggressive. An intelligent interviewee should anticipate the questions asked in a typical employment interview and rehearse the answers. To prepare, record yourself on video. This is a helpful way to practice your responses and gain confidence. When you review the video, be aware of any weaknesses or areas in which you might improve. Are you able to communicate effectively in clear and logical sentences? Do you use correct and accurate diction? Many judgments are made about other people's intellectual achievements by the way they talk.

While viewing your video, also be mindful of nonverbal communication. This can include facial expressions, fidgeting, hand and arm movements and lack of eye contact. Try to keep nervous mannerisms under control. Sometimes you say more with nonverbal communication than you realize. After all, how does a good investigator get that "gut feeling" when talking to a potential suspect?

You will be asked questions relating to your experience and any special skills or abilities you may possess. You probably have much more going for you than you think. Try to think of experiences where you demonstrated your abilities and skills.

With all these tips on how to sell yourself during an interview, you're still trying to present your unique self. A phony personality will be spotted by any seasoned interviewer. Sincerity and enthusiasm can go a long way in selling yourself as THE right person for the job.

Brenda P. Maples is a lieutenant with the Memphis (Tennessee) Police Department and has 23 years' experience in the criminal justice field. She holds a B.S. from Middle Tennessee State University, is the national president of the Law Enforcement Alliance of America and the vice chairman of the Tennessee Peace Officers and Standards Commission.

MIND STRETCHES

1. What three things have made you feel accepted by another person while you attempt to break the four-minute barrier? What three things have made you feel unaccepted by another person while you attempt to break the four-minute barrier?

2. How would you work your responses to Question #1 into the job application process?

3. List opportunities you could create to sell yourself besides the traditional resume and interview.

4. Why is it important to approach the elements of the interview as a whole rather than looking at the pieces separately?

5. Why is it important to develop a *strategy* rather than just jumping into the interview process?

6. Who could you ask for constructive feedback on how you come across to others by your clothing? Your handshake? Your cover letter and resume? Their initial reaction to you?

7. Which elements of the interview do you think you need to work on? How will you do so for each?

8. How might videotaping yourself be beneficial in preparing for an interview?

REFERENCES

Frerkes, Larry R. *Becoming a Police Officer: A Guide to Successful Entry Level Testing.* Incline Village, NV: Copperhouse Publishing Company, 1998.

Mullins, Terry. "Search Skills: How to Land a Job." *Psychology Today,* September/October 1994, pp. 12–13.

Reece, Barry L. and Brandt, Rhonda. *Effective Human Relations in Organizations,* 3rd ed. Boston, MA: Houghton Mifflin Company, 1987.

Wallach, Janet. *Looks that Work.* New York: Viking Penguin, Inc., 1986.

Wharton, David. "Fit to Be Hired." *Men's Fitness*, November 1997, pp. 58–60.

Yate, Martin John. *Knock 'em Dead with Great Answers to Tough Interview Questions.* Boston: Bob Adams, 1998.

CHAPTER 13

THE INTERVIEW: A CLOSER LOOK

Whenever you are asked if you can do a job, tell 'em, "Certainly I can"—and get busy and find out how to do it.

—Theodore Roosevelt

Do You Know

➢ What the definition of *interview* is?
➢ What purposes the interview serves?
➢ What five types of interviews you may encounter and how they differ?
➢ How likely you'll be able to negotiate your salary?
➢ How you should close an interview?
➢ What the importance of follow-up is?

INTRODUCTION

The interview. It even sounds ominous. Fear of the unknown can be paralyzing. So take a good look at what you might expect because the interview *is* what it's all about in the job-hunting game.

Webster's defines *interview* as: "A formal consultation usually to evaluate qualifications (as of a prospective student or employee). A meeting at which information is obtained." Here are some facts about job interviews:

➢ Interviews are anxiety provoking.
➢ Interviews are necessary.
➢ Everyone has to have them.
➢ Everyone working has had them.

> An interview is a meeting between someone who has a job opening and someone who needs a job, at which information is obtained and exchanged.

PURPOSES OF THE JOB INTERVIEW

For you, the purposes of the interview are to show the panel the "real" you and to find out who the "real" employer is. Ask any employer, and they will have stories of applicants who looked nothing short of spectacular on their resumes but were absolutely unacceptable in person. A good resume, in addition to the other preparatory material and contacts, is just your ticket *into* the interview. An advantage of the preliminary phases of the job-seeking process is that you can get help from friends, for example, proofreading your written material. But once you are led into the interview room, you are on your own. It is completely up to you—as it should be. For employers, the purpose of an interview is to get to know you. Simple? Your entire future based on a brief interview? Simple?!

Bolles (1998) likens the interview to the "dating game." He notes: "*Both* of you have to like the other, before you can get on to the question of 'going steady.'" According to Bolles, employers have four key questions:

➤ Why are you here? (Why did you pick us?)
➤ What can you do for me?
➤ What kind of person are you?
➤ How much are you going to cost me?

The main thrust of any interview is to see how you interact on a personal level. This is extremely important. The process of getting a job and developing a strategy to meet this challenge boils down to two critical aspects:

➤ Having a resume that can withstand the "weeding out" process.
➤ Developing a strategy to not only withstand the interview process, but to emerge victoriously.

The Purposes—Up Close

The personal interview can fulfill several purposes.

The primary purposes of the personal interview are for the employer to:

➤ Get a look at you.
➤ Listen to you.
➤ See how you perform under stress.
➤ Observe how you analyze problems.
➤ Test your people skills.
➤ Test your knowledge.

Looking at You. Employers would no more hire an unknown person than they would purchase a home or a car they had never seen. They want to see what they are getting. Particularly for a job in criminal justice or private security, you do not want to make a negative impression by presenting yourself in an extreme manner. If hired, you will represent the agency. To most future clients you will *be* the agency. Think about it! The interviewers will be thinking about it, rest assured.

Remember the importance of grooming. Find the restrooms on your way into the building to make that final check: comb your hair, straighten your tie, adjust your slip, zip up your zipper. *Look sharp. Be sharp.* Also get a drink of water.

Listening to You. No matter how great your resume looks or how sharp you look, employers want to know that you also speak English well. There will probably never be a better test of this than during the job interview. In addition to testing your general grammatical skills, employers want to hear how you sound. They want their employees to sound *normal.* If you get uptight during an interview (and understand that everyone does), just be yourself. Do not try to cover up your anxiety by being cute, funny, smart-alecky or a host of other facades you've probably seen people try when uptight.

What if you *sound* nervous? Your voice may crack, you may say something you did not intend to, or you may just plain forget where you were or what the question was. Don't panic. It is reassuring to employers to see you as capable of recognizing a mistake and being able to reorganize and continue. Do not fake it. If a major goof occurs, simply proceed as follows:

➢ Grip the side of your chair.
➢ Take a deep breath.
➢ Admit to the interviewer(s): "This job is really important to me, and I guess I'm more nervous than I thought."
➢ Continue with your answer.

There is nothing wrong with being honest. If you are really nervous, admit it; 99.99999% of the time interviewers are sympathetic. Your honesty will make a positive impression. Also, they just may be easier on you.

Take a moment before you answer a question, especially if the question is *not* one you "practiced." What may seem like an eternity will probably be only a matter of seconds. Never answer without thinking through your response.

Seeing How You Perform Under Stress. Some employers use a "stress interview." The rationale is that the job you are seeking is stressful, so they want to see what you do under stress. Such interviews often involve "rapid-fire" questions during which you have little or no time to think about your response. The interviewers may appear hostile or demanding to you. They may ask questions you just can't answer—either because you lack the expertise or because there *is* no answer.

Because the purpose of stress interviews is to see how you will act, do your best to keep your wits about you. Brainstorm all the possible weird things that could be set up in an interview. Ask others what they have undergone in interviews, and you will be as well prepared as you can be for this experience. Fortunately, these interviews are not too common. Stress interviews are discussed further on page 265.

Observing How You Analyze Problems. You may be asked to solve problems presented to you. Particularly at an entry-level position, you are *not* expected to know every exact answer. For example, an interview for a police dispatcher might include such questions as, "What would you do if 25 747s crashed in various parts of the city at once?" A potential corrections officer might be asked, "What would you do if you were the only guard in your pod and, during a power outage, 21 inmates became embroiled in a massive knife fight?" Or a potential security officer might be asked, "What if you were accosted by 17 chapters of Hell's Angels demanding a solution to world hunger?" Remember that even if there is an answer, in all probability you are not expected to know it.

Prospective employers want to know if and how you think. A good strategy is to begin your answers with your own variation of the "policy/will learn" statement. That is, you understand that every company/department is likely to have its own policy on how to handle most situations and that you are also eager to learn.

For example, if asked, "How would you handle a situation in which you find an open door to an office after hours, and the boss is inside with his partner's wife?" A reasonable answer could be: "Because I have had no previous security experience, that situation is certainly a difficult one. Based on the information you have given me, I would follow the applicable company policy; for instance, filling out an incident report if required, as well as immediately advising my supervisor. In addition, I would anticipate learning how the company would want me to handle such sensitive situations during my training period. If it is not brought up, I will bring it up now that you've asked me about it." During such analytical interviews, rather than looking for a right answer, the interviewers are interested in the *process* you use in coming to some conclusions.

Testing Your People Skills. Your resume may look spectacular, but if you cannot come across as friendly, sincere and at least somewhat appealing, you will not get the job. No matter how nervous you get, no matter how frustrating the interview is, do not forget your manners. Let the interview board know that you appreciate their time and that you appreciate the challenging questions raised. Shake hands with each interviewer, smile, say "yes" not "yeah," and use *common sense*.

This is all more easily said than done. Whether or not the interview is specifically intended to create stress, it will! The "little things" are so easily forgotten. Well before the interview, make a list of what you want to do. For example:

➢   Shake hands with everyone when introduced.
➢   Look at everyone personally during your responses.
➢   Thank the group at the end of the interview and again shake the hand of each interviewer.

Thinking about it all ahead of time will put it in your head. It is then easier to remember during the pressure of the interview.

Testing Your Knowledge. You may also be asked questions to check your knowledge in specific areas, depending on the state in which you are applying. For police officers, you could be asked about very basic statutes, for example, the deadly force law. You should be prepared to answer as many of these questions as possible, but do not panic if you cannot. In such a situation admit that you do not know, but that you would look it up in the state statute book, or the traffic code or wherever it is likely to be found. *Do NOT guess.* If you draw a blank, admit it. In such a case, you may want to follow up with a letter providing the answer to show you can find needed information. According to Mounts (1997, p. 65):

> What is the reason for an oral interview? Is it to test your technical knowledge? Generally speaking, the answer is no. In most cases, your technical knowledge will be, or has already been, addressed in the written examination and through various performance evaluations. However, some interviews do test part of your technical knowledge coupled with your conceptual skills, such as: quality of work experience and training, stability, ambition, ability to work with others, communication skills, manner, speech, decision making, and interpersonal skills.

Most of the important purposes of an interview can be addressed during one question posed by the panel. A common question for police officer applicants is: "What would you do if you stopped an off-duty officer for drunk driving?" Try the "policy/will learn" approach to come up with an answer. For example, "If the department had a policy, I would follow it. I would certainly advise my supervisor. Recognizing that DWI is a serious offense and that police officers are not above the law, I would . . . ." You get the idea. Such a question gives you a great chance to appear at your best—or worst.

Imagine you are an employer seeking to fill the position of either police, corrections or security officer. An applicant has just walked into the room. List in your journal five things that would turn you off immediately.

Next, list five things that would strike you positively.

A San Francisco financial recruiting firm surveyed 100 large corporations to find out how some job applicants performed during the interview. Among the responses were the following:

➢ Said he was so well qualified, if he didn't get the job it would prove that the company's management was incompetent.
➢ Asked to see the *interviewer's* resume to see if the personnel executive was qualified to judge the candidate.
➢ Announced she hadn't had lunch and proceeded to eat a hamburger and french fries in the interviewer's office.
➢ Wore a Walkman and said she could listen to me and the music at the same time.
➢ Dozed off and started snoring during the interview.

Unbelievable, but true. What should you do during the interview? Bolles suggests paying attention to not only *what* you say but also *how* you say it. According to Bolles, various studies have shown that the people who get hired are typically those who speak half the time in the interview and let the employer speak the other half of the time. He also advises, based on similar studies, that when it is your turn to speak in the interview, you should talk no shorter than twenty seconds and no longer than two minutes at any one time.

TYPES OF INTERVIEWS

Interviews provide employers with a chance to observe you from a variety of perspectives. The majority of interviews can be classified as:

> ➢ Informational
> ➢ Mass
> ➢ Stress
> ➢ Unnecessary
> ➢ Courtesy

Informational Interviews

This is the "classical" interview, where you are asked to come in to give employers a chance to check you out in the areas previously outlined. These interviews are straightforward. Presumably you enter this interview in a relatively equal position with the other applicants. You have no say about what format your interview will take, so "go with the flow." The interview may be formal, relaxed or somewhere in between. You may have only one interviewer, or there may be several.

The formal interview is rather rigid, with questions being asked one after another and the interviewers giving little or no response to tip you as to how you are doing. They purposely do not respond so that you will not have any advantage over other applicants. This can be rather disconcerting since everyone likes feedback, but just continue on. On the other extreme, you may find yourself caught off guard by the informality of your interview. Your interviewers may be so laid-back, it may seem they don't even care. While possible, don't let a group that likes to have fun throw you off. In either case, provide your interviewer with as accurate a picture of yourself as you can. Just because you find yourself in a formal setting doesn't mean you must perform as rigidly as a stick, nor should informality lull you into a false sense of security and make you lose your edge.

> The informational interview is the classical interview. These interviews are straightforward and are typically one-on-one, although there may be more than one interviewer present.

Mass Interviews

The number of individuals that employers like to interview varies. One or two applicants may be invited to be interviewed if they are exceptionally strong candidates, or many people may be asked in. So many applicants present themselves so poorly that a general informational meeting can serve to weed out a number of them.

"Assembly line" interviews are hard on everyone, including those conducting the interviews. Applicants seem to melt together, making it difficult to remember who was who. This is when it is critical to not only provide a very strong interview, but to also pay particular attention to your follow-up.

> Mass interviews involve several candidates being interviewed in rapid succession, or in "assembly line" fashion. In these situations, candidates may blur together in the interviewers' minds, and you must pay particular attention to your follow-up to stand out from the crowd.

Stress Interviews

Here you have good news and bad news. The good news first: True "stress interviews" are seldom conducted. The bad news is that criminal justice and private security do lend themselves to this type of interview. These jobs involve a great deal of stress, so the approach is justified to see how applicants respond under stress. Don't expect these to be comfortable. They are designed not to be. You cannot do anything about it. Go into the interview with the commitment that, regardless of the type of interview you are confronted with, you will do your best.

During stress interviews rapid-fire questions give you little time to think about your answers or to regroup before the next question. The interviewer may seem harsh, if not downright mean. Furniture may be placed in unusual configurations; for instance, your chair may be put in a corner—or maybe you won't even have a chair.

Recognize what the game is here—to get you uptight. You *should* feel tension. In fact, you have much more reason to be concerned if you *don't* respond nervously to this setup. Draw energy from a stress interview and maintain your cool. Use the strength that brought you this far. When you get the job, you'll find yourself confronted with similar stress. The interviewers want to be sure you won't become overly defensive, hostile or panicky. While many interviewees would tell you that *every* interview is a stress interview, in fact, few are set up to purposely get you uptight.

> The stress interview's purpose is to get you uptight so the interviewers can evaluate how you handle stress. Rapid-fire questioning, interviewer hostility and unusual furniture configurations may all be parts of the stress interview.

Unnecessary Interviews

Many jobs are filled before they are even advertised. Letting this fact influence you too greatly is similar to not trying to get a job because the world is eventually bound to end. There is always a chance you'll survive. What if the job is promised to someone else? Who's to say that person will accept it? If they do, who's to say it will work out? What if someone even higher up at that agency doesn't like that person? Most important, what if they like *you* better?

No interview is unnecessary. It's just that some seem more necessary than others. At the very least, it is a chance to practice your interview skills and find out you can survive rejection. Both opportunities are valuable. Because you are unique, you may be the perfect candidate. Never let an opportunity pass by. You have no way of knowing if this job will be *the one*. A lot can be said for the person who tries, even in the face of adversity.

"Unnecessary" interviews may be conducted when the position is already filled but policy demands the position still be advertised or that a certain number of people be interviewed. Make the most of this opportunity—no interview is truly needless.

Courtesy Interviews

Never say, "Ah, I only got this interview because the chief knows my dad. He did it as a favor to him." So what? It doesn't matter *how* you got into an interview, just that you did. Once you're there, it's all up to you. Some opportunities to interview do result because the applicant knew someone or was related to someone in the agency. So what?

You've heard the saying, "It's not *what* you know but *who* you know." All that matters is that *now* you have the chance to impress the interview panel. Worrying about how you got there consumes valuable energy. Go for it!

Courtesy interviews are done as favors or because of "connections," but they are still legitimate interviewing opportunities. Again, make the most of them.

Teleconferencing—A New Twist

Technology is changing the way jobs are pursued and found. A trend today is using video technology for conducting interviews. While face-to-face meetings between job seekers and prospective employers are still most common, any of the preceding types of interviews may also be conducted through teleconferencing. Healy (1996, p. D4) notes: "Although video teleconferencing has been on the market for several years, the video job interview is a fairly recent development." The two primary reasons for the growing popularity of this method are that others beyond the formal process can view the interview and that applicants a long distance away from a potential employer can effectively compete for a position without having to travel extensively.

Such "interviews" may consist simply of a candidate's videotaped responses to questions or it may be a "live" interview via video hookups, such as is done routinely on the national evening news. Internet technology is going to make it equally convenient for prospective employees or employers to communicate, interview and negotiate long-distance.

Police Chief Len Harrell in Mound, Minnesota, has discussed strategies to optimize this opportunity. He suggests applicants present themselves in different modes to set off their personality. For example, some questions could be answered in a dress uniform, others in a suit, and yet others more casually in a sweater. He tells of a fire chief who answered questions with a fireplace or fire truck behind him. This is a chance to plan how to present yourself in your best light and to be far more in control of the situation than in most conventional interviews.

TYPICAL QUESTIONS

Countless lists have been compiled of questions you should anticipate and be prepared for during job interviews. Some of these questions are construed as quite "self-incriminating," as noted by Weiss and Dresser (1998, p. 48):

> Kill questions relate to being fired, arrested, experiencing discontent with an employer, problems with a supervisor, being too slow and so on. Red flag questions are those that can place the interviewee on the defensive, or in a negative light. These go on forever and can include:
>
> > "My worst characteristic is . . ."
> > "If I could change one trait about myself . . ."
> > "People criticize me because . . ."
>
> And
>
> > "My weakest point is . . . ."
>
> An applicant must be honest and answer the questions. Many people are not shrewd enough to provide a positive illustration of a success in dealing with a shortcoming.

Kinsman (1996, p. D4) offers tips on how to respond to some "chilling" questions:

Why should I hire you? . . .
Start by talking about your work experience that has prepared you for this job and then talk about your educational background that will lend an understanding on the job.

Why have you been out of work for so long? . . .
Say that you were trying to approach your period of unemployment as a career opportunity and that you were looking for a position that truly matched your talents.

What are your future plans? . . .
A potential employer usually wants to find out if you have a commitment to this job . . . . Employers want to hire individuals who have a vision of their future.

Why were you fired from your last job? . . .
Prepare an honest, thoughtful description of the reasons behind your firing. Make certain, however, that you don't begin to weave together a detailed defense of your position or bad-mouth your former employer . . . . Most employers are less concerned about why you were fired than in how you respond to questions about it.

To tackle the common interview question of "What is your biggest weakness?" Nelson and Dauten (1996, p. D3) recommend: "Just name your best attribute, then put the word 'too' in front of it." Pearson (1998, p. 57) suggests some other questions that might be asked during an interview:

How can your skills and abilities meet the needs of this position?
What was the most enjoyable part of your previous position?
Why did you leave your last position?
What are your career goals?
What are some of the things you look for in a job?
If you could have an ideal job, what would it be?

Following are some typical questions. As you read through them, consider this particularly relevant comment from Yate (1998): "To some of the toughest questions, there is never a 'right' answer—that's what makes them the toughest—but there is always a right approach."

 You'll notice that most of the questions call for more than a mere "yes" or "no" answer. Concentrate on *your* approach to each question. What would make a good response to each? Write your responses in your journal.

1.   What makes you think you would be an asset to this agency?

2.   When did you first consider joining the police/corrections/security field?

3.   What public service organizations or clubs do you belong to?

4.   Do you realize that your previous training will be of little value in the job you are applying for?

5.   Do you have applications in at other agencies?

6.   Are you married? If so, what does your spouse think of your career choice? The odd hours you'll be working?

7.   Are any of your friends members of this agency?

8.   Do you have any relatives who are members of this agency?

9.   When did you first think about becoming a police/corrections/security officer?

10. Have you ever taken any tests for law enforcement/corrections/security positions?

11. Have you ever considered the hazardous nature of the work we perform?

12. Have you talked over the conditions, opportunities and the attitudes of members of this agency with the agency?

13. What are your hobbies?

14. Have you trained for this position by going to any coaching schools, taken any courses or the like?

15. If you are chosen for the job, would you make it your lifetime career?

16. Has the security of the job or the desire for service been your main reason for applying for this position?

17. What is your attitude about unions in police/corrections/security fields?

18. You are a member of this agency and a fellow officer has been injured along with civilians. To whom would you give your first attention?

19. You are a member of this agency and you suspect that a fellow officer is committing thefts in the district/office/business while off duty. What action would you take?

20. You are patrolling on the midnight-to-morning watch and have been walking hours without seeing anyone. Would you find an unoccupied auto and rest?

21. You receive an order you believe to be in error from your superior. What action would you take?

22. Who would you rather please in your work, your superior officer or the public?

23. What kind of job do you feel this agency is doing?

24. How would you improve the quality of work in this agency after you have been trained?

25. What is your present occupation? Do you feel the training you have received will benefit you if selected to join this agency?

26. What do your friends think of you joining this agency?

27. Have you ever had difficulty with any law enforcement agency either as a juvenile or as an adult?

28. Give us a brief idea of what a good law enforcement/corrections/security officer should be in the way of character, knowledge and physical condition.

29. What are your greatest strengths? Your greatest weaknesses?

30. Where do you expect to be 10 or 20 years from now?

31. Why should we hire you?

32. What are your strongest attributes?

33. Are there things we should be concerned about?

34. I there anything else you would like to say or ask?

The following questions should be anticipated by those seeking positions in law enforcement.

35. Why did you choose the police department instead of the fire department?

36. Have you ever stood around when you saw a crowd gathered about a serious accident or when a police officer was investigating a crime or making an arrest?

37. Do you listen to police calls on shortwave radio? If yes, and you hear a call that sounds serious, do you go to where the officers were sent?

38. You are off duty and a purse-snatcher runs past you with the victim in pursuit. What action would you take?

39. You find that your superior drinks to excess and is drunk on the job. The place your superior drinks is on your beat. What action would you take? Would you say anything to the bartender who serves your superior?

40. Should the police and fire departments be integrated into a single unit known as a public safety department?

41. Should this agency perform such tasks as letting locked-out people into their homes, escorting single women home at late and unusual hours, removing from the street debris that has accidentally fallen from moving vehicles?

42. What is this agency's responsibility in respect to juvenile delinquents?

43. Under the authority of government you would represent, could you use deadly force against a citizen where your life or the life of someone else was threatened? Could you take another person's life under any other circumstances?

Guidelines for Replies to Commonly Asked Interview Questions

Having studied these questions and formulated answers, see how close you come to the following guidelines.

1. Indicate such items as interest in working with people, interest in serving the public and having completed so many hours of related course work.

2. Frequently the oral board gives great weight to someone who has considered law enforcement/corrections/security as a career for a long time.

3. You might mention Rotary, Lions, Kiwanis, various veterans' organizations, as well as such high school organizations as Key Club or anything similar.

4. This is a "loaded" question. Politely take exception. All training you have received in citizenship, first aid, governmental organizations and the like is important. Rifle club memberships are also important. The value lies in understanding the functions of departments, etc.

5. Answer frankly, but indicate that the agency in question is your first choice.

6. It is hoped that your "significant other" enthusiastically backs your decision.

7. Be able to recall the names of police/corrections/security officers you know.

8. Answer truthfully, even if the relationship is extremely remote.

9. Again, the oral board may give great weight to someone who has been considering that particular career over time.

10. Answer frankly. It might be best to indicate that this agency is your first choice.

11. Indicate that you are aware of the hazards in dealing with the criminal element and in driving a patrol vehicle, such as handling aggressive prisoners or driving at pursuit speeds, but that you do not consider law enforcement/corrections/security to be any more hazardous than any other occupation. You might indicate that some training you have received and some experience you've had in observing procedures have helped alleviate this hazard.

12. Talk to members of the agency before the interview. Know the agency's salary range and something about the agency itself and the city/industry, such as its approximate size, its type of government/management and so on.

13. Organize your thinking so your answer stresses activities related to law enforcement/corrections/security. Among these may be target shooting, skeet shooting, hunting, youth activities such as scouting, or sports, particularly wrestling, boxing and the martial arts.

14. This is a good chance to list the related courses you have successfully completed.

15. Answer this question affirmatively.

16. Job security and service to the public are two factors in your decision. Other factors might be the chance for advancement, growth in a professional organization and the satisfaction of doing a worthwhile job.

17. Generally officers do not feel that police unions contribute to professionalization. Be careful, however, a member of the oral board may also be the primary union representative.

18. The most seriously injured person should get first attention.

19. Recommended action depends on the basis for the suspicion. If you have sufficient evidence to be considered reasonable cause, you have no alternative but to report your facts to a superior. This is for your own sake and the good of law enforcement/private security. Without sufficient facts, severe damage could be done, and the reporting officer could be open to civil damages.

20. Officers are not paid to "rest" on duty. Alternatives might be to stop in at a restaurant for a cup of coffee where you would still be considered on duty and available for assignment.

21. Follow the order if not seriously in error. An alternative is to call the error to the superior's attention and, after doing so, abide by that decision. Officers who refuse to obey orders do so at their own peril. Officers should refuse any order that involves an illegal act. Short of an illegal act, it would be the superior's responsibility if he/she gave an erroneous order.

22. This question is similar to "have you stopped beating your wife yet?" Chances are the superior's objectives are the same as yours in public service. If pleasing the public means overlooking offenses and violations, this is wrong.

23. You feel the agency is a good one or you would not be applying. Have some basis for this belief, however, such as conversations with officers, articles in the paper or conversations with citizens, particularly people who have had some dealing with the agency.

24. Such things as continued education, home study and in-service training would help improve the quality of your work after being hired.

25. In addition to specialized knowledge, law enforcement/corrections/security officers should know something about a great many things. Therefore, most experiences and training you have had will be of some benefit.

26. Generally, your friends would approve of your joining the agency.

27. Answer frankly.

28. Because of the nature of the work, criminal justice and security officers in effect "live in a fishbowl." Therefore, they must make sure their character and activities are beyond reproach. They must maintain excellent physical condition and continue to search for knowledge throughout their careers.

29. Strengths should be very apparent from your resume. Employers are especially interested in such characteristics as leadership, ability to communicate, compassion, loyalty and the like. And since you may be asked to list as many weaknesses as you did strengths, don't get too carried away on your strengths. Stick to around three. Make the

weaknesses portion of this question work to your advantage. Do not be negative, but be honest, and pick a strength that you have perhaps carried to extremes, for example, "I sometimes pay too much attention to details." Or "I am a perfectionist."

30. Take your time on this one. You should indicate that you expect to grow and develop professionally and be promoted accordingly.

31. Be prepared to explain what you can contribute to the agency. This is a favorite interview question.

32. Blow your own horn. List some positives like "enthusiastic," "professional," etc. Know what the word *attribute* means! See the response for #29, discussing strengths.

33. If there is a problem in your background, be honest about it. But there is not a need to list every issue you may wish you had handled differently.

34. See the upcoming "Closing the Interview" section.

35. Law enforcement is a challenging, interesting, diversified career with great opportunity for service and working with people.

36. Be sure your answer does not indicate you have interfered with any police/security activities. Confine your answer to incidents in which you helped by furnishing license numbers, relating the direction of flight of a suspect, pointing out witnesses, identifying participants and the like.

37. Such activity is usually frowned on by law enforcement officers and might indicate that the person is overzealous.

38. In such instances, an officer is never off duty. Appropriate action should be taken depending on if you and/or the probable purse-snatcher is armed. Officers in plain clothes should identify themselves, probably by pinning their badges on their lapels, etc. At least, get an accurate description of the suspect.

39. The answer depends on the circumstances and how obviously drunk the superior would appear to others and if he or she is known as a police officer. Know department policy. If any police officer, regardless of rank, indulges in activity that might discredit the agency, it is the officer's responsibility to report the matter to a superior. Be careful to state only facts. Record the time, date and to whom such a report is made.

40. Traditionally, both fire and police service are opposed to integration. While the concept has some merit in financial savings, frequently the objectives of the two agencies are so different that it makes the idea impractical.

41. Opinions differ considerably as to the responsibility of law enforcement relative to this area. Generally, this kind of public service is good public relations and may have some crime prevention value as well. The public expects help in emergencies.

42. Since juvenile delinquency is a serious problem in our society, it is a major responsibility of law enforcement officers. There is disagreement as to the amount of rehabilitative activity in which a law enforcement agency should engage. Generally, authorities agree that law enforcement personnel should handle the law and leave rehabilitation to other agencies whose personnel are better qualified.

43. Answer in the affirmative to the first question. The answer to the second question would depend on the law, department policy and procedures and circumstances.

Rigdon (1995, pp. 132–136) asked some of America's toughest interviewers to share their most frequent questions, as well as their suggestions on how to respond. Here is some of what they said:

> ➤ *What exactly do you want from us? Describe your ideal job.*
> Many people dodge these types of questions by giving a generic, safe answer. To make a better impression . . . prepare by writing an "employment ad" that describes your dream job. . . . [forcing] you to focus on exactly what you want and what you have to offer.

> ➤ *Where do you want to be five years from now?*
> The best way to botch this one is to not have an answer . . . make long-term goals a part of [your] answer but . . . focus on the short term.

> ➤ *What's your greatest accomplishment?*
> Many candidates flub this question. . . . [by] responding with responsibilities rather than *results*. . . . "[Describe] the big picture, not just the activities."

> ➤ *What are your weaknesses?*
> Many candidates try to highlight vague weaknesses that can be viewed as assets. They say "I'm impatient," . . . or, "I work such long hours that my family life is out of balance." Don't try it. Interviewers are sick of hearing these stock answers. Instead, be honest, but emphasize the actions you've taken to deal with a weakness. . . . [Try] this type of answer: "Sometimes I would push back deadlines to turn in higher quality work. However, I've learned to delegate more, and I've only slipped once in the past year."

What all the interviewers' suggestions have in common is taking a good, hard look at yourself and what you want *before* going to the interview and preparing yourself to handle tough questions such as these. Think about them and decide how you will answer, and don't worry about making a mistake. As Rigdon (p. 136) tells:

> It *is* possible to recover from an honest faux pas. When Fred Benson of Weyerhaeuser applied for a White House fellowship in 1973, he took a red-eye flight from overseas to make his interview on time. Walking bleary-eyed into the room, he was blinded by the sun glinting off a glass table and could make out only the silhouettes of the panelists. Extending his hand to the chairman, he knocked a pitcher of water into the man's lap.
>
> In that instant he gave up all hope of getting the position. "I have a feeling that I have nowhere to go but up from here, so I'm going to be very relaxed in this interview," he told the panel. He was—and got the job. Now he helps interview finalists for the fellowships.

NEGOTIATING

Negotiating is sometimes not possible. The majority of criminal justice jobs are union jobs, or at least are positions that bargain collectively. Therefore, you will have little room to negotiate, particularly at entry-level positions. Likewise, security positions generally permit little room for you to make demands. As you work your way upward in either the public or private sector, you may find room to negotiate. At almost all entry-level, and even mid-level lateral movements, you could easily appear too demanding if you want too much. Be realistic. Recognize the limitations of these careers. If you have specific needs, however, pursue them as far as you can.

The opportunity to negotiate a salary in these fields, particularly in entry-level jobs, is very limited.

CLOSING THE INTERVIEW

The final impression you make on your way out is also important. Here is an opportunity to shine as the ideal, enthusiastic candidate. The interview is likely to close with the interviewer asking, "Is there anything you would like to ask?" Every other candidate will say something like, "Well, no, not really." Boring. Unmemorable.

Your strategy should include having several closing questions . . . *if* you want the answers. The questions should *not* be about salary or benefits, at least at this time. For many employers, it's a real turnoff to be asked about how many sick days or vacation days there are or how long the coffee breaks are. Similarly, don't ask questions you should have already researched, for example, the size of the city or the department. Certainly, don't ask any questions just for the sake of asking questions. It shows through clearly. Good questions could be about the starting date or a likely assignment.

Always leave on an assertive, upbeat, energetic note. Regardless of the words you choose, make sure the message comes across loud and clear: *I want this job, and I'll be spectacular at it!* One of the strongest conclusions an applicant ever gave me was to simply say, "You'll never regret hiring me!" Don't be too brash or boastful. Make your closing statement brief and to the point. Any last minute chance you have will be ruined if you drag it out with question after question or statement after statement. As is true throughout your overall strategy, seek a balance.

In summary, let the interviewer know that you *want* the job. You would be astonished by how few applicants ever communicate that they've applied for the job because they *want* the job! Recall that this was one of my mistakes when applying for a police job—I assumed they *knew* I wanted that job rather than one with a law firm.

You should close the interview on an upbeat note by asking about a starting date or what a typical assignment might be. Never close by asking about salary or benefits. Finally, let the interviewer know that you really *want* the job.

FOLLOW-UP

Punctuate your interest with a follow-up. Follow-up is an easy way to score points during the hiring process because few applicants have developed a strategy that includes plain old courtesy. At the least, send a letter telling the interviewer(s) you appreciate the time and opportunity to meet. Such a letter not only demonstrates politeness but also offers one more chance to impress the employer with your strong points. Anything in addition, within reason, will probably benefit you.

Do not forget to follow up. As stressed in previous chapters, following up helps you score points in the hiring process by demonstrating your courtesy and getting your name in front of the interviewer one more time.

MAKING A DECISION

Making a decision is something you probably can't imagine would be a problem. Selecting from several jobs would be a great problem, right? If this does become your "problem," take your time before deciding. Usually employers are happy to give you a reasonable time to make a decision.

If you are a final contender in some other agencies, you now have a card to play. There is nothing wrong with contacting these other employers to let them know you would like to work for them, but you have been offered another job elsewhere. Suddenly you have increased your desirability, since someone else wants you too.

At some point you need to decide. Weigh as many factors as you are aware of. Seek input from others, and then take that risk and make your final decision. The *Occupational Outlook Handbook* (1998, pp. 16–17) provides the following guidance: "There are many issues to consider when assessing a job offer. Will the organization be a good place to work? Will the job be interesting? Does the employer offer good benefits? Where is the job located?"

The workplace culture is also a major consideration. According to an article entitled "How to Get a Read on Corporate Culture" (1998, p. J33):

> One of the greatest determinants of job satisfaction is also the most difficult to pin down during interviews. A good fit comes from first looking inside yourself, then into an organization's culture.
>
> Workplace culture is like the air you breathe: essential to the operation of all systems yet nearly invisible to the eye.
>
> Having accepted a position, an organization's values and expectations will define your days. But beforehand, when all parties are on good interview behavior, the truth of what working there is like can get lost amid their smiling descriptions and your hopeful ears. . . .
>
> An environment is neither good nor bad. One individual's dream is another's disaster, which makes understanding yourself the first piece to the puzzle.

The *Occupational Outlook Handbook* (p. 16) recommends: "If possible, speak to current or former employees of the organization." This will provide invaluable insight into the workplace culture and help you determine if it's a good fit for you. If you are the kind of person who prefers a more relaxed environment, accepting a position in a very formal agency where socializing is frowned upon and little after-hours camaraderie exists can feel very unfulfilling. If, on the other hand, you prefer a very "buttoned-down," more impersonal type of work climate, where little mixing of professional and private life exists, taking a job in an agency where coworkers openly share and discuss their families and like to hang out together after hours can leave you feeling alienated when you choose not to participate. You must know these things about yourself.

Even if you are not going to accept a position with an agency, let them know you appreciate them. Who knows, maybe you'll join them in the future.

A QUICK REVIEW

Quickly review these job interview tips given in the *Occupational Outlook Handbook* (p. 16) and review them again when you have an interview lined up:

Preparation:
- ➤ Learn about the organization.
- ➤ Have a specific job or jobs in mind.
- ➤ Review your qualifications for the job.
- ➤ Prepare answers to broad questions about yourself.
- ➤ Review your resume.
- ➤ Practice an interview with a friend or relative.
- ➤ Arrive before the scheduled time of your interview.

Personal Appearance:
- ➤ Be well groomed.
- ➤ Dress appropriately.
- ➤ Do not chew gum or smoke.

The Interview:
- ➤ Answer each question concisely.
- ➤ Respond promptly.
- ➤ Use good manners. Learn the name of your interviewer and shake hands as you meet.
- ➤ Use proper English and avoid slang.
- ➤ Be cooperative and enthusiastic.
- ➤ Ask questions about the position and the organization.
- ➤ Thank the interviewer, and follow up with a letter.

Test (if employer gives one):
- ➤ Listen closely to instructions.
- ➤ Read each question carefully.
- ➤ Write legibly and clearly.
- ➤ Budget your time wisely and don't dwell on one question.

Information to Bring to an Interview:
- ➤ Social Security number.
- ➤ Driver's license number.
- ➤ Resume. Although not all employers require applicants to bring a resume, you should be able to furnish the interviewer with information about your education, training and previous employment.
- ➤ Usually an employer requires three references. Get permission from people before using their names, and make sure they will give you a good reference. Try to avoid using relatives. For each reference, provide the following information: Name, address, telephone number and job title.

CONCLUSION

The interview is what the job-hunting game is all about. Prepare by anticipating commonly asked questions and practicing your responses to these questions. Also prepare a few questions of your own to ask the interviewers. Close the interview on an upbeat note by asking about a starting date or what a typical assignment might be. Never close by asking about salary or benefits, and realize that the opportunity to negotiate a salary in these fields, particularly in entry-level jobs, is very limited. Finally, let the interviewer know that you really *want* the job. And *do not* forget to follow up.

AN INSIDER'S VIEW

YOUR TURN TO STAR

Jim Chaffee
Director of International Security
Walt Disney Company

BEFORE THE INTERVIEW

I would suggest you type all correspondence, including your application. One of my greatest "turnoffs" is to receive an application that is not typed. This is not to say I won't look at it, but when you are in competition with a hundred other candidates, every little edge will help.

I don't mean to suggest that if you type all correspondence that's all you need to worry about. Correspondence should be neat and organized and *should not* contain spelling errors or noticeably improper grammar. Some people have their resumes professionally done, which looks very nice and can be impressive. A resume does not have to be done professionally, however. With today's computers, a professional-looking resume can be done with little effort.

Do not include a poorly typed cover letter to go with a professional resume. This only points out in a glaring fashion that the resume was done professionally and for obvious reasons. When responding to a job announcement, try to include in the cover letter all your attributes that mesh with what was indicated in the ad. For instance, if the ad listed "map reading" as a desirable trait, be sure to highlight your qualifications and/or experience in map reading. As a general rule, the cover letter should not be more than one page long and should cover what the announcement asked for.

THE ORAL INTERVIEW

There is not a lot you can do to prepare for an oral interview. Unless you know the type of interview and the questions being asked, you are going in blind, so to speak. *Don't* worry about being nervous. Everyone is. Try not to be overly nervous though, where your voice cracks and breaks and you perspire profusely.

On the other hand, *don't* be too relaxed and nonchalant. It does not look good in the interview process to sit back with your legs crossed and your arm draped over the back of the chair. *Remember* that the interviewers are not only listening to what you have to say, but they are surveying your mannerisms, posture, dress, grooming and the like. The interviewers may not have ever seen you before, and first impressions are lasting impressions.

Absolutely be on time. If you are late for an interview, it is almost like a kiss of death for that particular job. There may always be a reasonable excuse that caused your tardiness, but the burden will be squarely on you to show why you were late. Some examples of reasonable excuses are: "I was robbed, beat-up and sent to the hospital on my way over here," or "I was caught in a flood where several people were swept away, and I ended up saving all of them." If you *do* have a reasonable excuse for your tardiness, if at all possible telephone and try to let someone know. If you flat out miss the interview and don't call and explain why, you have just indicated your desire not to continue in the selection process.

Do dress appropriately. That does not always mean a suit or sport coat and tie, but it almost always does. Wear conservative clothing without loud colors or patterns. A white shirt, neutral tie and dark suit (gray, black or dark blue) is most appropriate. *Do not* forget about shoes and socks—you are being evaluated in totality, which includes your shoes and socks. Make sure your shoes are shined and your socks match whatever you are wearing. Try to make sure that your entire outfit is color coordinated and pleasing to the eye. *Do* make sure you are neatly groomed, e.g., hair is combed and not too long. Also, women should not wear an overabundance of makeup or perfume.

ANSWERING QUESTIONS

Do *not* attempt to answer a question when you clearly do not know the answer. It is OK to ask to have the question repeated or to ask for clarification. Look the interviewer in the eyes, but not aggressively. If there are several interviewers, look at them also while answering the question. Try not to fidget.

TRICKS OF THE TRADE

When being introduced to the panel, repeat each interviewer's name. For example, "Good morning (or afternoon), Lt. Adams. Pleased to meet you." Doing this should help you remember each interviewer's name as you go through the process. It is impressive when you can repeat the interviewer's name some time during the interview. For example, you may need the second part of a question reread, and you could say, "I'm sorry, Lt. Adams, but I did not understand the second part of the question." Try to work in each interviewer's name some time during the process, but don't do it unless it sounds natural.

Be prepared for trick questions that may or may not have anything to do with the job. Sometimes a question may be thrown in just to see what your reaction is. Sometimes it will be a humorous type of question, but be sure that it *is* before you laugh.

Also, be prepared for the unexpected. During one interview session we placed a lone chair way out in the middle of the room for the applicant to sit in. This very definitely causes stress to the interviewee. We were trying to see how the person coped with the situation. Some sat in the chair very appropriately, and others were obviously very nervous. We even had several drag the chair up to the interview table before sitting down. One candidate just stood and would not, or could not, sit in the chair. Some candidates appeared really perplexed when trying to decide the appropriate action to take regarding the chair.

Always follow up your interview with thank-you letters to the interview panel.

Jim Chaffee is the director of international security for the Walt Disney Company. He has 23 years' experience in the field of criminal justice, including four years with the United States Air Force Security Police, eleven years as a police officer in Minnetonka, Minnesota, and three years as the public safety director in Chanhassen, Minnesota. Mr. Chaffee holds an MBA and is a certified fraud examiner. He has been happily married for 18 years and has three children.

AN INSIDER'S VIEW

PROMOTION INTERVIEWS*

Albert J. Sweeney
Captain Commanding, Training and Education Division
Boston (Massachusetts) Police Department

The night that never seemed to end. The letter kept creeping into the nightmare. "You are scheduled for your promotional assessment center interview at 9:00 am Tuesday morning. Be prompt!" Like they needed to throw that in, just to increase the pressure. Yikes! I hate mornings. Why couldn't I get an afternoon appointment? My eyes don't open until 11:00 am. Oh my God—what am I going to do?

Okay, okay, calm down. There's a system to this, right? After all, I have seen some of the winners who have been promoted in the past. I can do this! I can do this! So what is this system?

First, calm down. I need to convince myself this is going to be okay before I can convince anyone else to give me this promotion. Self-confidence seems to be a key. It must begin now, before the interview comes down on me.

Somebody told me a list of positive characteristics about myself would help. I can do that! Let's see, I know the job—that's knowledge. I successfully scored high enough on the written exam—that's technical and subject matter expertise. I've worked on the job for the last several years—that's experience! What about all those commendations and letters from the people out there who I have helped? How about the commendations from my supervisors and my good work out there? And then there are the courses I have taken at the University to improve my education.

Wow! I'm better off than I thought. So if they start with that tough question, "Tell us why you are better qualified for the job than are the other candidates," I have a great list to begin with: knowledgeable, educated, experienced, successful, commended and confident!

But what happens if they give me a tougher one to start? Calm, calm, that's the key. No matter how tough the question, I can work it through. In fact, someone told me that they put this stress on you on purpose. Well, I got this one down. Breathing—that's the secret. Good thing I took those birthing classes! Slow, controlled breathing with slow exhale. Focus on the question, take a deep breath and ask them to repeat it if I need time. I can handle that.

But what the heck are they looking for with a question like that? Is it specific, technical knowledge from the rules and procedures manual? Well, I'd better read up on some of the more current and relevant procedures. There seems to be a lot of emphasis on operating under the influence these days. That's one. What about sexual harassment issues like "Quid pro quo" and all that? Uh oh, I need some brushing up on that and the definition of "hostile

---

* Although geared to the promotional interview, this advise also applies to entry-level interviews.

working environment." What's a little more reading now, anyway? Domestic violence in the workplace! Good topic. I would put one in front of that for sure. What if the suspect is one of my employees? Tough one. Better think this one out in advance.

Okay, do I tell them what they want to hear or tell them the truth? I wonder if they can tell the difference. What if I start with the stated written policy or directive on that? I need to show them I am current on the policy, of course. Then I need to show that I understand that sometimes what is written is not what is always done. Will I hurt myself with this honesty? I don't think so! In fact, maybe I will score some points for integrity. Besides, I am not going to violate the policy, rather I am going to show my compassion and creativity.

Compassion. I read somewhere that this is one of the top-rated qualities of a good supervisor. So I need to find the opportunity in the question to show this compassion piece. Look for cues in the question that allow me to see what is going on in the subordinate's life and work. Always ask for their side of the issue. Seek their opinion on how to remedy the situation. Don't jump to conclusions and come down like a hammer. Isn't that what the books said anyway?

How does this work in an oral board? I am confused! You mean those concepts in the books can be worked into an oral interview? What was one of those other qualities of value in a supervisor? Feeling "in on" things? Yeah, that's it. Feeling in on things! I have to remember to keep everyone informed of changes, updates, procedures and rules. I guess that's also part of the training function they talk about all the time. By showing the testers I am up on things and telling them how I would find various ways to keep everyone informed, I could score some heavy points.

The other one was sympathy and understanding, I think. If they ask me what I liked best in a previous supervisor, I can work this one in. After all, everyone has personal problems sometimes. And most people appreciate that someone in charge cares enough just to ask. Maybe by showing how much I care about the people and their personal problems, they will see that I would be a better supervisor than some of the other contenders. I will remember to work that one into the interview, too.

Wow—I didn't realize I'd remembered all these points from the readings. This isn't as terrifying as I originally thought. I think I'm beginning to see how they score these things. They must have a checklist with qualities and characteristics on it. Then they simply put checkmarks beside the ones I score on and leave blank the ones I forget. I wonder what the checklist could consist of for promotion. I have some already listed from above. Knowledge, experience and understanding rules and procedures are some. Compassion, sympathy and understanding are some more. Ability to express or communicate these must be another.

This reminds me, if I work on writing down some of these answers before I go in there, it will really calm me down. Even if I just write some key points or phrases, this will give me more confidence to get through this thing. I'll start a small notebook right now.

Oh, yeah, calm and confidence are two more I remembered. When I take my time to understand the question and show them that the question doesn't throw me, I can pick up more points. This goes hand in hand with the leadership trait that must be on there too. Being calm and collected in a stress interview gives the testers more confidence that I can handle the stresses of the actual promotion. I have to remember that this is important too.

Control is critical as well. I must remember to show them I have the toughness and fortitude to exert the authority that goes with the position. After all, each time, the promotion carries with it increased responsibility to exert proper control over people and situations. So, if the situation comes down to a choice between the organization's policy and someone's personal preference, I have to remember to land on the side of policy. After all, in this age of litigation, a mistake can cost a lot!

Oh well, that notice of the 9:00 am appointment isn't so bad now. Just needed time to practice my own control techniques. I will get all the items I need to bring with me two days before. From pencils to forms—I want it all ready. I will choose the proper outfit to wear that flatters my professional look. I wonder if leisure suits are back, especially the one with the black string tie. That laid-back look. Maybe NOT!

I also have to remember the feeding part that day. What is it that will hold me well enough for several hours in case they are backed up, yet won't repeat on me? I read that certain foods are better brain foods than others. Maybe one of those granola bars or earthy crunchy things as a backup might help.

Okay, okay, I'm much more calm and ready for this thing than I thought. After all, I got this far, right? And this is only the beginning. Remember, I have seen the ones already doing this job, and I've bested a number of my peers just to get this far. Okay, world, bring on these monster testers! I'm ready!

Albert J. Sweeney is the captain commanding for the Training and Education Division at the Boston (Massachusetts) Police Department. He holds a B.A. in Psychology from University of Massachusetts in Boston and an M.A. in Public Administration from Northeastern University. His first job was as a guidance counselor in a junior high, then he went to the Boston Police Department, where he's been for 28 years. Captain Sweeney has held all ranks up to and including superintendent. He does extensive consulting and training for the International City Managers Association (ICMA) and for the National Institute of Justice (NIJ). His specialty is community policing. Captain Sweeney has been married 28 years to Wendy; they have two college-age daughters, Christine and Suzanne.

 MIND STRETCHES

1. Why would a mass interview put you at a disadvantage? An advantage?

2. How could you make the interview process more enjoyable and memorable for an employer?

3. At what point during any phase of the hiring process can you become a pest rather than an impressive, aggressive candidate? How can you maintain an awareness of this and prevent it?

4. What could you do to remain cool during a "stress" interview?

5.   What could you do if you really blew an interview?

6.   What techniques could you use to deal with the understandable stress and anxiety everyone experiences during interviews?

7.   Why should you follow up with an employer you've applied to, even if you take a different job?

8.   List your three greatest concerns about being interviewed. How can you reduce these concerns?

REFERENCES

Bolles, Richard Nelson. *What Color Is Your Parachute? A Practical Manual for Job-Hunters and Career Changers.* Berkeley, CA: Ter Speed Press, 1998.

Healy, Thomas. "Via Video: Companies Employ New Way to Interview Students." (Minneapolis/St. Paul) *Star Tribune*, February 18, 1996, p. D4.

"How to Get a Read on Corporate Culture." (Minneapolis/St. Paul) *Star Tribune*, January 11, 1998, p. J33.

Kinsman, Michael. "Even When Expected, Questions at Job Interview Can Be Chilling." (Minneapolis/St. Paul) *Star Tribune*, April 14, 1996, p. D4.

Mounts, Harry C. "The Oral Interview." *Law Enforcement Technology*, July 1997, pp. 65–71.

Nelson, Mark and Dauten, Dale. "Your Biggest Weakness? Try Your Greatest Strength." (Minneapolis/St. Paul) *Star Tribune*, May 5, 1996, p. D3.

Occupational Outlook Handbook. 1998–1999 Edition. U.S. Department of Labor. Bureau of Labor Statistics. Washington, DC: U.S. Government Printing Office, April 1998.

Pearson, Robert. "Effective Interviewing." *Security Technology and Design*, November 1998, pp. 56–58.

Rigdon, Joan E. "Ace That Job Interview: What You Say Is Important, But How You Say It Is Crucial." *Reader's Digest,* July 1995, pp. 132–136. [condensed from *The Wall Street Journal*]

Weiss, Jim and Dresser, Mary. "Job Hunt Karate." *Law and Order*, May 1998, pp. 47–52.

Yate, Martin John. *Knock 'em Dead with Great Answers to Tough Interview Questions.* Boston: Bob Adams, 1998.

SECTION FOUR

YOUR FUTURE IN YOUR CHOSEN PROFESSION

The future comes one day at a time.

—Dean Acheson

Destiny is not a matter of chance, it is a matter of choice; it is not a thing to be waited for, it is a thing to be achieved.

—William Jennings Bryan

What is the recipe for successful achievement? To my mind there are just four essential ingredients: Choose a career you love . . . .Give it the best there is in you . . . . Seize your opportunities . . . . And be a member of the team.

—Benjamin F. Fairless

The road to happiness lies in two simple principles: find what it is that interests you and that you can do well, and when you find it, put your whole soul into it—every bit of energy and ambition and natural ability you have.

—John D. Rockefeller, III

There are no secrets to success. It is the result of preparation, hard work, and learning from failure.

—General Colin L. Powell

Once you've landed your "dream job," another challenge begins. How do you not only make certain you keep the job, but also make certain you excel? Chapter 14 addresses this major challenge. Chapter 15 discusses how you can enhance your chances for promotion, and Chapter 16 looks at job loss and starting the job-seeking process all over.

Preparation for the future is critical because that's where you'll be spending the rest of your life!

CHAPTER 14

AT LAST! YOU'VE GOT THE JOB!
CONGRATULATIONS!!!

When you are making a success of something, it's not work. It's a way of life. You enjoy yourself because you are making your contribution to the world.

—*Andy Granatelli*

Do You Know

- ➢ What needs to be done once you get the job?
- ➢ As you keep trying to do well, what is important?
- ➢ How to be "appropriate" on the job?
- ➢ What the likely effects of "knowing it all" will be?
- ➢ How to approach politics on the job?
- ➢ How to respond to criticism?
- ➢ Why being yourself is critically important?
- ➢ How to maintain yourself?

INTRODUCTION

By the time you get to this chapter, you will have covered an exceptional amount of material that should give you a genuine edge during your job search. You have taken a look at where to find jobs, how to write a resume, how to best present yourself, how to interview, how to follow up and even how to deal with those inevitable rejections. Hopefully you were able to assimilate all this information and emerge victorious.

Hold everything! The race is not over yet. In a sense, it is just beginning. The only thing expected of the unsuccessful candidate is to be a good loser. But for the successful candidate, the ultimate challenge is just ahead. Getting a job brings a whole new set of problems, especially in fields where you usually face a six-month to one-year probationary period.

Entry-level employees, in particular, are subject to a multitude of unwritten rules. Because criminal justice and private security are fields traditionally closed to outsiders, you have no basis to understand the expectations. You'll learn all too soon that the expectations are extremely high.

Starting a new job is like going to court. It doesn't happen all that often, but when it does, officers are expected to know what to do without having to be told ahead of time. To make an error could be very serious. The same with getting the job. Do you act like the old-timers? Do you act like the rookies? It is imperative that you have at least some idea of what to expect. Call it learning from others' mistakes.

What a bitter disappointment it must be to be successful in the pursuit of that dream job—only to lose it because you don't know what these circumstances demand. While many job applicants who could probably do the job just fine never get the chance because they cannot interview adequately, the opposite is true as well. Many people who cannot perform adequately get the job because they came across very well during the interview. You have to balance this situation.

Being successful in an interview does not guarantee success on the job. You must have some idea of what to expect and what the circumstances demand if you want to hold on to the job.

Here's what needs to be done once you get the job:

➤ Keep trying.
➤ Be appropriate.
➤ Know nothing.
➤ Wait until you are asked.
➤ Understand politics.
➤ Accept criticism maturely.
➤ Be yourself.
➤ Maintain yourself.

KEEP TRYING

Do not stop putting forth your best effort just because you have the job. If anything, make even greater attempts to fit into the new job than you did to get it. As Abraham Lincoln was fond of saying: "Things may come to those who wait, but only the things left by those who hustle." This is particularly true for those who have not had a professional-type job before. Criminal justice and security jobs are demanding, both in expectations and workload. You will be expected to perform as a professional, even at an entry-level position. Most employers expect you to know the basics. They seldom take time to ask if you do.

It's a far greater error to *not* ask questions than to, for whatever reasons, be afraid to ask and then make a mistake. It is far better to ask a "dumb" question than to make a dumb mistake. No one likes to appear unintelligent. But any employer knows that no one knows it all. Employers want to have employees who are intelligent enough to direct themselves while knowing enough to stop and ask for help when needed. In effect, there are no dumb questions.

Keeping a job takes constant effort. You must not be afraid to ask questions, for not doing so may lead to mistakes that may cost you your job.

BE APPROPRIATE

This aspect of easing into your new job may seem terribly simplistic, but it's not. The job you have landed is a far cry from most other entry-level jobs such as working at a fast-food restaurant, washing cars or bagging groceries. The usual horseplay and immature attitudes frequently found at such jobs are simply not tolerated in any criminal justice or security job. Anything short of professional behavior is not good enough. These fields are constantly seeking to prove their professional image and demand employees who will help in this mission.

It is hard for new employees to know just what *is* appropriate behavior, unless they have been police explorers, reserve officers, interns or have had some other association with the criminal justice or security fields. Few outsiders know what goes on "inside." For a newly hired individual, a conservative, low-key, quiet approach is not only appropriate, it's key to survival.

The best way to discover what behavior is appropriate is to simply assume a wait-and-see approach and take the necessary time to observe what is happening around you. You will see what behavior is approved of and disapproved of. A quiet approach for a new employee is always appreciated, while giving you a chance to ease into an admittedly uncomfortable new role. As Fought (1998, p. 36) explains: "New officers are trying so hard to fit in that this very effort causes them to stand out. . . . If the neophyte officer observes two senior officers in conversation with their forearms resting on their sidearm, you will be sure he or she will practice this salty stance in the mirror at home."

Particularly younger people who have had little experience in the job world are susceptible to starting out with some rather "extreme" behavior. An overconfident, "cocky" attitude is often a cover-up for some very natural feelings of discomfort, self-doubt and personal reservations. Coming on too strong, however, can be very abrasive to fellow workers. Such an attitude tends to keep people at a distance when you really need them to reassuringly welcome you to your new job.

Learn appropriate behavior by assuming a conservative, low-key, wait-and-see approach, taking the necessary time to observe what is happening around you and observing what behavior is approved of and disapproved of.

KNOW NOTHING

It is frequently easy to tell who the new kids on the block are. They are often overbearing and brash, seeming to go out of their way to show the world they know it all—or at least *think* they know it all. Actually, the more experienced officers become, the more those officers acknowledge that there is always more to learn.

Fact: a hierarchy exists in every police department, correctional facility and security corporation. Entry-level employees, especially *new* entry-level employees, are at the bottom of the ladder. You may never recover from the damage unintentionally done by telling anyone above you how *they* should be doing something. Many rookies destroy relationships with senior officers (maybe senior by only a year) by advising them on a better holster to carry, or a safer way to make a traffic stop, or which lights to use on the squad car during a motorist assist.

Maybe the rookie was correct. Rookies usually have received up-to-date training that reflects better ways of doing things and have not had time to develop bad habits. *This is not the point.* You will have plenty of time to do it your own way. Irritate anyone early on and word will spread that you are a "know it all."

This is definitely not advice to "play stupid." If you are asked for an opinion, give it. If you have to make a decision, make it. Show interest and a desire to learn. It may be difficult to admit to yourself and others that you *are* new and really do *not* know it all. But if you pretend that you do, you will have shot yourself in the foot. Not only will others not think you are dumb if you ask questions, they will appreciate the fact that you really want to learn.

Being a "know it all" will likely earn you a negative reputation and delay your being accepted by others in the department, institution or agency.

WAIT UNTIL YOU ARE ASKED

This is a continuation of "know nothing." Officers in law enforcement, corrections or private security are in positions of respect. They tend to expect it and generally receive it. Particularly as a new employee, you will get more respect from other employees if you show respect for them. They deserve it. They have passed those difficult early stages of the job. They are now "regulars" and have a great deal to offer you as a newcomer. Give them the opportunity to share their wisdom with you.

"Now that I get this job I'm gonna' tell these old guys where to get off."

Show respect, and make it clear you know you have much to learn. Ask questions. Take advantage of your unique opportunity to learn. Do not, however, ask questions that are personally or professionally challenging to the individual (for example, "Why would you wear a holster everyone *knows* is dangerous *and* ugly?"). A better way might be to ask what equipment the officer would suggest you consider when you purchase your gear.

It will not make a positive impression to say to an officer you are riding with, "My instructor told us to tag such a violator for speeding. Why didn't you?" Rather, you might ask what other violations could have been written or how the officer decided what to write on that particular stop. Many officers feel their own department or agency does not adequately recognize them for their knowledge and ability. To have someone new ride with them and ask well-thought-out, inquisitive questions is flattering to that officer. We all like to be able to "strut our stuff." Your presence can be a positive experience for both of you *if* you take full advantage of it.

Keep in mind that people working in criminal justice and security make their living getting lied to by the best. Do not pretend to be interested or ask questions to "set up" the officer to tell you something for an alternative purpose. You will be spotted before you get the question completed, and you will be off to a terrible start.

Is it possible to ask *too many* questions? This is difficult to answer. Determine this on your own. Teachers *want* students to ask appropriate questions, but also come to cringe at those always-present students who chronically ask questions for the sake of hearing themselves talk.

UNDERSTAND POLITICS

Every organization has its own politics. Webster's defines *politics* as: "competition between interest groups or individuals for power and leadership in a government or other group." That is a fitting definition, but the complexities are so deep you can be caught in the political web before ever being aware of its existence.

To understand politics, recognize that politics are impossible to understand. This is an area to be particularly careful of. Even seasoned veterans can easily fall prey to internal politics. Politics can be a deadly game and should be avoided.

The biggest problem is that newcomers do not know where the political lines are drawn. While certain people tend to be more than willing to give advice, such advice may not turn out to be at all sound. Eventually you will learn who you can talk to openly. Some people are willing to share helpful insights; others may well set you up for a fall. Some things you might innocently say may offend someone. *You just do not know*, so don't take a chance. For example, if someone talks negatively about another employee, don't get involved. You may want to nod or grunt appropriately, but if you also start making comments about others, you will quickly expose yourself as a gossip.

Experienced officers learn that it is best to never write anything they do not want to show up because it inevitably will surface. Similarly, it is a good practice to never say things you don't want heard because statements always seem to get repeated. People will tell you things in confidence. An eight-hour shift in a squad car, on a cell block or on security duty lends itself to sharing a lot of thoughts and ideas. Should you make the mistake of telling others what was told to you, you may cause some serious relationship problems for yourself and others. Never say anything you do not want repeated, and never repeat what is told to you in confidence.

> Do not play politics. Do not try to understand politics. Do not get yourself drawn into politics. This is important advice for anyone on the job, but absolutely crucial for a newly hired individual.

Dauten and Nelson (1997, p. D5) observe: "Performing well and playing politics may not be enough when [the] time comes for reducing [the] work force." They advise that the best way to keep a job is to cultivate relationships by developing skills involving rapport and getting people to like you.

ACCEPT CRITICISM MATURELY

A natural aspect of getting into any new job or position is learning. Considering that most people learn from their mistakes, you, too, should want to learn from *your* mistakes—they present great opportunities. Everyone (yes, *everyone*) makes mistakes at work. Naturally, the newer you are, the more mistakes are likely to occur. Employers expect this and would probably feel you weren't trying if mistakes weren't made.

So what's the big deal about making mistakes? The problem is that many people can't deal with thinking they are capable of making mistakes. Whether ego or just plain embarrassment, many individuals react inappropriately to being told they did something wrong. Failure to respond appropriately to criticism received at work can negatively affect a critical phase of the new job.

As discussed earlier, seemingly "negative" events may open up great opportunities to end up looking better than before. This is even more true in the case of learning at work. Frequently, part of field training or the probationary period is seeing how recruits or new employees handle constructive criticism. Assuming you learn from your mistakes and are able to prevent them from reoccurring too often, what is really critical is that you can maturely accept critical comments and process them, hopefully improving as a result.

To argue with a trainer or superior is a poor choice for those who have been at the job for awhile. It could prove fatal for someone on probation. Take advantage of the occasional times someone offers criticism to not only improve the particular skill at issue, but to make sure the person leaves thinking about how professionally you handled the situation.

One aspect of this process that people often fail to recognize is that offering criticism is frequently as difficult to do, or more so, than receiving it. If you accept the comments in a positive way, even thanking the person for offering the comments, you may well end up scoring far more points than you will ever realize.

It would be a serious mistake to get angry, challenge the superior, have a temper tantrum or go shooting your mouth off to others, even if you felt wronged. In the unlikely event that you genuinely do feel you are being harassed or ill-treated, discuss this with the person first, and only then proceed up the proper chain of command to deal with it. In some situations, new employees have, for whatever reason, not hit it off with a trainer. Personality conflicts do occur, as do outright illegal discrimination and harassment. But the real issue will be how you choose to handle it.

For example, a newly hired individual had extremely offensive body odor. When the supervisor suggested that perhaps a change in deodorant might be in order, the new employee became incensed and stormed out of the building. When she returned to work the next day, she was told that she no longer had a job there. It was *not* the body odor that caused her to lose the job—that was correctable. It was her immature, hostile reaction to the suggestion that cost her the job.

> Accept criticism maturely for such instances provide great opportunities for you to learn from your mistakes. Recognize also that offering criticism is frequently as difficult as receiving it, and if you accept the comments in a positive way, you may score far more points than you will ever realize.

BE YOURSELF

This advice is very important. You managed to get the job by being yourself, and you will succeed by being yourself. Recognize from the start that it is very uncomfortable to start a new job, particularly in a field you're not used to. That's just another "job fact," so don't fight it. Accept it, and don't get down on yourself because you're nervous, afraid or feel inadequate—we all feel this way when we start new jobs. The first few weeks *are* going to be rough. Draw energy from it rather than allowing it to exhaust you.

> It is important for you to be yourself. The fact is, starting a new job, particularly in a field you are not used to, is uncomfortable and requires an adjustment. You will become exhausted if you spend energy putting on an act. Save your energy for learning the job and just *be yourself*.

Police, corrections and security officers make their livings dealing with people who are trying to run scams on them. Many of these individuals are very good and may be able to fool the professionals at first. You will not be able to. Trying to do so will only result in your being labeled as someone trying to be someone you are not. Officers must be honest!

Peer pressure is always difficult to cope with. As a rookie, you will be expected to do as you are told. If you are unfortunate enough to get drawn into a bad group of fellow employees, you will be faced with some tough decisions. Do not engage in brutality. Use the minimum force necessary under the circumstances to accomplish the objective. Do not let peer pressure cause you to violate this important principle. Also recognize that to stand by and watch unethical, possibly illegal, behavior is only slightly less devious than actually participating. If you don't think you can resist the temptations from within or without, get out now.

If you are not happy, do something about it. These jobs are *not* for everyone. If you are unhappy, or if you can foresee problems for whatever reason, admit this to yourself as soon as you become aware of it. It is sad to see people suffer for years at jobs they dislike—especially those in jobs that provide the individual with a great deal of power and authority. Perhaps some officers "go bad" by becoming terribly abusive or sarcastic because the job is just no longer right for them . . . and it shows. Further, consider that professionals who dislike their work do not have the necessary concentration to be safe. Many horrible things can result from remaining in an unfulfilling job for too long.

Do not become cynical because of the nature of the work, the clientele or opinions expressed by fellow officers. Watch out for "burnout." Use R&R time effectively to relieve stress. Do not become a "mooch," sponging off cooperative retailers, which usually begins with free coffee. Remember the concept of *quid pro quo*, that is *those who give usually expect something in return.*

The longer you remain in a job, any job, the harder it is to let go of the benefits. You will be much further ahead if you are honest with yourself and leave if the work does not suit you. Similarly, the work may suit you just fine, but the job may not. For a variety of reasons, not every employment opportunity will fit everyone. If you know you want to be a police, corrections or security officer, but personalities or any other factors make this particular job less than satisfying, do *not* stay around. It is unlikely that things will improve. There *is* a job out there for you. Your job is to find it.

MAINTAIN YOURSELF

Burnout. We've all heard about it. Maybe you've been there. Most of us have at one time or another. When starting a new job, consider ways of balancing it to keep it as attractive as it was when you first heard about it. Don't overdo it. Keep up your other friendships, activities and interests. Take care of your physical self: eat right, exercise and get enough sleep.

It is also important to keep your guard up, to stay on your toes and be mentally sharp. This also means not getting too lazy, comfortable or complacent in your position. Messmer (1995, p. 31) advises: "Without getting too paranoid, keep yourself mentally prepared for the possibility that the job may not work out. Stay in touch with recruiters. Maintain your networking activities. Keep current. Be visible. And be alert to signs that your company is in trouble or that your job may be in jeopardy."

Maintain yourself physically and mentally. Stay current not only with things related to the job but also with things that interest you outside of work. This helps prevent burnout.

CONCLUSION

Congratulations! You've got the job! These words will, and should, be a deserved conclusion to a significant amount of work. Relish them. You are well on your way to professional career fulfillment. Don't let your guard down, and don't give up pursuing excellence. Set exceptional goals for yourself and you will be exceptional.

Bear in mind, your success during the interviews will not guarantee you success on the job. You must have at least some idea of what to expect and what the circumstances demand if you want to hold on to the job. Remember, keeping a job takes constant effort. You must not be afraid to ask questions, for not doing so may lead to mistakes that may cost you your job. Work in criminal justice, security and related fields is important. It is satisfying. It says something about you that people working in other fields cannot boast. Congratulations on choosing these fields to pursue employment in and for making the effort to do it well.

YOUR GAME PLAN FOR EXCELLING ON THE JOB

 Take time *now* to write out, on a *separate* piece of paper, three goals to help you excel in your new position. Put the paper someplace you will see it often. Let these goals guide you as you embark on your exciting new career. And again, congratulations!

AN INSIDER'S VIEW

SURVIVING PROBATION

Linda S. Miller
Sergeant, Bloomington (Minnesota) Police Department
Project Director, Minnesota Community Policing Institute

Now that you have landed that job, you probably think you can relax. Think again. You are about to undergo a period of the most intense scrutiny you've ever experienced. It's called *probation*. Usually a period of six months to a year, it gives the department a chance to see you in action and to evaluate your work, your judgment and your style of relating to others. You don't have that job wrapped until you "make probation." Think of this period as a time to apply what you've learned in school and what you will learn on the job. Advice from veteran officers as you begin your probationary period would surely include the following:

➤   Don't be a know-it-all. You may have been the star of the academy, but keep it to yourself or you may alienate your colleagues.
➤   Learn the basics well. Fancy shooting or exotic defensive tactics moves won't be of much help to you unless you can also write a good report and make a proper car stop.
➤   Concentrate on report writing. Carry a pocket dictionary if you are not a good speller.
➤   Don't be a "gadget" person. One can often tell a rookie by the surprising number of pieces of equipment hanging from the gunbelt.
➤   Watch respected veteran officers do their job and learn from them. Don't, however, adopt their "bad" work habits.
➤   Don't take short cuts. These are for veterans willing to live with the consequences. You can't afford it.
➤   Don't get a reputation for being too aggressive. You want to be a willing worker, very interested in doing your job, but not a crusader chosen to rid the world of criminals.
➤   Treat the public and co-workers with respect. Displaying your personal prejudices can be detrimental to your continued employment. Don't make derogatory racial or sexual remarks, even if you hear others doing so.
➤   Try to develop a reputation of being cooperative and nonargumentative. Be a team player.
➤   You may be in social situations with co-workers where alcohol is served. Drink conservatively. You can be sure that what you say and do under the influence of alcohol will be the talk of the department by the next day at the latest. Alcohol abuse is a serious problem in this society and in law enforcement. Most departments will not be impressed with a rookie who displays even a hint of alcohol abuse.
➤   The same goes for sexual behavior. Keep your personal life personal. Above all, don't sleep around with fellow employees.

Remember, your training officer and the department's supervisors have your future in their hands. In many departments, probationary employees can be let go for *any* reason. With a little forethought, you can avoid providing a reason. You have what it takes for the job or you wouldn't have been hired. And the department wants you to "make it" too. They have invested time and money in your hiring and training. They need you to assure them they've made the right choice.

Linda S. Miller *is a sergeant with the Bloomington (Minnesota) Police Department. She has been with the department 23 years and has been a police dispatcher, patrol officer, crime prevention officer, patrol supervisor and head of the planning, research and crime prevention division. She is currently on loan from the Bloomington Police Department to serve as the project director for the newly created Minnesota Community Policing Institute. Sergeant Miller is a member of the Minnesota Peace and Police Officers Association, the International Police Association, the Midwest Gang Investigator's Association, the International Association of Women Police and the Minnesota Association of Women Police. She was a member of the People-to-People's Women in Law Enforcement delegation to the Soviet Union in 1990. Sgt. Miller is a frequent presenter to community groups and is also an instructor.*

AN INSIDER'S VIEW

LET'S BE HONEST

Lawrence J. Fennelly
Sergeant, Crime Prevention Specialist
Harvard University Police Department

So, you want to get into law enforcement. Why?

You like working nights, being off Tuesday and Wednesday nights, finishing your shift at 8 am and then going to court until noon, sleeping 4½ hours and then going back in for the next shift.

You get married. Your wife works days; you work nights. You have children . . . you remember when they were born. You get to visit your wife in the hospital when you finish work, and you both get to have coffee and a donut together.

A couple of years later you get divorced (possibly). You get married again and have some of the guys on the force in your wedding party. It seems now that all of your friends are cops. Your second wife is a nurse. Ever wonder why cops marry nurses?

While on the job, you get beaten up. You don't get shot but you wear that vest every day, even in the summer, and it's HOT. You *almost* got stabbed and say to yourself, "Boy, I'm glad I had the vest on."

You just used OC Spray Pepper Mace and the wind shifted and your almost prisoner got away; you go home sick. You take a shower, and OC is in your hair, and then your eyes and your wife wonders why you are screaming and have a headache.

Six months later you give CPR to a woman only to find out that she has AIDS. Four months later you arrest a woman who has tuberculosis, and your supervisor doesn't tell you to get tested because she was only a carrier.

You transport to the hospital a sick person who is coughing from the time she gets in your car until the time she leaves your car. In 48 hours you are sick. Your wife, the nurse, thinks you have some kind of strange flu because she heard the nurses talking about a patient who came into the hospital the other day with a rare flu diagnosis.

Your children grow up so fast you can't even remember when they learned to walk and talk. You were too busy working details, doing court time, etc. . . . .

* * * * *

I am not a negative person. I am not a "doom and gloom" type. I don't think my department is totally messed up. I am just being honest with you. Law enforcement is a great career; however, when you go to the academy for 26 weeks and graduate, you will then be prepared to start that career.

Then set personal goals such as:

➢ Getting into a special unit (CID, CPU, COPS, IA).
➢ Continuing in school to get your Master's degree.
➢ Taking those promotional exams.
➢ Going to law school.
➢ Teaching in the local academy.

Setting goals and exploring your educational benefits after the academy should be your first objective to climb your way to the top. Start young and study, study, study. That's how it is done. You must continue to grow personally, professionally and academically *after* you get your job.

Getting into an academy is actually only the beginning of your career. Yes, you are going to take an exam and then be interviewed—all of which is an art. The academy is where you learn all the theory and you get all the required certifications. The street is where you learn by experience and where you apply the theory and concepts.

Let me give you the advice an old Cambridge police officer gave me on a snowy, miserable night. He said, "Remember, kid, a good cop is never cold, doesn't get wet, and has sunglasses in the summertime."

Lawrence J. Fennelly is a nationally recognized authority on crime prevention, security planning and analysis. Mr. Fennelly is a sergeant and crime prevention specialist at Harvard College, employed by the Harvard University Police Department in Cambridge, Massachusetts. He is also the department's training officer and assistant court officer. He, like all police officers at Harvard, is a deputy sheriff in both Suffolk and Middlesex counties. Mr. Fennelly is also a security practitioner, involved not only in administration but in all aspects of Harvard's security and security planning for more than 500 pieces of property. In 1982, Mr. Fennelly was appointed to President Reagan's Task Force on Crime Prevention and Violent Crime. He was trained in Los Angeles by the 1984 Olympic Security Committee and placed in charge of security for the Olympic Village at Harvard College. He is an active member of the American Society for Industrial Security (ASIS) and lectures for them frequently.

MIND STRETCHES

1.   Have you ever been "too enthusiastic" at a new job? Why do you think you were? Did it hurt you?

2.   What behaviors have you observed in people in uncomfortable situations (like in a new job)?

3.   Why do you think important people often seem so "down to earth"? Conversely, why do you think many "not-so-important" people act so brash?

4.   How long does it take to fit in at a new job? What helps you fit in?

5.   Have you ever felt pressured at a job to behave in a way you did not feel comfortable? How did you handle this situation?

6.   Why do you think people, particularly officers, seem to like to complain or be negative? What traps can this create for new employees?

7.   What dangers are there in "taking sides" in an office dispute? How can you avoid becoming involved?

8.   Can people who work together get along "too well"? Are "office romances" good or bad? Can they be avoided, or do they "just happen"?

9.   How would you handle a situation in which you knew a co-worker was doing something illegal, immoral or unethical? Would you respond differently if the person was a peer or your supervisor?

10.   At what point do you think people stop growing and developing professionally? What opportunities exist to help you maintain your own personal and professional vitality?

REFERENCES

Dauten, Dale and Nelson, Mark. "Best Way to Keep a Job Is to Cultivate Relationships." (Minneapolis/St. Paul) *Star Tribune*, March 2, 1997, p. D5.

Fought, Richard. "Growing Pains: Career Development Follows Predictable Path for Most." *Police*, October 1998, pp. 34–40

Messmer, Max. *Job Hunting for Dummies*. Foster City, CA: IDG Books Worldwide, Inc., 1995.

CHAPTER 15

THE CAREER LADDER: INSIGHTS INTO PROMOTIONS

If you can dream it, you can do it.

—*Walt Disney*

Do You Know

➢ Whether the promotional process differs from initial job seeking?
➢ What changes, besides promotions, may lead to personal and professional growth?
➢ What factors motivate people to seek change in their professional lives?
➢ Which basic job-seeking skills apply?
➢ Whether changing jobs can help or hurt future job-seeking efforts?
➢ If you can ever have "too much" education or education in the wrong area?
➢ How important "off duty" activities are?
➢ When networking is important (other than during the job search)?
➢ How important the oral interview is to the promotional process?

INTRODUCTION

While this book began as a book to help individuals get into the criminal justice or security employment force, it has introduced you to information regarding the employment process as well. For the newcomer, just *getting* the job is the dream. But eventually everyone develops higher aspirations, or just a desire to keep from being bored at doing the same old thing. This chapter provides some suggestions on how to prepare yourself for the promotional process and what to expect. As Bernstein (1998, p. 67) succinctly states: "The road to promotion is one of hard work and personal commitment."

You need to keep in mind several important aspects of the promotional process. First and foremost, the basic job-seeking skills and strategies that you are developing will serve you well throughout your job-seeking—and promotional—ventures. Regardless of the level of the job you are looking towards, you will still need to provide information about yourself that will present you as THE one to promote. Promotional interviews are similar to initial job interviews. Almost all of what you learned about getting your first job will continue to be important throughout your working life. This speaks to the importance of developing a job-seeking strategy that will work well for you. Remember how many careers people normally have during their lives. When you consider all the promotions or job changes people experience, it is easy to see how important it is to know how to prepare for opportunities.

Second, it is important to create a plan for yourself. Life itself presents numerous opportunities, as does work. By thinking ahead, you not only develop some ideas of where you want to go in life (and work), but how to recognize the many opportunities that present themselves.

Third, recognize that in criminal justice and security positions seniority and "paying your dues" also play an important role in promotions.

Promotion-seeking skills are very similar to the basic job-seeking skills and strategies you are developing. Both scenarios demand you present yourself as THE one to hire/promote.

PROMOTIONS: WHAT THEY ARE AND WHERE THEY ARE

Traditionally, promotions are considered to be upward moves, usually within the same organization where one is presently employed. This is a valid concept for many promotions, but try thinking of promotions in a much broader way. Any promotion is a change, but is every change a promotion? Take it one step further. Obviously, every promotion provides new challenges, but so does every change. . . even those that don't initially appear to be upward. Think of *any* job change as an employment opportunity. This includes promotions, transfers and, yes, even demotions or dismissals.

Think about it for a moment. Many people who have confronted what appeared to be overwhelming adversity end up saying it was the best thing that ever happened to them. Why? Because they grew from the experience. Any change, even one that appears negative, presents an opportunity. The bigger the challenge, the greater the opportunity for personal and professional growth.

Promotions are but one type of change that provides new professional challenges and allows for growth. Often the most adversarial changes, such as demotions or dismissals, lead to the greatest amount of personal and professional growth.

MOTIVATIONS FOR SEEKING CHANGE

The chapter on rejection addresses how you should strive to obtain energy from the process, and how you should control the process rather than let it control you. It *can*, *should* and (eventually) *will* result in growth for you. Richard Obershaw, Director of the Burnsville (Minnesota) Counseling Center of Grief, is fond of saying "a rut is a groove with the ends knocked out." And it is this feeling that frequently compels people to set their sights on bigger, better, or at least different, careers.

Of course, considerations like better pay, more benefits or even a desire to move to another community motivate people to change their job status. Other reasons may not present themselves as "positive" reasons for the change. Downsizings, reorganizations, closings and even involuntary terminations force people to change.

Motivations for seeking change include better pay, better benefits, the desire to live and work in another community, downsizing, reorganizations, closings and involuntary terminations. Some of these reasons originate in the individual; some are forced upon the individuals—all lead the individual to change.

So whether a change results from unanticipated factors or your desire to better yourself professionally, seek a better paycheck with improved benefits, or move to a more desirable place, remember that your job-seeking skills will serve you a lifetime.

SIMILAR SKILLS

Take time to reflect on the entry-level job search and the promotional process, and you can see the similarities. In fact, both are going to result in different jobs. . . new jobs, and the skills you will need are the same:

> Cover letters (sometimes called "letters of interest" in the promotional process).
> Resumes (now providing more specific training and experience records).
> Test-taking skills.
> Interview skills.
> An overall positive appearance as THE one to hire.

> The job-seeking skills needed during the promotional process include writing effective cover letters and resumes, taking tests, interviewing and presenting yourself positively as THE one to hire or promote.

The changes you will notice as you work on your promotional strategies are simply a fine-tuning of the skills you developed earlier. It is through explaining how you have developed professionally and why you want the change that makes this job-seeking process different from an entry-level job search.

INCREASING YOUR CHANCES FOR PROMOTION

Rachlin (1995, pp. 25–27) suggests several ways to increase one's chances of being promoted:

Broaden your experience. Take advantage of opportunities as they present themselves, and avoid spending your entire career in one area. While running the bicycle safety rodeos may not be the most exhilarating police experience, it provides one with the opportunity to develop administrative experience and learn more about yet another area of the business. And, perhaps most importantly, it shows you are a contributor to your agency, and that says a lot about your level of professionalism. Obtain experience in as many areas of the agency as possible, including operations, administrative services and budget planning. If rotational opportunities are available, take them!

Grow in your job. You can always learn more about a position, but to do so often requires applying innovative ideas and a fresh perspective. Never stop trying to expand your horizons.

Take on challenging assignments. This might include implementing new programs (safety, training, etc.), acquiring new equipment or technology, or undertaking a variety of other special projects. Think about ways to improve the agency and how to go about making the improvements. Let supervisors know you want challenging responsibilities that will benefit the entire agency. Recognize that most people do only what is expected of them—what is asked of them. I frequently advise newly hired people that it truly is not difficult to be a star!

First, do that which is, indeed, expected of you. Many don't. Second, take the occasional opportunity to do something beyond what is expected of you. It will get you noticed.

Accomplish things. Finish what you start and do the task well. Develop a reputation for follow-through, dependability and quality—these are things you'll be evaluated on. Keep in mind it is far better to be selective in taking on tasks than to take on so many you end up failing to complete them.

Move on to other agencies. While not always possible, it may present a great opportunity to expand your range and depth of experience. Again, be discriminating and don't hop frivolously from one agency to another. Seek out ones that present wise career steps and will further your managerial experience. There is a challenge in knowing how, what and where to move to. While in the corporate world it is almost expected that the really good people will seek for and be sought by other organizations, this is not necessarily the case in traditional criminal justice and security positions. In fact, it may be viewed as a detriment by some agencies that an applicant has been a "job jumper." Be selective!

This is not a big problem for people employed in larger agencies. Employment in federal, state and large agencies permit many opportunities for change, new challenges and promotional advancement. Smaller agencies may demand that the motivated employee take new jobs outside their agency. These changes should be pursued as a part of your plan for achieving your employment goals, just like all other areas of developing your strategy. Change merely for the sake of change may become self-defeating. If you don't stay at a new job or a new assignment long enough to really benefit from it (or be of benefit to your employer), this may cause understandable concern to those doing the hiring.

Take opportunities that further your planned career path, but do not get carried away, jumping from one job to another. Be selective in your moves, or such job jumping may damage your future options in your profession.

Further your education. Obtain as much education as you can. With standards rising all the time, and more and more qualified people acquiring advanced education, you must keep up to stay competitive. Take courses that will help you in your profession. The possibilities are almost endless!

Education is akin to experience—you cannot acquire "too much" education or education in the wrong area.

It is difficult to understand how anyone's education could be viewed negatively, but it may. The two reasons that surface most frequently are a fear the applicant will soon move on to a "bigger and better" job and the fear of intimidating those "above." It is difficult to view this as anything more than jealousy, but some supervisors don't want their subordinates to have more education than they have. Do not fail to acquire advanced education because of what others might think, but be prepared to defend the choice, as well as to assure others that such education will benefit the department. Never stop learning.

Obtain special training. Take advantage of special training programs offered by various institutions and organizations. Individuals who have attended a number of such programs demonstrate a commitment to stay current on topics that relate to their field, a desirable attribute in those seeking promotions. Once you obtain a degree, do not rest on your laurels. Take every opportunity to add to your knowledge. This makes you attractive to a promoter.

So many training opportunities are available that to merely list every class becomes overwhelming. Don't let your really important message get lost in reams of photocopied course certificates. Pick and choose both the classes you take and the course documentation you present during the promotional process. Develop an overall strategy to get you where you want to go. Rather than taking every class you can get into, determine which will serve you best.

Be active in associations. Promoters look favorably upon those actively involved in fraternal, federal, state or other types of associations. Such participation demonstrates a commitment to the profession. Even officers serving at the entry level have many opportunities to join professional organizations. Membership in these groups not only provides a superb opportunity to keep on the cutting edge of your profession, but it shows you are willing to make the extra commitment to develop your professionalism. Again, "too many" may not be as helpful as selecting several organizations that speak to your commitment to better yourself.

Being actively involved in such "off duty" activities as professional organizations and associations demonstrates a commitment to your profession, which is looked upon favorably by promoters.

Develop a network of contacts. As with the job search, networking to get a promotion is very important. The more people you know, and the more people who know you, the better off you'll be. Again, becoming involved in professional organizations and associations is a great way to learn more and to get your name out there.

Networking is as essential to promotion efforts as it is to job-seeking efforts.

Collect letters of commendation. These tools reflect positive actions in which a candidate was involved. For promotional purposes, letters that highlight leadership abilities or management skills are particularly valuable. Don't be shy about asking for letters. Many people will tell you they appreciate your work but may need some encouragement to document it. You have a responsibility to yourself to do everything you can do to best convey your excellence. A good supply of such personal recommendations will put you in a great position to include the best and most applicable for your next effort.

Be a spokesperson. "Enhance your reputation (and resume) by delivering speeches at conferences and writing articles. Have something important to relate, and be selective where you relate it. Speak at professional and civic conferences, and write for general publications and professional journals" (Rachlin, p. 26). Give careful consideration to the issues facing your profession and how you or your agency have addressed such issues. Use your knowledge and experience to offer solutions to problems facing your industry.

Develop a public appearance image. Take every opportunity to improve your public speaking skills. When you are associating with those you work with, or with people who could be called on to comment on you as a candidate, NEVER let your guard down. All the effort you have made to develop a positive reputation can be destroyed with one error in judgment. More often than not, alcohol is involved. Even at a social gathering, eyes are on you. Innocent comments, too, can come back to haunt you. Recall that the job-seeking process is a job in and of itself. So is grooming yourself for promotion. Keep this in mind when associating with others who may, in any way, influence your career development. If you are engaging in any activities away from work that could be construed as unprofessional—reevaluate it.

Research your interview. As with the initial job-seeking interview, research your potential future path by gathering as much information about the interviewing department or agency and the surrounding community. Know how the agency is organized, what the various divisions are and what they do, and any special circumstances or programs the agency is involved in.

Promote yourself. Keep track of your accomplishments and add them to your resume. These achievements are what promoters are looking for, so you must be certain to provide documentation.

Be a leader. Leadership may be demonstrated in many ways, including developing and implementing new programs, taking charge in an emergency situation or supervising assignments and projects within your agency. Showing leadership shows you care. Employers, your co-workers and the community—all want to know you care. So step out and be a leader.

(Adapted from Harvey Rachlin. "How to Improve Your Chances of Getting Hired." Part of "The Hiring of a Police Chief." *Law and Order,* March 1995, pp. 25–27. Reprinted by permission.)

Seek Feedback

Feedback is always beneficial, particularly for those have not gotten the promotions they sought. Face it, most people are either too polite or too intimidated to tell an applicant if there is a problem he or she is simply unaware of. It takes guts to ask for honest feedback. The most difficult thing is once you ask for feedback, being willing to accept it.

Seek A Mentor

Along with feedback, it is helpful to develop a relationship with someone you respect who can provide support and advice and lend an ear during the frequently stressful, sometimes discouraging, process of seeking employment goals. Support is considerably more important than many think, and the friendships that develop as a result of these mentoring relationships are a great benefit as well.

PREPARE FOR PROMOTION

Garner (1998, p. 82) notes: "Years ago, there were very few programs or products for helping you get promoted. Today, there are books, videos and courses to help you pass promotional exams, oral boards and assessment centers. The officers who take advantage of such resources are more likely to get promoted than those who rely on their own perceptions of what it takes to be promoted." Fulton (1999, p. 28) adds:

> The serious candidate for promotion will have given a great deal of careful thought to the pending career milestone before he elects to take the plunge.
>
> He will have conducted an honest self-assessment and determined that he's making the right choice for the right reasons.
>
> He will have looked carefully at what his agency expects of its first-line supervisors and reached the determination that he is both willing and able to measure up.

He will have examined his former peers who have preceded him into supervisory ranks and concluded that he would fit in well as a contributing member of the work group.

IMPROVING PROMOTIONAL EXAM PERFORMANCE

DiVasto (1990, p. 24) notes: "There may be nothing in the work life of an experienced police officer that can generate as much anxiety as a promotional exam. Officers who face armed hoodlums without so much as a blink will lose sleep for weeks worrying about a promotional exam." DiVasto (pp. 24, 29) suggests some strategies to help reduce text anxiety. These strategies are to be implemented before and during the exam as follows:

Part I—Before the Exam

1. Have a clear idea of what material the exam will cover. Some departments publish reading lists, some circulate written materials, others just rely on word of mouth. . . .
2. Commit yourself to buy, borrow or share the books you'll need. Many of these, such as state codes and S.O.P. manuals, you might already have. Other materials, such as textbooks, you might have to buy or borrow. . . .
3. Determine what the test format will be. Find out, for example, if you'll be required to answer essay questions, true-false questions, multiple-choice questions, or a combination of these. . . .
4. "Train" for the exam. . . . Set out . . . a training plan . . . [including these] elements . . .:
   a. Commit yourself to study a minimum of 100 hours for your exam. . . . only eight hours a week for the three months prior to the exam. . . .
   b. Begin studying not less than three months before the exam date.
   c. Set out your study plan on a calendar. . . .
   d. Find the time that is best for you to study. . . .
   e. Don't take on any major responsibilities, projects, or other energy-consuming activities while you're studying. . . .
   f. Give yourself time to relax a few days prior to test day. . . .
5. Before the test day arrives, be sure you know the time, place and what you're expected to bring. . . .
6. On the day of the exam, allow for extra time to drive to the test site, and plan on being there early. . . .

Part II—Taking the Exam

The most common type of written promotional examination is multiple-choice. . . .

1. Divide the test into hour-long segments. If there are one hundred questions and two hours in which to do them, plan on spending an hour on each fifty questions. If there's no time limit, allow yourself about a minute and a half per question or forty questions an hour.
2. Read each question very carefully and restate it to yourself in its most basic terms. If there are "distracters" in the question, eliminate them as you read. . . .
3. Answer each question by supplying the correct answer before you look at the choices. Your answer should match up with one of the choices listed.
4. Answer every question in your one-hour block before you go on to the next block. . . .
5. If you can't come up with the correct answer, eliminate the obvious wrong answers. . . .
6. Once you've eliminated the wrong answers, your choices will generally be down to two. Reread the question, restate it to yourself and take your best guess.
7. If you're taking a test made up from standard textbooks, forget the "real world" answer. . . . the test maker doesn't ride in your patrol car. He is going by what the text writer said is correct, not how you would do it on the street.
8. Beware of the right answer to the wrong question. . . .
9. Take a few minutes of break time between each of your one-hour segments.

(Adapted from Peter V. DiVasto, "Improving Promotional Exam Performance." *Law and Order,* May 1990, pp. 24, 49. Reprinted by permission.)

IMPROVING PROMOTIONAL INTERVIEW PERFORMANCE

Narramore (1991, pp. 161–162) has written a comprehensive review on how to prepare for a promotional interview:

> The people involved in an interview to evaluate your qualifications try to ascertain three basic facts about you. These are the most important traits you will need to convey to the panel:
>
> ➢   You can handle the job.
> ➢   You will do the job to the best of your ability.
> ➢   You are a manageable team player.
>
> Candidates who communicate to the evaluators "yes" to the above questions will score the highest. You must be able to demonstrate willingness and ability during the interview process.
>
> The first time I competed for the position of police sergeant was a disappointment I will always remember. I felt very comfortable after taking the written examination. I had scored high and was in an excellent position. Because I felt so confident, I did nothing to prepare for the oral interview. I felt showing up in all my glory and answering the questions to the best of my ability would be enough. That was a very big mistake. I finished in the top five overall, but I was not in the winner's circle. I looked back and learned from my mistake. That experience taught me to take that extra step of preparedness for every phase of the testing process.
>
> The interview is the most important part of the promotional process. A successful candidate will make the "question and answer period" an exchange of ideas between law enforcement professionals. Accomplishing this means you are qualified and prepared.
>
> The foundation for a successful interview comes from the following areas:
>
> **Knowledge.** This is not power, but rather a good working knowledge of the position for which you are applying. Simply having correct information.
>
> **Wisdom.** This is knowing where you want to go and what to do with the knowledge you have acquired to get you there.
>
> **Action.** This is the key element to the plan. Taking your thoughts and ideas and putting them into motion.
>
> **Belief.** The most powerful element is persuasion. You must believe in yourself and feel confident you are supervisory material. Imagine yourself in the position and believe you will get there.
>
> **Repetition (The Mother of Skill).** The best way to be mentally prepared is through repetition. The more you repeat something, the more skillful you will become.
>
> Law enforcement agencies look for specific traits in individual profiles to help determine the type of supervisor a candidate may become. Being more skilled and more qualified does not prove they will be a team player. Education and experience alone does not guarantee they will fit into the scheme of the organization. Several traits are reviewed during an interview:
>
> **Ambition**: An eager desire for distinction. Inner drive to get things done and succeed in doing them.
>
> **Motivation**: A mental force that induces enthusiasm and willingness to ask questions.
>
> **Communication Skills**: Ability to speak and write effectively.
>
> **Devotion**: Energy and dedication to provide the organization.
>
> **Conviction**: Belief and determination not to back down from a problem no matter what obstacles arise.
>
> **Confidence**: An assured state of mind that enhances the ability to get the job done and done right. This is not a cocky attitude, but rather an attitude of optimism.

Now that you are aware of what an interview board looks for, let's talk about the basic "traps" so many well qualified candidates fall prey to. Some of these traps are so damaging, recovery is next to impossible.

Failure To Listen To the Question. Every question asked by an interviewer demands a specific answer. Do not ramble on with superfluous responses. Be brief, yet concise. For example: if asked how many years you have been in law enforcement, provide a specific number. However, if you are asked to relate your feelings about illegal drugs, provide a more general answer.

Take Your Time Answering Questions. Do not answer a question immediately. Think about what you are going to say. This gives the impression you consider your responses and do not respond spontaneously.

Don't Answer Questions Not Asked. Answering a question not asked is annoying. When the board wants more information, they will ask for it.

Be Brief and To the Point. The board does not want drawn out answers providing little information. If you do not know the answer, don't attempt to deceive the board with flowered responses. Be brief and to the point.

Turn a Negative Into a Positive. You may be asked a question regarding a negative area of your career, or be asked to discuss a major weakness. Try to turn the atmosphere into something positive. Admit you had a certain weakness, but were able to recognize it and took the steps necessary to correct it.

Don't Be Flippant or a Joker. Oral boards do not like flippant responses. One improper response could ruin the entire interview.

It is not always the best person who receives the promotion. The ones who receive the promotions are usually those who have qualities of efficiency, hard work and reliability. If you follow the above suggestions, you will have a much better opportunity receiving that promotion you deserve.

(From Randy E. Narramore. "Preparing for a Promotional Interview." *Law and Order,* September 1991, pp. 161–162. Reprinted by permission.)

Mahoney (1991, p. 89) describes a category of applicant known as the "I'm Ready But Don't Understand How to Express It" candidate. According to Mahoney (p. 89):

This group is normally comprised of a few candidates who at just about every interview process, initially appear to be front-runners for promotion but who end up falling somewhere in the middle of the pack. This is not because they aren't qualified, but because they made some basic errors in preparation, errors that repeat themselves time and time again.

Mahoney (pp. 89–92) notes reasons candidates fail to perform well during the oral interview, including:

Not Knowing the Questions. It's almost a given that [the candidates] will be asked, "Tell us about yourself and why you are the best candidate," "What have you done to prepare yourself for the promotion?" . . . .

Yet, time after time, when asked, candidates look at the panel members as though they've been asked to expound on the Theory of Relativity. . . . Every applicant for promotion should have a 2–3 minute "commercial" prepared . . . .

"Narrow Focus" Response. Candidates working in specialized assignments tend to see the entire organization from the limited perspective of their own job. . . .

Candidates that view their job or department through only a narrow focus are not going to be perceived by an interview panel as being ready for promotion. Successful applicants must be able to perceive their department in broad terms and understand the internal and external forces that affect day-to-day operations.

Interacting with Board Members. Generally, oral interview board members are conservative, middle-aged law enforcement managers, predominantly male . . . .

Board members frown on the use of even the mildest of profane words or phrases during an interview. . . . Avoid interjecting things of a personal nature into opening or closing statements. . . . Don't wear jewelry that proclaims allegiance to a particular college or organization . . . consider the length of your responses . . . [and] pace yourself accordingly.

> The oral interview is the most important part of the promotional process. Prepare for it as enthusiastically as you did for your initial job-seeking interview.

As you prepare for your promotion interview, you may also want to reread the *Insider's View* by Sweeney on pages 279–281 of Chapter 13. This may also help you organize your thoughts.

CONCLUSION

Because work is such a significant part of life, job satisfaction is vital. Not only do satisfactory jobs provide monetary and other employment-related benefits to enable you to live the lifestyle you desire, but your job helps you feel the way you do about yourself.

Promotion-seeking skills are very similar to the basic job-seeking skills and strategies you are developing. Both scenarios demand you present yourself as THE one to hire/promote. Additional job-seeking skills needed during the promotional process include writing effective cover letters and resumes, taking tests and interviewing. Networking and researching the interviewing department or agency are also important elements. Whatever your reasons for seeking a new job or a change in the job you have, your ability to develop successful job-seeking strategies will help you realize your goals. Promotions and professional advancement require a well-thought-out plan that you will implement over time.

AN INSIDER'S VIEW

**WHAT ARE THEY LOOKING FOR?
TIPS ON THE PROMOTIONAL PROCESS IN
LAW ENFORCEMENT AGENCIES**

Luis Velez
Captain
Colorado Springs (Colorado) Police Department

At some point in our careers, we inevitably realize that the promotional ladder may hold the key to several unachieved dreams. As is the case in every public and private sector agency, those who get promoted are the exception rather than the rule. A common thread separates those who are promoted from those who compete year after year and, for whatever reasons, are passed over for promotion. Early on, I can tell you that if you are one of those officers who feel you should be rated on only your abilities to do "police work," then you should also realize you may be setting yourself up for a great disappointment.

WHAT ARE THEY LOOKING FOR? What must you do to place yourself in a position to be promoted? What is it that your agency wants from its supervisors, its managers and its directors? Answers to those questions are the focus of this article.

WHAT ARE THEY LOOKING FOR? Several immediate answers come to mind, but they all start with this basic premise: it is not the similarities among people which will determine who will be chosen, but rather, the decisions will be based on the differences exhibited by the respective candidates. Differences in education, differences in assignments, differences in knowledge, skills and abilities, coupled with differences in attitude, optimism and the ability to bring what I refer to as a "stepstool" into the arena.

You can do many things to position yourself for promotion. The first step is to ask yourself, "Am I ready to make this commitment?" It takes time and a great deal of personal effort to get promoted. To start this journey, you must have the proper mindset, and you must be willing to sacrifice that precious commodity called time. Certain aspects of the time with your family, time with your friends and even some of your leisure time will invariably disappear. However, if you have made the conscious decision that you intend to compete against your peers and to get promoted, please read on.

ATTITUDE is a disposition. It is a manner, a demeanor, a feeling, a bearing, a temperament, a spirit, but most importantly, it is a positive approach by which some individuals carry themselves. We have all encountered people who had the technical expertise or the necessary decision-making skills at their fingertips, but they would never be considered for promotion because they lacked the proper *attitude*. This characteristic feature may very well be the first difference viewed or perceived by those who make promotional decisions.

OPTIMISM can be viewed as the embodiment of confidence, hopefulness or faith, all of which seem to propel those individuals who have this trait into the forefront. Police work can be demanding, and it can take its toll on the psyche. Optimism can be viewed as the dam that can hold back the pressures of the job. We can easily pick out those officers who have *optimism*. They invariably stand a better chance of getting promoted.

EDUCATION can be used as a predictor of future potential. In and of itself, educational achievements must be viewed in conjunction with other promotability factors. However, given two candidates with similar backgrounds, similar time on the job and similar skills, *education* may prove to be a key determinant in the selection process. Some agencies are increasing their entry-level criteria for police officers, while other agencies are looking at the feasibility of tying promotional consideration to the educational level attained. This is an area where you should scan your competition and go after an educational level at least equal to your peers.

COMMUNICATION is the most important talent that can be readily displayed by candidates seeking promotion. This area truly separates the proverbial wheat from the chaff. Whether verbal or written, the ability to communicate is paramount in law enforcement. Officers must be able to speak to citizens who represent every level of education and every culture in our society. Those officers who also distinguish themselves in their ability to paint a clear, distinct image through the written word will prove to be the best contenders for promotion.

LISTENING has become a lost art. We are usually too busy trying to make a point or control a conversation. A Roman slave once said that we were given two ears and one mouth, so that we should listen twice as much as we speak. That notion has seemingly lost its rightful place in our modern organizations. Nevertheless, it may prove to be another deciding factor in the promotional process.

APPEARANCE, much like PRESENCE, is crucial for officers seeking promotion. We all make almost instantaneous decisions about people when we first see them. The public makes similar cognitive leaps when confronted by police officers. A professional appearance, either in uniform or business attire, will generally promote a positive interaction rather than creating a negative or confrontive situation. Having a "command presence" may mean the difference between having to talk to someone for 30 minutes or having to fight them for 30 seconds. That type of presence becomes a tangible factor, particularly during promotional oral boards.

Last, but certainly not least, is how the candidates conduct themselves daily. We can call it their VALUE SYSTEM. If you are a good person, then you can hardly help but be a good police officer. If the scrutiny of a video camera poses no anxiety in how you normally conduct yourself, if your decisions are based on what is right rather than what is expedient, if your associations are made in the sunlight rather than the darkness, then you will be hard pressed not to place yourself in a position to be noticed, let alone be promoted.

Earlier in this article, I mentioned "bringing a stepstool into the arena." Let me explain. If you could envision a stadium full of candidates for promotion and you are tasked with trying to pick out a particular individual, it would become an exhaustive, quite possibly futile search. If, on the other hand, the individual in question brought a stepstool to the arena, placed it on the ground and stood upon it, even in a crowd of thousands, it would be easy to pick him/her out. They would have separated themselves from their competition, and they now would hold a vantage point which gives them a different perspective of the same stadium. That new vantage point, that ability to scan the environment, is what is needed by candidates for promotion.

They need to take their unique perspectives, and hopefully that will include a vision more global than that of their peers. That "stepstool" makes it easier for others to notice you.

WHAT ARE THEY LOOKING FOR? As you can see, the factors viewed as being important for promotability in law enforcement are the same factors important for promotability in any organization.

The makeup of an individual, their vision of the future, their philosophical perspective on their role and how it relates to their organization and, obviously, their knowledge of the job all factor into the equation. In short, anyone who can deal with the necessities of the present, while always looking at the possibilities for the future, will be a good candidate for promotion.

Luis Velez is a 23-year veteran of the Colorado Springs (Colorado) Police Department. He has been married to his wife, Joyce, for 28 years, and they have two children, Christine and Marc. Captain Velez was born in Puerto Rico and grew up on the lower east side of New York City. He served in both the Army and the Marine Corps, completing a tour of duty in South Vietnam between 1969–1970.

Captain Velez holds a Master's degree in Public Administration from the University of Colorado and a Bachelor's degree in Sociology from the University of Southern Colorado. He is a graduate of the FBI National Academy, Session #171. He has held a number of staff-level positions as lieutenant (shift commander), sergeant (community relations, vice/narcotics), detective (homicide unit), hostage negotiator, captain (Office of Professional Standards) and commander (Gold Hill Division). Currently, he is the commander for Central Division, which houses all specialized uniformed assignments, such as the SWAT team, Bomb Unit, Canine Unit, Mounted Patrol, Air Support, Park Police, Volunteer Enforcement and the Traffic Section, including the Motorcycle Unit.

AN INSIDER'S VIEW

MAKING THE MOST OF YOUR LAW ENFORCEMENT CAREER

Richard D. Beckman
Sergeant
Cloverdale (California) Police Department

Let's assume that you have passed all your tests, been appointed to the position of a law enforcement officer, successfully completed the academy and are performing well in your FTO program. Sounds like a dream, sounds like a long ways off, hard to imagine. With a strong set of values, persistence and a good, well thought-out set of goals, you can do it.

By now you have figured out that law enforcement is not all the glitter and glamour of television, and all your expectations of the job have been shattered or changed considerably. With the academy behind you and your newly gained knowledge as an experienced trainee, you now have a unique opportunity to assess your career, re-evaluate your goals based on your newfound knowledge and plan your future.

Law enforcement is a noble profession. We all had different ideas the first time we climbed into the passenger seat of that police car next to a seasoned veteran. With our eyes wide open, we were about to go through a transformation that would affect us the rest of our life. The old standard oral-board answer of, "I want to be a police officer so I can help people," took on a new meaning when you encountered the *real* world. You will learn and see many new things. You will see the worst and the best in people. Remember, we are all part of the same human race. The old adage, "Don't judge a person until you've walked in their shoes," has a lot of hidden meaning to those of us in law enforcement. Don't take things at face value. Look inside things, find out why they happen. Dig deep and you will be surprised by what you find and how it will affect your attitude. As the guardian of the public peace, you will do what is expected of you and do it to the best of your abilities.

Having a strong set of personal values is essential for a successful career. Basic values come from your parents, siblings, life experiences, interactions with others and your inner self. Some of the personal values required of a successful law enforcement professional would fall into the following categories:

Integrity. The lack of integrity destroys the effectiveness of the individual and can affect the entire organization. Honesty and law enforcement are two words that are inseparable. Integrity is the backbone of what we do and who we are. There is no room for dishonesty in our profession, and any breach of the public trust must be dealt with immediately and severely.

Loyalty. Loyalty is the hinge that ties the individual to his environment and creates the flow of power between employees and management. It is important to understand the prioritization of loyalties and the nuances of loyalty conflicts to be able to make decisions consistent with existing values.

Humility. Humility is one of the strongest values an individual can possess. On occasion where you have erred, nothing demonstrates your positive values so powerfully as a simple, humble apology. You must recognize that errors or failures will occur in life. You must be willing to accept the failure or apology of others if you expect others to tolerate your own human nature. Humility includes the recognition of the need to learn.

Tenacity. Tenacity tempered with patience gives the individual the ability to focus on long-term goals and creates consistency of purpose and successful change.

Courage. Courage is demonstrated most often as the result of a strong personal value system that supports action in the face of adversity. It requires "strength of character," or more simply, a strong moral fiber, which denotes a strong sense of values and ethics. Courage is not something that can be taught but comes from combining skills with your entire value system.

Responsibility. To be an effective law enforcement professional, you must accept responsibility for all that occurs in your purview. Responsibility ties directly into integrity and courage and, if you are wrong, humility.

Confidence. Confidence is a state of mind that exists in particular situations when an individual's knowledge or experience dictates a high likelihood of success or acceptable consequences in the event of failure. Confidence cannot be taught, but can be gained through repeated experiences in specific areas of knowledge. Confidence is your tool of survival. Confidence is one of the key elements of a successful career.

Setting Goals. You have obviously set some goals for yourself as you have been successful in your quest for a law enforcement career. Goals are not something you set, attain and forget. To grow in your life and career, you must constantly reassess your goals. Set a goal for your career, reach that goal and then set another one. You may want to set long-range and short-range goals, such as being an FTO by the time you have three years on the job, or making sergeant within five years. You must work for these goals; they will not come to you. When you reach a goal, set another one. Do not become complacent in your career. Get as much overall, broad-based experience as you can. Don't be afraid to try. Avoid being stereotyped or stuck in a rut. See what you want and go after it, keeping in mind the basic values you have set for yourself and your career.

Expectations. Know what is expected of you at all times. Constantly communicate with your fellow officers about what you expect of each other. Don't be afraid to go to your supervisor and ask what is expected of you. This is an integral part of building your confidence and maintaining your value system.

Survival. During my 30-year law enforcement career, I saw many changes, both good and bad, in our profession. Early on, while driving around solo on those long night shifts, I started playing a mind game with myself that later on enabled me to survive encounters which could have been deadly. After each call, as I got back in my car and drove off, I would mentally go through the call and play a "what if" game with myself. What if the guy had a gun? What if the lady attacked me? I would change the scenario several times and play it over in my mind along with my reactions to the situations. What I was doing (unknown to me) was building up a computer program in my mind as to what I would do and how I would react in hundreds, if not thousands, of situations. When confronted with a real-life, deadly encounter, I was (during a 30-second period) able to save the life of a fellow officer, a 17-year-old hostage and take out an armed suspect by reacting to that mental computer program.

Never stop playing that "what if" game, have confidence in your ability and live by a good set of values, and I hope your career will be as successful as mine.

Sgt. Richard D. Beckman is a 30-year veteran of California law enforcement, now retiring from the Cloverdale (California) Police Department. In 1988 he received the "Police Officer of the Year" award from the International Association of Chiefs of Police for his actions in saving the lives of a fellow officer and a 17-year-old hostage. In 1990 he received the Medal of Valor from the Attorney General of the State of California. Sgt. Beckman was referred to as a "true American hero" by President Ronald Reagan. He is a founding board member and president of the Law Enforcement Alliance of America, and travels extensively throughout the country promoting officers', citizens' and victims' rights as well as other pro-constitutional issues.

AN INSIDER'S VIEW

IDENTIFYING YOUR WORST JOB-SEEKING ENEMY . . . IT ISN'T WHO YOU THINK IT IS!

J. Scott Harr, JD

I am a self-proclaimed law book junkie. My bookshelves at home are lined with case books, texts on American and foreign law and, best of all, police novels. It is from the novels that I glean some of my most important information! One of my favorite novels is Joseph Wambaugh's *The Blue Knight*. In it, the main character, Officer Bumper Morgan, explains that more people talk themselves into jail than get there any other way. That caused me to come up with a saying of my own: more people cause themselves to not be hired than because of anyone else.

I have seen job applicants do some amazing things over the years. Occasionally, they are amazingly outstanding things that cause me to take particular notice of an applicant. This happens so rarely that these individuals really do stand out!

More frequently, however, are examples of job-seeking skills that make me take notice of an applicant, but not for the reasons that an applicant would hope for. Usually when I take a second look at an application these days, it is because I simply can't believe anyone would exercise such poor judgment as to submit some of the material I have seen.

I can't think of a better way to demonstrate this than to discuss the applications I received for a law enforcement-related position. It was the type of job discussed in this book—one that provided excellent on-the-job training while getting one's foot in the door. It was an important job, and our expectations were that applicants would put careful consideration into their effort to get the job—to develop a job-seeking strategy that would help them stand out as THE applicant to hire.

I ran an ad one Sunday in the metropolitan newspaper under the heading POLICE, explaining the job and instructing applicants to submit a resume and cover letter by a certain cut-off date. There were to be no phone calls. After reading this book, you will understand exactly why the ad ran as it did, but let me briefly explain:

➤ *Why does the ad run one day in one large metro area paper*? You should check ALL papers in your area, not just your own local paper.
➤ *Why do we require a cover letter and resume?* To learn as much as we can about you in the few brief moments we have to review the material submitted with many, many others.
➤ *Why not a standard application form?* Because anyone can "fill in the blanks." We want to see how you write and how organized you can develop a resume.
➤ *Why no phone calls?* Because we don't have time.

In addition, the ad ran as it did because we are purposely trying to see who can and can't follow simple instructions. Yes, we do make note of who calls, who submits a form application and whose material comes in late.

A significant number of applicants did not follow the ad's simple instructions, which was noted on their files. But more extreme errors in judgment were also noted. One resume was printed on the back of a wedding invitation. Over half the cover letters were not signed. One did not have a return address or phone number. One was handwritten. Many had significant grammatical and spelling errors that leapt off the page. Several were late. Some people couldn't resist the temptation to call. Several applicants dropped off standard application forms without the required cover letter and resume. Some people delivered only a resume, and some only a letter. Some people *called* for an *application form*!

When all was said and done, of all 50+ interested applicants in one of the country's most glutted law enforcement and criminal justice job markets (where the average time people spend looking for work before being hired is over two years!), I had ONE application worthy of consideration. ONE!

The simple fact that you have taken the time to read this book will give you a significant edge over other applicants you will compete against. The mere fact that you are THINKING about how to successfully seek a job puts you far beyond most of your competition. Your competition may have more, or better, experience. They may have a better grade point average or more schooling. They may be more physically fit, smarter or have a ton of volunteer experience. . . *but if they don't know how to get past the very first hurdle, does any of it matter? NO!*

Not a day goes by that people looking for work call me and complain about how hard it is to find work. Yes, it is, but it isn't nearly as difficult as they are usually making it for themselves. I can provide many more examples of just plain foolish things applicants have done to eliminate themselves as viable candidates for work, and every other employer could add to my list.

So why do people who genuinely want work in the field of their dreams do such silly things? Simply because they haven't taken the time to develop their own job-seeking strategy. It is so simple, but so critical, to understand that even though *you* know you have so much to offer an employer, you first have to get in the door to TELL them!

This reminds me of the cartoon that shows a person trying to enter a door marked "pull" by pushing. It's funny because it's so simple, so silly and so ridiculous. This couldn't happen in real life, right? Well, it does—routinely. People looking for work (and such important work to both them and our society) are so eager to achieve their goals they overlook what should be very obvious and simple—getting the employer to recognize them for who they really are. Most people simply can't get in the first door.

So, who is your worst enemy when seeking employment? Lots of people think it's the "system"—one that sets people up for failure or favors less-qualified applicants in the name of affirmative action, appearance, nepotism or the myriad of other excuses unsuccessful candidates come up with. It always boils down to "it's just not fair." Often, the real reason is that the applicant did a substandard job of applying. (Note: In no way do I want to imply or state that inappropriate discrimination does not exist. It does, and it is both illegal and wrong. These are not the cases I am talking about here.)

But so many qualified applicants are their own worst enemies. They have no one else to blame but themselves for not getting the job they want, and perhaps a job they would be terrific at. Failing to develop a successful job-search strategy affects *all concerned* and leads to a lose/lose situation for both the applicant and the employer.

Developing a successful job-search strategy may well be as much an art as it is a science. You may have noticed that even some of the contributors to this book have differing opinions on what works and what doesn't. There are different applications, different employers and different ways that will work for you in preparing for your job-seeking journey.

Continue to learn: read books and talk to others seeking work, including those who have either been through it or actually do the hiring. Continue to learn more, better and different ways to search for work.

You are doing two things by taking the time and making the effort to read this book. First, you are developing a skill that will serve you a lifetime, whether it be for the seeking of work in a different career or striving for promotions in your present work. Second, the mere fact that you are interested in bettering your chances in the job-seeking world truly sets you apart from all the other applicants. It is so tempting to tell yourself you could not have anything over the hundreds of candidates who are competing for the job you want. Untrue! Most of them have given absolutely no thought to how to present themselves. So, even if they do happen to have different, maybe even better, credentials than yours, they probably have little idea how to present those credentials and themselves as well as you do, because you have given this important element of the job-seeking process your attention. You now know how to present yourself as THE one to hire!

J. Scott Harr is a private investigator, attorney at law and licensed police officer. He has over 20 years' experience in the criminal justice field, including positions as a police officer, a police/school liaison officer, investigator for Canterbury Downs (a horseracing track), firefighter and emergency medical technician, public safety director for the City of Chanhassen, Minnesota, law enforcement instructor, social worker, private detective and textbook author.

Mr. Harr holds a J.D., a B.S., an A.A. and a chemical dependency counseling certificate. He is married to Diane and has two children, Ricky and Kelsey.

MIND STRETCHES

1. What promotions do you see as being of interest to you now? In one year? Five years? Ten years?

2. If you were promoting someone, what characteristics would you look for?

3. Why would actions "off duty" influence employers?

4. Name the things you are doing now that employers would view favorably.

5. Name the things that they could view unfavorably.

6. Do you think someone could be "overeducated"? Why or why not?

7. What schooling do you think could help you in your job pursuits?

8. Consider those around you who have been promoted. What have they done to benefit themselves?

REFERENCES

Bernstein, Jeff. "Preparing for Promotion." *Law and Order*, February 1998, pp. 67–68.

DiVasto, Peter V. "Improving Promotional Exam Performance." *Law and Order,* May 1990, pp. 24, 49.

Fulton, Roger. "Moving Up the Ladder." *Law Enforcement Technology*, February 1999, p. 82.

Garner, Gerald W. "Are You Ready for Promotion?" *Police*, July 1998, pp. 22–24, 28.

Mahoney, Tom. "How (Not) to Fail an Oral Interview." *Law and Order,* March 1991, pp. 89–92.

Narramore, Randy E. "Preparing for a Promotional Interview." *Law and Order,* September 1991, pp. 161–162.

Rachlin, Harvey. "How to Improve Your Chances of Getting Hired." Part of "The Hiring of a Police Chief." *Law and Order,* March 1995, pp. 25–27.

CHAPTER 16

JOB LOSS AND CHANGE: THE ROAD LESS TRAVELED

In the middle of difficulty lies opportunity.

—*Albert Einstein*

Success is how high you bounce when you hit bottom.

—*General George Paton*

Do You Know

➢ What besides death and taxes is inevitable?
➢ How common job-loss grief is?
➢ What myths about employment are common?
➢ Why an effective strategy to deal with job loss is needed?
➢ What basic survival strategies are needed?
➢ What emotions are normally experienced following job loss?
➢ What depression is? What to do if it occurs?
➢ When you should begin your job search after losing your current job?
➢ Whether to sue your former employer or not?

INTRODUCTION

With all the excitement attached to getting a job, losing that job should also be addressed. Why? Because it will happen to you. It happens to everyone. Sometimes leaving a job is unexpected and unwanted. Sometimes it's a desired change. Sometimes it's a promotion or a demotion. Eventually it will be retirement. There is no escaping it. Maybe it has just happened to you, which is why you are focusing on this chapter. If so, we hope to lend support.

This chapter is titled *Job Loss <u>and</u> Change* because even desired, positive changes in employment status provide challenges. People often are surprised at the sadness accompanying these changes. They needn't be. In fact, the stress and fear of change prevents some people from pursuing promotions or other job opportunities, or to turn them down when offered. This may not make sense now, but it will. Ask anyone who has been there. As Pulley (1997, p. 144) advises:

> Everyone who loses a job goes through a transition. It is impossible to avoid. We go through transitions throughout our life; they accompany the passage of time. Transitions always involve a loss. Something must be left behind in order to usher in something new. This is why endings and beginnings are the two sides of the same coin. You can't have one without the other. An ending is a beginning, and a beginning is an ending.

It is so exciting to develop a strategy to get that job or promotion. Why put a cloud over it by thinking about losing it? Because it can happen to anyone. So it's best to be prepared and to develop a strategy for responding to and managing the emotions that accompany job loss or change.

> Transition is inevitable. And job loss is inevitable. It happens to everyone.

Who are you?" said the caterpillar.

I—I hardly know, Sir, just at present," Alice replied rather shyly, "at least I know who I *was* when I got up this morning, but I think I must have been changed several times since then."

—Lewis Carroll, *Alice's Adventures in Wonderland*

Stop to think about this. You, too, have experienced transitions and loss to one degree or another. Everyone has. Maybe not a job loss—yet—but a loss, even if only resulting from change. As noted by Birkel and Miller (1998, p. 35):

> Job-loss grief is a universal experience.

Analogies sometimes help explain areas of life we have limited experience with, like losing a job. Bridges (1980, p. 4) paints a vivid picture of what job loss might feel like: "Being in between . . . careers takes on a particularly painful quality when those things themselves are changing profoundly. It is as if we launched out from a riverside dock to cross to a landing on the opposite shore—only to discover in midstream that the landing was no longer there. (And when we looked back at the other shore, we saw the dock we left from had just broken loose and was heading downstream.) Stuck in transition between relationships and identities that are themselves in transition, many Americans are caught in a semipermanent condition of transitionality."

Another analogy comes from Ms. Jane Bankester of Tacoma, Washington, a well-respected skydiver who uses her sport as an analogy in counseling clients experiencing job loss. She explains that the shock of the loss of employment is like falling out of an airplane. Lacking experience, you tumble earthward with absolutely no control, fearing for your life. Skydivers, however, have learned to control themselves during a free fall by adjusting themselves so that they *are* in control. They have developed a strategy to manage the descent. They return safely to earth, exhilarated. The key is *control.*

If you are reeling from job loss, you will find—like the skydiver—that when you are ready, the chute will pop open, and you will make a gradual, controlled descent (if you are prepared). The previous weeks or months may be a blur, but it's all part of dealing with job-loss emotions. Once you've slowed down and are more in control, you can reset your sights on where you want to land and get yourself there. But, as with skydiving, you don't just jump out of the plane without thinking. It requires thought and planning. And if, or when, you get shoved out the door, it becomes even more important that you have a plan—quickly.

This chapter is intended to help you develop a plan. It addresses several important points: anticipating change, responding to and surviving change, and growing from change. The chapter begins with some "Myths About Work" to demonstrate that the working world is not always what you think it is.

MYTHS ABOUT WORK

Employment has changed drastically in the past decades. Despite these changes, people continue to believe in several myths about their employment.

Myth #1: My employment is secure—after all, I got the job, didn't I?

Myth #2: If I do a good job, I'll continue to be recognized for it and be assured of a secure future.

Myth #3: Job loss can only happen to someone else—not me.

Myth #4: Even if it does happen to me, I'll be able to handle it without a problem.

Myth #1: My Employment Is Secure—After All, I Got the Job, Didn't I?

What is meant by *secure*? If it means you will always have your current job, this is incorrect. At most you will retire. Or you could be fired. You could be promoted, transferred to another division or even find yourself on long-term disability after being injured on the job. Or you might move for one reason or another. But you will *not always* have a particular job just because you once got it.

No one is immune from the possibility of losing their job. And those who think they are may well be most at risk. It doesn't matter if you are union, senior, government employed, or really, really good at your job. There *are* circumstances that could, and eventually will, cause you to lose your job sometime or another. The big question is: *How will you handle it*?

Of course, it is everyone's hope that any particular job will end when *we* want it to. After all, it's *our* job. It belongs to us. It's a part of us, and we're a part of it. But unless you are truly self-employed, you do *not* own your job. Even the self-employed do not necessarily have a job that will last a lifetime.

It is dangerous to think you are above and beyond what has occurred to so many who have gone before and who are sure to follow. Job loss is becoming an increasingly familiar scenario and one that must at least be acknowledged. To do otherwise will lull you into a complacency that makes you even more susceptible to risk. As Pulley (p. 12) notes:

> A recent poll shows that since 1980, three-quarters of American adults have been affected by job loss, either personally or within their own family, and one in ten says that a lost job has precipitated a major crisis at home. Within the country, this growing tide is swelling into a tidal wave that threatens to engulf us with anxiety and insecurity. [A 30-year employee of Xerox] said, "Losing my job was the most shocking experience I've ever had in my life. I almost think it's worse than the death of a loved one, because at least we learn about death as we grow up. No one in my age group ever learned about being laid off."

Myth #2: If I Do a Good Job, I'll Continue to Be Recognized for It and Be Assured of a Secure Future

This is an old paradigm. It's the way things might have been for our parents or grandparents, but it's no longer what employees can expect. In fact, it's just the opposite. Here is a frightening prediction: Almost 30 years ago, in 1970, Alvin Toffler published *Future Shock*, in which he anticipated societal change. In it he stated: "In the three short decades between now and the twenty-first century, millions of ordinary, psychologically normal people, will face an abrupt collision with the future. Citizens of the world's richest and most technologically advanced nations will find it increasingly painful to keep up with the incessant demand for change that characterizes our time. For them the future will have arrived too soon."

The future is now, and more and more people have had their employment collide with this future, and they *are* in shock. No doubt you know some of these people. If not, you will. And you may well find yourself among them.

A study in *The Top 10 Career Strategies for the Year 2000 & Beyond* (Grappo, 1997, p. 3) reveals that employees with strong stability (those with only one or no job changes in a 10-year period) decreased from 67 percent in the 1970s to 52 percent in the 1980s. The percentage of employees with weak stability (those changing jobs at least three times in a 10-year period) *doubled* to 24 percent during the 1980s.

Cutbacks, downsizing and other synonyms for *job loss* are not only occurring in corporate America. Perhaps no other campaign platform rings louder than: "Lower taxes!" Programs, personnel, and even entire departments are increasingly finding themselves part of the tax-reduction "solution" in the public sector, once the bastion of security. No shield can fully protect employees from inevitable change—not unions, not job performance, not popularity.

Myth #3: Job Loss Can Only Happen to Someone Else—Not Me

Wrong. Remember, that "someone else" is a "me." In 1999, *Caregivers Quarterly* (Lindgren, 1999, p. 1) reported that for the first time in the publication's history of providing grief and bereavement services, they were focusing on a loss not directly relating to death and dying, but on a loss being experienced by increasingly large numbers of people: job loss.

Lindgren goes on to state that the "heartless layoff" story has become part of the mythology of America, evidenced by the 3 million layoffs in the United States over the past decade: "For a worker who mourns the past, the new relationship with the work world is not one of hope and promise, but of compromise and anxiety." How we deal with job loss is vitally important.

Myth #4: Even if It Does Happen to Me, I'll Be Able to Handle It without a Problem

It's always easier looking in from the outside. It is all too easy to judge those experiencing the natural range of emotions resulting from job loss as "weak" or otherwise not up to the task. Anyone who has lost a job will tell you that it takes significant courage to address this change. And when Birkel and Miller (p. 44) cite that the typical "white collar" worker will experience at least one involuntary job loss, you cannot ignore the possibility, even the probability, that it will be you . . . someday.

We do not want to paint too bleak of a picture. Loss and change are a part of life, and one that actually builds character for most who experience it. It is just an area all too often ignored until it is on our own front doorstep. Every one of us who has "been there" have a whole new appreciation for the intensity of emotions that surface and a willingness to extend an understanding hand to those who will need it.

WHY IS HAVING A STRATEGY SO IMPORTANT?

It is as important to develop a strategy to deal with job loss as it was to get the job in the first place. Why? Because it *will* happen, and it can be significant and downright painful.

> An effective job-loss strategy will not only enable you to feel more in control of very difficult circumstances, but it will allow you to move on in a healthy manner to the next job.

And there *will be* another job.

DEVELOPING A STRATEGY

It's always better to have a plan in place before the emergency strikes, so if you happen to be reading this chapter *before* you need it—good for you. But human nature as it is, you'll probably give it a lot more consideration when you find yourself needing it. Even then you can get a plan in place quickly and benefit from it. You'll find yourself needing just a few basics, but they are very important.

> Basic job-loss survival strategies include:
>
> ➤ Building a support network now.
> ➤ Building a "survival nest egg" of at least six months' living expenses, maybe longer.
> ➤ Balancing your life so your job isn't the only important thing to you.

As you build your network, consider volunteering for an organization you are interested in. As Wendleton and Dauten (1999, p. 1J) suggest, networking at its best is "not hunting, but helping."

 List in your journal individuals you want to keep in contact with not only for future job networking, but because you enjoy them. Can you help any of them now? Can they help you?

 What volunteer opportunities might interest you and might also benefit you in a job search?

 How much money would you need if you suddenly lost your job?

 What interests or hobbies have you put off due to lack of time or money?

Smith (1993, p. 59) suggests the following additional survival strategies:

> ➢ Set aside a regular time to explore and plan your life.
> ➢ Get as much information as possible about the new situation.
> ➢ Know yourself—how you react, how you make decisions, how you relax.
> ➢ List all the useful people you know—a network for support, for fun, for closeness, and for information.
> ➢ Take care of yourself and your body.
> ➢ Express your feelings—use anger constructively; keep the best memories, but live in the present and let go of the past.
> ➢ Set new goals, make decisions, and look for alternatives to replace what is missing.
> ➢ Practice relaxation and deep breathing; become calm.

Survival strategies set a foundation for you to proceed. While they may seem elementary, they can be overlooked in the midst of chaos. They address the areas that need to be worked with and worked through: awareness, acceptance, support, putting the past behind you, and finally, moving ahead. You need to progress through all these areas. And that's one of the most challenging parts of the process. You cannot go around the emotions of job loss; you've got to go through them. There is no shortcut. It is no different than going on a trip. You know where you are, and where you want to get—the challenge is how to get there. It is vitally important that you *manage* your response to the loss. To end up taking it out on others who don't deserve it will only add to your difficulties. Be aware of how you respond to the changes and how you respond to those around you.

THE SEQUENTIAL REACTION TO JOB LOSS AND CHANGE

Chapter 10, which dealt with *not* getting a job, discussed the predictable process most people experience when they lose something important. Whatever begins the sequence of emotional, sometimes physical, responses to job loss, the emotions are so universal that we know they've got to be worked through. Failure to do so will keep you stuck in that phase (e.g., becoming overly angry or sad), and it will affect all other areas of your life.

The normal emotions experienced following job loss are denial, anger, sadness, searching, withdrawal and reorganization. The sequence in which these emotions occur may vary and emotions may repeat themselves.

Denial

Denial is normally experienced as, "I can't believe this happened to me." We all operate our lives in somewhat of a denial state. If we didn't, we probably couldn't cross the street, drive a car, fly in a plane, or even attach ourselves to a job or a relationship for fear of failing or being hurt. We all need to believe to a certain degree that "it can't happen to me." That's normal. But in the denial stage of loss, the ability to *accept* the loss is a necessary step on the journey to being able to continue on with life.

Anger

Why me? You lost your job—who wouldn't be upset? It's another expected emotion, but the danger is in lashing out at those who are susceptible, but not responsible, like friends and family. There is even more danger in lashing out at those you may feel *are* responsible. It's in your best interest to not burn those bridges where you left. As tempting as it may be—keep quiet. Hold your head high. Odds are all your yelling and screaming will get you nowhere, except identified as a hothead. Show some class. Do not turn people even further away from you. Should another opportunity arise there in the future, or when your former employer is called for a reference, you don't want to have already managed to ruin either possibility. But the anger has to be dealt with. The challenge is to find an appropriate outlet.

Sadness

Sadness is another emotion to expect along the way. The tendency is to ignore it because being "sad" may not be your style. But neither is being unemployed. You need to work through the sadness, but not let it consume you and keep you from moving on.

Searching

This phase may outwardly appear quite unreasonable. You might go back to your place of employment, even if only to drive by. You might call. You keep hoping that you'll get your old job back, that "they" will come to their senses since you've been gone and miss you and your contribution. It's like survivors going back to the disaster scene or people driving past the old family homestead. It helps verify the reality and provides a reality check. You may find yourself doing this without thinking; suddenly you are there.

Some reaching out for contact with former co-workers is understandable, even necessary. But you've got to cut the tether sometime. There is no point in complaining or trying to rally the troops. Fair or not, it's done, and unless you have legal recourse, you probably aren't going to be able to change things. Give yourself time to check out the old as you prepare to move on to the new.

Withdrawal

If the searching phase is hard for family and friends to understand, your inevitable withdrawal will be even more difficult to understand. Your pulling away from people will create stress for everyone. What's happening here is that you are doing your emotional work inside. You've stepped back and are assessing where you fit into the world now. This takes time, too, and only you can do it. So when your friends see you as more quiet and withdrawn, no one need worry. It's simply another part of the process.

Reorganization

Here is where you are getting closer to the pot of gold at the end of the rainbow. Having worked through the previous emotional stages, you're ready to rebuild. Here the excitement finally begins to unfold in a positive direction. Having looked at, or been through, this exhausting set of emotions, makes it understandable why people resist change—good or not. Young police officers have difficulty understanding why they keep getting called back to the same address on domestic disturbance calls. "If it's so bad, why doesn't one of them just leave?" The answer is that even as difficult as the situation is, it's known. It's secure and predictable. What's on the other side of that door is unknown. Only when the pain exceeds the risk will change occur.

> All changes, even the most longed for, have their melancholy; for what we leave behind is part of ourselves; we must die to one life before we can enter another.   —Anotole Frarie, writer.

Change is hard. To expect anything less is unrealistic. The emotions experienced are normal, natural.

Managing the Responses

It is not enough to know and anticipate the feelings you will experience. It is vitally important that you effectively *manage* them as well. This is *not* easy because of the intensity of the emotions and (fortunately) the relative lack of experience most people have dealing with such significant loss. What you do not want to do is add to your difficulties by letting the emotions overtake you. You will feel anger, but don't make inappropriately hostile phone calls or confront a former employer you blame for your job loss. Does this happen? Yes, even to extremes. We hear more frequently about former employees who act their anger out with violence, sometimes even killing former employers. It's probably not coincidence that workplace violence is increasing at the same time job loss is increasing across the country.

Nor do you want to take the emotions out on people trying to support you. This is a difficult area to understand because it doesn't make much sense at the time. You're angry. You're sad. The denial factor may not even allow you to understand that it's your lost job that is causing it. But those feelings *will* come out. They have to, or they will eat you alive. If friends and family around you don't deserve to be subject to these feelings, don't allow yourself to make up problems that aren't there or to otherwise justify taking your feelings out on them. Think you've got problems having lost your job? You don't want to lose those close to you, too. It is possible to "grieve other people right out of your life." Here is where you will benefit from objective help, professional or otherwise. Get it!

Understanding, accepting, and managing the emotions associated with job loss is a huge step in moving forward. However, you must guard against one emotion that can be devastating: depression.

DEALING WITH DEPRESSION

The numbers of people suffering from depression is far greater than people may realize. It can be a miserable state to be in, and left untreated, can become debilitating and lead to illness and even suicide.

> Depression is not about being sad. It's about being in a cloud that casts a dark shadow over everything. The hopelessness associated with it may become devastating.

Those who experience it will never again tell someone else that "others have it worse," or "you just need to tell yourself it will all be O.K." If it were this easy, no one would be depressed. It's not that easy.

Allow yourself to feel all of what you are going through—to accept it, but not to like it, and to accept help. Perhaps no other group as a whole is less willing to reach out for help than criminal justice professionals. After all, they are there to help others, people who can't help themselves. It's surely not the stereotypic macho cop who admits to another person, much less to themselves, that they need help.

Depression to some degree *will* result from job loss. The associated negativity and hopelessness can cast a bleak shadow over everything. Following are some thoughts from Byron's study of people in transition and their advice to others (1995, pp. 171–177) that may help you as you walk a path that may seem unbearably long. It's helpful to know that others have been there and survived.

> ➤ Don't be too hard on yourself, or set too many demands; this, like everything, will be resolved one way or another, sooner or later.
> ➤ Expect rejection. Don't take it personally.
> ➤ Be positive and work hard at the search (a new job won't just happen).
> ➤ Let your pride push you rather than hold you back.
> ➤ You are not simply what you do, and you should realize that the job revolution has resulted in people being out who have done nothing wrong.
> ➤ You are not what you own or your title.
> ➤ Never, ever believe your job is secure.
> ➤ Only a positive attitude will propel you into a good job that is the right job for you.
> ➤ Have your network in place before you ever need it.
> ➤ Nothing is forever. Things change. People change.
> ➤ Hang in there.

A Matter of Life and Death

Things can get away from you. Don't try to go it alone. If you were a police, corrections or security officer, you'd never respond to a call alone if you knew you'd need additional officer-power and firepower at the scene. You'd never hesitate to call for help on the street, so don't hesitate to call for help now if you need it.

> If you are depressed and need help—get it.

Talk to friends, see a counselor or psychologist, join a support group, see a psychiatrist and get on medication if need be. Ask anyone. And if you don't like one answer, keep asking. But whatever you do, GET HELP. It takes a strong, courageous person to reach out in the midst of despair. But you can do it. You can!

Another way to break out of depression is to tackle the job search for your next job.

GOTTA GET WORKING

You know how to get a job. After all, you got the job(s) you no longer have.

> As you move through the emotional steps of job loss, keep working at finding new work. As your energy level permits, keep developing the job search.

As you move on, you'll develop increasing energy to be even more creative in this effort. Birkel and Miller belong to an organization called Professionals in Transition (PIT). They set forth what they refer to as "PIT's Top Ten Guerrilla Job-Hunting Tactics" (pp. 144–147):

1. Remind yourself to be a winner.
2. Conduct a multilevel campaign (work with job-hunting allies, market yourself, and conduct informational interviews).
3. Create a business card (front: name, address, phone and general area of expertise; back: career objective and bulleted list of key strengths/skills).
4. Meet employers' needs (cover letter with left column headed "Your Needs" taken from advertisement and right column headed "My Qualifications").
5. Use large mailing envelopes (to stand out from other mail received).
6. Volunteer (there's always someone worse off than you).
7. Get out and meet people (to find advocates in your job search).
8. Recruit a coach (find a personal advocate to encourage and support you).
9. Keep a journal (to spot trends and learn from them).
10. Stay proactive (control your job search; reemployment possibilities are everywhere).

 Write in your journal which of the preceding tactics you'd like to try.

One tactic some people who have lost their jobs seriously consider is a lawsuit against the former employer.

TO SUE OR NOT TO SUE

No one who has lost their job thinks it was fair. It may well have not been. But unless it was illegal, no judge will care. Even then, you need to think whether a lawsuit is the way to proceed.

It doesn't hurt to consult with a lawyer. It would help you put this possibility to rest. A discussion of when a dismissal is illegal is beyond the scope of this book. Employment law is very complex. It depends on your particular circumstances. Do you have a contract? Are you a veteran? What does your employee handbook include? Are you union? And the list goes on. You need legal counsel for answers. Even if you have a legal cause of action, consider the consequences of suing a previous employer.

Questions to answer when considering a lawsuit include:

➤ What is the likelihood of prevailing?
➤ What will future prospective employers think of this action?
➤ Will a lengthy lawsuit prolong my agony and prevent me from beginning my healing process?
➤ How much might it cost?

All these questions need to be considered. A competent attorney will be able to help with this, which is why they are also called counselors at law. But know that suing solely out of anger is never a good idea.

THE SCOTT HARR STORY

This chapter was not based on only academic research. If some of it feels heartfelt, it is. Up until recently, all my job changes were positive, moving up the occupational ladder. True, I felt some loss with each change, but most of the emotions were positive. Then, like a thunderbolt, I lost my position as Public Safety Director of one of Minneapolis' fastest growing suburbs. I'd held that position for over 11 years and had a sterling record. I never thought job loss could happen to me. It did though, and I experienced every single emotion addressed in this chapter, and then some, including embarrassment and humiliation.

I had to step outside my usual roles of police officer, chief, boss, lawyer, and helper of others, and admit that now it was I who needed help. That was hard! The good news was that I had some idea of what was to come.

My strategy was to immediately get my safety net of support in place. I connected with as many friends and colleagues as I could, letting them know I would appreciate their support by remaining in contact with me and helping with my networking effort, which I knew would be important.

Another action I took was to sign up with the Leukemia Society of America's Team in Training. This unique program trains you to run a marathon in exchange for your acquiring donations for the organization. By running in the San Diego Rock 'n Roll marathon the previous year, I learned what a great experience it was, and when I lost my job I thought it would be a good one to repeat—but for different reasons. This year they were training for the Anchorage, Alaska, marathon. The charitable fundraising, getting to know the cancer patients I was running for, and having to get out every day to train, all helped me to keep moving on positively. If running isn't your thing, look around. There will be other opportunities for you to manage the experience as best you can.

I also attended two support groups. One consisted of all police personnel who understood the unique policing profession. The other was a group sponsored by my church dealing with employment issues. Group support provides significant benefits. It's a safe place to process thoughts and feelings while helping others do the same. A story told at one group meeting helped me a great deal. Perhaps it will do the same for you.

> A man was walking along the road one day and was unexpectedly and undeservedly hit with an arrow. This man had absolutely no idea who shot the arrow, why, or why he was the target. He'd done nothing wrong. But the doctors told him that unless the arrow was removed and the wound allowed to heal, he would die. The victim refused to have the arrow taken out until he had answers to his questions. Why did this happen? Why him? Why, when he had done nothing wrong? Then he died. The question: Whose fault was it that the man died—the fault of the unknown assailant who might never be found or his reasons known? Or was it the victim's fault for being unwilling to have the arrow removed to allow the wound to heal?

For me, this was an important lesson because I, too, demanded to know "why?" One blessing I had was incredible public support for a firing that was politically motivated. I spent a lot of energy trying to figure out why. Finally I had to let it go. The arrow needed to be removed.

And so it was. How? In my case, I had to be creative. Since I didn't have a traditional "good-bye" party and I didn't even get to say good-bye to many people I'd worked with for over a decade, I needed to create my own ritual. I needed to draw the line to effectively say, "This is the end; it's time to leave the past behind so I can move ahead." And I wasn't the only one who needed this "funeral" for what was. Several of us invited anyone who felt they could benefit from an opportunity to attend an informal picnic with a formal purpose: to bid farewell to what we had all shared. At last the arrow was out, and the healing began.

CONCLUSION

All endings result in new beginnings. It just might not seem like it at the time. But you've got to believe that there will be another side—a brighter side, a new job, new opportunities, new friends, a whole new world.

Job loss can also increase your awareness of the importance of workplace dignity when changes need to occur. Perhaps you'll be the one to explain positive ways to help employees through a period of loss or change. For sure, you'll be better able to walk the path again, as change continues to be a part of our lives.

A fitting close to this chapter can be found in the words of Pulley (pp. 24–26):

> The American Dream is a myth that puts us in danger . . . . The irony is that in pursuing. . . part of the American Dream, we often lose ourselves. We lose touch with our true nature and our real passion. We lose touch with the inner resources that provide us with energy and feed our soul. We lose touch with our real gifts and with the source of those gifts. . . .
>
> Not only do we risk losing sight of our own gifts but also we find they get lost in the sight of others. . . .We become our position, while our spirit quietly bleeds from inattention . . . . The loss of a job can bring forth new questions. We ask fewer questions when things are going well, or when we are too busy to stop. Often we keep ourselves busy to avoid the void. When that busyness stops, things come out of the shadows. . . .
>
> We are afraid that if we lose our job, we will lose our self. Yet it is when a crack develops that the soul has an opening, a doorway, to get in and be seen. It's when things are falling apart that we look again.
>
> When things are coming apart, it feels bad and frightening, and it can be devastating. But therein lie the hope and the promise. Recovery from job loss means rediscovering our gifts. It means reclaiming the fragmented parts of ourselves that were ignored while we were working. It means healing the splits: It means putting Humpty Dumpty back together again.

The upside of job loss is also examined in the first Insider's View for this chapter. In fact, if you are currently in a position that is unfulfilling for you, Mr. Driggs contribution may even make you consider losing your current position voluntarily. It certainly builds a strong case for making sure you give adequate consideration to the work you choose to do.

AN INSIDER'S VIEW

WHO'S IN CONTROL: YOU OR YOUR WORK?

John Driggs, LICSW

Work used to be like walking the family dog—you did it out of a sense of duty and it was good for your soul. Nowadays, work is more like walking a pit bull—you hang on to the leash for dear life as it drags you along. Too many of us are overworked, threatened with job insecurity through downsizing and corporate restructuring, and expected to perform the same tasks that several of our co-workers used to do. The American Dream has transformed too many of us into "wage slaves."

Since 1991, 2.5 million workers have fallen victim to corporate restructuring and re-assignment (Family Networker, 1996), causing many families to be relocated and breaking down the formation of community roots so precious to quality family life. Too many of us have become, in Vance Packard's poignant words, a "nation of strangers." We dare not invest ourselves in our communities if we expect to be uprooted later. The unpredictable demands of our workplace cause us to live in a state of perpetual uncertainty and disconnection as we become estranged from ourselves and our children.

All of us suffer on a more personal level, too. More than 45 million American adults take prescription psychotropic medications just to get through the workday (*Utne Reader*, 1999) .

Why Do We Stay in Dysfunctional Situations?

Problems with work originate both within ourselves and outside ourselves. Those of us with hefty mortgages and family responsibilities may have prepared all our lives for the dynamic challenges of our careers only to have our certainty cut out from under us through job restructuring, downsizing, and managed care. Our fatigue, numbness, and inattentiveness to our families may have less to do with personal shortcomings and more to do with the massive and often impossible work demands placed on our shoulders as well as our buying into the cultural myths of consumerism. To offset our emotional oblivion, many of us work harder at our frantic workplaces, consume more, and see no other options. Many healthy family members have been done in by the vicious cycle of overwork, fatigue, numbness, and capitulation so inherent in the modern workplace and consumer treadmill.

Other Options

In 1851, John Ruskin, an English social critic said that work happiness was determined by three factors: we must be fit for our work, we must not do too much of it, and we must find meaning in it. To make ends meet, we simply need to have a job that pays our bills. However, to get a sense of fulfillment from our work, we need to find ourselves a career. Each of us has something unique to contribute to life. People who find their calling in life often say, "Gee, do I really get paid for this?" Often, the process of defining and re-defining our careers is a lifetime endeavor. This endeavor is made more difficult if we are out of touch with our emotional selves or are trapped in our parents' dreams. However, finding a career is not optional. Our self-esteem depends on it.

Each day take small steps in facing work problems. Read *What Color Is Your Parachute* (Richard Bolles, Ten Speed Press, 1999). Allow yourself to image your dream job. Interview people who already work at your dream job and see what your dreams are made of. Convene a group of your friends over dinner to give you advice on what kind of work you would be good at. If you're caught in a dream job that's gone haywire, consider other options. Perhaps it's time for you to strike out on your own to downsize your lifestyle. Doing what you love and eating peanut butter sandwiches may be a lot better than dining on caviar on the corporate treadmill. . . . You may need to reinvent yourself and your life to have a life. Whatever your direction, don't let your work push you around. Stand up for yourself. When your work is becoming more important than yourself, it's time to tighten the leash on the dog. You are not your work and there's a lot more to you than any job could define.

John H. Driggs, LICSW, is a licensed clinical social worker in private practice in St. Paul and co-author of Intimacy between Men (Penguin Books, 1990). This Insider's View is excerpted from his article "Who's in Control: You or Your Work?" published in The Phoenix, Vol. 19, No. 2, February 1999, pp. 9, 14), reprinted by permission of the author. Mr. Driggs can be reached at 651.699.4573.

AN INSIDER'S VIEW

JOB LOSS AND GRIEF

Richard J. Obershaw, LICSW, MSW, ACSW
Founder and Director of the Grief Center, Burnsville, Minnesota

Our job is a lot about who we are. When we lose our job we lose who we *were*—not who we *are*. When we lose our job, we often lose our identity, our security, our friends, our co-workers, our financial security, our sense of accomplishment, our lifestyle, our routine, our sense of productivity, and sometimes we lose the reason for getting out of bed in the morning.

We often select "our work" because of who we *were*. For example, perfectionists seldom take on jobs that can't be done perfectly. If they do, they soon learn to look for another job. Individuals who enjoy people usually select jobs that involve people. During those years at the job we all change. The changes come because of maturational issues in our life as well as situational occurrences. But because of financial factors we seldom elect to leave our first job of choice. We learn to "live with the way I am now in a job that was selected for the way I was then." We adapt by mixing the *new me* with the *old me.*

Then the day comes when someone says you are no longer wanted, needed, or capable of performing this job, or your job is eliminated because of (1) a change in the workplace, (2) economic factors, or (3) interpersonal differences.

It is at this point in our life that we have to once again ask, "Who am I now as an individual and what do I need for a job that matches this 'now' individual?"

This is the process of grief—letting go of the *old me* and learning who the *new me* will be. It is the job of re-identifying the self. After many studies on the topic of change and grief, we have come to learn that the process is somewhat predictable. No one follows the process in exactly the same pattern as others, but the overall general idea may help you understand your "normally crazy" thoughts, ideas, feelings, and behavior during this period of re-identifying yourself.

Initially we find it difficult to accept the reality of our loss. Our **denial** system starts to protect us from the stress created by change. It may seem like a bad dream, or we may wish, sometimes out loud, that the old familiar activities will once again return. This may look unhealthy to others around us, but it serves as a buffer for us as we go gently from the *old me* to the *new me*. We may even decide not to tell our family and friends about the job loss because they will want to discuss it. But we aren't ready to deal with a discussion about it because it makes it too real. This denial will fade gently as we become more aware that we can cope with this change in our lives.

As we become more aware of the reality of the loss, we become more aware of the effort it will take to re-identify ourselves. It is at this point we get **resentful** of the effort needed to change and we find ourselves with a general "anger all over" feeling. We get angry that we have to change. We get angry at the people who get to keep their jobs. We get angry at those who told us our job was ending. We get angry at God, and we get angry at ourselves. Because we are punched in the gut over this loss, we want to punch others. We want others to suffer with us.

Soon we find ourselves feeling quite restless and pacing around the house. Where do we belong? We awaken at the time we normally would to go to work, but find ourselves with no place to go.

Then comes the **search**—we may drive by and around the workplace feeling the need to check out if it's still there for us. We may search our minds and others to come up with the "real reason" this loss has been placed in our lives. We may search to find new meaning in our life without our old job. The term *job search* may also explain why initially we search to find a job—sometimes any job. And, because we find a job we take it—just to end the search and get a job back. These jobs often do not meet our new needs, our changed selves.

Another part of the grief process with job loss is **withdrawal**. We withdraw from our families, friends, former co-workers, and often from ourselves. We sleep to withdraw from life and ourselves. We withdraw into television and spend countless hours staring at brain-dead talk shows that help us escape from our own grief and re-identification process. In extreme cases we may withdraw into obsessive-compulsive behaviors, alcohol and other drugs, dangerous hobbies, sexual affairs, excessive spending, and even suicide.

If we survive all of the preceding, we begin the process of realizing we are new. Our thinking, our needs, and our goals are often new. We start to know the *new me* and become more comfortable being changed. It is at this point we should begin with a true job search that fits the *new us*. If everyone had the financial security to wait this long, life would be easier, but the reality is, jobs are needed to earn money to pay the bills. Perhaps what we need to do is reassess how we choose to live our lives. Is the job where we work about collecting money or is a job about meeting our needs to be who we are?

Richard Obershaw, LICSW, MSW, ACSW, is an internationally renowned expert on loss and change, grief and bereavement. He travels extensively, lecturing and consulting on these subjects in addition to his clinical practice. He is also founder and director of the Grief Center in Burnsville, Minnesota.

MIND STRETCHES

1. If you needed them today, who makes up your support network?

2. What losses have you experienced? How did you work through the steps?

3. Why does job loss effect more than just the individual?

4. Why do you think job loss is more common now than in years past?

5. Do you think job loss can be harder to deal with than death? Why or why not?

6. Why do people think job loss can't happen to them?

7. What would you do to help yourself if you lost your job today?

8. Why do people feel bad even if they choose to leave their jobs?

9. If you were to lose your job now, would you say, "That's what I was" or "That's what I did?"

10. Why do you think some people put more emphasis on their jobs than on the rest of their lives?

REFERENCES

Birkel, J. Damian with Miller, Stacey J. *Career Bounce-Back! The Professionals in Transition*^{SM} *Guide to Recovery & Reemployment.* New York: AMACOM: American Management Association, 1998.

Bridges, Willliam. *Transitions: Making Sense of Life's Changes.* Reading, MA: Addison-Wesley Publishing Company, 1980.

Byron, William J. *Finding Work without Losing Heart: Bouncing Back from Mid-Career Job Loss.* Holbrook, MA: Adams Publishing, 1995.

Grappo, Gary Joseph. *The Top 10 Career Strategies for the Year 2000 & Beyond.* New York: Berkley Books, 1997.

Lindgren, Amy. "*Grief and Loss in the 'New Workplace.'*" *Caregivers Quarterly*, Vol. 14, No. 1, Winter, 1999, pp. 1–2.

Smith, Maggie. *Changing Course: A Positive Approach to a New Job or Lifestyle.* San Diego: Pfeiffer and Company, 1993.

Pulley, Mary Lynn. *Losing Your Job—Reclaiming Your Soul: Stories of Resilience, Renewal, and Hope.* San Francisco: Jossey-Bass Publishers, 1997.

Wendleton, Kate and Dauten, Dale. "Networking Isn't Just Stalking a Resume." (Minneapolis/St. Paul) Star Tribune, May 23, 1999, p. 1J.

APPENDIX A

DEFINITIONS OF SCANS KNOW-HOW
(WORKPLACE COMPETENCIES AND FOUNDATION SKILLS)

WORKPLACE COMPETENCIES

Resources

Manages Time—Selects relevant, goal-related activities; ranks them in order of importance; allocates time to activities and understands, prepares and follows schedules.

Manages Money—Uses or prepares budgets, including making cost and revenue forecasts; keeps detailed records to track budget performance and makes appropriate adjustments.

Manages Material and Facility Resources—Acquires, stores and distributes materials, supplies, parts, equipment, space or final products in order to make the best use of them.

Manages Human Resources—Assesses knowledge and skills, distributes work accordingly, evaluates performance and provides feedback.

Interpersonal

Participates as a Member of a Team—Works cooperatively with others and contributes to group efforts with ideas, suggestions and effort.

Teaches Others—Helps others learn needed knowledge and skills.

Serves Clients/Customers—Works and communicates with clients and customers to satisfy their expectations.

Exercises Leadership—Communicates thoughts, feelings and ideas to justify a position, encourage, persuade, convince or otherwise motivate an individual or groups, including responsibly challenging existing procedures, policies or authority.

Negotiates to Arrive at a Decision—Works towards an agreement that may involve exchanging specific resources or resolving divergent interests.

Works with Cultural Diversity—Works well with men and women and with people from a variety of ethnic, social or educational backgrounds.

Information

Acquires and Evaluates Information—Identifies a need for data, obtains the data from existing sources or creates them and evaluates their relevance and accuracy.

Organizes and Maintains Information—Organizes, processes and maintains written or computerized records and other forms of information in a systematic fashion.

Interprets and Communicates Information—Selects and analyzes information and communicates the results to others using oral, written, graphic, pictorial or multimedia methods.

Uses Computers to Process Information—Employs computers to acquire, organize, analyze and communicate information.

Systems

Understands Systems—Knows how social, organizational and technological systems work and operates effectively within them.

Monitors and Corrects Performance—Distinguishes trends, predicts impacts of actions on system operations, diagnoses deviations in the functioning of a system/organization and takes necessary action to correct performance.

Improves and Designs Systems—Makes suggestions to modify existing systems in order to improve the quality of products or services and develops new or alternative systems.

Technology

Selects Technology—Judges which sets of procedures, tools or machines, including computers and their programs, will produce the desired results.

Applies Technology to Task—Understands the overall intents and the proper procedures for setting up and operating machines, including computers and their programming systems.

Maintains and Troubleshoots Technology—Prevents, identifies or solves problems in machines, computers and other technologies.

THE FOUNDATION SKILLS

Basic Skills

Reading—Locates, understands and interprets written information in prose and documents—including manuals, graphs and schedules—to perform tasks; learns from text by determining the main idea or essential message; identifies relevant details, facts and specifications; infers or locates the meaning of unknown or technical vocabulary and judges the accuracy, appropriateness, style and plausibility of reports, proposals or theories of other writers.

Writing—Communicates thoughts, ideas, information and messages in writing; records information completely and accurately; composes and creates documents such as letters, directions, manuals, reports, proposals, graphs and flow charts with the language, style, organization and format appropriate to the subject matter, purpose and audience; includes, where appropriate, supporting documentation and attends to level of detail and checks, edits and revises for correct information, appropriate emphasis, form, grammar, spelling and punctuation.

Arithmetic—Performs basic computations; uses basic numerical concepts such as whole numbers and percentages in practical situations; makes reasonable estimates of arithmetic results without a calculator and uses tables, graphs, diagrams and charts to obtain or convey quantitative information.

Mathematics—Approaches practical problems by choosing appropriately from a variety of mathematical techniques; uses quantitative data to construct logical explanations for real world situations; expresses mathematical ideas and concepts orally and in writing and understands the role of chance in the occurrence and prediction of events.

Listening—Receives, attends to, interprets and responds to verbal messages and other cues such as body language in ways that are appropriate to the purpose—for example, to comprehend, learn, critically evaluate, appreciate or support the speaker.

Speaking—Organizes ideas and communicates oral messages appropriate to listeners and situations; participates in conversation, discussion and group presentations; selects an appropriate medium for conveying a message; uses verbal language and other cues such as body language in a way appropriate in style, tone and level of complexity to the audience and the occasion; speaks clearly and communicates a message; understands and responds to listener feedback and asks questions when needed.

Thinking Skills

Creative Thinking—Generates new ideas by making nonlinear or unusual connections, changing or reshaping goals and imagining new possibilities and uses imagination freely, combining ideas or information in new ways, making connections between seemingly unrelated ideas and reshaping goals in ways that reveal new possibilities.

Decision Making—Specifies goals and constraints, generates alternatives, considers risks and evaluates and chooses best alternatives.

Problem Solving—Recognizes that a problem exists (i.e., that there is a discrepancy between what is and what should be); identifies possible reasons for the discrepancy and devises and implements a plan of action to resolve it and evaluates and monitors progress, revising the plan as indicated by findings.

Mental Visualization—Sees things in the mind's eye by organizing and processing symbols, pictures, graphs, objects or other information—for example, sees a building from a blueprint, a system's operation from schematics, the flow of work activities from narrative descriptions or the taste of food from reading the recipe.

Knowing How to Learn—Recognizes and can use learning techniques to apply and adapt existing and new knowledge and skills in both familiar and changing situations and is aware of learning tools such as personal learning styles (visual, aural, etc.), formal learning strategies (notetaking or clustering items that share some characteristic) and informal learning strategies (awareness of unidentified false assumptions that may lead to faulty conclusions).

Reasoning—Discovers a rule or principle underlying the relationship between two or more objects and applies it in solving a problem—for example, uses logic to draw conclusions from available information, extracts rules or principles from a set of objects or a written text or applies rules and principles to a new situation (or determines which conclusions are correct when given a set of facts and conclusions).

Personal Qualities

Responsibility—Exerts a high level of effort and perseverance toward goal attainment; works hard to become excellent at doing tasks by setting high standards, paying attention to details, working well even when assigned an unpleasant task and displaying a high level of concentration and displays high standards of attendance, punctuality, enthusiasm, vitality and optimism in approaching and completing tasks.

Self-Esteem—Believes in own self-worth and maintains a positive view of self, demonstrates knowledge of own skills and abilities, is aware of one's impression on others and knows own emotional capacity and needs and how to address them.

Sociability—Demonstrates understanding, friendliness, adaptability, empathy and politeness in new and ongoing group settings; asserts self in familiar and unfamiliar social situations; relates well to others; responds appropriately as the situation requires and takes an interest in what others say and do.

Self-Management—Accurately assesses own knowledge, skills and abilities; sets well-defined and realistic personal goals; monitors progress toward goal attainment and motivates self through goal achievement and exhibits self-control and responds to feedback unemotionally and nondefensively.

Integrity/Honesty—Recognizes when being faced with making a decision or exhibiting behavior that may break with commonly held personal or societal values; understands the effects of violating these beliefs and codes on an organization, oneself and others and chooses an ethical course of action.

IACP POLICE CODE OF CONDUCT*

All law enforcement officers must be fully aware of the ethical responsibilities of their position and must strive constantly to live up to the highest possible standards of professional policing.

The International Association of Chiefs of Police believes it is important that police officers have clear advice and counsel available to assist them in performing their duties consistent with these standards, and has adopted the following ethical mandates as guidelines to meet these ends.**

Primary Responsibilities of a Police Officer

A police officer acts as an official representative of government who is required and trusted to work within the law. The officer's powers and duties are conferred by statute. The fundamental duties of a police officer include serving the community; safeguarding lives and property; protecting the innocent; keeping the peace and ensuring the rights of all to liberty, quality and justice.

Performance of the Duties of a Police Officer

A police officer shall perform all duties impartially, without favor or affection or ill will and without regard to status, sex, race, religion, political belief or aspiration. All citizens will be treated equally with courtesy, consideration and dignity.

Officers will never allow personal feelings, animosities or friendships to influence official conduct. Laws will be enforced appropriately and courteously and, in carrying out their responsibilities, officers will strive to obtain maximum cooperation from the public. They will conduct themselves in appearance and deportment in such a manner as to inspire confidence and respect for the position of public trust they hold.

Discretion

A police officer will use responsibly the discretion vested in the position and exercise it within the law. The principle of reasonableness will guide the officer's determinations and the officer will consider all surrounding circumstances in determining whether any legal action shall be taken.

Consistent and wise use of discretion, based on professional policing competence, will do much to preserve good relationships and retain the confidence of the public. There can be difficulty in choosing between conflicting courses of action. It is important to remember that a timely word of advice rather than arrest—which may be correct in appropriate circumstances—can be a more effective means of achieving a desired end.

---

* Adopted by the Executive Committee of the International Association of Chiefs of Police on October 17, 1989, during its 96th Annual Conference in Louisville, Kentucky, to replace the 1957 code of ethics adopted at the 64th Annual IACP Conference.

** The IACP gratefully acknowledges the assistance of Sir John C. Hermon, former chief constable of the Royal Ulster Constabulary, who gave full license to the association to freely use the language and concepts presented in the RUC's "Professional Policing Ethics," Appendix 1 of the Chief Constable's Annual Report, 1988, presented to the Police Authority for Northern Ireland, for the preparation of this code.

SOURCE: Reprinted with permission from the International Association of Chiefs of Police, Alexandria, Virginia. Further reproduction without express written permission from IACP is strictly prohibited.

Use of Force
A police officer will never employ unnecessary force or violence and will use only such force in the discharge of duty as is reasonable in all circumstances. Force should be used only with the greatest restraint and only after discussion, negotiation and persuasion have been found to be inappropriate or ineffective. While the use of force is occasionally unavoidable, every police officer will refrain from applying the unnecessary infliction of pain or suffering and will never engage in cruel, degrading or inhuman treatment of any person.

Confidentiality
Whatever a police officer sees, hears or learns of, which is of a confidential nature, will be kept secret unless the performance of duty or legal provision requires otherwise. Members of the public have a right to security and privacy, and information obtained about them must not be improperly divulged.

Integrity
A police officer will not engage in acts of corruption or bribery, nor will an officer condone such acts by other police officers. The public demands that the integrity of police officers be above reproach. Police officers must, therefore, avoid any conduct that might compromise integrity and thus undercut the public confidence in a law enforcement agency. Officers will refuse to accept any gifts, presents, subscriptions, favors, gratuities or promises that could be interpreted as seeking to cause the officer to refrain from performing official responsibilities honestly and within the law. Police officers must not receive private or special advantage from their official status. Respect from the public cannot be bought; it can only be earned and cultivated.

Cooperation with Other Officers and Agencies
Police officers will cooperate with all legally authorized agencies and their representatives in the pursuit of justice. An officer or agency may be among many organizations that may provide law enforcement services to a jurisdiction. It is imperative that a police officer assist colleagues fully and completely with respect and consideration at all times.

Personal/Professional Capabilities
Police officers will be responsible for their own standard of professional performance and will take every reasonable opportunity to enhance and improve their level of knowledge and competence. Through study and experience, a police officer can acquire the high level of knowledge and competence that is essential for the efficient and effective performance of duty. The acquisition of knowledge is a never-ending process of personal and professional development that should be pursued constantly.

Private Life
Police officers will behave in a manner that does not bring discredit to their agencies or themselves. A police officer's character and conduct while off duty must always be exemplary, thus maintaining a position of respect in the community in which he or she lives and serves. The officer's personal behavior must be beyond reproach.

APPENDIX C

ASIS SECURITY CODE OF ETHICS[*]

PREAMBLE

Aware that the quality of professional security activity ultimately depends upon the willingness of practitioners to observe special standards of conduct and to manifest good faith in professional relationships, the American Society for Industrial Security adopts the following Code of Ethics and mandates its conscientious observance as a binding condition of membership in or affiliation with the Society:

ARTICLE I

A member shall perform professional duties in accordance with the law and the highest moral principles.

Ethical Considerations

I-1   A member shall abide by the law of the land in which the services are rendered and perform all duties in an honorable manner.

I-2   A member shall not knowingly become associated in responsibility for work with colleagues who do not conform to the law and these ethical standards.

I-3   A member shall be just and respect the rights of others in performing professional responsibilities.

ARTICLE II

A member shall observe the precepts of truthfulness, honesty and integrity.

Ethical Considerations

II-1   A member shall disclose all relevant information to those having a right to know.

II-2   A right to know is a legally enforceable claim or demand by a person for disclosure of information by a member. Such a right does not depend upon prior knowledge by the person of the existence of the information to be disclosed.

II-3   A member shall not knowingly release misleading information, nor encourage or otherwise participate in the release of such information.

ARTICLE III

A member shall be faithful and diligent in discharging professional responsibilities.

Ethical Considerations

III-1   A member is faithful when fair and steadfast in adherence to promises and commitments.

III-2   A member is diligent when employing best efforts in an assignment.

---

[*] Reprinted with permission from the American Society for Industrial Security.

III-3   A member shall not act in matters involving conflicts of interest without appropriate disclosure and approval.

III-4   A member shall represent services or products fairly and truthfully.

ARTICLE IV

A member shall be competent in discharging professional responsibilities.

Ethical Considerations

IV-1   A member is competent who possesses and applies the skills and knowledge required for the task.

IV-2   A member shall not accept a task beyond the member's competence nor shall competence be claimed when not possessed.

ARTICLE V

A member shall safeguard confidential information and exercise due care to prevent its improper disclosure.

Ethical Considerations

V-1   Confidential information is nonpublic information the disclosure of which is restricted.

V-2   Due care requires that the professional must not knowingly reveal confidential information or use a confidence to the disadvantage of the principal or to the advantage of the member or a third person unless the principal consents after full disclosure of all the facts. This confidentiality continues after the business relationship between the member and his principal has terminated.

V-3   A member who receives information and has not agreed to be bound by confidentiality is not bound from disclosing it. A member is not bound by confidential disclosures made of acts or omissions which constitute a violation of the law.

V-4   Confidential disclosures made by a principal to a member are not recognized by law as privileged in a legal proceeding. The member may be required to testify in a legal proceeding to information received in confidence from his principal over the objection of his principal's counsel.

V-5   A member shall not disclose confidential information for personal gain without appropriate authorization.

ARTICLE VI

A member shall not maliciously injure the professional reputation or practice of colleagues, clients or employers.

Ethical Considerations

VI-1   A member shall not comment falsely and with malice concerning a colleague's competence, performance or professional capabilities.

VI-2   A member who knows, or has reasonable grounds to believe, that another member has failed to conform to the Society's Code of Ethics shall present such information to the Ethical Standards Committee in accordance with Article XIV of the Society's Bylaws.

APPENDIX D
RESUME WORKSHEETS

Name: _____

Current Address: _____

Permanent Address: _____

Phone Number(s): _____

Colleges: _____

_____

Professional Schools: _____

_____

Internships: _____

_____

Certificates Held: _____

_____

_____

Other Educational Experiences: _____

_____

_____

High School: _____

EMPLOYMENT HISTORY
(Note: Make as many copies of this page as you have had jobs so you can complete one page for each job you've had.)

Dates Employed: From _____ to _____

Employer: _____

      Address: _____

      Phone: _____

      Supervisor: _____

Position/Title: _____

Responsibilities: _____

_____

_____

_____

_____

Skills Acquired: _____

_____

_____

_____

_____

Achievements/Awards: _____

_____

_____

_____

Salary (NOT included in resume): _____

Reason for Change (NOT included in resume): _____

_____

Position Desired/Employment Objective: _____

_____

_____

Other information that may be put in your resume includes the following:

Birthdate: _____ Height: _____ Weight: _____

Health: _____

Travel (willing to travel?): _____

Location (willing to relocate?): _____

Military (service, dates, rank, honorable discharge): _____

_____

Reserve status: _____

Professional Memberships (committees served on, awards): _____

_____

_____

_____

Foreign Languages (read, write, speak fluently): _____

_____

Foreign Travel: _____

_____

Awards: _____

_____

Publications: _____

_____

Community Service/Involvement (organizations, offices held, etc.): _____

_____

Interests/Hobbies (avocations, non-business pursuits): _____

_____

Availability (immediate or extent of "notice" required): _____

Present Employer Contact: _____
(Is present employer aware of your prospective job change? May the employer be contacted?)

Salary Desired: _____
(NOT included in resume, but know what you'd expect.)

BUSINESS/PROFESSIONAL/ACADEMIC REFERENCES:

Full Name: _____

    Position: _____

    Address: _____

    Phone: _____

Full Name: _____

    Position: _____

    Address: _____

    Phone: _____

Full Name: _____

    Position: _____

    Address: _____

    Phone: _____

PERSONAL REFERENCE:

Full Name: _____

Relationship (neighbor, teammate, etc.): _____

    Address: _____

    Phone: _____

RESUME EVALUATION CHECKLIST

CATEGORY	Excellent	Average	Poor	How to Improve
APPEARANCE:				
Is the format clean?				
Is it easy to follow?				
Are headings effective?				
Does it make the reader want to read it?				
CONTENT:				
Do my qualifications stand out?				
Is the language clear and understandable?				
Have I used short phrases?				
Have I used verbs (action words)?				
Is it brief and to the point?				
Are all important skills and qualifications included?				
Does it create a true picture of me?				
Is irrelevant personal information left out?				
PROOFREADING:				
Is it error free?				
Spelling?				
Punctuation?				

SAMPLE RESUMES

Historical/Chronological Resume

WILLIAM A. SMITH
10 South First Street
Minneapolis, MN 55404

Home Phone: (612) 555-5650
Work Phone: (612) 555-9123

PERSONAL   Date of Birth: 6/3/69, 6'0", 175 lbs. Married, one child. Will relocate.

EDUCATION

1987 - 91   NORMANDALE COMMUNITY COLLEGE
Bloomington, Minnesota
Associate Arts Degree and Law Enforcement Certificate.
     Member of football team.
     Photographer for school paper.

1987   BLOOMINGTON HIGH SCHOOL
Bloomington, Minnesota
High school diploma. Honor student.
     Member of football team.

**WORK
EXPERIENCE**

1988 - present   SECURITY OFFICER
Dayton's Department Store
Minneapolis, Minnesota
Hired as store detective. Duties include plainclothes observation or retail sales area to observe and arrest shoplifters. Assist in loss prevention seminars for store employees.

1985 - 1988   WAITER
Fancy Joe's Burger Joint
Bloomington, Minnesota
Hired as dishwasher. Promoted to busboy and then waiter. Duties as waiter included taking customers' orders, delivering food and beverage items to the table, and assisting other wait staff.

References available on request.

Functional Resume

WILLIAM L. SMITH
10 South First Street
Minneapolis, MN 55404
Home Phone: (612) 555-5650

Personal Data: Date of Birth 6-3-62, 6'0", 175 lbs., Single.

Objective:
Position as a law enforcement officer.

Work History

1987 - present

Security Officer:

Southdale Shopping Center
Edina, Minnesota

- Hired as uniformed security officer. Duties include patron assistance, emergency first-aid response, enforcement of property rules and statutes. Assist in training new employees by providing presentations on company rules and state criminal statutes. Frequently appear as witness in court cases resulting from my position. Work with the area law enforcement officers hired to assist during holiday seasons. Act as company representative to Minnesota Loss Control Society.

1985-1987

Office Worker:

Kenny's Market, Inc.
Bloomington, Minnesota

- Hired as assistant to the vice-president. Duties included typing, filing, and telephone reception. In charge of confidential employee records. Assisted in organizing the company's first loss prevention program.

Education

1985-1987   BA, University of Minnesota, Minneapolis, Minnesota.

1983-1985   AA, Law Enforcement Certification, Normandale Community College, Bloomington, Minnesota.

1986   Emergency Medical Technical Technician Registration, Hennepin County Vo-Tech, Eden Prairie, Minnesota.

References available on request.

Analytical Resume

WILLIAM L. SMITH
10 South First Street
Minneapolis, MN 55404
Home Phone: (612) 555-5650
Work Phone: (612) 555-9123

Job Objective: Apply my proven ability in loss prevention.

Qualifications:

- Retail Security: Have developed knowledge and skills in the profession while employed as loss prevention officer for several retail stores. In addition to providing undercover and plainclothes loss prevention services as a store detective, have provided extensive training on the subject to store employees. Excellent performance reviews at each position. Continued increases in apprehension statistics. Received "Employee of the Month" award six times for excellent work as a security officer.

- Supervisory Skills: Promoted to supervisor of 17 loss prevention officers at most recent position. Duties included training, delegating duties, and scheduling. Performance statistics for the crew increased significantly.

- Organizational Skills: All jobs have required detailed activity reports. Hands-on-experience using computers to organize data. Often provided oral reports to supervisors.

Employers

1983 – present   Donaldson's Department Store, Edina, Minnesota.

1982 – 1983   Tom Thumb Stores, Inc., St. Paul, Minnesota.

1980 – 1982   Automobile Club of America, St. Louis Park, Minnesota.

Education

1983   Associate of Arts and Private Security Certificate, Normandale Community College, Bloomington, Minnesota.

Other

1984   Participated in organization of 1984 American Industrial Security Association National Convention.

References available on request.

APPENDIX F

SAMPLE COVER LETTER AND FOLLOW-UP LETTER

Sample Cover Letter

Ms. Jane Smith
1234 Second Avenue
Los Angeles, CA 90017

July 15, 1999

Lt. Pat Jones
Mytown Police Department
1234 First Avenue
Denver, CO 80203

Dear Lt. Jones:

I am responding to your ad in the *Los Angeles Times* for the position of police officer.

I am enclosing a resume highlighting my background, qualifications and experience. With an AA degree in law enforcement and three years' experience as a reserve officer with the Los Angeles Police Department, I am ready to enter the law enforcement profession and hope it will be with your department.

I will call you the week of July 29th to make sure my resume was, indeed, received and to arrange for a personal interview. I will look forward to talking with you then.

Sincerely,

Jane Smith

Encl. Resume

Sample Follow-Up Letter

Mr. Scott Anderson
1234 Second Avenue
Boulder, CO 23456

July 21, 1999

Protection Plus Security
1234 First Avenue
Denver, CO 12345

Attn: Mr. Ronald Smith,
        President

Dear Mr. Smith:

Thank you for the opportunity to participate in the hiring process for the position of security officer. I delivered my resume to your office yesterday and am sorry to have missed you.

I remain extremely interested in the position and look forward to the possibility of being considered for the job. Please call if you need any further information.

Very sincerely,

Scott Anderson

APPENDIX G

JOB INFORMATION SOURCES

HELPFUL HINTS FOR GETTING A JOB

Adapted from: Job Search. Career Information Series. Job Service, Minnesota Department of Employment Services.

From among the many sources of job information, you will have to select those most appropriate for you. The ones you choose will depend on the type of job you want, where you want to live and want to work and the demand in your field. Some sources of job information are listed below. Brief comments on their characteristics may help you choose the ones best suited to your needs.

STATE JOB SERVICE. It has more job listings in more occupational categories than any other single source. Using a computer, job openings in the entire state are compiled for use by placement specialists. Employment counseling and career consultation is also available. All services are provided free of charge.

FRIENDS AND RELATIVES. Through their work or social and business contacts, they may know of opportunities not listed by regular sources. But, of course, their knowledge is likely to be limited to their own, and perhaps a few other places of employment. If you're on good terms with a banker, insurance agent or others who have a lot of contact with people, check with them for possible leads.

LIBRARY. Librarians can show you various business directories, membership rosters of various trade associations, purchasing guides, professional journals, etc. They can help you zero in on companies that use your particular skills.

SCHOOL OR COLLEGE PLACEMENT SERVICE. This may be a productive source, but is generally available only to students and alumni.

WANT ADS IN NEWSPAPERS, PROFESSIONAL JOURNALS AND TRADE MAGAZINES. These provide a broad range of definite openings. A large share of listings in publications devoted to your field are likely to be for jobs you are qualified to fill. Analysis of the ads provides information about the extent of employment activity in your field throughout the area.

INDUSTRIAL AND CRAFT UNIONS. This is a productive source for members, particularly those with seniority. They may have exclusive hiring authority for some firms.

GOVERNMENT CIVIL SERVICE DEPARTMENTS. Federal, state, county and city civil service departments fill jobs in a wide variety of professional, technical, clerical, craft and other occupations.

PRIVATE EMPLOYMENT AND TEMPORARY SERVICES. Another source of current job openings for individuals. Some charge applicants a fee for placement; some collect fees from employers. If you use a private agency, observe the following advice: (1) Be sure it is licensed by the state; (2) check its reputation with the Better Business Bureau, large employers and friends; (3) before you sign a contract, be sure you understand it (ask if you may take it home to check it out) and (4) fees vary considerably, so make sure you understand what you must pay.

YELLOW PAGES OF TELEPHONE DIRECTORY, INDUSTRIAL DIRECTORIES AND CHAMBER OF COMMERCE LISTS. These provide names of firms that employ workers in your field and other useful information.

HOW TO GET MORE INFORMATION

The following is a list of agencies and organizations able to supply information about careers in the criminal justice system. Where specific listings of names and addresses cannot be given, other means of obtaining information are suggested. Although this listing of sources is not all inclusive, it does provide a base from which to start gathering career information. (From *Criminal Justice Careers Guidebook*. U.S. Department of Labor. Raymond J. Donovan, Secretary. Employment and Training Administration. 1982.)

LAW ENFORCEMENT

Federal Level

Bureau of Alcohol, Tobacco, and Firearms
U.S. Treasury Department
1111 Constitution Avenue NW
Washington, DC 20220

Drug Enforcement Administration
U.S. Department of Justice
1405 I Street NW
Washington, DC 20537

Federal Bureau of Investigation
U.S. Department of Justice
9th Street and Pennsylvania Avenue NW
Washington, DC 20535

General Services Administration
Office of Federal Protective Service
    Management
18th and F Streets NW
Washington, DC 20405

Immigration and Naturalization Service
U.S. Department of Justice
425 I Street NW
Washington, DC 20536

Internal Revenue Service
Criminal Investigations Division
U.S. Treasury Department
1111 Constitution Avenue NW
Washington, DC 20220

Internal Revenue Service
Internal Security Division
Career Development Section
U.S. Treasury Department
1111 Constitution Avenue NW
Washington, DC 20220

United States Civil Service Commission
1900 E Street NW
Washington, DC 20415

United States Customs Service
1301 Constitution Avenue NW
Washington, DC 20229

United States Department of Agriculture
14th Street and Independence Avenue SW
Washington, DC 20250

United States Department of Defense
The Pentagon
Washington, DC 20301

United States Department of Health and Human Services
200 Independence Avenue SW
Washington, DC 20201

United States Department of the Interior
C Street between 18th and 19th Sts. NW
Washington, DC 20240

United States Department of Labor
200 Constitution Avenue NW
Washington, DC 20210

United States Department of Transportation
400 7th Street SW
Washington, DC 20590

United States Marshals Service
One Tysons Corner Center
McLean, VA 22102

United States Postal Service
Chief Postal Inspector
475 L'Enfant Plaza SW
Washington, DC 20260

United States Secret Service
Personnel Division
U.S. Treasury Department
1800 G Street NW
Washington, DC 20223

* More information about federal employment can be obtained by contacting the Job Information Center in your area or by accessing www.usajobs.opm.gov.

State, County and Local Levels

Information about law enforcement jobs at the state, county and/or local level can be obtained by contacting the nearest state, county and/or local civil service commission. Specific information about job opportunities may also be found at the recruitment or personnel office at the local and/or county police department. Searches of local and state websites may also yield critical information regarding job opportunities.

THE SECURITY FIELD

American Society for Industrial Security (ASIS)
1655 North Fort Myer Drive
Arlington, VA 22209

THE JUDICIARY

Administrative Office of the State Courts
Division of Personnel
  (In the 50 States, American Samoa, Guam
  and Puerto Rico, these offices are usually
  located in the capital or principal city.)

Administrative Office of the U.S. Courts
Division of Personnel
Supreme Court Building
Washington, DC 20544

American Bar Association
1155 East 60th Street
Chicago, IL 60637

American Library Association
50 East Huron Street
Chicago, IL 60611

American Polygraph Association
P.O. Box 74
Linthicum Heights, MD 21090

Institute of Judicial Administration
1 Washington Square Village
New York, NY 10012

National Association of Legal Secretaries
3005 East Skelley Drive, Suite 120
Tulsa, OK 74105

National Association of Para-Legal Personnel
188 West Randolph Street
Chicago, IL 60601

National Business Education Association
1906 Association Drive
Reston, VA 22091

National Center for State Courts
300 Newport Avenue
Williamsburg, VA 23185

National Council on Crime and Delinquency
411 Hackensack Avenue
Hackensack, NJ 07601

National Shorthand Reporters Association
2361 South Jefferson Davis Highway
Arlington, VA 22202

* Specific information about job opportunities can be obtained by contacting a representative of the nearest local, county and/or state civil service commission office, Federal Job Information Center.

CORRECTIONS AND REHABILITATION

Federal Level

To find out more about correction occupations or general information on corrections at the federal level, write to any of the offices listed below:

American Correctional Association (ACA)
8025 Laurel Lakes Court
Laurel, MD 20707

Federal Bureau of Prisons
Central Office
Washington, DC 20534

North Central Regional Office
8800 Northwest 112st Street
K.C.I. Bank Building
Kansas City, MO 64153

Northeast Regional Office
Scott Plaza II
Industrial Highway
Philadelphia, PA 19113

South Central Regional Office
3883 Turtle Creek Boulevard
Dallas, TX 75219

Southeast Regional Office
3500 Greenbriar Parkway SW
Atlanta, GA 30331

Western Regional Office
330 Primrose Road – Fifth Floor
Crocker Financial Center Building
San Francisco, CA 94010

* Again, on-line searches of corrections agencies may provide much useful information.

State Level

To obtain information about occupations, or general information about corrections at the state level, contact the corrections agency in the capital city of the state in which you reside or wish to work.

Local and County Levels

To find out more about correctional programs in your community, get in touch with your city or county civil service commission, or apply directly to the program center.

APPENDIX H

SAMPLE APPLICATION FORM

PERSONNEL DEPARTMENT
CIVIL SERVICE COMMISSION
312 3RD AVENUE SOUTH
MINNEAPOLIS, MINNESOTA 55415

IMPORTANT EMPLOYMENT APPLICATION INSTRUCTIONS - PLEASE READ

1. **Read the Job Announcement carefully** to be sure that you meet all of the requirements.

2. **Type or print in ink.**

3. **Be sure to include** with your application all requested proofs of education, licenses, veteran's eligibility, etc. (such as trade licenses, drivers license, transcripts, etc).

4. Your application **must be completely** filled out and copies of all required documents must be included. Applications which are not complete will not be processed.

TITLE OF JOB:

EXAM NUMBER:

---

1 | **LAST NAME:** | **FIRST NAME:** | **MIDDLE NAME:**

---

2 | **PRESENT ADDRESS:** | **APARTMENT NO:** | **CITY:** | **STATE:** | **ZIP CODE:**

NOTE: If you should move after applying for this position, please notify the Personnel Department Office in writing immediately of your change of address.

---

3 | **PRESENT HOME TELEPHONE NUMBER:** AREA CODE - | **PRESENT WORK TELEPHONE NUMBER:** AREA CODE - | **4** | **SOCIAL SECURITY NUMBER:**

5

CIRCLE THE LAST GRADE OF SCHOOL COMPLETED	DID YOU GRADUATE (NOT MANDATORY)	DATE OF GRADUATION	NAME OF LAST ELEMENTARY OR HIGH SCHOOL ATTENDED	CITY OR POST OFFICE	STATE
5 6 7 8 9 10 11 12 GED					

6

ADDITIONAL EDUCATION AND TRAINING (Include names and locations of Colleges, Universities, Trade, Vocational or other schools attended)	DATES ATTENDED		CERT OR DEGREE	DATE REC'VD	MAJOR / MINOR SUBJECT(S)
	FROM	TO			

OTHER APPLICANT INFORMATION

AN AFFIRMATIVE ACTION-EQUAL OPPORTUNITY EMPLOYER, the City of Minneapolis will hire and promote without regard to such non-job related distinctions as race, creed, color, age, religion, sex (except when sex is a BFOQ), ancestry, marital status, status with regard to public assistance, national origin, physical or mental disability or affectional preference.

DATA PRIVACY: Except for requested race/ethnic data, the information on this application including social security number, is necessary to identify you and to determine your suitability for this position. You **must** supply this information in order to be considered for City employment. Racial/ethnic data is used by the Minneapolis Personnel and Affirmative Action Departments to monitor employment opportunities for protected classes. While we encourage you to provide this information, it is not required.

CS-1808 Rev. 10/89

7 EMPLOYMENT RECORD: List all your work history for at least the past ten years. Start with your PRESENT or MOST RECENT Job. Include both paid and job-related unpaid or volunteer experience.

EMPLOYER:		ADDRESS:		CITY:		STATE:	ZIP CODE:

SUPERVISORS NAME:	PHONE NUMBER:	DATES EMPLOYED (MONTH AND YEAR ONLY): FROM: TO:	HOURS PER WEEK:	IS THIS VOLUNTEER WORK? ☐ YES ☐ NO

YOUR JOB TITLE:	REASON FOR LEAVING:

Your Job Duties (include examples of the type of paid or volunteer work you performed): _____

If you are currently working, may we contact your PRESENT employer about your work?   ☐ YES   ☐ NO

PRIOR EMPLOYER

EMPLOYER:		ADDRESS:		CITY:		STATE:	ZIP CODE:

SUPERVISORS NAME:	PHONE NUMBER:	DATES EMPLOYED (MONTH AND YEAR ONLY): FROM: TO:	HOURS PER WEEK:	IS THIS VOLUNTEER WORK? ☐ YES ☐ NO

YOUR JOB TITLE:	REASON FOR LEAVING:

Your Job Duties (include examples of the type of paid or volunteer work you performed): _____

PRIOR EMPLOYER

EMPLOYER:		ADDRESS:		CITY:		STATE:	ZIP CODE:

SUPERVISORS NAME:	PHONE NUMBER:	DATES EMPLOYED (MONTH AND YEAR ONLY): FROM: TO:	HOURS PER WEEK:	IS THIS VOLUNTEER WORK? ☐ YES ☐ NO

YOUR JOB TITLE:	REASON FOR LEAVING:

Your Job Duties (include examples of the type of paid or volunteer work you performed): _____

IMPORTANT NOTICE

If you need more space, enclose or attach additional sheets, including, for each job, all information requested above.

YOU MUST COMPLETE THIS APPLICATION FORM FULLY, however, you may also include a resume or other related documentation relevant to this position.

8 Give dates and reasons, excluding disabilities, for any time in the last ten (10) years that is not accounted for in your employment history (e.g, unemployment, education, etc): _____

_____

_____

_____

9 Have you ever been discharged or asked to resign from any position for misconduct or unsatisfactory service? ☐ NO ☐ YES
If yes, please describe the situation. Use the back of this application if you need more space: _____

_____

_____

_____

10 Would you, in any of your listed education or experience, be known only under another name? ☐ NO ☐ YES
If yes, under what name: _____

11 Have you ever been convicted of any violation of the law (other than parking tickets)? ☐ NO ☐ YES - If yes, list **all convictions within the last seven years**. Do not list juvenile (under 18 years of age) convictions unless you were tried as an adult. The Minneapolis Civil Service Commission **does** not automatically reject applicants who have conviction records.

| DATE | | PLACE | | NATURE OF OFFENSE | RESULT |
MONTH	YEAR	CITY	STATE		

PERSONAL EXPERIENCE

12 City of Minneapolis employees serve the public. Please describe any work, volunteer or personal experience which is relevant to this position and in which you worked with persons of different races, sexes or ages or with a person with a disability? _____

_____

_____

_____

_____

_____

_____

_____

_____

_____

_____

13 Do you have any other personal experience (hobbies, other volunteer or training experiences, other coursework, etc.) which you feel may help you qualify for this position? _____

_____

_____

_____

_____

_____

_____

_____

_____

_____

PLEASE BE SURE TO SIGN THIS APPLICATION, AND READ THE FOLLOWING STATEMENTS CAREFULLY

1. I certify that all the information I have provided on this application is true and complete to the best of my knowledge. I understand that giving false information or omitting requested information could result in rejection of my application or dismissal if I am hired.

2. I authorize the City of Minneapolis Civil Service Commission to verify this information to determine whether or not I am qualified for the position for which I am applying.

3. I hereby authorize all current and previous employers to release job-related information upon the written request of the Minneapolis Civil Service Commission. However, I understand that if, in the Employment Record Section, I have answered "No" to the question, "May we contact your present employer?" contact with my current employer will not be made without my specific authorization.

PRINTED NAME:	SIGNATURE:	DATE SIGNED:

PLEASE COMPLETE A VETERAN'S PREFERENCE FORM (103A) IF YOU ARE A VETERAN OF THE U.S. ARMED FORCES.

CONFIDENTIAL DATA FORM - To be separated from application immediately upon receipt in the Personnel Office.

To be completed by applicant: The City of Minneapolis has an equal employment opportunity/affirmative action policy. Knowledge of your race, sex, age, handicap and medical status is necessary for monitoring the effectiveness of the program. Although you are not required to provide the information requested on this form, your cooperation is appreciated. Persons referred for employment may be required to verify race and citizenship.

LAST NAME:	FIRST NAME:	MIDDLE NAME:

TITLE OF JOB APPLYING FOR:	EXAM NUMBER:	SEX: ☐ MALE ☐ FEMALE	DATE OF BIRTH:

RACE

☐ 1. WHITE: All persons having origins in any of the peoples of Europe (including Spain), North Africa or the Middle East.

☐ 2. BLACK: All persons having origins in any of the Black racial groups of Africa.

☐ 3. HISPANIC: All persons of Mexican, Puerto Rican, Cuban, Central or South American or other non-European Spanish culture or origin (regardless of race) who retain cultural identification through name, community recognition, language and/or activities.

☐ 4. ASIAN OR PACIFIC ISLANDERS: All persons having origins in any of the original peoples of the Far East, Southeast Asia, the Indian subcontinent or the Pacific Islands. This area includes, for example, China, Japan, Korea, the Phillipine Islands and Samoa.

☐ 5. AMERICAN INDIAN OR ALASKAN NATIVE: All persons having origins in any of the original peoples of North America and who maintain cultural identification through tribal affiliation or community recognition.

WHERE DID YOU LEARN THAT THIS POSITION WAS OPEN FOR APPLICATION?

☐ Minneapolis Personnel Department (Civil Service)
☐ Hot Line 348-MPLS
☐ Minneapolis Star and Tribune
☐ State Job Bank
☐ City Employee
☐ Friend
☐ School - which one: _____

☐ Community Newspaper - which one: _____
☐ Community Agency - which one: _____
☐ TV Announcement - which station: _____
☐ City Department - which one: _____
☐ Radio Announcement - which station: _____
☐ Other: _____

FOR OFFICE USE ONLY

P-#:	F:	NSO-NSW-NST:	CODE:	DNA:	R:

.... CONTINUED ON REVERSE SIDE ....

CLAIM FOR VETERAN'S PREFERENCE

ELIGIBILITY: A person who is eligible to receive a monthly veteran's pension based on length of service will not qualify for preference. To qualify for preference for a competitive exam you must have been separated under honorable conditions from any branch of the armed forces of the United States after having served on active duty for 181 consecutive days or by reason of disability incurred while serving on active duty and be a United States citizen or resident alien; or be the spouse of a deceased veteran; or be the spouse of a disabled veteran who because of such disability is unable to qualify or earn a living. To qualify for preference on a promotional exam you must be entitled to disability compensation for a permanent service connected disability rated at 50 percent or more; or be the spouse of a veteran who is rated as 100 percent disabled and who because of such disability is unable to qualify or earn a living. Persons eligible for such preference may use it only for the 1st promotion after securing public employment.

NOTE: If you do not meet the eligibility requirements outlined above, do not complete this section.

Name of Veteran (Last, First, Middle): _____ Date of Birth: _____

Did you serve on active military duty without interruption for 181 days or more (does not include Active Duty for Training (ADT) in the Reserve or National Guard .... ☐ Yes ☐ No

Are you a U.S. citizen or resident alien .... ☐ Yes ☐ No

Date of entry into active duty: _____ Date of release from active duty: _____

Branch: _____

Type of separation (for verification purposes, furnish a copy of your DD-214, WD AG053-55, NAC. PERS., or other separation papers .... ☐ Honorable ☐ Medical ☐ Honorable release from active duty and transfer to reserves

Are you now receiving or are you eligible to receive a monthly veteran's pension based on length of military service .... ☐ Yes ☐ No

Disability claim number: ☐☐☐☐☐☐☐ Be sure this number is correct. If not available, put service serial number here _____

Percent of service connected disability _____ Currently existing: ☐ Yes ☐ No

Date and amount of most recent disability payment: Month - _____ Day - _____ Year - _____ $ _____

State in which filed _____

If not Minnesota, have records since been transferred to Fort Snelling: ☐ Yes ☐ No Where _____

Have you ever been promoted in the City service: ☐ Yes ☐ No

FOR SPOUSES OF DECEASED VETERANS		FOR SPOUSES OF DISABLED VETERANS	
DATE OF DEATH:	HAVE YOU REMARRIED: ☐ YES ☐ NO	VETERAN'S PRESENT OCCUPATION:	VETERAN'S TOTAL EARNINGS FROM EMPLOYMENT FOR PAST 12 MONTHS: $

I hereby claim veteran's preference for this examination and (swear/affirm) that the information given on this document is true and correct. I also authorize the release of necessary information by the Veteran's Administration to the City of Minneapolis Personnel Department.

SOCIAL SECURITY NO: _____

SIGNATURE: _____ DATE: _____

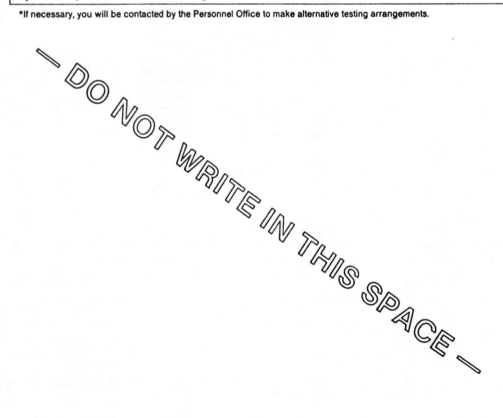

PART 2: CONFIDENTIAL DATA FORM - To be separated from application immediately upon receipt in Personnel Office.

The information requested below will **NOT** be stored with your employment application. Providing this information is voluntary and, by not doing so, you will not hurt your chances for employment. The City is requesting this information solely to track and improve the effectiveness of its Affirmative Action recruitment and testing efforts. This information will not be accessable to City personnel involved in the selection process. Such access would violate the Minnesota Human Rights Act.

For the purposes of this section, a disability is defined as a condition which limits one or more major life activities such as employment opportunities, access or testing.

Do you consider yourself to have any of the following disabilities, handicaps, or medical conditions?

☐ 8. No

☐ A. Joint Disability

☐ E. Post Polio Disability

☐ G. Speech Disability

☐ I. Hearing Disability

☐ J. Mental/Emotional Disability

☐ O. Back Injury or Disability

☐ L. Diabetes or Related Disability

☐ H. Communicative/Learning Disability

☐ B. Amputated or impaired limb

☐ C. Paraplegia, Quadriplegia or Hemiplegia

☐ D. Neuro Muscular Disability (Cerebral Palsy, Muscular Dystrophy, Multiple Sclerosis, etc.)

☐ F. Visual Disability (does not include corrected vision.)

☐ K. Epilepsy or other Seizure Disability

☐ Z. Other Medical Disability which limits employment opportunities and/or ability to perform all job tasks. If yes, explain: _____

_____

_____

If you have checked one or more of the disabilities above, it may be possible to arrange alternative testing accommodations. Do you need any alternative testing accommodations? ☐ NO   ☐ *YES - If yes, please explain _____

_____

_____

_____

_____

If you have a question about alternative testing, call 348-2292 or TDD 348-2157.

*If necessary, you will be contacted by the Personnel Office to make alternative testing arrangements.

— DO NOT WRITE IN THIS SPACE —

YOU MAY USE THIS SPACE TO PROVIDE ADDITIONAL INFORMATION WHICH YOU BELIEVE MAY HELP YOU QUALIFY FOR THIS POSITION OR WHICH MAY CLARIFY OTHER INFORMATION THAT YOU HAVE ALREADY PROVIDED.

========== DO NOT WRITE BELOW THIS LINE ==========

APPROVAL:			DATE:	INITIALS:
INCOMPLETE (REASON):			DATE:	INITIALS:
WITHDRAWAL (DATE):	INITIALS:	REJECTION (DATE):		INITIALS:
REMARKS:				

ACTION	DATE	BY
Application Indexed		
Rejection Notice		
NST-NSO-NSW		
Fail Notice		
Written Notice		
Oral Notice		
Practical Notice		
References Sent		
Other		
Final Results		

Final Average: _____   Rank: _____

NECESSARY PROOFS	DATE PRESENTED	RECEIVED BY	ITEM

EQUAL EMPLOYMENT OPPORTUNITY (EEO) GUIDELINES

Topic	Permitted Inquiries	Prohibited Inquiries
AGE	Whether candidate meets minimum age requirement or is under 65. Requirement that candidate submit proof of age after hired. Whether candidate can meet terms and conditions of job.	Age, birth certificate. Any inquiry for purpose of excluding persons between 40 and 70. Inquiries as to date of graduation from college or high school to determine age should also be avoided.
ARRESTS	None.	Any inquiry relating to arrest.
CONVICTIONS	Inquiries about actual convictions which relate reasonably to performing a particular job.	Inquiries regarding convictions that do not relate to performing the particular job under consideration.
CREDIT RATING	Inquiries about credit rating, charge accounts, etc., that relate reasonably to performing the particular job in question.	Any inquiries concerning charge accounts, credit rating, etc., that do not relate to performing the particular job under consideration.
DRIVER'S LICENSE	If required for the job, may ask if applicant possesses valid license.	Not permitted to ask applicant to produce or show a license.
EDUCATION	Inquiries regarding degrees or equivalent experience. Information regarding courses relevant to a particular job.	Disqualification of a candidate who does not have a particular degree unless employer has proven that the specific degree is the only way to measure a candidate's ability to perform the job in question.
HANDICAPS	Whether candidate has any disabilities which would prevent him or her from performing the job. Whether there are any types of jobs for which candidate should not be considered because of a handicap or health condition.	General inquiries that would elicit information about handicaps or health conditions which do not relate to job performance.
HEIGHT & WEIGHT	Inquiries regarding ability to perform a particular job. However, being a specific height or weight will not be considered a requirement unless the employer can show no employee with ineligible height or weight could do the work.	Inquiries are prohibited if they are not based on actual job requirements.
MARITAL & FAMILY STATUS	Whether candidate can meet work schedule or job. Whether candidate has activities, responsibilities or commitments that may hinder meeting attendance requirements. (Should be asked of candidates of both sexes.)	Childcare problems, unwed motherhood, contraceptive practices, spouse's preferences regarding job conditions. Inquiries indicating marital status, number of children, pregnancies. Any questions directly or indirectly resulting in limitation of job opportunity in any way.

Topic	Permitted Inquiries	Prohibited Inquiries
MILITARY RECORD	Type of experience and education in service as it relates to a particular job.	Discharge status, unless it is the result of a military conviction.
NAME	Whether candidate has ever worked under a different name.	Inquiries to determine national origin, ancestry or prior marital status.
NATIONAL ORIGIN	Whether candidate is legally eligible to work in the United States.	Lineage, ancestry, descent, mother tongue, birthplace, citizenship. National origin of spouse or parents.
NOTICE IN CASE OF EMERGENCY	Permitted after time of hire.	Not permitted before hire.
ORGANIZATIONS	Inquiries which do not elicit discriminatory information.	Inquiries about memberships to determine the race, color, religion, sex, national origin or age of candidates.
PHOTOGRAPHS	Photos may be requested after hiring for identification purposes.	Requests for photos at any time before hiring.
PREGNANCY	Inquiries regarding duration of stay on the job or anticipated absences which are made to males and females alike.	All questions regarding pregnancy and related medical history.
RACE OR COLOR	None.	Complexion, color, skin, hair, eyes, etc.
RELATIVES	Relatives' names already employed by the company or by a competitor.	No other inquiries regarding relatives permitted.
RELIGION	Whether candidates can meet work schedules of job with reasonable accommodation by employer if necessary.	Religious preference, affiliations, denomination.
RESIDENCE	Applicant's address with regard to being able to contact him or her during the selection process.	Owning or renting a home. Names or relationships of people residing with applicant.
SEXUAL PREFERENCE	None.	Number of male vs. female friends, roommates, living arrangements, etc.
WORK EXPERIENCE	Candidate's previous job-related experience.	None.

AUTHOR INDEX

SUBJECT INDEX